From our publishers

We at American School of Needlework® are proud to present our first volume of The Crochet Yearbook.

Crocheters love magazines—and this crochet yearbook gives you a whole year's worth of a quarterly magazine, all in one book!

How often have you received the newest issue of your favorite crochet magazine, and wished you didn't have to wait two whole months or more for an exciting new issue? How often have you waited for a new subscription to begin?

In ASN's new The Crochet Yearbook, four quarterly issues are combined so that you can choose to make a Christmas item in the spring, a bridal gift in December, or a sweater anytime! No waiting for seasonal issues to arrive by mail, no fussing with subscriptions.

The Crochet Yearbook is filled with crochet patterns, techniques, and interviews with interesting crochet people. You'll look at old stitches in new ways, and meet new stitches to add sparkle to your work.

The Crochet Yearbook, Volume 1, is a must for your own collection and the perfect gift for a crocheting friend! Let us know what you think.

Jean Leinhauser

Rita Weiss

©2000 by American School of Needlework®, Inc.; ASN Publishing, 1455 Linda Vista Drive, San Marcos, CA 92069

ISBN:0-88195-935-9   All rights reserved.   Printed in Hong Kong   3 4 5 6 7 8 9

American School of Needlework® presents

The Crochet Yearbook

We've included a year's worth of magazine-style projects and articles in this one colossal volume. Here's a sampling of what you'll find in each season's issue...

Let's Crochet for

Winter...

The season we all want to be inside and snuggle with yarn—featuring our luscious **For Baby & Me** mama and baby size afghans in pearly white yarn. Magnifique! Get ready for the holidays with elegant **Evening of Glamour** vest, shawl and evening bag and festive **Holiday Vest**. We've even included **Merry (Christmas!)-Go-Round Doily** to set your holiday table. Plus you'll find our **Rich and Warm** afghan, masculine enough to give your favorite man, and **Snowbound!** afghan, that's great for wrapping up in front of a cozy fire.

Let's Crochet for

Spring...

It wouldn't be Spring without a beautiful wedding so this issue offers everything from a breathtaking **Bridal Gown** to other bridal accessories. For golfers... there's **Tigers for Your Woods**. For a cool, carefree summer look...**Confetti Tunic** or a **Casual Striped Cardigan**. Create Wedgwood-look china with **Time for Tea** and dress up the boudoir with a **Tissue Box in Bloom** and **Pretty Pillow Talk** edgings.

Let's Crochet for

Summer...

Are you a Beanie Baby® collector? We have **fashions for Collectibles**! Create wonderful summertime fashions— **Desert Stripes** sweater, the **Weekend Cardigan**, and **An All-American Kid** vest. For picture-perfect projects, **In the Pink** sweaters are sized for both mom and daughter as are the **Sweet and Simple Shrugs**—in fact, we also have a shrug for the 18" doll that is an important part of the family.

Let's Crochet for

Fall...

Cold and wintry weather is just around the corner so you'll want to be ready with a **Back-To-School Plaid Afghan** for the school set and **Sporty Comfort** to wear for extra warmth at the football game. Men will enjoy the handsome look of our **Rugged Individualist** sweater. For the sweetest dresser drawers... our **Sunflower Sachet** is delightful!

A year's worth of crochet ideas and designs

American
School of
Needlework®
excellence
in instruction

Plus every issue has these features...

All You've Ever Wanted to Know About Crochet Stitches – Become an expert in all the basics and finer points of crochet. From the perfect starting chain to doing a half double crochet, we'll enjoy sharing our secrets and you'll be able to achieve the results you expect.

Winter: The Chain Stitch
Spring: Single Crochet
Summer: Double Crochet
Fall: Half Double Crochet

Recreate an Antique Treasure – Each issue features an absolutely wonderful crocheted treasure from our archive of museum-quality crocheted needlework.

Winter: Pretty as a Picture Apron
Spring: Pansy Bedspread
Summer: Patriotic Spirit Flag
Fall: Swirls Tablecloth

People and Places – There are some pretty interesting people who enjoy crocheting and related hobbies. Meet one in each issue!

Winter: Turn of the Century Crochet Hooks
by William Schmidt
Spring: Crocheting On Stage and Off with Ragtime
Summer: The Gifted Work of Elizabeth Hiddleston
Fall: Mini Crochet by Kathi Bacon

Tried-and-True Technique - Check out the special techniques that we have found and have fun trying something new!

Winter: Houndstooth, Scarf with Matching Hat
Spring: Starching, Time for Tea
Summer: Smooth Joinings, Summer Breeze Afghan
Fall: Bead Stringing, Little Treasure Amulet Bag

One Night Stand – Sometimes you want to finish your project in just one evening, so here are designs that are perfect for the person who doesn't have the patience to spend a month on every project.

Winter: Neck Cozy
Spring: Chenille Scrunchie
Summer: Cheery Stripes Dishcloth
Fall: Betwitching Boa

It Takes a Skein – Each issue has a project that takes no more than one skein of yarn.... Great ideas for gifts and craft sales!

Winter: Bounty of Buttons Necklace
Spring: Pure Elegance Bag
Summer: Classy Clotheshangers
Fall: Darling Baby Booties

Keeping You in Stitches – Learn a new stitch... They're like candy, there's always room for one more!

Winter: Popcorn and Diamond
Spring: The Bullion Stitch
Summer: Trio of Novel Fringes
Fall: Reverse Crochet

Fiber Fun – Try out some unusual yarns that you may not have heard about... projects will be quick to do and a step into the unknown.

Winter: Huggable Teddy in chunky chenille
Spring: Little Amulet Bag in lamé
Summer: Double-Take Scarves in eyelash yarn
Fall: Evening Bun Warmer in sparkly chenille

Animal Pairs – Soft huggable and very lovable... these animal couples have personality and style. Each pair is crocheted with worsted weight yarn and then dressed in matching crocheted outfits.

Winter: Kathy and Keith Kitty
Spring: Becca and Brian Bunny
Summer: Brittany and Bobby Bear
Fall: Patsy and Pierre Pig

The Crochet Yearbook

PUBLISHERS

Jean Leinhauser
Rita Weiss

EDITORIAL

Managing Editor
Bobbie Matela

Editorial Director
Mary Ann Frits

Editorial Staff
Sandy Scoville, Kathy Wesley, Kelly
Robinson, Stephanie Hill, Denise Black

Photography Stylist/Illustrations
Carol Mansfield

Charting
Carly Poggemeyer

Designer
Graphic Solutions inc-chgo

Photography
Norton Photography
Rick Starkman Photography

Pattern Testers
Donna Gonzales
Tammy Hebert
LaWanda Larner
Melody Long
Georgia Nordman
Carly Poggemeyer
Judie Scoville

ADVERTISING

Advertising Manager
Patricia Hodges-Brillon

How to Reach Us
ASN Publishing
1455 Linda Vista Drive
San Marcos, CA 92069

e-mail: asnpub@aol.com
web site: www.asnpub.com

If you would like to submit your original designs for future Yearbooks, please send snapshots and a brief description to Managing Editor.

Let's Crochet
for Winter

Huggable Teddy and Kitties

Keep Warm Neck Cozy, Hats and Scarves

Afghan Beauties For Baby & Me

Glamour Fashions for Evening and Holiday

Winter Contents

On our cover:
For Baby & Me Afghans by Ann Kirtley in two sizes, for baby and also for mother, see page 40.

Talented Hands Create
Heirloom Crochet Hooks

(7¹/₂ inches) gives them a nice balance. Bill does every step of the process himself.

Bill became fascinated by wood turning by watching a master turner. He developed his own methods using his background as a farm kid (always fixing things), engineering studies, and summer jobs in a tool and die shop.

In addition to crochet hooks, Bill and his partner, Dana Andra, create many other wonderful turned wood objects—chopsticks, hair ornaments, pens, lace bobbins, tatting shuttles, knitting needles, vases and bowls—which they sell at craft fairs throughout the country.

Despite Bill's often 80-hour work weeks, Turn of the Century hooks are in short supply. You can admire them and find ordering information on the Turn of the Century website, http://www.turn2001.com/tchome.htm

We wish Bill would make fewer chopsticks and more crochet hooks!

Exquisite crochet hooks—hand turned by an expert woodworker—are among the products created by Turn of the Century in Mansfield, Ohio.

Bill Schmidt, a professional wood turner since 1971, has won numerous awards and has crocheters waiting in line, eager to buy his hooks.

"Wood turning combines the power of the machine with the skill of hand tools," Bill explained. "It is one of the oldest applications of power to a machine."

Bill makes hooks in sizes from F through K, using woods with exotic coloring and graining from Brazil and Central America.

"I love all beautiful woods," Bill commented, "but my favorites for crochet hooks are the exotics, because of their strength and durability, as well as for their beauty."

Each hook is an individual work of art, and all designs are Bill's own originals. After turning, each is meticulously given a hand-rubbed finish. The hooks feel wonderful in the hand and their longer than usual length

Meet Kathy and Keith Kitty

*Boy and girl kitties
are sure to delight when
they're big and huggable
and dressed up in their
fine crocheted ensembles.*

— designed by Candy Clayton

Kathy Kitty

Size:
About 16¹/2" tall

Materials:
Worsted weight yarn, 7 oz (490 yds,
210 gms) grey; 3¹/2 oz (245 yds,
105 gms) pink; 2 oz (140 yds,
60 gms) white
*Note: Our photographed animal was
made with Red Heart®
Classic™, Silver #412,
Grenadine #730,
and White #001.*
Size F (3.75mm) crochet
hook, or size required
for gauge
Size 18 tapestry needle

Trimmings:
two sets of 30mm doll joints
two 15mm black animal eyes
9x22mm cat nose
18" length of black embroidery floss
tacky craft glue or hot glue
polyester fiberfill
black plastic eyelashes

1 large pink heart button
sewing needle and matching thread

Gauge:
4 sc = 1"

*Note: Kitties have plastic
face parts which are not
suitable for children under
three years of age. If for a
young child please embroider faces with floss.*

Find more Animal Pairs in our Spring, Summer, and Fall issues.

*Bunny Pair
in Spring, page 62*

*Bear Pair
in Summer, page 150*

*Pig Pair
in Fall, page 190*

Pattern Stitches

Front Post Double Crochet (FPdc):
YO, insert hook from front to back to front around post (see page 211) of st indicated, draw up lp, (YO, draw through 2 lps on hook) twice—FPdc made.

Back Post Double Crochet (BPdc):
YO, insert hook from back to front to back around post (see page 211) of st indicated, draw up lp, (YO, draw through 2 lps on hook) twice—BPdc made.

Front Post Single Crochet (FPsc):
Insert hook from front to back to front around post (see page 211) of st indicated, draw up lp, YO and draw through 2 lps on hook—FPsc made.

Instructions

Kitty

Arm (make 2):
With grey, ch 2.

Note: Rnds 1 through 25 are worked in continuous rnds. Do not join; mark beg of rnds.

Rnd 1 (right side): 6 sc in 2nd ch from hook.

Rnd 2: 2 sc in each sc—12 sc.

Rnd 3: (Sc in next sc, 2 sc in next sc) 6 times—18 sc.

Rnd 4: Sc in each sc.

Rnd 5: 2 sc in each of next 3 sc—thumb shaping made; sc in next 15 sc—21 sc.

Rnds 6 and 7: Rep Rnd 4.

Rnd 8: Sc dec over next 2 sc (to work sc dec: draw up lp in each of next 2 sc, YO and draw through all 3 lps on hook—sc dec made); (sc dec over next 2 sc) twice; sc in next 15 sc—18 sc.

Rnd 9: (Sc dec over next 2 sc) twice; sc in next 14 sc—16 sc.

Rnds 10 through 24: Rep Rnd 4.

Rnd 25: Sc in next 4 sc. Remove hook from lp. Cut yarn, leaving a 36" end (to be used for completing arm later). Set aside.

Leg (make 2):
With grey, starting at foot, ch 9.

Note: Rnds 1 through 30 are worked in continuous rnds. Do not join; mark beg of rnds.

Rnd 1 (right side): Sc in 2nd ch from hook and in next 6 chs, 5 sc in next ch; working in unused lps on opposite side of beg ch-9, sc in next 6 lps, 2 sc in next lp—20 sc.

Rnd 2: 2 sc in next sc; sc in next 6 sc, 2 hdc in each of next 5 sc—toe shaping made; sc in next 6 sc, 2 sc in each of next 2 sc—28 sts.

Rnd 3: 2 sc in next sc; sc in next 9 sts, 2 hdc in each of next 6 hdc; sc in next 10 sts, 2 sc in each of next 2 sc—37 sts.

Rnd 4: Sc in each st.

Rnd 5: Sc in next 14 sc, (sc dec over next 2 sc) 4 times; sc in next 15 sc—33 sc.

Rnd 6: Sc in next 13 sc, hdc dec over next 2 sc [to work hdc dec: (YO, draw up lp in next st) twice; YO and draw through all 5 lps on hook—hdc dec made]; (hdc dec over next 2 sc) twice; sc in next 14 sc—30 sts.

Rnd 7: Sc in each st.

Rnd 8: Sc in next 11 sc, (hdc dec over next 2 sc) 4 times; sc in next 11 sc—26 sts.

Rnd 9: Sc in next 10 sc, (hdc dec over next 2 sts) 4 times; sc in next 8 sc—22 sts.

Rnd 10: Sc in next 10 sc, (sc dec over next 2 sts) twice; sc in next 8 sc—20 sc.

Rnds 11 through 30: Sc in each sc.

Rnd 31: Sc in next 4 sc. Remove hook from lp. Cut yarn, leaving a 36" end (to be used for completing leg later). Set aside.

Note: Do not skip ahead, Arms and Legs Assembly needs to be completed before going further.

Arms and Legs Assembly:
Step 1: Stuff arms firmly with fiberfill to Rnd 21, leaving remaining rnds unstuffed.

Step 2: Using purchased doll joints, place a washer on each bolt. Hold arm with thumb pointing upward. To make left arm, place bolt through Rnds 23 and 24 to left of thumb; glue inside of washer to inside of arm. To make right arm, place bolt through Rnds 23 and 24 to right of thumb; glue inside of washer to inside of arm.

Step 3: Stuff legs firmly with fiberfill to Rnd 28, leaving remaining rnds unstuffed.

Step 4: Using doll joints, place a washer on each bolt. Hold leg with toes pointing upward. To make left leg, place bolt through Rnds 28 and 29 to left of toes; glue inside of washer to inside of leg. To make right leg, place bolt through Rnds 28 and 29 to right of toes; glue inside of washer to inside of leg.

Step 5: Stuff remainder of arms and legs firmly with fiberfill.

continued on page 4

Kathy Kitty
continued from page 3

To Complete Arms: Hold arm with bolt facing away from you and fold Rnd 25 of arm in half; insert hook in dropped lp; working through both thicknesses, sc dec over first 2 sc; sc in next 4 sc, sc dec over next 2 sc. Finish off and weave in ends. Repeat for other arm, holding arm with bolt facing you.

To Complete Legs: Hold leg with bolt facing away from you and fold Rnd 31 of leg in half; insert hook in dropped lp; working through both thicknesses, sc dec over first 2 sc; sc in next 6 sc, sc dec over next 2 sc. Finish off and weave in ends.

Repeat for other leg, holding leg with bolt facing you.

Head and Body:
HEAD:
With grey, ch 2.

Note: Rnds 1 through 54 are worked in continuous rnds. Do not join; mark beg of rnds.

Rnd 1 (right side): 6 sc in 2nd ch from hook.

Rnd 2: 2 sc in each sc—12 sc.

Rnd 3: (Sc in next sc, 2 sc in next sc) 6 times—18 sc.

Rnd 4: (Sc in next 2 sc, 2 sc in next sc) 6 times—24 sc.

Rnd 5: Sc in each sc.

Rnd 6: (Sc in next 3 sc, 2 sc in next sc) 6 times—30 sc.

Rnd 7: (Sc in next 4 sc, 2 sc in next sc) 6 times—36 sc.

Rnd 8: (Sc in next 5 sc, 2 sc in next sc) 6 times—42 sc.

Rnds 9 through 14: Rep Rnd 5.

Rnd 15: Sc in next 17 sc, 2 sc in each of next 7 sc—nose shaping made; sc in next 18 sc—49 sc.

Rnds 16 and 17: Rep Rnd 5.

Rnd 18: Sc in next 17 sc, sc dec over next 2 sc; (sc in next sc, sc dec over next 2 sc) 4 times; sc in next 18 sc—44 sc.

Rnd 19: Sc in next 17 sc, sc dec over next 2 sc; sc in next 6 sc, sc dec over next 2 sc; sc in next 17 sc—42 sc.

Rnd 20: (Sc in next 5 sc, sc dec over next 2 sc) 6 times—36 sc.

Rnd 21: Rep Rnd 5.

Rnd 22: (Sc in next 4 sc, sc dec over next 2 sc) 6 times—30 sc.

Rnd 23: (Sc in next 3 sc, sc dec over next 2 sc) 6 times—24 sc.

Rnd 24: (Sc in next 2 sc, sc dec over next 2 sc) 6 times—18 sc.

Rnd 25: Rep Rnd 5.

Rnd 26: (Sc in next 2 sc, 2 sc in next sc) 9 times—27 sc.

Rnd 27: Sc in next sc, (2 sc in next sc, sc in next sc) 13 times—40 sc. Remove hook from lp. Do not cut yarn.

Note: Do not skip ahead, Face Assembly needs to be completed before going further.

Face Assembly:
Step 1: Place eyelashes behind eyes; glue together. Place eyes between Rnds 11 and 12 on head about 1 1/4" apart.

Step 2: Glue nose between Rnds 16 and 17 of nose shaping.

Step 3: Stuff head firmly.

Body:
Insert hook through dropped lp of head.

Rnd 28: (Sc in next 4 sc, 2 sc in next sc) 8 times—48 sc.

Rnd 29: Sc in each sc.

Rnds 30 through 37: Rep Rnd 29.

Kathy likes to play with yarn.

continued on page 43

Keith Kitty

Keith looks dapper with his bowtie.

Size:
About 16½" tall

Materials:
Worsted weight yarn, 5 oz (350 yds, 150 gms) grey; 3½ oz (245 yds, 105 gms) pink; 2 oz (140 yds, 60 gms) white

Note: Our photographed animal was made with Red Heart® Classic™, Silver #412, Grenadine #730, and White #001.

Size F (3.75mm) crochet hook, or size required for gauge

Size 18 tapestry needle

Trimmings:
two sets of 30mm doll joints
two 15mm black animal eyes
9 x 22mm cat nose
18" length of black embroidery floss
polyester fiberfill

Gauge:
4 sc = 1"

Pattern Stitches

Front Post Double Crochet (FPdc):
YO, insert hook from front to back to front around post (see page 211) of st indicated, draw up lp, (YO, draw through 2 lps on hook) twice—FPdc made.

Back Post Double Crochet (BPdc):
YO, insert hook from back to front to back around post (see page 211) of st indicated, draw up lp, (YO, draw through 2lps on hook) twice—BPdc made.

Front Post Single Crochet (FPsc):
Insert hook from front to back to front around post (see page 211) of st indicated, draw up lp, YO and draw through 2 lps on hook—FPsc made.

Instructions

Kitty
Work same as Kathy Kitty beginning on page 3, omiting eyelashes and hair. Follow Finishing instructions on page 44, omitting Step 4.

Romper
Starting at neckline with white, ch 32.

Row 1 (wrong side): Sc in 2nd ch from hook and in next 2 chs, (2 sc in next ch, sc in next 3 chs) 7 times—38 sc. Ch 1, turn.

Row 2 (right side): Sc in first 6 sc, 2 sc in each of next 5 sc; sc in next 16 sc, 2 sc in each of next 5 sc; sc in next 6 sc—48 sc. Ch 1, turn.

Row 3: Sc in each sc. Ch 1, turn.

Row 4: Sc in first 6 sc; † 2 sc in next sc; 2 dc in each of next 9 sc; 2 sc in next sc †; sc in next 14 sc; rep from † to † once; sc in next 6 sc—70 sts. Ch 1, turn.

Row 5: Sc in first 7 sc; † 2 sc in next sc; dc in next 18 dc, 2 sc in next sc †; sc in next 16 sc; rep from † to † once; sc in next 7 sc—74 sts. Ch 1, turn.

Row 6: Sc in first 8 sc; † 2 sc in next sc; dc in next 18 dc, 2 sc in next sc †; sc in next 18 sc; rep from † to † once; sc in next 8 sc—78 sts. Ch 1, turn.

Row 7: Sc in first 9 sc; † 2 sc in next sc; dc in next 18 dc, 2 sc in next sc †; sc in next 20 sc; rep from † to † once; sc in next 9 sc—82 sts. Ch 1, turn.

Row 8: Sc in first 10 sc; † sc dec over next 2 sts; ch 4, sk next 16 dc, sc dec over next 2 sts †; sc in next 22 sc; rep from † to † once; sc in next 10 sc. Ch 1, turn.

Row 9: 2 sc in first sc; sc in each sc and in each ch to last sc; 2 sc in last sc—56 sc. Ch 1, turn.

Row 10: Sc in each sc. Ch 1, turn.

continued on page 45

Bounty of Buttons Necklace

— designed by Sandy Scoville

Perk up your winter woollies when you wear this fun designer necklace. A quick crochet in bedspread-weight Knit-Cro-Sheen®, the necklace features polished wooden buttons worked into the design for an earthy, natural look.

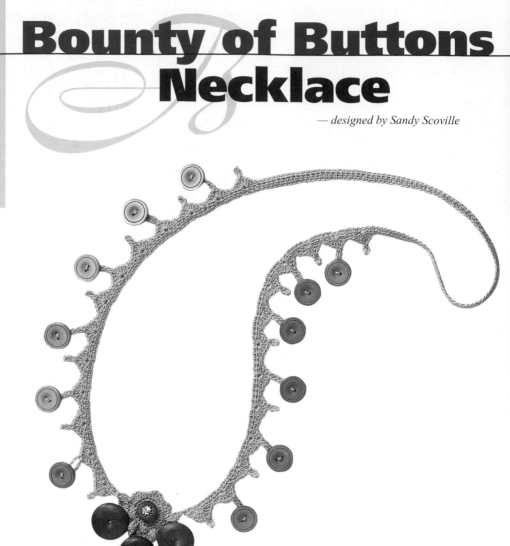

Size:
About 35" circumference

Materials:
Bedspread-weight crochet cotton,
 100 yds ecru
 ***Note:** Our photographed necklace was made with J. & P. Coats® Knit-Cro-Sheen®, New Ecru #61.*
Size 6 (1.80mm) steel crochet hook, or size required for gauge
12 wooden buttons each with 2 large holes,
 3/4"-diameter
3 wooden buttons with shank, 1" diameter
1 button with metal trim and shank,
 5/8" diameter
Size 18 tapestry needle
Sewing needle and matching thread

Gauge:
8 dc = 1"

Instructions

Medallion
Ch 6, join to form a ring.

Rnd 1 (right side)**:** Ch 3 (counts as a dc on this and following rnd), 23 dc in ring; join in 3rd ch of beg ch-3—24 dc.

Rnd 2: Ch 1, sc in same ch as joining; hdc in next dc, 3 dc in next dc; hdc in next dc; * sc in next dc, hdc in next dc, 3 dc in next dc; hdc in next dc; rep from * around; join in FL of first sc—36 sts.

Rnd 3: Ch 3, 2 dc in same lp; working in FLs only, 3 dc in each of next 2 sts; * † in next st work (2 dc, draw up long lp, remove hook, thread lp through tapestry needle, draw threaded lp through shank of 1" button, remove needle, insert hook, draw lp tight, dc) †; 3 dc in each of next 5 sts; rep

from * once more, then rep from † to † once; 3 dc in each of next 3 sts; ch 251; being careful not to twist ch and leaving rem sts unworked, join in 3rd ch of beg ch-3. Ch 2 (counts as first hdc on following rows), sk next dc on medallion, sl st in next dc, turn.

***Note:** Remainder of necklace is worked in rows.*

Row 1 (wrong side)**:** Working in ch-251, sk first ch, hdc in each rem ch; sk next dc on medallion, sl st in next dc—251 hdc. Turn.

Row 2 (right side)**:** Sk first 2 hdc; * † in next hdc work (4 dc, ch 5, sl st in last dc made, 3 dc); sk next 2 hdc, sc in next hdc, sk next 2 hdc, in next hdc work (4 dc, ch 5, draw up long lp; remove hook, thread long lp through tapestry needle, draw threaded lp

through one button from back to front to back, remove needle, insert hook in lp and draw lp tight, ch 5, sl st in last dc made, 3 dc); sk next 2 hdc, sc in next hdc, sk next 2 hdc; rep from * 5 times more; in next hdc work (4 dc, ch 5, sl st in last dc made, 3 dc); sk next 2 hdc †; sc in next 97 hdc, sk next 2 hdc; rep from † to † once; join in last sl st made on medallion.

Finish off and weave in all ends.

Finishing
Insert shank of 3/4" button through center ring of medallion. With sewing needle and matching thread, secure shank on wrong side of medallion.

Holiday Vest

The busy social weeks
during the holiday
season are filled with
opportunities for
special looks like this
stylish chenille vest.
Worn with a long
formal skirt, tailored
slacks or even jeans,
this vest will be enjoyed
for its comfort, for
its versatility and
for the compliments
you'll receive.

— designed by Darla Sims

Sizes:

	Small	Medium	Large
Chest Measurement:	30"- 32"	34"- 36"	38"- 40"
Finished Chest Measurement:	36"	40"	44"

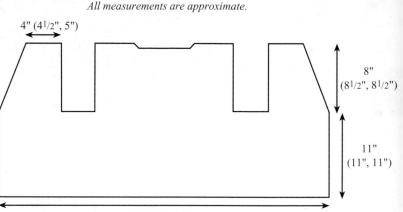

All measurements are approximate.

4" (4½", 5")

8" (8½", 8½")

11" (11", 11")

36" (40", 44")

Materials:

Worsted weight chenille yarn, 10 (12, 14) skeins red; 1 (1, 1) green
Note: Our photographed vest was made with Lion Chenille Senations, Garnet #113 and Forest Green #131.
Size G (4.25mm) crochet hook, or size required for gauge
Size F (3.75mm) crochet hook
Nine 5mm pearl beads
Size 18 tapestry needle

Gauge:

7 dc = 2"
2 dc rows = 1"

Instructions

Note: Instructions are written for size small; instructions for larger sizes are in parentheses.

Body

Beginning at lower edge with larger size hook and red, ch 149 (165, 181).

Row 1 (right side)**:** Dc in 5th ch from hook (beg 4 skipped chs count as a dc and a ch-1 sp)—beg V-st made; * sk next 3 chs, 5 dc in next ch—shell made; sk next 3 chs, in next ch work (dc, ch 1, dc)—V-st made; rep from

* 17 (19, 21) times more—18 (20, 22) shells. Ch 3 (counts as first dc on following rows), turn.

Row 2: 2 dc in next ch-1 sp; V-st in 3rd dc of next shell; * shell in next ch-1 sp; V-st in 3rd dc of next shell; rep from * 16 (18, 20) times more; 3 dc in sp formed by beg 4 skipped chs—17 (19, 21) shells. Ch 4 (counts as first dc and ch-1 sp on following rows), turn.

Row 3: Dc in first dc—beg V-st made; * shell in next ch-1 sp; V-st in 3rd dc of next shell; rep from * 16 (18, 20) times more; shell in next ch-1 sp; V-st in 3rd ch of turning ch-3. Ch 3, turn.

Rows 4 through 21: Rep Rows 2 and 3 nine times more. At end of Row 21, ch 3, turn.

Left Front

Size Small Only:

Row 1 (wrong side)**:** Dc in next ch-1 sp; * dc in next 7 dc and in next ch-1 sp; rep from * twice more; dc in next 4 dc—30 dc. Ch 3, turn, leaving rem sts unworked.

Row 2 (right side)**:** Dc in each dc and in 3rd ch of turning ch-3. Ch 3, turn.

Row 3: Dec over next 2 dc [to work dec: (YO, draw up lp in next dc, YO, draw through 2 lps on hook) twice; YO and draw

through all 3 lps on hook—dec made]; dc in each rem dc and in 3rd ch of turning ch-3—29 dc. Ch 3, turn.

Row 4: Dc in each dc to last dc and turning ch-3; dec over last dc and 3rd ch of turning ch—28 dc. Ch 3, turn.

Rows 5 through 16: Rep Rows 3 and 4 six times more—16 dc. At end of Row 16, do not ch 3. Finish off, leaving an 18" end for sewing.

Continue with Back on page 50.

Size Medium Only:

Row 1 (wrong side)**:** Dc in next ch-1 sp; * dc in next 7 dc and in next ch-1 sp; rep from * 3 times more—34 dc. Ch 3, turn.

Row 2 (right side)**:** Dc in each dc and in 3rd ch of turning ch-3. Ch 3, turn.

Row 3: Dec over next 2 dc [to work dec: (YO, draw up lp in next dc, YO and draw through 2 lps on hook) twice; YO and draw through all 3 lps on hook—dec made]; dec over next 2 dc; dc in each rem dc and in 3rd ch of turning ch-3—32 dc. Ch 3, turn.

Row 4: Dc in each dc to last 3 dc and turning ch-3; dec over next 2 dc; dec over last dc and 3rd ch of turning ch-3—30 dc. Ch 3, turn.

Row 5: Dec over next 2 dc; dc in each rem dc and in 3rd ch of turning ch-3—29 dc. Ch 3, turn.

Row 6: Dc in each dc to last dc and turning ch-3; dec over last dc and 3rd ch of turning ch—28 dc. Ch 3, turn.

Rows 7 through 16: Rep Rows 5 and 6, five times more. At end of Row 16—18 dc.

Row 17: Rep Row 5. At end of row—17 dc.

Flower is embellished with pearl bead center.

continued on page 50

Merry (Christmas!)-Go-Round Doily

— designed by Hartmut Hass

Six snow-laden trees dance around a golden star, making this holiday doily exceptionally elegant and cheerful. Designer Hartmut Hass delivers this sensational season's greeting in fluent filet crochet.

Size:
About 28" diameter

Materials:
Size 20 crochet cotton, two 442-yd balls
   white; 20 yds gold metallic floss
   *Note: Our photographed doily was made
   with J. & P. Coats® Big Ball size 20,
   White #1.*
Size 10 (1.30mm) steel crochet hook,
   or size required for gauge

Gauge:
10 squares x 10 squares = 2¹/₄"

Pattern Stitches
Double Triple Crochet (dtrc):
YO 3 times; draw up lp in stitch indicated, (YO, draw through 2 lps on hook)
4 times—dtrc made.

Cluster (CL):
Keeping last lp of each dc on hook, 3 dc
in sp or st indicated or dc in next 3 sts
indicated; YO and draw through all
4 lps on hook—CL made.

Triple Crochet Cluster (trc CL):
Keeping last lp of each trc on hook,
3 trc in st indicated; YO and
draw through all 4 lps on hook—
trc CL made.

Instructions
*Note: If you are not familiar with working
filet from a chart, please read "Filet
Review" on page 214.*

*Design Note: Each of the six trees is
worked separately. Beginning with the second tree, connect the end of each branch
with an sc in the two places indicated by
the + symbol on Diagram A on page 46.
After all six trees are completed, add the
crocheted star in the center. To help you
start your doily, follow the written instructions for Rows 1 through 3. Continuing in
same manner, work Rows 4 through 57
from Chart A on page 46.*

Tree Section

First Tree:
Starting at bottom of tree with white, ch 96.

Row 1 (right side): Dc in 9th ch from hook;
* ch 2, sk next 2 chs, dc in next ch; rep
from * 28 times more. Ch 11, turn.

Row 2: Dc in 9th ch from hook, ch 2, sk
next 2 chs, dc in next dc, (dc in next 2 chs
and in next dc) 8 times; (ch 2, dc in next dc)

4 times; (dc in next 2 chs and in next dc) 6
times; (ch 2, dc in next dc) 4 times; (dc in
next 2 chs and in next dc) 7 times; dc in
next 3 chs of beg 8 skipped chs, ch 2,
dtrc (see Pattern Stitches) in same ch as
last dc made; ch 2, dtrc in side of dtrc just
made. Ch 11, turn.

Row 3: Dc in 9th ch from hook, ch 2, sk
next 2 chs, (dc in next dtrc and in next
2 chs) twice; dc in next 25 dc, (dc in next
2 chs and in next dc) twice; (ch 2, sk next
2 chs, dc in next dc) twice; ch 2, sk next
2 dc, dc in next 13 dc, ch 2, sk next 2 dc, dc
in next dc, (ch 2, sk next 2 chs, dc in next
dc) twice; (dc in next 2 chs and in next dc)
twice; dc in next 24 dc, dc in next 2 chs and
in next dc, dc in next 3 chs of turning ch-11,
ch 2, dtrc in same ch as last dc made; ch 2,
dtrc in side of dtrc just made. Ch 9, turn.

Referring to **Chart A** on page 46, work
Rows 4 through 57. At end of Row 57,
finish off.

Second through Sixth Trees:
Work same as first tree, joining each branch
of completed tree to working tree with an sc

(indicated by the + symbol on **Diagram A**).
When joining last tree to first tree, be careful not to twist trees.

Star Center
With gold metallic thread, ch 8; join to form
a ring.

Rnd 1 (right side): Ch 3 (counts as a dc on
this and following rnds), 17 dc in ring; join
in 3rd ch of beg ch-3—18 dc.

Rnd 2: Ch 3, dc in same ch as joining;
* † dc in next dc, 2 dc in next dc; ch 2 †;
2 dc in next dc; rep from * 4 times more,
then rep from † to † once; join in 3rd ch of
beg ch-3.

Rnd 3: Ch 3, dc in next 4 dc; * † ch 2,
CL (see Pattern Stitches) in next ch-2 sp;
ch 2 †; dc in next 5 dc; rep from * 4 times
more, then rep from † to † once; join in 3rd
ch of turning ch-3—6 CLs.

Rnd 4: Ch 2, dc in next dc; * † dc in next
dc, keeping last lp of each dc on hook, dc in
next 2 dc, YO and draw through all 3 lps on
hook; ch 4, CL in next CL; ch 4 †; keeping

continued on page 46

11

Snowbound!

Snuggle up with your snowman under this pretty blue and white afghan that looks just like snowflakes falling out of the clear blue sky.

— designed by Nanette Seale

Size:
About 51" x 64"

Materials:
Worsted weight yarn, 30 oz (2100 yds, 900 gms) white; 18 oz (1250 yds, 540 gms) blue

Note: Our photographed afghan was made using Caron® Dazzleaire®, White #2601 and Celestial Blue #2885.

Size H (5mm) crochet hook, or size required for gauge

Size 16 tapestry needle

Gauge:
4 dc = 1"

Pattern Stitches

Beginning Cluster (beg CL):
Ch 3, keeping last lp of each dc on hook, 2 dc in st indicated; YO and draw through all 3 lps on hook— beg CL made.

Cluster (CL):
Keeping last lp of each dc on hook, 3 dc in st indicated; YO and draw through all 4 lps on hook—CL made.

Double Crochet Cluster (dc CL):
Keeping last lp of each dc on hook, 2 dc in sp or st indicated; YO and draw through all 3 lps on hook—dc CL made.

Beginning Triple Crochet Cluster (beg trc CL):
Ch 4, keeping last lp of each trc on hook, 2 trc in sp or st indicated; YO and draw through all 3 lps on hook— beg trc CL made.

Triple Crochet Cluster (trc CL):
Keeping last lp of each trc on hook, 3 trc in sp or st indicated; YO and draw through all 4 lps on hook— trc CL made.

Instructions
Note: Instructions for motifs follow assembly instructions.

Assembly
Beg at lower left corner of afghan, work Motif A. Work Motif B, joining to Motif A in last rnd. Referring to **Diagram A** on page 49 for placement of motifs, work remainder of Row 1 of afghan; continue with Rows 2 through 6. Border instructions follow Motif E.

Motif A
With white, ch 6; join to form a ring.

Rnd 1 (right side): Ch 3 (counts as a dc on this and following rnds), 15 dc in ring; join in 3rd ch of beg ch-3—16 dc.

Rnd 2: In same ch as joining work beg CL (see Pattern Stitches); ch 3, sk next dc; * CL (see Pattern Stitches) in next dc; ch 3; rep from * 6 times more; join in beg CL— 8 CLs.

Rnd 3: Beg CL in same CL; ch 3, sc in next ch-3 sp, ch 3; * CL in next CL; ch 3, sc in next ch-3 sp, ch 3; rep from * 6 times more; join in beg CL.

Rnd 4: In same CL work (beg CL, ch 3, CL, ch 3, CL); * † ch 5, sk next 2 ch-3 sps,

trc CL (see Pattern Stitches) in next CL; ch 5, sk next 2 ch-3 sps †; in next CL work (CL, ch 3) twice; CL in same CL; rep from * twice more, then rep from † to † once; join in beg CL.

continued on page 49

Part One – The Chain Stitch

— by Jean Leinhauser

The humble chain stitch is the basis of crochet.

Nearly all crochet work begins with a chain; the chain helps us move from place to place, lets us add open, airy affects to our work, and provides the base on which we build the crochet fabric.

Making the starting chain

Most of us have already learned—sometimes the hard way—that the starting chain needs to be looser than the work that will follow it.

We accomplish this either by chaining very loosely, or working the starting chain with a larger size hook than the body of the project.

But there are many other things to learn about the chain. Here are some questions we've been asked, with their answers.

1. I have trouble keeping accurate count of the starting chains when working a large number of them. What should I do?

You can keep track by putting a small safety pin through every 10th or 25th chain; or, make the starting slip knot leaving a long yarn end. Then on the first row if you run out of chains, just add however more chains you need with the yarn end. To do this, follow these steps:

Step 1: After working the last stitch, drop lp from hook; insert hook in beginning slip knot (**Fig 1**).

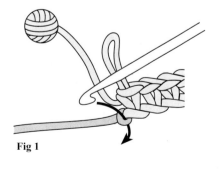

Fig 1

Step 2: YO with yarn end and draw through slip stitch (**Fig 2**). One new chain made.

Fig 2

Step 3: For each additional chain, YO with same end and draw through lp on hook (**Fig 3**). When enough new chs have been added, reinsert hook in last st made and continue working sts in the added chs.

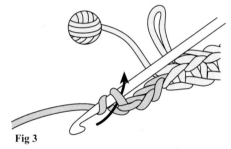

Fig 3

Note: Be sure to use the same hook size used for the original chains.

2. If you have a really long starting chain, maybe several hundred stitches, is there any way to make the starting chain and work the first row at the same time?

Yes! That is if the first row can be single crochet.

Here's how:

Step 1: Make a slip knot on hook and ch 2.

Step 2: Insert hook in 2nd ch from hook (**Fig 4**), YO and pull lp through—2 lps on hook; YO and pull through both lps on hook (**Fig 5**)—first sc made.

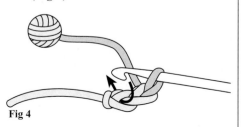

Fig 4

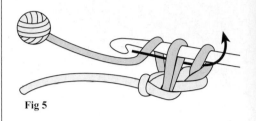

Fig 5

Step 3: Insert hook in long strand of last sc (**Fig 6a**), YO and pull lp through— 2 lps on hook; YO and pull through both lps on hook: another sc made.

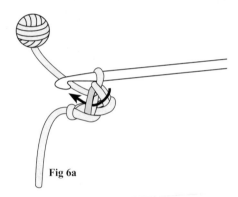

Fig 6a

Repeat Step 3 for each required stitch (**Fig 6b**). To make counting easier, place a small safety pin in every 10th or 25th stitch.

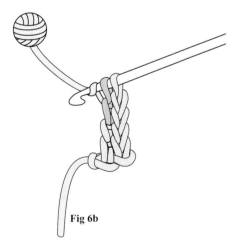

Fig 6b

When you have the desired number of stitches, ch 1 and turn. Work the next row of sc under both lps of each sc of the preceding row. If the next row is to be in dc or any other stitch, simply make the appropriate turning chain.

3. Can I possibly eliminate the starting chain?

Yes, if you really have trouble making a long starting chain loose enough, here is a "chainless" way to get started. You do have to know how wide your finished piece will be.

Let's say an afghan is to be 40 inches wide. Measure off about 60" of yarn, then make a slip knot on the hook. Holding the long yarn end in your left hand, sc over the yarn end (see **Figs 7** and **8**) until you have the specified number of stitches given in the pattern—such as, "Ch 161; sc in 2nd ch from hook and in each rem ch—160 sc." In this case, work 160 sc over the yarn length, not the 161 specified for the starting chain.

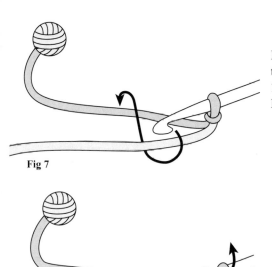

Fig 7

Fig 8

This beginning sc row counts as the starting chain, not as the first row of the pattern. Now you can go on and work Row 1 of the pattern.

Work a few rows, then stretch the beginning sc row out evenly; finish off the excess yarn. In this method, the foundation row should always be worked in sc, no matter what the pattern stitch will be on Row 1.

4. Where do I put my hook when I work into the starting chain?

Let's say a pattern directs you to ch 16, sc in 2nd ch from hook and in each ch across. But did you know that there are three places in the chain that you can work that first row?

Method 1: Insert hook under back loop only of each chain (**Fig 9**). This method provides the most stretch for the beginning row.

Fig 9

Method 2: Insert hook into the center of the V and back bump of each chain (**Fig 10**). This gives a neater finished edge than Method 1.

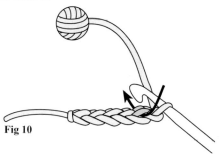

Fig 10

Method 3: This is my personal favorite. Insert hook in back bump behind each chain (**Fig 11**). This is a good choice for projects in which you will be working on both sides of the starting chain. I also like the way the finished edge looks, and it will be easier to work a row of single crochet around the edge.

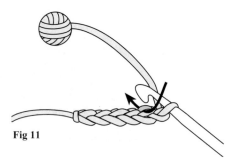

Fig 11

5. Sometimes a pattern reads "Ch 50; join in a ring, being careful not to twist chain." I find it hard to keep the chain from twisting. Is there an easy way?

Since it is difficult to keep a long chain from twisting, do not join it into a ring. Instead, work the first row of the pattern, then join with a sl st in first st. When weaving in the ends, just sew the first row lower edge together.

6. I love to make filet crochet, but is there a way to be sure my squares are really square?

Many crocheters find they can get the row gauge in filet, but not the stitch gauge. Chances are this is because the one or two chains used to create open blocks are worked too tightly. So loosen up the chains to square up the stitches!

7. When I crochet lacy doilies with lots of chain repeat sections, I find the work becomes distorted. Why is this?

Lacy doilies often have repeat sections of chains. If these chains are worked too tightly or too loosely, the doily will be distorted. Keep the chains firm and even, but not tight.

For additional lessons on basic crochet stitches, see the following articles.

Part Two – Single Crochet on page 83

Part Three – Double Crochet on page 124

Part Four – Half Double Crochet on page 176

Neck Cozy

What a stylish way to keep the wind off your neck without adding bulk to your silhouette! Enjoy a productive evening crocheting this flattering scarf.

— *designed by Nancy Brown*

Size:
About 4$\frac{1}{2}$" wide x 32" long

Materials:
Worsted weight yarn, 2$\frac{1}{2}$ oz (175 yds, 75 gms) dark rose
> *Note: Our photographed scarf was made using Lion Brand® Wool-Ease®, Dark Rose Heather #139*

Size I (5.5mm) crochet hook, or size required for gauge
Size 18 tapestry needle

Gauge:
1 shell = $\frac{3}{4}$"

Instructions

Left Side
Ch 2.

Row 1 (right side): In 2nd ch from hook work (sc, 2 dc)—shell made. Ch 1, turn.

Row 2: Shell in first dc; sk next dc, shell in next sc—2 shells. Ch 1, turn.

Row 3: Shell in first dc; sk next dc, shell in next sc; sk next 2 dc, shell in next sc—3 shells. Ch 1, turn.

Row 4: Shell in first dc; sk next dc, shell in next sc; * sk next 2 dc, shell in next sc; rep from * once more—4 shells. Ch 1, turn.

Row 5: Shell in first dc; sk next dc, shell in next sc; * sk next 2 dc, shell in next sc; rep from * twice more—5 shells. Ch 1, turn.

Row 6: Shell in first dc; sk next dc, shell in next sc; * sk next 2 dc, shell in next sc; rep from * 3 times more—6 shells. Ch 1, turn.

Row 7: Shell in first dc; sk next dc, shell in next sc; * sk next 2 dc, shell in next sc; rep from * 4 times more—7 shells. Ch 1, turn.

Row 8: Shell in first dc; sk next dc, shell in next sc; * sk next 2 dc, shell in next sc; rep from * 5 times more—8 shells. Ch 1, turn.

Row 9: Shell in first dc; sk next dc, shell in next sc; * sk next 2 dc, shell in next sc; rep from * 5 times more; sk next 2 dc, sc in next sc—8 shells. Ch 1, turn.

Row 10: Shell in first sc; * sk next 2 dc, shell in next sc; rep from * 6 times more; sk next 2 dc, sc in next sc— 8 shells. Ch 1, turn.

Rows 11 through 13: Rep Row 10.

Row 14: * Dec over first 3 sts (to work dec: draw up lp in next sc and in each of next 2 dc, YO and draw through all 4 lps on hook—dec made); rep from * 7 times more; sc in next sc—9 sc. Ch 1, turn.

Row 15: 2-sc dec over first 2 sc (to work 2-sc dec: draw up lp in each of next 2 sc, YO and draw through all 3 lps on hook—2-sc dec made); sc in next 5 sc, 2-sc dec over next 2 sc—7 sc. Ch 1, turn.

Row 16: Sc in each sc. Ch 1, turn.

Rows 17 through 22: Rep Row 16.

Row 23: Shell in each of next 6 sc; sc in next sc—6 shells. Ch 1, turn.

Rows 24 through 45: Rep Row 23. At end of Row 45, do not ch 1.

Finish off and weave in ends.

Right Side

Scarf Front Opening:
Ch 2.

Rows 1 through 15: Rep Rows 1 through 15 of Left Side.

Row 16: Working in FLs only, sc in each sc. Ch 1, turn.

Row 17: Sc in each sc. Ch 1, turn.

Rows 18 through 22: Rep Row 17. At end of Row 22, do not ch 1.

Finish off and weave in ends.

Scarf Back Opening:

Hold piece with right side facing you and Row 22 at top; join yarn in first unused lp of Row 15.

Row 1 (right side)**:** Ch 1, working in rem unused lps, sc in each lp—7 sc. Ch 1, turn.

Row 2: Sc in each sc. Ch 1, turn.

Rows 3 through 7: Rep Row 2.

Row 8 (joining row)**:** Holding wrong side of scarf front opening facing wrong side of back opening and working through both thicknesses, sc in each sc. Ch 1, turn.

Rows 9 through 31: Rep Rows 23 through 45 of Left Side. Finish off, leaving an 18" end for sewing.

Finishing

Hold left and right sides with wrong sides together and last rows worked at top. With tapestry needle and 18" end, sew together through both lps.

Weave in ends.

Huggable
Chenille Teddy

The way into a child's heart may very well be through a furry crocheted Teddy Bear. This comforting creature is quickly created with plush Lion Brand®'s Chenille "Thick & Quick".

— designed by Kelly Robinson

Size:
About 17" high (sitting)

Materials:
Bulky weight chenille yarn, 20 oz (400 yds, 560 gms) tan; small amount of worsted weight black chenille
   Note: Our photographed teddy was made with Lion Brand® Chenille "Thick and Quick", Khaki #124 and Chenille Sensations, Black #153.
Size K (6.5mm) crochet hook, or size required for gauge
Size 18 tapestry needle

Trimmings:
two 18mm animal eyes
one flocked animal nose
tacky craft glue or hot glue
15 oz polyester fiberfill
1 yd red satin ribbon, 1"-wide

Gauge:
5 sc = 2"

Instructions

Head
Note: Rnds 1 through 24 are worked in continuous rnds. Do not join; mark beg of rnds.

Starting at center of nose, ch 3.

Rnd 1 (right side)**:** 11 hdc in 3rd ch from hook (beg 2 skipped chs count as an hdc)—12 hdc.

Rnd 2: (Sc in next hdc, 2 sc in next hdc) 6 times—18 sc.

Rnd 3: Sc in each st.

Rnd 4: Rep Rnd 3.

Rnd 5: (Sc in next sc, 2 sc in next sc) 9 times—27 sc.

Rnd 6: Sc in next 3 sc, (sc in next 2 sc, 2 sc in next sc) 6 times; sc in next 6 sc—33 sc.

Rnd 7: Rep Rnd 3.

Rnd 8: Sc in next 5 sc, 2 sc in each of next 23 sc; sc in next 5 sc—56 sc.

Rnd 9: Rep Rnd 3.

Rnd 10: Dec over next 2 sc (to work dec: draw up lp in each of next 2 sc, YO and draw through all 3 lps on hook—dec made); dec over next 2 sc; sc in next 48 sc, (dec over next 2 sc) twice—52 sc.

Rnd 11: Dec twice; sc in next 44 sc, dec twice—48 sc.

Rnds 12 through 14: Rep Rnd 3.

Rnd 15: Sc in next 19 sc; † hdc in FL of next sc, 3 dc in FL of next sc; 5 trc in FL of next sc; 3 dc in FL of next sc; hdc in FL of next sc—ear made †; sc in next 7 sc; rep from † to † once; sc in next 12 sc.

continued on page 18

Huggable Chenille Teddy

continued from page 17

Rnd 16: Sc in next 19 sc; keeping ear piece folded forward, sc in next 5 unused lps and in next 7 sc; keeping next ear folded forward, sc in next 5 unused lps and in next 12 sc—48 sc.

Rnd 17: Rep Rnd 3.

Rnd 18: (Sc in next sc, dec) 16 times—32 sc.

Rnd 19: Rep Rnd 3.

Rnd 20: (Dec, sc in next sc) 10 times; dec—21 sc.

Note: It is easier to attach nose and eyes at this point before continuing. With right side facing you, insert nose shank into center sp formed by Rnd 1; secure with washer on wrong side. Place eyes on Rnd 5 in same manner, with four stitches in between them.

Rnd 21: Rep Rnd 3.

Rnd 22: (Dec, sc in next sc) 7 times—14 sc.

Note: Stuff head firmly with fiberfill.

Rnd 23: Rep Rnd 3.

Rnd 24: Dec 7 times—7 sc. Finish off, leaving a 6" end for sewing.

Body

Note: Rnds 1 through 24 are worked in continuous rnds. Do not join; mark beg of rnds.

Starting at top of body and leaving a 20" end for sewing, ch 18; join to form a ring.

Rnd 1 (right side): Ch 1, 18 sc in ring.

Rnd 2: Sc in each sc.

Rnd 3: 2 sc in each sc—36 sc.

Rnds 4 through 9: Rep Rnd 2.

Rnd 10: * Sc in next sc, 2 sc in next sc; rep from * 17 times more—54 sc.

Rnds 11 through 19: Rep Rnd 2.

Rnd 20: Dec over next 2 sc [to work dec: draw up lp in each of next 2 sc, YO and draw through 2 lps on hook—dec made]; sc in next sc; * dec over next 2 sc; sc in next sc; rep from * 16 times more—36 sc.

Rnd 21: Rep Rnd 2.

Rnd 22: (Dec, sc in next sc) 12 times—24 sc.

Rnd 23: Rep Rnd 2.

Rnd 24: (Dec, sc in next sc) 8 times—16 sc.

Rnd 25: Dec 8 times; join in first sc. Finish off, leaving a 12" end for sewing.

Arm (make 2)

Note: Rnds 1 through 20 are worked in continuous rnds. Do not join; mark beg of rnds.

Ch 8.

Rnd 1 (right side): Sc in 2nd ch from hook and in next 5 chs, 2 sc in next ch; working in unused lps on opposite side of beg ch, sc in next 6 lps—14 sc.

Rnd 2: Sc in each sc.

Rnds 3 through 18: Rep Rnd 2.

Rnd 19: (Dec, sc in next sc) 4 times; dec—9 sc.

Note: Stuff arm with fiberfill.

Rnd 20: Rep Rnd 2.

Rnd 21: Dec 4 times; sc in next sc; join in first sc. Finish off, leaving a 12" end for sewing.

continued on page 47

CHENILLE
Thick & Quick
A super soft plush yarn that
works up very quickly.
Perfect for luxurious
fashions and afghans.
*Available at leading yarn
and craft stores.*

Evening of Glamour

— *designed by Joyce Nordstrom*

Make a lasting impression your next night on the town in glamorous and glitzy accessories made with Luster Sheen® yarn. Three tantalizing pieces include an alluring vest and a bewitching shawl (shown here), and a dazzling little evening bag (shown on page 24).

Vest

Sizes:

	Small/Medium	Large/X-Large
Finished Measurements:	38"	44"

Materials:

Sport weight yarn, 8 (10) oz [700 (900) yds,
230 (295) gms] black/pearl
*Note: Our photographed vest was
made with J. & P. Coats® Luster Sheen®,
Black/Pearl #2P.*
Size E (3.5mm) crochet hook, or size
required for gauge
Four black buttons, 1/2" diameter
Sewing needle and matching thread

Gauge:

In pattern stitch (sc in next st, ch 4):
4 ch-4 sps = 31/2"

Instructions

*Note: Vest is worked in one piece to under-
arm, then split for back and front.*

Starting at lower edge, ch 170 (202).

Row 1 (right side): Sc in 2nd ch from hook;
* ch 4, sk next 3 chs, sc in next ch; rep from
* 41 (49) times more—42 (50) ch-4 sps.
Ch 4 (counts as first dc and ch-1 sp on following rows), turn.

Row 2: Dc in first sc; * † sc in next ch-4 sp,
ch 4, sk next sc, sc in next ch-4 sp †; in next
sc work (dc, ch 1, dc, ch 1, dc)—shell
made; rep from * 19 (23) times more, then
rep from † to † once; in next sc work (dc,
ch 1, dc)—20 (24) shells. Ch 1, turn.

Row 3: Sc in first dc, shell in next sc; * † sc
in next ch-4 sp, shell in next sc †; sk next dc
and next ch-1 sp, sc in next dc, sk next ch-1
sp and next dc, shell in next sc; rep from
* 19 (23) times more, then rep from † to
† once; sk next dc and next ch of turning
ch-4; sc in next ch. Ch 4, turn.

Row 4: Dc in first sc; * † sc in 2nd dc of
next shell, ch 4, sk next sc, sc in 2nd dc of
next shell †; shell in next sc; rep from * 19
(23) times more, then rep from † to † once;
in next sc work (dc, ch 1, dc)—half shell
made. Ch 1, turn.

Row 5: Sc in first dc, ch 4, sk next ch-1 sp,
next dc and next sc; * sc in next ch-4 sp,
ch 4, sc in 2nd dc of next shell, ch 4, sk next
sc; rep from * 19 (23) times more; sc in

next ch-4 sp,
ch 4, sk next ch
of turning ch-4,
sc in next ch—
42 (50) ch-4 sps.
Ch 4, turn.

**Rows 6 through
21:** Rep Rows 2
through 5 four
times more.

Right Front

Row 1 (wrong side): Dc in first sc; * sc in
next ch-4 sp, ch 4, sk next sc, sc in next ch-
4 sp, shell in next sc; rep from * 3 (4) times
more; sc in next ch-4 sp, ch 4, sc in next
ch-4 sp—4 (5) shells. Ch 1, turn, leaving
rem sts unworked.

Row 2 (right side): Sc in first ch-4 sp, shell
in next sc; * † sc in 2nd dc of next shell,
shell in next sc; sc in next ch-4 sp †; shell in
next sc; rep from * 2 (3) times more, then
rep from † to † once; shell in next sc; sk
next dc and next ch of turning ch-4, sc in
next ch—9 (11) shells. Ch 1, turn.

Row 3: Sk first dc and next ch-1 sp, sc in
next dc, ch 4, sc in 2nd dc of next shell,
shell in next sc; * sc in 2nd dc of next shell,
ch 4, sc in 2nd dc of next shell, shell in next
sc; rep from * 2 (3) times more; sk next dc,
sc in next dc. Ch 1, turn.

Row 4: Sk first sc, sc in 2nd dc of
next shell, ch 4, sc in next ch-4
sp; * ch 4, sc in 2nd dc of next
shell, ch 4, sc in next ch-4
sp; rep from * 2 (3) times
more; ch 4, sc in next sc—
8 (10) ch-4 sps. Ch 1, turn.

Row 5: Sc in first ch-4 sp, ch 4, sk next sc;
* sc in next ch-4 sp, shell in next sc; sc in
next ch-4 sp, ch 4; rep from * 2 (3) times
more; sc in next ch-4 sp, half shell in next
sc. Ch 1, turn.

Row 6: Shell in next sc; * sc in next ch-4
sp, shell in next sc; sc in 2nd dc of next
shell, shell in next sc; rep from * 2 (3) times
more; dc in next sc—7 (9) shells. Ch 1, turn.

Row 7: * Sc in 2nd dc of next shell, shell in
next sc; sc in 2nd dc of next shell, ch 4; rep
from * 2 (3) times more; sc in 2nd dc of
next shell. Ch 4, turn.

Row 8: * † Sc in next ch-4 sp, ch 4, sc in
2nd dc of next shell †; ch 4; rep from * once
(twice) more, then rep from † to † once; dc
in next sc—6 (8) sc. Ch 4, turn.

continued on page 22

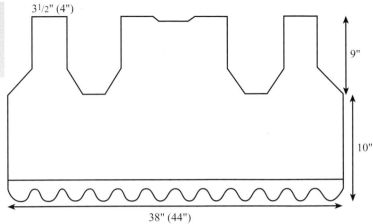

All measurements are approximate.

31/2" (4")

9"

10"

38" (44")

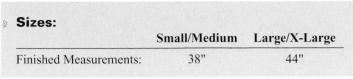

Lower edge of vest.

Evening of Glamour – Vest

continued from page 21

Row 9: Dc in first dc, sc in next ch-4 sp; * ch 4, sc in next ch-4 sp, shell in next sc; sc in next ch-4 sp; rep from * once (twice) more; half shell in next sc. Ch 1, turn.

Row 10: Sc in first dc; * shell in next sc; sc in 2nd dc of next shell, shell in next sc; sc in next ch-4 sp; rep from * once (twice) more; shell in next sc; sk next ch of turning ch-4, sc in next ch— 5 (7) shells. Ch 1, turn.

Row 11: Sk first sc, next dc, and next ch-1 sp; sc in next dc; * ch 4, sc in 2nd dc of next shell, shell in next sc; sc in 2nd dc of next shell; rep

from * once (twice) more; half shell in next sc. Ch 1, turn.

Row 12: Sc in first dc; * ch 4, sc in 2nd dc of next shell, ch 4, sc in next ch-4 sp; rep from * once (twice) more; sc in next sc— 4 (6) ch-4 sps. Ch 4, turn.

Row 13: Dc in first dc; * † sc in next ch-4 sp, shell in next sc; sc in next ch-4 sp †; ch 4; rep from * 0 (1) time more, then rep from † to † once; half shell in next sc. Ch 1, turn.

Row 14: Sc in first dc; * † shell in next sc; sc in 2nd dc of next shell, shell in next sc †; sc in next ch-4 sp; rep from * 0 (1) time more, then rep from † to † once; sk next ch of turning ch-4, sc in next ch. Ch 4, turn.

Row 15: Dc in first sc; * † sc in 2nd dc of next shell, shell in next sc; sc in 2nd dc of next shell †; ch 4; rep from * 0 (1) time more, then rep from † to † once; half shell in next sc— 1 (2) ch-4 sps. Ch 1, turn.

Row 16: Sc in first dc; * † ch 4, sc in 2nd dc of next shell, ch 4 †; sc in next ch-4 sp; rep from * 0 (1) time more, then rep from † to † once; sk next ch of turning ch-4, sc in next ch—4 (6) ch-4 sps. Ch 4, turn.

Rows 17 through 20: Rep Rows 13 through 16.

Rows 21 through 23: Rep Rows 13 through 15. At end of Row 23, do not ch 1; do not turn. Finish off.

Back

Hold piece with wrong side facing you, sk next 3 unused ch-4 sps from right front; make lp on hook and join with an sc in next ch-4 sp.

Row 1 (wrong side)**:** Shell in next sc; sc in next ch-4 sp; * ch 4, sk next sc, sc in next ch-4 sp, shell in next sc; sc in next ch-4 sp; rep from * 6 (8) times more—8 (10) shells. Ch 1, turn, leaving rem sts unworked.

Row 2 (right side)**:** Sk first sc, next dc, and next ch-1 sp; sc in next dc, shell in next sc; sc in next ch-4 sp; * shell in next sc; sc in 2nd dc of next shell, shell in next sc; sc in next ch-4 sp; rep from * 5 (7) times more; shell in next sc; sc in 2nd dc of next shell— 14 (18) shells. Ch 4, turn.

Row 3: Dc in first sc, sc in 2nd dc of next shell, ch 4, sc in 2nd dc of next shell; * shell in next sc; sc in 2nd dc of next shell, ch 4, sc in 2nd dc of next shell; rep from * 5 (7) times more; half shell in next sc. Ch 1, turn.

Row 4: Sc in first dc; * ch 4, sc in next ch-4 sp, ch 4, sc in 2nd dc of next shell; rep from * 5 (7) times more; ch 4, sc in next ch-4 sp, ch 4, sk next ch of turning ch-4, sc in next ch— 14 (18) ch-4 sps. Ch 3, turn.

Row 5: Sc in next ch-4 sp; * ch 4, sc in next ch-4 sp, shell in next sc; sc in next ch-4 sp; rep from * 5 (7) times more; ch 4, sc in next ch-4 sp, dc in next sc. Ch 1, turn.

Row 6: Sc in first dc, shell in next sc; sc in next ch-4 sp; * shell in next sc, sc in 2nd dc of next shell, shell in next sc; sc in next ch-4 sp; rep from * 5 (7) times more; shell in next sc; sc in 3rd ch of turning ch-3—14 (18) shells. Ch 3, turn.

Row 7: Sc in 2nd dc of next shell, ch 4; * sc in 2nd dc of next shell, shell in next sc; sc in 2nd dc of next shell, ch 4; rep from * 5 (7) times more; sc in 2nd dc of next shell, dc in next sc. Ch 4, turn.

continued on page 52

Shawl

Size:
About 88" wide x 44" long

Materials:
Sport weight yarn, 20 oz (1700 yds, 560 gms) black/pearl

Note: Our photographed shawl was made with J. & P. Coats® Luster Sheen®, Black/Pearl #2P.

Size E (3.5mm) crochet hook, or size required for gauge

Gauge:
In pattern stitch (sc in next st, ch 4): 4 ch-4 sps = 3½"

Pattern Stitch
Double Triple Crochet (dtrc): YO 3 times; draw up lp in st indicated, (YO and draw through 2 lps on hook) 3 times—dtrc made.

Instructions
Starting at center back, ch 24.

Row 1 (right side)**:** Sc in 6th ch from hook, ch 3, sk next 6 chs, in next ch work (trc, ch 2, trc, ch 4, trc, ch 2, trc); ch 3, sk next 6 chs, sc in next ch, ch 3, sk next 3 chs, sc in next ch. Ch 1, turn.

Row 2: Sc in next ch-3 sp, 3 dc in next ch-3 sp; dc in next trc, 2 dc in next ch-2 sp; dc in next trc, in next ch-4 sp work (3 dc, ch 1, 3 dc); dc in next trc, 2 dc in next ch-2 sp; dc in next trc, 3 dc in next ch-3 sp; sc in sp formed by beg 6 skipped chs. Ch 7, turn.

Row 3: Sc in first sc; † ch 4, sk next 3 dc, sc in next dc, ch 4, sk next 2 dc, sc in next dc, ch 4, sk next 3 dc †; in next ch-1 sp work (sc, ch 6, sc)— mark for center sp; rep from † to † once; in next sc work (sc, ch 4, dc)—edge sp made. Ch 7, turn.

Row 4: Sc in edge sp—beg edge sp made; ch 4, sc in next ch-4 sp, in next sc work (dc, ch 1, dc, ch 1, dc)—shell made; (sc in next ch-4 sp, ch 4) twice; in next center ch-6 sp work (sc, ch 6, sc)—center sp made; (ch 4, sc in next ch-4 sp) twice; in next sc work (dc, ch 1, dc, ch 1, dc)—shell made; sc in next ch-4 sp, ch 4, edge sp in turning ch-7— 2 shells. Ch 7, turn.

Row 5: Sc in edge sp, ch 4, sc in next ch-4 sp, shell in next sc; sc in 2nd dc of next shell, shell in next sc; (sc in next ch-4 sp, ch 4) twice; in next center ch-6 sp work center sp; (ch 4, sc in next ch-4 sp) twice; shell in next sc; sc in 2nd dc of next shell, shell in next sc; sc in next ch-4 sp, ch 4, edge sp in turning ch-7—4 shells. Ch 7, turn.

Row 6: Sc in edge sp, ch 4, sc in next ch-4 sp, ch 4, sc in 2nd dc of next shell, shell in next sc; sc in 2nd dc of next shell, (ch 4, sc in next ch-4 sp) twice; ch 4, center sp in next center sp; (ch 4, sc in next ch-4 sp) twice; ch 4, sc in 2nd dc of next shell, shell in next sc; sc in 2nd dc of next shell, ch 4, sc in next ch-4 sp, ch 4, edge sp in turning ch-7— 2 shells. Ch 7, turn.

Row 7: Sc in edge sp, (ch 4, sc in next ch-4 sp) twice; ch 4, sc in 2nd dc of next shell, (ch 4, sc in next ch-4 sp) 3 times; ch 4, center sp in next center sp; (ch 4, sc in next ch-4 sp) 3 times; ch 4, sc in 2nd dc of next shell, (ch 4, sc in next ch-4 sp) twice; ch 4, edge sp in turning ch-7. Ch 7, turn.

Row 8: Sc in edge sp, (ch 4, sc in next ch-4 sp) 3 times; shell in next sc; sc in next ch-4 sp, (ch 4, sc in next

continued on page 53

Evening Bag

Size:
About 8" wide x 8" high, including edging

Materials:
Sport weight yarn, 2¹/₂ oz (200 yds,
65¹/₂ gms) black/pearl
*Note: Our photographed bag was
made with J. & P. Coats® Luster Sheen®,
Black/Pearl #2P.*
Size E (3.5mm) crochet hook, or size
required for gauge
black fabric, 18" x 15" piece (for lining)

Gauge:
In pattern stitch (sc in next st, ch 4):
4 ch-4 sps = 3¹/₂"

Instructions
Note: Bag is worked in one piece.

Ch 34.

Row 1 (right side)**:** Sc in 2nd ch from hook;
* ch 4, sk next 3 chs, sc in next ch; rep from
* 7 times more. Ch 4 (counts as a dc and a
ch-1 sp on following rows), turn.

Row 2: Dc in first sc; * † sc in next ch-4 sp,
in next sc work (dc, ch 1, dc, ch 1, dc)—
shell made; sc in next ch-4 sp †; ch 4, sk
next sc; rep from * twice more, then rep
from † to † once; in next sc work (dc, ch 1,
dc)—half shell made. Ch 1, turn.

Row 3: Sc in first dc; * † shell in next sc; sc
in 2nd dc of next shell, shell in next sc †; sc
in next ch-4 sp; rep from * twice more, then
rep from † to † once; sk next ch of turning
ch-4, sc in next ch—8 shells. Ch 4, turn.

Row 4: Dc in first sc; * † sc in 2nd dc of
next shell, shell in next sc; sc in 2nd dc of
next shell †; ch 4; rep from * twice more,
then rep from † to † once; half shell in next
sc. Ch 1, turn.

Row 5: Sc in first dc; * † ch 4, sc in 2nd
dc of next shell, ch 4 †; sc in next ch-4 sp;
rep from * twice more, then rep from † to
† once; sk next ch of turning ch-4, sc in
next ch—8 ch-4 sps. Ch 4, turn.

Rows 6 through 37: Rep Rows 2 through
5 eight times more. At end of Row 37, do
not ch 4.

Finish off and weave in all ends.

Finishing
Fold piece in half with right sides together
and matching beg ch and Row 37. Sew side
seams with overcast stitch (see Crochet
Stitch Guide, page 213) matching corresponding rows. Turn right side out.

Border
Hold bag with opening at top and right side
of beg ch facing you; join yarn in first
unused ch-3 sp of beg ch.

Rnd 1: Ch 3 (counts as a dc), 2 dc in same
sp; working in unused lps of beg ch and in
sps formed by skipped chs, dc in next lp;
* 3 dc in next sp; dc in next lp; rep from
* 6 times more; dc in next seam; working
across Row 37, ** 3 dc in next ch-4 sp; dc
in next sc; rep from ** 7 times more; dc
in next seam; join in 3rd ch of beg ch-3—
66 dc.

Rnd 2: Ch 4 (counts as first dc and ch-1
sp), sk next dc; * dc in next dc, ch 1, sk
next dc; rep from * around; join in 3rd ch of
beg ch-4.

Rnd 3: Ch 3, dc in each ch-1 sp and in each
dc; join in 3rd ch of beg ch-3.

Rnd 4: Ch 1, sc in same ch as joining; sk
next 2 dc, shell in next dc; sk next 2 dc; * sc
in next dc, sk next 2 dc, shell in next dc; sk
next 2 dc; rep from * around; join in first sc.

Finish off and weave in ends.

Lining
These instructions are for a double layer lining with seams enclosed between layers.

Fold lining fabric in half lengthwise and
sew a ¹/₂" seam along two sides (18"-long
side and one 7¹/₂" side). Press under ¹/₂"
seam allowance on open end. Bring the
open end down over stitched end with all
seam allowances inside; hand stitch the
open end closed. Adjust double lining so
that one half is folded inside the other half
and seams of 7¹/₂" sides are matching.
Place inside the bag and stitch the top fold
to first row of dc border below ch-1 sps.

Drawstring (make 2)
Cut two 125" lengths of yarn. Following
Twisted Cord instructions on page 46, make
2 twisted cords about 25" long. Weave
through ch-1 sps of border, having ends at
opposite sides of border. Tie ends tightly.

continued on page 46

Touch A Life
Make a Difference

Crochet or Knit a Square

Warm Up America!

Valentine Chair Hugs

How about a special chair for your honeybuns? Little things mean a lot, so feather your love nest with little handcrafted touches, such as romantic Valentine Chair Hugs in filet crochet.

— *designed by Linda Mershon*

Size:
Chair Back: 18" x 15"
Armcover: 10" x 12"

Materials:
Bedspread-weight crochet cotton,
one 225-yd ball ecru
*Note: Our photographed set was made
with J. & P. Coats® Knit-Cro-Sheen®,
New Ecru #61.*
Size 6 (1.80mm) steel crochet hook, or size
required for gauge

Gauge:
8 dc = 1"

Instructions

Chair Back

Center:
Ch 138.

Row 1 (right side): Dc in 4th ch from hook
(beg 3 skipped chs count as a dc) and in
each rem ch—136 dc. Ch 3 (counts as first
dc on following rows), turn.

Following **Chart A**, work Rows 2 through
45. At end of Row 45, ch 1. Do not turn.

Border:

Rnd 1: Sc in last dc made, working along
side in sps formed by edge dc and turning
chs, (ch 5, sk next sp, sc in next sp) 22
times; ch 5; working along next side in
unused lps of beg ch, sc in first lp, (ch 5, sk
next 4 lps, sc in next lp) 26 times; ch 5, sk
next 4 lps, sc in next ch of beg 3 skipped
chs; working along next side in sps formed
by turning chs and edge dc, (ch 5, sk next
sp, sc in next sp) 22 times; ch 5; working
across Row 45, sc in first dc, (ch 5, sk next
4 dc, sc in next dc) 26 times; ch 5; join in
first sc.

Rnd 2: Ch 3 (counts as a dc), 2 dc in same
sc; † (sl st in 3rd ch of next ch-5 sp, ch 3,
dc in next 2 chs of same ch-5 sp) 23 times;
3 dc in next sc; (sl st in 3rd ch of next ch-5
sp, ch 3, dc in next 2 chs of same ch-5 sp)
27 times †; 3 dc in next sc; rep from † to
† once; join in 3rd ch of beg ch-3.

Finish off and weave in ends.

Arm Cover (make 2)

Center:
Ch 78.

Row 1 (right side): Dc in 4th ch from hook
(beg 3 skipped chs count as a dc) and in
each rem ch—76 dc. Ch 3 (counts as first
dc on following rows), turn.

Following **Chart B**, work Rows 2 through
39. At end of Row 39, ch 1. Do not turn.

Border:

Rnd 1: Sc in last dc made, working along
side in sps formed by edge dc and turning
chs, (ch 5, sk next sp, sc in next sp) 19
times; ch 5; working along next side in
unused lps of beg ch, sc in first lp, (ch 5, sk
next 4 lps, sc in next lp) 14 times; ch 5, sk
next 4 lps, sc in next ch of beg 3 skipped
chs; working along next side in sps formed
by turning chs and edge dc, (ch 5, sk next
sp, sc in next sp) 19 times; ch 5; working
across Row 39, sc in first dc, (ch 5, sk next
4 dc, sc in next dc) 14 times; ch 5; join in
first sc.

Rnd 2: Ch 3, 2 dc in same sc; † (sl st in 3rd
ch of next ch-5 sp, ch 3, dc in next 2 chs of
same ch-5 sp) 20 times; 3 dc in next sc;
(sl st in 3rd ch of next ch-5 sp, ch 3, dc in
next 2 chs of same ch-5 sp) 15 times †;
3 dc in next sc; rep from † to † once; join
in 3rd ch of beg ch-3.

Finish off and weave in ends.

Finishing
Following Blocking instructions on page
216, starch and block pieces.

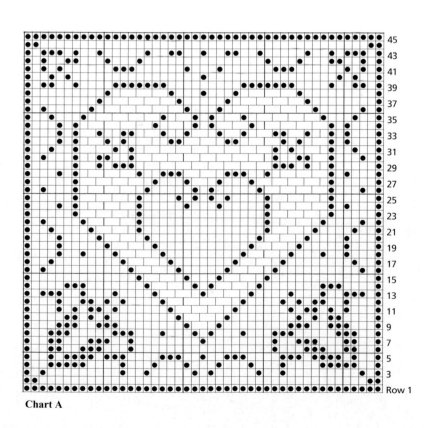

Chart A

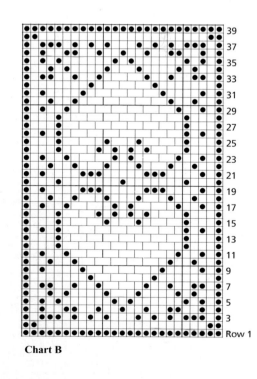

Chart B

Tried-and-True Technique

If you've been avoiding patterns that require you to change colors, follow our tips here for creating a houndstooth pattern. You'll learn to carry two colors of yarn and change from one color to another with ease!

Check Out This
Houndstooth Scarf
with Matching Hat

— designed by Sandy Scoville

Changing Colors

To change from working color to a new color, work the last stitch to be done in working color until 2 loops remain on the hook (**Photo A**). Draw new color through the 2 loops on hook. Drop working color (**Photo B**) and continue to work in the new color. This method can be used when change of color is at the end of a row or within the row.

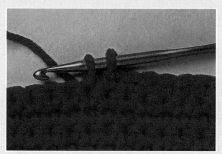
Photo A

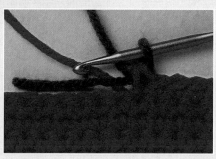
Photo B

Carrying Colors

To create a pattern such as the houndstooth one, it is necessary to change colors frequently within a row. To do this, you will carry one color behind the work for several stitches and then change back to it. To carry a color means to carry the strand on the side away from you. To prevent having loops of unworked yarn, it is helpful to work over the strand of the carried color. To do this, consider the strand a part of the stitch being worked into and simply insert hook in stitch and draw new color through (**Photo C**).

Hint: When changing from working color to a color that has been carried, always bring the carried color under the working color. This is very important as it prevents holes in your work.

Photo C

Houndstooth Scarf with Matching Hat

Size:
Scarf: About 8" wide x 45" long before fringe
Hat: Fits 20" to 21" circumference

Materials:
Worsted weight yarn, 7 oz (490 yds, 200 gms) each, red and black
Note: Our photographed scarf and hat were made with Bernat® Berella®, Scarlet #8933 and Black #8994.
Size H (5mm) crochet hook, or size required for gauge
Size G (4.25mm) crochet hook
3" x 3" piece of cardboard (for pompon)
Size 16 tapestry needle

Gauge:
Scarf: With larger size hook, 7 sc = 2"
Hat: With smaller size hook, 8 sc = 2"
4 sc rows in BLs only = 1"

Instructions

Scarf

With red, ch 165.

Row 1 (right side)**:** Sc in 2nd ch from hook and in next 3 chs, changing to black in last sc made; * † sc in next ch, changing to red; sc in next ch, changing to black; sc in next ch, changing to red †; sc in next 5 chs, changing to black in last sc made; rep from * 18 times more, then rep from † to † once; sc in next 5 sc—164 sc. Ch 1, turn.

Row 2: Sc in first 4 sc, changing to black in last sc made; * † sc in next sc, changing to red; sc in next sc, changing to black; sc in next sc, changing to red †; sc in next 5 sc, changing to black in last sc; rep from * 18 times more, then rep from † to † once; sc in next 5 chs. Ch 1, turn.

continued on page 30

Houndstooth Scarf with Matching Hat

continued from page 29

Row 3: Rep Row 2.

Row 4: Rep Row 2, changing to black in last sc. Ch 1, turn.

Row 5: Sc in first sc, changing to red; * sc in next sc, changing to black; sc in next sc changing to red; sc in next sc, changing to black; sc in next 5 sc, changing to red in last sc; rep from * 19 times more; sc in next sc, changing to black; sc in next sc, changing to red; sc in next sc, changing to black. Ch 1, turn.

Rows 6 and 7: Rep Row 5.

Row 8: Rep Row 5; do not change to black in last sc. Ch 1, turn.

Rep Rows 2 through 8 in sequence three times.

Rep Rows 2 through 5 once. At end of Row 5, finish off.

Weave in all ends.

Fringe:
Following Fringe instructions on page 211, make Single Knot Fringe. Cut 26" strands of each color; use 6 strands of each color for each knot. Tie nine knots evenly spaced across each short end of scarf. Trim ends even.

Hat

Cuff:
With smaller size hook and red, ch 25.

Row 1 (right side): Sc in 2nd ch from hook and in each rem ch—24 sc. Ch 1, turn.

Row 2: Working in BLs only, sc in each sc. Ch 1, turn.

Rows 3 through 84: Rep Row 2.

Joining Row: Hold Row 84 and beg ch tog, matching sc and unused lps of beg ch; sl st in each st through both thicknesses. Change to black by drawing lp through; cut red.

Crown:

Rnd 1: Ch 1, working along side in each edge sc, sc in each row; join in first sc—84 sc.

Rnd 2: Ch 1, sc in same sc and in each rem sc; join in first sc.

Rnd 3: Rep Rnd 2.

Rnd 4: Ch 1, dec over same sc and next sc (to work dec: draw up lp in each of 2 sc indicated, YO and draw through all 3 lps on hook—dec made); sc in next 5 sc; * dec over next 2 sc; sc in next 5 sc; rep from * around; join in first sc—72 sc.

Rnds 2 through 13: Rep Rnd 2.

Rnd 14: Ch 1, dec over same sc and next sc; sc in next 2 sc; * dec over next 2 sc; sc in next 2 sc; rep from * around; join in first sc—54 sc.

Rnd 15: Ch 1, sc in same sc; dec over next 2 sc; * sc in next sc, dec over next sc; rep from * around; join in first sc—36 sc.

Rnd 16: Ch 1, dec over same sc and next sc; sc in next sc; * dec over next 2 sc; sc in next sc; rep from * around; join in first sc—24 sc.

Rnd 17: Ch 1, dec over same sc and next sc; * dec over next 2 sc; rep from * around; join in first sc—12 sc.

Rnd 18: Ch 1, dec over same sc and next sc; * dec over next 2 sc; rep from * around; join in first sc—6 sc.

Rnd 19: Ch 1, dec over same sc and next sc; * dec over next 2 sc; rep from * once more.

Finish off and weave in all ends.

Finishing

Step 1: Fold cuff up about 3".

Step 2: Make pompon as follows:

Cut two 1¼"-diameter cardboard circles. Cut a hole in the center of each circle, about ½" in diameter. Thread a tapestry needle with 36" length of red and black, doubled. Then holding both circles together, insert needle through center hole, over outside edge, through center again (**Fig 1**) until entire circle is covered and center hole is filled (thread more lengths of yarn as needed).

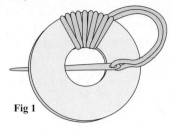

Fig 1

With sharp scissors, cut yarn between the two circles all around the circumference (**Fig 2**).

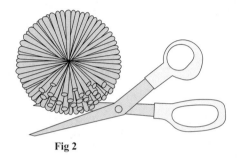

Fig 2

Using two 12" strands of yarn, one red and one black, slip yarn between circles and overlap yarn ends 2 or 3 times (**Fig 3**) — (prevents tying knot from slipping), pull tightly and tie into a firm knot. Remove cardboards and fluff out pompon by rolling it between your hands. Trim evenly with scissors, leaving tying ends for attaching pompon to hat.

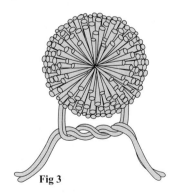

Fig 3

Sew pompon to top of hat.

Pretty as a Picture
Apron

Size:
Fits 8-10 year old

Crocheted piece:
waist - about 13"
length, top to bottom - about 24"

Materials:
Size 20 cotton crochet thread, four
225-yd balls white
*Note: Our photographed apron was
made with J. & P. Coats® Knit-Cro-
Sheen®, White #001.*
Size 10 (1.30mm) steel crochet hook,
or size required for gauge
Size 16 tapestry needle

Trimmings:
2 7/8 yds white satin ribbon, 1"-wide
two white buttons, 3/8"-diameter
1 yd white satin ribbon, 1/2"-wide
sewing needle and matching thread

Gauge:
15 trc = 1"

*Note: If you are not familiar with work-
ing filet from a chart, please read Filet
Review beginning on page 214. However,
on the charts for this apron, all open
squares are formed by ch-3 sps, not ch-2
sps as described in the review.*

Instructions

Top
Ch 86.

Row 1 (right side): Dc in 4th ch from
hook and in next 3 chs, (ch 3, sk next
2 chs, dc in next ch) 25 times; dc in next
4 chs. Ch 3, turn.

Row 2: Dc in next 4 dc, (ch 3, sk next
3 chs, dc in next dc) 25 times; dc in next
3 dc and in 3rd ch of beg 3 skipped chs.
Ch 3, turn.

Conjure up memories of a bygone era when painstaking hours were invested crocheting every sort of lovely finery—such as this petite beribboned apron we discovered in a antique shop. Filet crochet bib and skirt are finished with lacy crochet ruffles.

Heirloom apron discovered in antique shop.

Following **Chart A**, work Rows 3 through 28.

Edging

Hold top with wrong side facing you and Row 1 to right; join thread in sp formed by edge dc.

Row 1 (wrong side): Ch 1, 3 sc in same sp; working in sps formed by edge dc and turning chs of each row, † 4 sc in next row; 3 sc in next row †; rep from † to † 9 times more; * sc in next 2 dc, 3 sc in next row; rep from * 5 times more; sc in next 7 dc, 3 sc in next row; working along top edge, sc in next 44 dc and in 3rd ch of turning ch-3; working along next side in sps formed by turning chs and edge dc of each row, 3 sc in same row as last sc worked; sk next dc, sc in next 7 dc, 3 sc in next row; †† sk next dc, sc in next 2 dc, 3 sc in next row ††; rep from †† to †† 5 times more; rep from † to † 10 times—271 sc. Ch 3 (counts as first dc on following rows), turn.

Row 2 (right side): Dc in next 4 sc; † ch 3, dc in next 5 sc †; rep from † to † 25 times more; ch 3, sk next sc, dc in next 5 sc; rep from † to † 26 times—fifty-four 5-dc groups. Ch 6 (counts as first dc and a ch-3 sp on following rows), turn.

Row 3: Sk next 3 dc, dc in next dc, 3 dc in next ch-3 sp; dc in next dc, ch 3, sk next 3 dc, dc in next dc; * † ch 5, sk next ch-3 sp, dc in next dc, ch 3, sk next 3 dc, dc in

next dc, 3 dc in next ch-3 sp; dc in next dc, ch 3, sk next 3 dc †; dc in next dc; rep from * 24 times more, then rep from † to † once; dc in 3rd ch of turning ch-3. Ch 3, turn.

Row 4: 3 dc in next ch-3 sp; dc in next dc, ch 3, sk next 3 dc, dc in next dc, 3 dc in next ch-3 sp; dc in next dc; * † ch 7, sk next ch-5 sp, dc in next dc, 3 dc in next ch-3 sp; dc in next dc, ch 3, sk next 3 dc, dc in next dc †; 3 dc in next ch-3 sp; dc in next dc; rep from * 24 times more, then rep from † to † once; 4 dc in turning ch-6 sp. Ch 6, turn.

Row 5: Sk next 3 dc, dc in next dc, 3 dc in next ch-3 sp; dc in next dc, ch 3, sk next 3 dc, dc in next dc; * † ch 9, sk next ch-7 sp, dc in next dc, ch 3, sk next 3 dc, dc in next dc, 3 dc in next ch-3 sp; dc in next dc, ch 3, sk next 3 dc †; dc in next dc; rep from * 24 times more, then rep from † to † once; dc in 3rd ch of turning ch-3. Ch 3, turn.

Row 6: 3 dc in next ch-3 sp; dc in next dc, ch 3, sl st in 3rd ch from hook—picot made; sk next 3 dc, dc in next dc, 3 dc in next ch-3 sp; dc in next dc; * † dc in next ch of next ch-9 sp, picot; (sk next ch, dc in next next ch) 4 times; dc in next dc, 3 dc in next ch-3 sp; dc in next dc, picot; sk next 3 dc, dc in next dc †; 3 dc in next ch-3 sp; dc in next dc; rep from * 24 times more, then rep from † to † once; 4 dc in turning ch-6 sp.

Finish off and weave in all ends.

Waist Band

Ch 22.

Row 1 (wrong side): Sc in 2nd ch from hook and in each rem ch—21 sc. Ch 1, turn.

Row 2 (right side): Sc in each sc. Ch 4 (counts as first trc on following rows), turn.

Row 3: Trc in next 20 sc—21 trc. Ch 4, turn.

Row 4: Trc in next 20 trc and in 4th ch of turning ch-4. Ch 4, turn.

Row 5: Rep Row 4.

Row 6: Trc in next 3 trc, ch 13, sk next 13 trc, trc in next 3 trc and in 4th ch of turning ch-4. Ch 4, turn.

Row 7: Trc in each trc, in each ch and in 4th ch of turning ch-4—21 trc. Ch 4, turn.

Rows 8 through 47: Rep Rows 4 through 7 ten times more.

Rows 48 and 49: Trc in each trc and in 4th ch of turning ch-4. Ch 1, turn.

Row 50: Sc in each trc and in 4th ch of turning ch-4. Ch 1, turn.

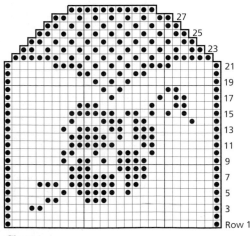

Chart A

continued on page 47

Keeping You in Stitches

Popcorns and Diamonds

If you have wanted to expand your collection of stitches, here are two popular ones which have been combined to create the interesting fisherman look that Becky Stevens uses in her hat and scarf designs.

The first is the traditional popcorn stitch. In our example we will be making a popcorn using double crochets. The second is the front post double crochet stitch which is used to form the diamond pattern.

— designed by Becky Stevens

Sizes:
Hat: One size fits most
Scarf: About 6^{1}/^{2}" wide x 60" long

Materials:
Scarf:
Worsted weight yarn, 10^{1}/^{2} oz (735 yds, 315 gms) off white

Hat:
Worsted weight yarn, 3^{1}/^{2} oz (245 yds, 105 gms) off white
Note: Our photographed scarf and hat were made using Patons Canadiana, Off White #104.
Size G (4.25mm) crochet hook, or size required for gauge
Size 18 tapestry needle

Gauge:
9 sc = 2"

Pattern Stitches
Note: See page 35 for stitch lesson.

Front Post Double Crochet (FPdc):
YO, insert hook from front to back to front around post (see page 211) of st indicated on 2nd row below; (YO and draw through 2 lps on hook) twice—FPdc made. Always sk st behind FPdc.

Double Front Post Double Crochet (dFPdc):
Keeping last lp of each FPdc on hook, 2 FPdc around same st indicated on 2nd row below; YO and draw through all 3 lps on hook—dFPdc made. Always sk st behind dFPdc.

Popcorn (PC):
4 dc in st indicated; drop lp from hook, insert hook in first dc made, draw dropped lp through—PC made.

continued on page 36

Keeping You in Stitches

Popcorn (PC)

Step 1: Work 4 double crochet stitches into one stitch (**Photo A**).

Step 2: Remove hook from loop and insert it from front to back in first double crochet made (**Photo B**).

Step 3: Pick up dropped loop and draw it through (**Photo C**). One popcorn stitch is completed (**Photo D**). *(Note: If necessary, work one chain stitch to secure popcorn.)*

Photo A

Photo B

Photo C

Photo D

Front Post Double Crochet (FPdc)

Step 1: YO, insert hook from front to back to front around post of the stitch (**Photo E**).

Step 2: (YO and draw through 2 lps on hook) twice. One front post double crochet stitch made (**Fig A** and **Photo F**).

In our pattern, a diamond-shaped pattern is created by working the front post stitch around the stitches indicated.

Photo E

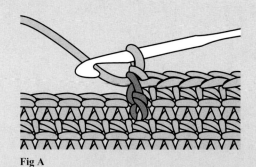

Fig A

Photo F

Popcorns and Diamonds

continued from page 34

Instructions

Scarf

Ch 30.

Row 1 (right side)**:** Sc in 2nd ch from hook and in each rem ch—29 sc. Ch 1, turn.

Row 2: Sc in each sc. Ch 1, turn.

Row 3: Sc in first 2 sc, FPdc (see Pattern Stitches on page 34) around next sc in 2nd row below; sc in next sc, PC (see Pattern Stitches on page 34) in next sc; sc in next sc, FPdc around next sc on 2nd row below; sc in next 7 sc, dFPdc (see Pattern Stitches on page 34) around next sc on 2nd row below; sc in next 7 sc, FPdc around next sc on 2nd row below; sc in next sc, PC in next sc; sc in next sc, FPdc around next sc on 2nd row below; sc in next 2 sc. Ch 1, turn.

Row 4: Sc in each st. Ch 1, turn.

Row 5: Sc in first 2 sc, FPdc around next FPdc; sc in next 3 sc, FPdc around next FPdc; sc in next 6 sc, dFPdc around next dFPdc; sc in next sc, dFPdc around same dFPdc; sc in next 6 sc, FPdc around next FPdc; sc in next 3 sc, FPdc around next FPdc; sc in next 2 sc. Ch 1, turn.

Row 6: Sc in each st. Ch 1, turn.

Row 7: Sc in first 2 sc, FPdc around next FPdc; sc in next sc, PC in next sc; sc in next sc, FPdc around next FPdc; sc in next 5 sc, dFPdc around next dFPdc; sc in next 3 sc, dFPdc around next dFPdc; sc in next 5 sc, FPdc around next FPdc; sc in next sc, PC in next sc; sc in next sc, FPdc around next FPdc; sc in next 2 sc. Ch 1, turn.

Row 8: Sc in each st. Ch 1, turn.

Row 9: Sc in first 2 sc, FPdc around next FPdc; sc in next 3 sc, FPdc around next FPdc; sc in next 4 sc, dFPdc around next dFPdc; sc in next 5 sc, dFPdc around next dFPdc; sc in next 4 sc, FPdc around next FPdc; sc in next 3 sc, FPdc around next FPdc; sc in next 2 sc. Ch 1, turn.

Row 10: Sc in each st. Ch 1, turn.

Row 11: Sc in first 2 sc, FPdc around next FPdc; sc in next sc, PC in next sc; sc in next sc, FPdc around next FPdc; sc in next 3 sc, dFPdc around next dFPdc; sc in next 3 sc, PC in next sc; sc in next 3 sc, dFPdc around next dFPdc; sc in next 3 sc, FPdc around next FPdc; sc in next sc, PC in next sc; sc in next sc, FPdc in next FPdc; sc in next 2 sc. Ch 1, turn.

Row 12: Sc in each st. Ch 1, turn.

Rows 13 and 14: Rep Rows 9 and 10.

Rows 15 and 16: Rep Rows 7 and 8.

Rows 17 and 18: Rep Rows 5 and 6.

Row 19: Sc in first 2 sc, FPdc around next FPdc; sc in next sc, PC in next sc; sc in next sc, FPdc around next FPdc; sc in next 7 sc, keeping last lp of each FPdc on hook, 2 FPdc around each of next 2 dFPdc; YO and draw through all 5 lps on hook—joined dFPdc made; sc in next 7 sc, FPdc around next FPdc; sc in next sc, PC in next sc; sc in next sc, FPdc around next FPdc; sc in next 2 sc. Ch 1, turn.

Row 20: Sc in each st. Ch 1, turn.

Rep Rows 5 through 20 fifteen times.

Rep Rows 5 through 19 once.

Finish off and weave in ends.

Fringe

Following Fringe instructions on page 211, make Single Knot Fringe. Cut 30" strands; use 8 strands for each knot. Tie 11 knots evenly spaced across each short end of scarf. Trim ends even.

Hat

Ribbing:

Ch 26.

Row 1 (right side): Sc in 2nd ch from hook and in each rem ch—25 sc. Ch 1, turn.

Row 2: Working in BLs only, sc in each sc. Ch 1, turn.

Rows 3 through 82: Rep Row 2. At end of Row 82, turn ribbing sideways.

Crown:

Row 1: Working in side of edge sc of each row, sc in each row—82 sc. Ch 1, turn.

Row 2: Sc in each sc. Ch 1, turn.

Row 3: Sc in first 8 sc, dFPdc (see Pattern Stitches on page 34) around next sc in 2nd row below; * sc in next 7 sc, FPdc (see Pattern Stitches on page 34) around next sc in 2nd row below; sc in next 7 sc, dFPdc around next sc in 2nd row below; rep from * 3 times more; sc in next 7 sc, FPdc around next sc in 2nd row below; sc in next sc. Ch 1, turn.

Row 4: Sc in each st. Ch 1, turn.

Row 5: Sc in first 7 sc; * † dFPdc around next dFPdc; sc in next sc, dFPdc around same dFPdc; sc in next 6 sc, FPdc around next FPdc †; sc in next 6 sc; rep from * 3 times more, then rep from † to † once; sc in next sc. Ch 1, turn.

Row 6: Sc in each st. Ch 1, turn.

Row 7: Sc in first 6 sc; * † dFPdc around next dFPdc; sc in next 3 sc, dFPdc around next dFPdc; sc in next 5 sc, FPdc around next FPdc †; sc in next 5 sc; rep from * 3 times more, then rep from † to † once; sc in next sc. Ch 1, turn.

Row 8: Sc in each st. Ch 1, turn.

Row 9: Sc in first 5 sc; * † dFPdc around next dFPdc; sc in next 5 sc, dFPdc around next dFPdc; sc in next 4 sc, FPdc around next FPdc †; sc in next 4 sc; rep from * 3 times more, then rep from † to † once; sc in next sc. Ch 1, turn.

Row 10: Sc in each st. Ch 1, turn.

Row 11: Sc in first 4 sc; * † dFPdc around next dFPdc; sc in next 3 sc, PC (see Pattern Stitches on page 34) in next sc; sc in next 3 sc, dFPdc around next dFPdc; sc in next 3 sc, FPdc around next FPdc †; sc in next 3 sc; rep from * 3 times more, then rep from † to † once; sc in next sc. Ch 1, turn.

Row 12: Sc in each st. Ch 1, turn.

Rows 13 and 14: Rep Rows 9 and 10.

Rows 15 and 16: Rep Rows 7 and 8.

Rows 17 and 18: Rep Rows 5 and 6.

Row 19: Sc in first 2 sc, dec over next 2 sc (to work dec: draw up lp in each of next 2 sc, YO and draw through all 3 lps on hook—dec made); sc in next sc, dec over next 2 sc; sc in next sc; * † keeping last lp of each FPdc on hook, 2 FPdc around each of next 2 dFPdc; YO and draw through all 5 lps on hook—joined dFPdc made; sc in next sc, (dec over next 2 sc, sc in next sc) twice; FPdc around next FPdc; sc in next sc †; (dec over next 2 sc, sc in next sc) twice; rep from * 3 times more, then rep from † to † once—62 sts. Ch 1, turn.

Row 20: Sc in first sc; * sc in next st, dec over next 2 sts; rep from * 19 times more; sc in next sc—42 sc. Ch 1, turn.

Row 21: Sc in first sc; * sc in next sc, dec over next 2 sc; FPdc around next joined dFPdc; sc in next sc, dec over next 2 sc; FPdc around next FPdc; rep from * 4 times more; sc in next sc—32 sts. Ch 1, turn.

Row 22: Sc in each st. Ch 1, turn.

Row 23: Sc in first sc, dec over next 2 sc; * FPdc around next FPdc; dec over next 2 sc; rep from * 8 times more; FPdc around next FPdc; sc in next sc—22 sts. Ch 1, turn.

Row 24: Sc in each st. Ch 3, turn.

Row 25: Keeping last lp of each st on hook, dc in first 2 sts; (FPdc around next FPdc, dc in next sc) 10 times; YO and draw through all 23 lps on hook; ch 1. Finish off, leaving a 24" end for sewing.

Finishing

Step 1: Sew seam, matching rows. Weave in ends. Turn ribbing up to form cuff.

Step 2: Following Pompon instructions on page 30, make one 3"-diameter pompon. Sew pompon to top of hat.

Sometimes a more rustic and comfortable kind of afghan like this one is needed to curl up with on a sofa—rather than a pretty lacy or flower design. Even a rugged outdoorsman would be at home with our rich, warm afghan. This mile-a-minute design is a snap to crochet with simple shells and popcorns—a reminder of the popcorn you'll soon be nibbling on while snuggled under this beauty.

— designed by Kathy Wesley

Size:
About 48" x 65"

Materials:
Worsted weight yarn, 34 oz (2380 yds, 1020 gms) beige; 16 oz (1120 yds, 480 gms) burgundy; 20 oz (1400 yds, 600 gms) variegated

Note: Our photographed afghan was made with Bernat® Berella® "4", Beige #8764, Burgundy #8927, and Rolling Meadows (variegated) #9300.

Size H (5mm) crochet hook, or size required for gauge

Gauge:
7 dc = 2"
4 rows = 2"

Pattern Stitch
Popcorn (PC):
4 dc in st indicated; drop lp from hook, insert hook in first dc made, draw dropped lp through—PC made.

Instructions

Center Panel (make 8)
With beige, ch 20.

Row 1 (wrong side): In 4th ch from hook (beg 3 skipped chs count as a dc) work (dc, ch 1) twice; sk next 3 chs, sc in next ch, ch 1, sk next 3 chs, in next ch work (dc, ch 1) 3 times; sk next 3 chs, sc in next ch, ch 1, sk next 3 chs, in next ch work (dc, ch 1, 2 dc). Ch 3 (counts as first dc on following rows), turn.

Row 2 (right side): Sc in next dc, ch 3, sk next dc, PC (see Pattern Stitch) in next sc; ch 3, sk next dc, sc in next dc, ch 3, sk next dc, PC in next sc; ch 3, sk next dc, sc in next dc, dc in 3rd ch of beg 3 skipped chs. Ch 3, turn.

Row 3: In next sc work (dc, ch 1) twice; sc in next PC; ch 1, in next sc work (dc, ch 1) 3 times; sc in next PC, ch 1, in next sc work (dc, ch 1, dc); dc in 3rd ch of turning ch-3. Ch 3, turn.

Row 4: Sc in next dc, ch 3, sk next dc, PC in next sc; ch 3, sk next dc, sc in next dc, ch 3, sk next dc, PC in next sc; ch 3, sk next dc, sc in next dc, dc in 3rd ch of turning ch-3. Ch 3, turn.

Rows 5 through 132: Rep Rows 3 and 4.

Row 133: Rep Row 3. At end of row, do not ch 3; do not turn. Finish off.

Panel Border:
Hold center panel with right side facing you and beg ch at top; with burgundy make lp on hook and join with an sc in first unused lp of beg ch.

Rnd 1: 2 sc in same lp—corner made; working in rem unused lps of beg ch; † sk next lp, sc in next lp, 2 sc in next lp; sc in next lp, sk next lp †; 2 sc in next lp; sk next lp, sc in next lp, sk next lp, 2 sc in next lp; rep from † to † once; 3 sc in next lp—corner made; †† working along next side in sps formed by edge dc and turning chs, 2 sc in each of next 133 sps ††; working across Row 133, 3 sc in first dc—corner made; sc in next dc, 2 sc in next dc; sc in next sc, 2 sc in next dc; sc in next dc, 2 sc in next dc; sc in next sc, 2 sc in next dc; sc in next dc, 3 sc in 3rd ch of turning ch-3—corner made; rep from †† to †† once; join in joining sc, sl st in next sc changing to variegated by drawing lp through; cut burgundy.

Rnd 2: Ch 4 (counts as first dc and ch-1 sp), in same sc work (dc, ch 1) twice—beg corner made; sk next sc; * sc in next sc, ch 1, sk next 2 sc, in next sc work (dc, ch 1) 3 times; sk next 2 sc; rep from * once more; sc in next sc, ch 1, sk next sc, in next sc work (dc, ch 1) 3 times—corner made; working along next side, sk next sc, sc in next sc; ch 1; † sk next 2 sc, in next sc work (dc, ch 1) 3 times; sk next 2 sc, sc in next sc, ch 1 †; rep from † to † 43 times more; sk next 2 sc; working along next side, in next sc work (dc, ch 1) 3 times—corner made; sk next sc; ** sc in next sc, ch 1, sk next sc, in next sc work (dc, ch 1) 3 times—corner made; rep from ** once more; sc in next sc, ch 1, sk next sc, in next sc work (dc, ch 1) 3 times—corner made; working across next side, sk next sc, sc in next sc, ch 1; rep from † to † 44 times; sk next sc and next sl st; join in 3rd ch of beg ch-4.

Rnd 3: Ch 1, sc in same ch as joining and in next ch-1 sp, ch 1, PC in next dc—corner made; ch 1; † sc in next ch-1 sp and in next dc, PC in next sc; †† sc in next dc, (sc in next ch-1 sp and in next dc) twice; PC in next sc ††; rep from †† to †† once more; sc in next dc and in next ch-1 sp, ch 1, PC in next dc—corner made; ch 1, sc in next ch-1 sp and in next dc, PC in next sc; rep from †† to †† 44 times †; sc in next dc and in next ch-1 sp; ch 1, PC in next dc—corner made; ch 1; rep from † to † once; ch 1; join in first sc. Change to burgundy by drawing lp through; cut variegated.

Rnd 4: Ch 1, sc in same sc and in next sc, 3 sc in next PC—corner made; * sc in each ch, in each sc, and in each PC to next corner PC; 3 sc in next PC—corner made; rep from * twice more; sc in ch, in each sc, and in each PC to first sc; join in first sc.

Finish off and weave in all ends.

For Baby & Me Afghans

This sweet pair of afghans is designed in two sizes—one for baby and one for mother. Differing only in the weight of the yarn required, both charming designs feature generous ruffling pineapple borders festooned with dimensional roses.

— designed by Ann Kirtley

Sizes:
Mother afghan: About 62" x 90"
Baby afghan: About 44" x 51"

Materials:
For Mother:
Worsted weight yarn, 105 oz (7350 yds, 3150 gms) off white
Note: Our photographed afghan was made with Patons Canadiana, Off White #104.
Size H (5mm) crochet hook, or size required for gauge

For Baby:
Sport weight yarn, 48 oz (3840 yds, 1440 gms) off white
Note: Our photographed baby afghan was made with J. & P. Coats® Luster Sheen®, Vanilla #7.
Size E (3.5mm) crochet hook, or size required for gauge
Size 16 tapestry needle

Gauge:
In pattern
With size H hook:
5 reps = 5 1/2"
With size E hook:
8 reps = 6"

Pattern Stitches
Cluster (CL):
Keeping last lp of each trc on hook, trc in 2 ch-1 sps indicated, YO and draw through all 3 lps on hook—CL made.

Double Triple Crochet (dtrc):
YO 3 times; draw up lp in st indicated (YO, draw through 2 lps on hook) 4 times—dtrc made.

Instructions
Note: Instructions written for mother afghan. Changes for baby afghan are in parentheses ( ).

continued on page 42

For Baby & Me Afghans

continued from page 40

Center

Ch 120 (132).

Row 1 (right side): Sc in 2nd ch from hook and in next 2 chs; * ch 1, sk next ch, sc in next 3 chs; rep from * 28 (31) times more. Ch 3 (counts as first dc on following rows), turn.

Row 2: Dc in each sc and in each ch—119 (131) dc. Ch 1, turn.

Row 3: Sc in first dc, trc in first ch-1 sp on 2nd row below; on working row, sk next dc (behind trc just made), sc in next dc, ch 1, sk next dc, sc in next dc; * CL (see Pattern Stitches on page 40) over same ch-1 sp on 2nd row below as last trc worked and next ch-1 sp; on working row, sk next dc (behind CL just made), sc in next dc, ch 1, sk next dc, sc in next dc; rep from * 27 (30) times more; trc in same ch-1 sp as last trc worked; on working row, sk next dc (behind trc just made), sc in 3rd ch of turning ch-3. Ch 3, turn.

Row 4: Dc in each st and in each ch. Ch 1, turn.

Row 5: Sc in first dc, trc in first ch-1 sp on 2nd row below; on working row, sk next dc (behind trc just made), sc in next dc, ch 1, sk next dc, sc in next dc; * CL over same ch-1 sp on 2nd row below and next ch-1 sp; on working row, sk next dc (behind CL just made), sc in next dc, ch 1, sk next dc, sc in next dc; rep from * 21 (30) times more; trc in ch-1 sp on 2nd row below as last trc worked; on working row, sk next dc (behind trc just made), sc in 3rd ch of turning ch-3. Ch 3, turn.

Rows 6 through 135 (131): Rep Rows 4 and 5, 65 (61) times more. At end of Row 135 (131), do not ch 3.

Finish off and weave in all ends.

Border

Hold center with right side facing you and Row 135 (131) at top; join yarn in first sc in upper right-hand corner.

Rnd 1 (right side): Ch 1, 3 sc in same ch as joining—corner made; sc in next 117 (129) sts, 3 sc in next sc—corner made; working along next side in ends of rows in sps formed by edge dc and turning chs, and in edge sc, sk end of Row 135 (131); † 2 sc in next row; sc in next row †; rep from † to † 65 (61) times more; 2 sc in next row; sk end of Row 1; working along lower edge in unused lps of beg ch, 3 sc in next lp—corner made; sc in each lp across to last lp; 3 sc in last lp—corner made; working along next side in ends of rows in sps formed by edge dc and turning chs, and in edge sc, sk end of Row 1; rep from † to † 66 (62) times; 2 sc in next row; sk end of Row 135 (131); join in BL of first sc—646 sc.

Rnd 2: Ch 3 (counts as a dc on this and following rnds), working in BLs only, 3 dc in next sc—dc corner made; * dc in each sc to 2nd sc of next corner; 3 dc in next sc—corner made; rep from * twice more; dc in each sc to beg ch-3; join in 3rd ch of beg ch-3—654 dc.

Rnd 3: Ch 3, in same ch as joining work (dc, ch 3, 2 dc)—beg shell made; sk next 2 dc; * in next dc work (2 dc, ch 3, 2 dc)—shell made; sk next 2 dc; rep from * around; join in 3rd ch of beg ch-3—218 shells.

Rnd 4: Sl st in next dc and in next ch-3 sp, beg shell in same sp; † sk next dc of same shell, in sp between next dc of same shell and first dc of next shell work shell; in next ch-3 sp work shell †; in ch-3 sp of each of next 40 (45) shells work shell; rep from † to † once; in ch-3 sp of each of next 67 (64) shells work shell; rep from † to † once; in ch-3 sp of each of next 40 (45) shells work shell; rep from † to † once; in ch-3 sp of each of next 66 (63) shells work shell; join in 3rd ch of beg ch-3—222 shells.

Rnd 5: Sl st in next dc and in next ch-3 sp, beg shell in same sp; shell in each rem shell; join in 3rd ch of beg ch-3.

Rnd 6: Sl st in next dc and in next ch-3 sp, beg shell in same sp; ch 1; * shell in next shell; ch 1; rep from * around; join in 3rd ch of beg ch-3.

Rnd 7: Sl st in next dc and in next ch-3 sp, beg shell in same sp; ch 2; * shell in next shell; ch 2; rep from * around; join in 3rd ch of beg ch-3.

Rnd 8: Sl st in next dc and in next ch-3 sp, beg shell in same sp; ch 3; * shell in next shell; ch 3; rep from * around; join in 3rd ch of beg ch-3.

Rnd 9: Sl st in next dc and in next ch-3 sp, ch 3, in same sp work (dc, ch 6, 2 dc); ch 1, (shell in next shell, ch 1) twice; * in ch-3 sp of next shell work (2 dc, ch 6, 2 dc); ch 1, (shell in next shell, ch 1) twice; rep from * around; join in 3rd ch of beg ch-3.

Rnd 10: Sl st in next dc and in next ch-6 sp, ch 3, 9 dc in same sp—base of beg pineapple made; ch 2, shell in each of next 2 shells; ch 2; * 10 dc in next ch-6 sp—base of pineapple made; ch 2, shell in each of next 2 shells; ch 2; rep from * around; join in 3rd ch of beg ch-3—74 pineapple bases.

Rnd 11: Ch 4 (counts as a dc and a ch-1 sp), (dc in next dc, ch 1) 8 times; dc in next dc, ch 2, sk next ch-2 sp, 2 dc in each of next 2 ch-3 sps; ch 2, sk next ch-2 sp; * (dc in next dc, ch 1) 9 times; dc in next dc; ch 2, sk next ch-2 sp, 2 dc in each of next 2 ch-3 sps; ch 2, sk next ch-2 sp; rep from * around; join in 3rd ch of beg ch-4.

Rnd 12: Sl st in next ch-1 sp, ch 1, sc in same sp; (ch 3, sc in next ch-1 sp) 8 times; ch 3, sk next ch-2 sp, sc in sp between next two 2-dc groups, ch 3, sk next ch-2 sp and next dc; * (sc in next ch-1 sp, ch 3) 9 times; sc in sp between next two 2-dc groups, ch 3; rep from * around; join in first sc. Finish off.

First Pineapple:

Note: Remainder of each pineapple is worked in rows.

Hold border with right side facing you; join yarn in last ch-3 sp of Rnd 12.

Row 1: Beg shell in same sp; ch 3, (sc in next ch-3 sp, ch 3) 8 times; shell in next ch-3 sp. Turn, leaving rem sts unworked.

Row 2: Sl st in next dc and in next ch-3 sp, beg shell in same sp; ch 3, sk next ch-3 sp, (sc in next ch-3 sp, ch 3) 7 times; sk next ch-3 sp, shell in next shell. Turn.

Row 3: Sl st in next dc and in next ch-3 sp, beg shell in same sp; ch 3, sk next ch-3 sp, (sc in next ch-3 sp, ch 3) 6 times; shell in next shell. Turn.

continued on page 43

For Baby & Me Afghans

continued from page 42

Row 4: Sl st in next dc and in next ch-3 sp, beg shell in same sp; ch 3, sk next ch-3 sp, (sc in next ch-3 sp, ch 3) 5 times; shell in next shell. Turn.

Row 5: Sl st in next dc and in next ch-3 sp, beg shell in same sp; ch 3, sk next ch-3 sp, (sc in next ch-3 sp, ch 3) 4 times; shell in next shell. Turn.

Row 6: Sl st in next dc and in next ch-3 sp, beg shell in same sp; ch 3, sk next ch-3 sp, (sc in next ch-3 sp, ch 3) 3 times; shell in next shell. Turn.

Row 7: Sl st in next dc and in next ch-3 sp, beg shell in same sp; ch 3, sk next ch-3 sp, (sc in next ch-3 sp, ch 3) twice; shell in next shell. Turn.

Row 8: Sl st in next dc and in next ch-3 sp, beg shell in same sp; sk next ch-3 sp, dc in next ch-3 sp, shell in next shell. Turn.

Row 9: Sl st in next dc and in next ch-3 sp, ch 2, keeping last lp of each dc on hook, dc in same sp; sk next 2 dc, dc in next dc, sk next 2 dc, 2 dc in ch-3 sp of next shell; YO and draw through all 5 lps on hook. Finish off. Mark this pineapple.

Remaining Pineapples:

Hold border with right side facing you; join yarn in next unused ch-3 sp on Rnd 12 from last completed pineapple. Work same as First Pineapple.

Outer Edging

Hold afghan with right side facing you; join yarn in tip of Row 3 of marked pineapple.

Rnd 1: Working around pineapple, * † (ch 5, sl st in tip of next row) 5 times; ch 5, sl st in side of first st of Row 9, ch 5, sl st in side of last st of Row 9, (ch 5, sl st in tip of next row) 6 times †; sl st in tip of Row 3 of next pineapple; rep from * 72 times more, then rep from † to † once; join in joining sl st.

Rnd 2: Sl st in next 5 chs of next ch-5 sp and in next sl st; ch 3 (counts as a dc), 2 dc in same sl st; * † sl st in next sl st, (7 dc in next sl st, sl st in next sl st) twice; 7 dc in next ch-5 sp; sl st in next sl st, (7 dc in next sl st, sl st in next sl st) twice; 3 dc in next sl st; dtrc (see Pattern Stitches on page 40) in next joining sl st on next pineapple †; 3 dc in next sl st; rep from * 72 times more, then rep from † to † once; join in 3rd ch of beg ch-3.

Rnd 3: Sl st in next 2 dc; * † sk next sl st, sl st in BL of next dc, (ch 3, sk next dc, sl st in BL of next dc) 3 times †; rep from † to † 4 times more; sk next sl st, (draw up lp in BL of next st, sk next 2 sts) twice; draw up lp in BL of next st, YO and draw through all 4 lps on hook; rep from * around; join in first sl st. Finish off.

Inner Edging

Hold afghan with right side facing you; join yarn in unused lp of first sc of Rnd 1 of border; ch 3, dc in 3rd ch from hook; working in rem unused lps, * sk next lp, sl st in next lp, ch 3, dc in 3rd ch from hook; rep from * around; join in joining sl st.

Finish off and weave in all ends.

Rose (make 74)

Ch 6, join to form a ring.

Rnd 1 (right side)**:** Ch 1, (sc in ring, ch 3) 6 times; join in first sc—6 ch-3 sps

Rnd 2: Sl st in next ch-3 sp, ch 3 (counts as a dc on this and following rnds), 2 dc in same ch-3 sp; (sl st in next sc, 3 dc in next ch-3 sp) 5 times. Do not join.

Rnd 3: Working behind Rnd 2, sc around post (see page 211) of first sc of Rnd 1, ch 4, (sc around post of next sc on Rnd 1, ch 4) 5 times. Do not join.

Rnd 4: Sl st in next ch-4 sp of Rnd 3, ch 3, 3 dc in same ch-4 sp; sl st in next sc, (4 dc in next ch-4 sp, sl st in next sc) 4 times; 4 dc in next ch-4 sp; join in beg sl st. Finish off, leaving a 12" end for sewing.

Weave in other end.

Finishing

Referring to photo on page 40 or page 42, sew roses to afghan.

Kathy Kitty

continued from page 4

Rnd 38: Sc in next 23 sc, (sc in next sc, 2 sc in next sc) 7 times— belly shaping made; sc in next 11 sc—55 sc.

Rnds 39 and 40: Rep Rnd 29.

Rnd 41: Sc in next 5 sc, (2 sc in next sc, sc in next sc) 5 times—bottom made; sc in next 40 sc—60 sc.

Rnds 42 through 45: Rep Rnd 29.

Rnd 46: (Sc in next 4 sc, sc dec over next 2 sc) 10 times—50 sc.

Rnd 47: (Sc in next 7 sc, sc dec over next 2 sc) twice; sc in next 32 sc—48 sc.

Rnd 48: (Sc in next 6 sc, sc dec over next 2 sc) 6 times—42 sc.

Rnd 49: (Sc in next 5 sc, sc dec over next 2 sc) 6 times—36 sc.

Rnd 50: Rep Rnd 29.

Rnd 51: (Sc in next 4 sc, sc dec over next 2 sc) 6 times—30 sc.

Rnd 52: (Sc in next 3 sc, sc dec over next 2 sc) 6 times—24 sc. Remove hook from lp. Do not cut yarn.

Note: Do not skip ahead. Body assembly needs to be completed before going further.

Body Assembly:

Step 1: Hold piece with right side facing you and head at top; place bolt of one arm through Rnds 29 and 30 on side of body, sk next 23 sc and place other arm between next sc and between Rnds 29 and 30.

Step 2: Hold each arm in place and push each locking washer through the bolt from inside of body.

Step 3: Hold piece with right side facing you and head at top; place bolt of one leg through Rnds 47 and 48 on side of body; sk next 23 sc on Rnd 47, place other leg between next sc and between Rnds 47 and 48.

Step 4: Hold each leg in place and push each locking washer through the bolt from inside of body.

Step 5: Stuff body firmly.

Note: Insert hook through dropped lp of body.

Rnd 53: Rep Rnd 29.

Rnd 54: (Sc in next 2 sc, sc dec over next 2 sc) 6 times—18 sc.

Rnd 55: (Sc in next sc, sc dec over next 2 sc) 6 times; join in first sc.

Finish off, leaving a 10" end for sewing.

continued on page 44

Kathy Kitty

continued from page 43

Ear (make 2):
With grey, ch 2.

Note: Rnds 1 through 7 are worked in continuous rnds. Do not join; mark beg of rnds.

Rnd 1 (right side): 6 sc in 2nd ch from hook.

Rnd 2: Sc in each sc.

Rnd 3: (Sc in next sc, 2 sc in next sc) 3 times—9 sc.

Rnd 4: (Sc in next sc, 2 sc in next sc) 4 times; sc in next sc—13 sc.

Rnd 5: Sc in each sc.

Rnd 6: Rep Rnd 5.

Rnd 7: (Sc in next 2 sc, 2 sc in next sc) 4 times; sc in next sc—17 sc.

Rnd 8: Sc in next 17 sc; join in first sc.

Rnd 9: Fold Rnd 8 flat; working through both thicknesses, sc in next 9 sc.

Finish off, leaving an 18" end for sewing.

Hair:
With grey, leaving a 12" end for sewing, ch 2.

Rnd 1 (right side): 6 sc in 2nd ch from hook; join in FL of first sc.

Rnd 2: Ch 6, 3 sc in 2nd ch from hook and in next 4 chs—curl made; working in FLs only, * sl st in next sc, ch 6, 3 sc in 2nd ch from hook and in next 4 chs—curl made; rep from * 4 times more; working over Rnd 1, sl st through center between last curl made and first curl, ch 6, 3 sc in 2nd ch from hook and in next 4 chs—curl made—7 curls.

Finish off and weave in end.

Finishing

Step 1: Stuff body firmly with fiberfill. With tapestry needle and 10" end of body, weave in and out through 12 sts of Rnd 55. Pull, to close opening. Weave in end.

Step 2: Cut 6" length of floss; set aside. Referring to photo for placement, with tapestry needle and floss, make mouth using straight stitches (see Embroidery Stitch Guide on page 211).

Step 3: Sew ears to head between Rnds 4 and 11 about 1 3/4" apart.

Step 4: On crocheted hair piece, twist each curl down and tack to secure. Sew hair to head between ears.

Step 5: For whiskers, stiffen remaining floss with starching solution (see Starching Supplies on page 216). Insert behind nose and separate strands as desired.

Dress

Starting at neckline with white, ch 32.

Row 1 (wrong side): Sc in 2nd ch from hook and in next 2 chs, (2 sc in next ch, sc in next 3 chs) 7 times—38 sc. Ch 1, turn.

Row 2 (right side): Sc in first 6 sc, 2 sc in each of next 5 sc; sc in next 16 sc, 2 sc in each of next 5 sc; sc in next 6 sc—48 sc. Ch 1, turn.

Row 3: Sc in each sc. Ch 1, turn.

Row 4: Sc in first 6 sc; † in next sc work (sc, dc); [in next sc work (2 dc, ch 2, 2 dc)—shell made; dc in next sc] 5 times; sc in same sc as last dc worked †; sc in next 14 sc; rep from † to † once; sc in next 6 sc. Ch 1, turn.

Row 5: Sc in first 6 sc; † 2 sc in next sc; [BPdc (see Pattern Stitches on page 3) around next sc, in ch-2 sp of next shell work shell] 5 times; sk next 2 dc—underarm opening; BPdc around next dc; 2 sc in next sc †; sc in next 14 sc; rep from † to † once; sc in next 6 sc. Ch 1, turn.

Row 6: Sc in first 7 sc; † 2 sc in next sc; [FPdc (see Pattern Stitches on page 3) around next BPdc, shell in next shell] 5 times; sk next 2 BPdc—underarm opening; FPdc around next BPdc; 2 sc in next sc †; sc in next 16 sc; rep from † to † once; sc in next 7 sc. Ch 1, turn.

Row 7: Sc in first 8 sc; † 2 sc in next sc; (BPdc around next FPdc, shell in next shell) 5 times; sk next 2 FPdc—underarm opening; BPdc around next FPdc; 2 sc in next sc †; sc in next 18 sc; rep from † to † once; sc in next 8 sc. Ch 1, turn.

Row 8: Sc in first 10 sc; † sc dec over next sc and next ch-2 sp (to work sc dec: draw up lp in each of next 2 sts or sps indicated, YO and draw through all 3 lps on hook—sc dec made); ch 4, sk next 19 sts, dec over 5th ch-2 sp and next dc †; sc in next 22 sc; rep from † to † once; sc in next 10 sc. Ch 1, turn.

Row 9: 2 sc in first sc; sc in each sc and in each ch to last sc; 2 sc in last sc—56 sc. Ch 1, turn.

Row 10: Sc in each sc. Ch 1, turn.

Row 11: 2 sc in first sc; sc in next 54 sc, 2 sc in next sc—58 sc. Ch 1, turn.

Rows 12 and 13: Rep Row 10.

Row 14: Sc in each sc; join in FL of first sc. Change to pink by drawing lp through; cut white.

Note: Remainder of dress is worked in rnds.

Rnd 1: Ch 3 (counts as a dc on this and following rnds), in same lp work (dc, ch 2, 2 dc)—beg shell made; working in FLs only, in next sc work (dc in next sc, shell in next sc) 28 times; dc in next sc; join in 3rd ch of beg ch-3—29 shells.

Rnd 2: Sl st in next dc and in next ch-2 sp; beg shell in same sp; (FPdc around next dc, shell in next shell) 28 times; FPdc around next dc; join in 3rd ch of beg ch-3.

Rnds 3 through 23: Rep Rnd 2.

Rnd 24: Sl st in next dc and in next ch-2 sp, ch 1; * 4 sc in same sp; ch 1, FPsc (see Pattern Stitches on page 3) around next dc; ch 1; rep from * around; join in first sc. Finish off.

Collar:
Hold dress with right side of back opening facing you and beg ch at top; join pink in first unused lp of beg ch-32 to left of back opening.

Row 1: Ch 3, working in unused lps of beg ch, shell in next lp; sk next lp, (dc in next lp, shell in next lp) 3 times; † sk next lp, dc in next lp, shell in next lp †; rep from † to † 3 times more; (dc in next lp, shell in next lp) 3 times; dc in next lp, sk next lp, shell in next lp; dc in next lp. Ch 1, turn.

Row 2: Sc in first dc; * † ch 1, 4 sc in next shell; ch 1 †; FPsc around next dc; rep from * 10 times more, then rep from † to † once; sc in 3rd ch of beg ch-3. Finish off.

Back Opening Trim and Ties:
Hold dress with right side facing you and neck edge to right; working in edge sc of each row on back opening, join white in first edge sc to right of back opening; ch 1, sc in same sc; † in next sc work (sl st, ch 24, sl st in 2nd ch from hook and in next 23 chs, sl st) †; sc in next 6 rows; rep from † to † once; sc in next 5 rows; working along next side in edge sc of each row, sc in next 5 rows; rep from † to † once; sc in next 6 rows; rep from † to † once; sc in next sc.

Finish off and weave in all ends.

Finishing

Sew heart button to center of dress.

Keith Kitty

continued from page 5

Row 11: 2 sc in first sc; sc in each sc to last sc; 2 sc in last sc—58 sc. Ch 1, turn.

Rows 12 and 13: Rep Row 10.

Row 14: Sc in each sc; join in first sc. Change to pink by drawing lp through; cut white.

Note: Remainder of romper is worked in rnds.

Rnd 1: Ch 3 (counts as a dc on this and following rnds), in same sc work (dc, ch 2, 2 dc)—beg shell made; sk next sc, dc in next sc, sk next sc; * in next sc work (2 dc, ch 2, 2 dc)—shell made; sk next sc, dc in next sc, sk next sc; rep from * 12 times more; in next sc work (2 dc, ch 2, 2 dc)—shell made; dc in next sc; join in 3rd ch of beg ch-3—15 shells.

Rnd 2: Sl st in next dc and in next ch-2 sp, beg shell in same sp; FPdc (see Pattern Stitches on page 5) around next dc; * in ch-2 sp of next shell work shell; FPdc around next dc; rep from * 13 times more; join in 3rd ch of beg ch-3.

Rnd 3: Sl st in next dc and in next ch-2 sp, beg shell in same sp; FPdc around next FPdc; * shell in next shell; FPdc around next FPdc; rep from * 13 times more; join in 3rd ch of beg ch-3.

Rnds 4 through 6: Rep Rnd 3. Finish off.

Back Flap:

Hold piece with right side of back opening facing you and Rnd 6 at top; join pink in 2nd FPdc to right of joining.

Row 1: Ch 3, (shell in next shell, FPdc around next FPdc) twice. Ch 3, turn.

Row 2: Shell in next ch-2 sp; BPdc (see Pattern Stitches on page 5) around next FPdc; shell in next shell; dc in 3rd ch of beg ch-3. Finish off, leaving a 10" end for sewing.

Front Flap:

Hold piece with right side of back opening facing you and Rnd 6 at top; sk next 5 shells to left of back flap; join pink in ch-2 sp of next shell.

Row 1: Ch 3, 2 dc in same sp; FPdc around next FPdc; shell in next shell; FPdc around next FPdc; 3 dc in next shell. Ch 3, turn.

Row 2: Sk first dc, dc in next 2 dc, BPdc around next FPdc; shell in next shell; BPdc around next FPdc; dc in next 2 dc and in 3rd ch of beg ch-3. Ch 3, turn.

Row 3: Sk first dc, dc in next 2 dc, FPdc around next BPdc; shell in next shell; FPdc around next BPdc; dc in next 2 dc and in 3rd ch of turning ch-3. Finish off, leaving a 10" end for sewing.

Left Leg:

Hold piece with right side facing you and Rnd 6 at top; join pink in next shell to left of back flap.

Rnd 1: Beg shell in same sp; (FPdc around next FPdc, shell in next shell) 4 times; FPdc around next FPdc; working in sps formed by turning chs and in edge dc of each row, shell in next row; dc in next row, shell in next row; FPdc around next FPdc; join in 3rd ch of beg ch-3—7 shells.

Rnd 2: Sl st in next dc and in next ch-2 sp; beg shell in same sp; FPdc around next FPdc; (shell in next shell, FPdc around next FPdc) 6 times; join in 3rd ch of beg ch-3.

Rnds 3 through 6: Rep Rnd 2.

Rnd 7: Sl st in next dc and in next ch-2 sp, 4 sc in same sp; FPsc (see Pattern Stitches on page 5) around next FPdc; (4 sc in next shell, FPsc around next FPdc) 6 times; join in first sc. Finish off.

Right Leg:

Hold piece with right side of front facing you and Rnd 6 at top; join pink in next shell to left of front flap.

Rnds 1 through 7: Rep Rnds 1 through 7 of Left Leg.

COLLAR TRIM:

Hold romper with right side of back opening facing you; working in unused lps on opposite side of beg ch-32, join pink in first unused lp; ch 1, sc in same lp; (2 sc in next lp, sc in next lp) 15 times—46 sc. Finish off.

Back Opening Trim and Ties:

Hold romper with right side facing you and legs to left; working in edge sc of each row, join white in first edge sc to right of back opening; ch 1, sc in same sc; † in next sc work (sl st, ch 24, sl st in 2nd ch from hook and in next 23 chs, sl st) †; sc in next

6 rows; rep from † to † once; sc in next 5 rows; working along next side in edge sc of rows, sc in next 5 rows; rep from † to † once; sc in next 6 rows; rep from † to † once; sc in next sc.

Finish off and weave in ends.

Bow Tie:

FIRST HALF:

With pink, ch 4.

Row 1 (right side): Sc in 2nd ch from hook and in next 2 chs—3 sc. Ch 1, turn.

Row 2: Sc in each sc. Ch 1, turn.

Row 3: Rep Row 2.

Row 4: 2 sc in first sc; sc in next sc, 2 sc in next sc—5 sc. Ch 1, turn.

Row 5: Sc in each sc. Finish off.

SECOND HALF:

Hold first half with right side facing you and unused lps of beg ch-4 at top; join pink in first unused lp.

Row 1: Ch 1, sc in same lp and in next 2 lps—3 sc. Ch 1, turn.

Rows 2 through 5: Rep Rows 2 through 5 of first half. At end of Row 5, do not finish off. Ch 1, turn.

Edging:

2 sc in first sc; † sc in next 3 sc, 2 sc in next sc; working in edge sc of each row of second and first halves, 2 sc in same row just worked; sc in next 8 rows, 2 sc in next row †; working across Row 5, 2 sc in same sc just worked; rep from † to † once; join in first sc.

Finish off and weave in ends.

Knot:

With pink, ch 3.

Row 1: Sc in 2nd ch from hook and in next ch—2 sc. Ch 1, turn.

Row 2: Sc in each sc. Ch 1, turn.

Rows 3 through 5: Rep Row 2. At end of Row 5, do not ch 1. Finish off, leaving an 8" end for sewing.

Finishing

Step 1: With tapestry needle and yarn ends, sew front and back flaps together; sew each front flap seam to each leg. Sew each back flap seam to each leg.

Step 2: Sew knot to center front of bow. Sew bow tie to center front of romper.

Merry (Christmas!)-Go-Round Doily

continued from page 11

last lp of each dc on hook, dc in next 2 dc, YO and draw through all 3 lps on hook; rep from * 4 times more, then rep from ‡ to ‡ once; join in first dc.

Rnd 5: Ch 2, keeping last lp of each dc on hook, dc in next 2 dc, YO and draw through all 3 lps on hook; * † ch 3, in next CL work [trc CL (see Pattern Stitches on page 11), ch 4, sc, ch 4, trc CL]; ch 3 †; CL over next 3 dc; rep from * 4 times more, then rep from † to † once; join in first st.

Rnd 6: Ch 4 (counts as a dc and a ch-1 sp); * † in next trc CL work (trc CL, ch 4, sc); ch 4, sc in next sc, ch 4, in next trc CL work (sc, ch 4, trc CL); ch 1 †; dc in next CL, ch 1; rep from * 4 times more, then rep from † to † once; join in 3rd ch of beg ch-4.

Rnd 7: Sl st in next ch-1 sp and next trc CL; ch 1, sc in same trc CL; ch 4, (sc in next sc, ch 4) 3 times; in next trc CL work (sc, ch 4, trc CL); hold tree section with wrong side facing wrong side of star; sc in 2nd dc on Row 57 of any tree, on star, in next trc CL

work (trc CL, ch 4, sc); * † ch 4, (sc in next sc, ch 4) 3 times; in next trc CL work (sc, ch 4, trc CL); sc in 2nd dc on Row 57 of next tree †; on star, in next trc CL work (trc CL, ch 4, sc); rep from * 3 times more, then rep from † to † once; on star, trc CL in next trc CL; ch 4; join in first sc.

Finish off and weave in all ends.

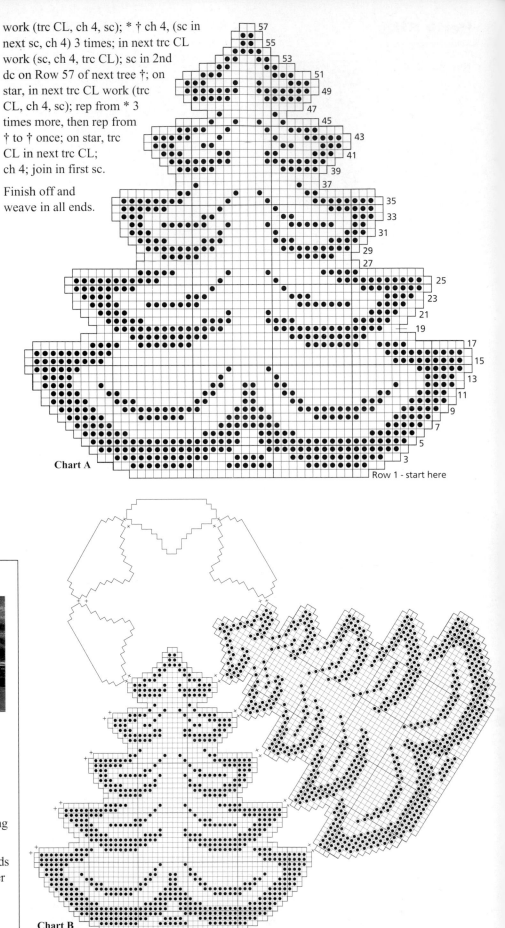

Chart A

Row 1 - start here

Evening of Glamour – Evening Bag

continued from page 24

Making Twisted Cord

Step 1: Fold length of yarn in half; tie ends in knot.

Step 2: Place knotted end over door knob or onto a wall hook to anchor.

Step 3: Slip loop at opposite end onto index finger.

Step 4: Holding strands taut, twist strands to your right until there is a firm even twist along the entire length.

Step 5: Keeping strands taut, fold twisted strands in half lengthwise, slipping loop off index finger and onto knob or hook with other end.

Step 6: Form cord by smoothing the twisted strands doubled in a downward direction from knob or hook.

Step 7: Knot each end of cord; trim ends even.

Chart B

Huggable Chenille Teddy

continued from page 18

Leg (make 2)

Note: Rnds 1 through 28 are worked in continuous rnds. Do not join; mark beg of rnds.

Starting at center of foot, ch 6.

Rnd 1 (right side): 3 sc in 2nd ch from hook; sc in next 3 chs, 3 sc in next ch; working in unused lps on opposite side of beg ch, sc in next 3 lps—12 sc.

Rnd 2: Working in BLs only, 2 sc in next sc; 3 sc in next sc; 2 sc in next sc; sc in next 4 sc, 3 sc in next sc; sc in next 4 sc—18 sc.

Rnd 3: Working in BLs only, sc in next 2 sc, 2 sc in next sc; 3 sc in next sc; 2 sc in next sc; sc in next 7 sc, 3 sc in next sc; sc in next 5 sc—24 sc.

Rnd 4: Working in BLs only, sc in each sc.

Rnd 5: Sc in each sc.

Rnds 6 and 7: Rep Rnd 5.

Rnd 8: Dec 6 times; sc in next 12 sc—18 sc.

Rnds 9 through 16: Rep Rnd 5.

Rnd 17: (2 sc in next sc, sc in next sc) 6 times; sc in next 6 sc—24 sc.

Rnds 18 and 19: Rep Rnd 5.

Rnd 20: (2 sc in next sc, sc in next sc) 10 times; sc in next 4 sc—34 sc.

Rnds 21 through 24: Rep Rnd 5.

Rnd 25: (Sc in next sc, dec) 10 times; sc in next 4 sc—24 sc.

Rnd 26: Sc in next 2 sc, (dec, sc in next sc) 6 times; sc in next 4 sc—18 sc.

Rnd 27: (Sc in next sc, dec) 4 times; sc in next 6 sc—14 sc.

Note: Stuff leg with fiberfill.

Rnd 28: Dec 7 times—7 sc.

Rnd 29: Sc in each sc; join in first sc. Finish off, leaving a 12" end for sewing.

Finishing

Step 1: Stuff head with fiberfill; with tapestry needle and 6" end on head, weave in and out of 7 stitches on Rnd 24; pull to close. Weave in end.

Step 2: Place washer on shank of joint; hold one leg with right side facing you; push shank through from wrong side of leg between Rnds 26 and 27 (on inside of leg). Add more fiberfill. Be careful that each shank is on inside of each leg. With tapestry needle and 12" end, weave in and out of Rnd 29; pull to close. Repeat for other leg. Set aside.

Step 3: Place washer on shank of joint; hold one arm with right side facing you, push shank through from wrong side of arm between Rnds 18 and 19 (on inside of arm). Add more fiberfill. Be careful that each shank is on inside of each arm. With tapestry needle and 12" end, weave in and out of Rnd 21; pull to close. Repeat for other arm. Set aside.

Step 4: Stuff with fiberfill lightly to shape body. With tapestry needle and 12" end on body, weave in and out of stitches on Rnd 25; pull to close. Hold one leg to corresponding side of lower body; place shank through from right side of body to wrong side of Rnds 17 and 18 of body; hold fastener from wrong side of body; push shank on fastener. Repeat for other leg. Hold arm to corresponding side of upper body; place shank through from right side of body to wrong side of Rnds 5 and 6 of body; hold fastener from wrong side of body; push shank on fastener. Repeat for other arm.

Stuff firmly. With tapestry needle and 20" end, sew head to Rnd 1 of body.

Step 5: Referring to photo for placement, with tapestry needle and black, using straight stitches (see Embroidery Stitch Guide on page 211) make lines for mouth on head and toes on each arm and leg.

Step 6: Wrap ribbon around neck and tie in bow. Trim ends.

Pretty as a Picture Apron

continued from page 33

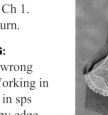

Row 51: Sc in each sc. Ch 1. Do not turn.

EDGING:

Row 1 (wrong side): Working in edge sc, in sps formed by edge trc, and in turning chs of each row, sc in side of last sc worked and in next row; 2 sc in each of next 47 rows; sc in next 2 rows—98 sc. Ch 2 (counts as a dc on following rows), turn.

Row 2 (right side): Dc in next 4 sc; * ch 3, dc in next sc; rep from * 88 times more; dc in next 4 sc—89 ch-3 sps. Ch 2, turn.

Row 3: Dc in next 4 dc; * ch 3, dc in next dc; rep from * 88 times more; dc in next 3 dc and in 2nd ch of turning ch-2. Ch 2, turn.

Skirt:

Following Chart B on page 48, work Rows 1 through 52. At end of Row 52, finish off.

Assembly

Hold waistband and top with right sides together; pin top to waistband between Rows 10 and 42; with tapestry needle and thread, sew using overcast st (see Crochet Stitch Guide on page 213) across top.

Skirt Edging:

Hold skirt with wrong side facing you and Row 55 at top; join thread in first dc on Row 40.

Row 1 (wrong side): Ch 1, sc in same dc and in next dc; working in sps formed by edge dc and turning chs of each row, 3 sc in next row; * 3 sc in next row; sc in next 2 dc; rep from * 6 times more; 3 sc in next row; sc in next 2 dc, (sk next 2 dc, sc in next 2 dc) twice; sk next 3 dc, 3 sc in next row; sc in next 57 dc, 3 sc in next ch-3 sp; sc in next 12 dc, (3 sc in next row, sc in next 6 dc) 3 times; 3 sc in next row; sc in next 11 dc, 3 sc in next row; working along top edge, sc in next 60 dc and in 3rd ch of turning ch-3, working along next side in sps formed by turning chs and edge dc of each row, 3 sc in same row as last sc worked; sk next dc, sc in next 11 dc, 3 sc in next row; † sk next 3 dc, sc in next 6 dc, 3 sc in next row †; rep from † to † twice more; sc in next 12 dc, 3 sc in next ch-3 sp; sc in next 57 dc, 3 sc in next row; sk next 3 sc, (sc in next 2 dc, sk next 2 dc) twice; sc in next 2 dc, (3 sc in next row, sk next 2 dc, sc in next 2 dc) 7 times; 3 sc in each of next 2 rows; sc in next 2 dc—397 sc. Ch 3 (counts as first dc on following rows), turn.

Row 2 (right side): Dc in next 4 sc; † ch 3, dc in next 5 sc †; rep from † to † 38 times more; ch 3, sk next 2 sc, dc in next 5 sc; rep from † to † 38 times—seventy-nine 5-dc groups. Ch 6 (counts as first dc and a ch-3 sp on following rows), turn.

continued on page 48

Pretty as a Picture Apron

continued from page 47

Row 3: Sk next 3 dc, dc in next dc, ch 5, sk next ch-3 sp, dc in next dc, ch 3, sk next 3 dc, dc in next dc, 3 dc in next ch-3 sp; dc in next dc, ch 3, sk next 3 dc, dc in next dc; * † ch 5, sk next ch-3 sp, dc in next dc, ch 3, sk next 3 dc, dc in next dc, 3 dc in next ch-3 sp; dc in next dc, ch 3, sk next 3 dc †; dc in next dc; rep from * 36 times more, then rep from † to † once; dc in 3rd ch of turning ch-3. Ch 3, turn.

Row 4: 3 dc in next ch-3 sp; dc in next dc, ch 3, sk next 3 dc, dc in next dc, 3 dc in next ch-3 sp; dc in next dc; * ch 7, sk next ch-5 sp, dc in next dc, 3 dc in next ch-3 sp; dc in next dc, ch 3, sk next 3 dc, dc in next dc; 3 dc in next ch-3 sp; dc in next dc; rep from * 37 times more; ch 7, sk next ch-5 sp, dc in next dc, 4 dc in turning ch-6 sp. Ch 6, turn.

Row 5: Sk next 3 dc, dc in next dc; * † ch 9, sk next ch-7 sp, dc in next dc, ch 3, sk next 3 dc, dc in next dc, 3 dc in next ch-3 sp; dc in next dc, ch 3, sk next 3 dc †; dc in next dc; rep from * 37 times more, then rep from † to † once; dc in 3rd ch of turning ch-3. Ch 3, turn.

Row 6: 3 dc in next ch-3 sp; dc in next dc, ch 3, sl st in 3rd ch from hook—picot made; sk next 3 dc, dc in next dc, 3 dc in next ch-3 sp; dc in next dc; * † dc in next ch of next ch-9 sp, picot; (sk next ch, dc in next next ch, picot) 4 times; dc in next dc †; 3 dc in next ch-3 sp; dc in next dc, picot; sk next 3 dc, dc in next dc, 3 dc in next ch-3 sp; dc in next dc; rep from * 37 times more, then rep from † to † once; 4 dc in turning ch-6 sp. Do not finish off.

Side Edging:

Picot in last dc made; working along side of apron in sps formed by edge dc and turning ch of each row, 3 sc in last dc worked; 3 sc in each of next 2 rows; picot; * 3 sc in each of next 3 rows; picot; rep from * 13 times more; sk next edge sc, working along edge of waistband in unused lps of beg ch-22, (sc in next 7 lps, picot) 3 times; working along edge of waistband, in sps formed by turning chs and edge trc, sk next edge sc; 3 sc in next row; in next row work (2 sc, picot, sc); 3 sc in next row; in next row work (sc, picot, 2 sc); in next row work (3 sc, picot); 3 sc in next row; in next row work (2 sc, picot, sc). Finish off.

Hold apron with right side facing you and waistband at top; join thread in first unworked edge dc to left of apron top; ch 1, in same sp work (2 sc, picot, sc); working in sps formed by edge trc and turning ch of each row, 3 sc in next row; in next row work (sc, picot, 2 sc); in next row work (3 sc, picot); 3 sc in next row; in next row work (2 sc, picot, sc); 3 sc in next row; working along edge of waistband, sc in first sc, picot; (sc in next 7 sc, picot) twice; sc in next 6 sc; working along skirt, sk next edge sc; * in next row work (sc, picot, 2 sc); 3 sc in each of next 2 rows; rep from * 14 times more; in same sp as last 3 sc worked work (sc, picot).

Finish off and weave in all ends.

Finishing

Step 1: Cut two 14" lengths of 1" wide ribbon; tie each into a bow. Trim ends. Place button over knot; with sewing needle and matching thread, sew button and bow to apron top as in photo.

Step 2: Weave 2 yds of 1" wide ribbon through waistline slits. Tie bow at back.

Step 3: Cut two 18" lengths of 1/2" wide ribbon. With sewing needle and matching thread, sew one end of each length to wrong side behind bows.

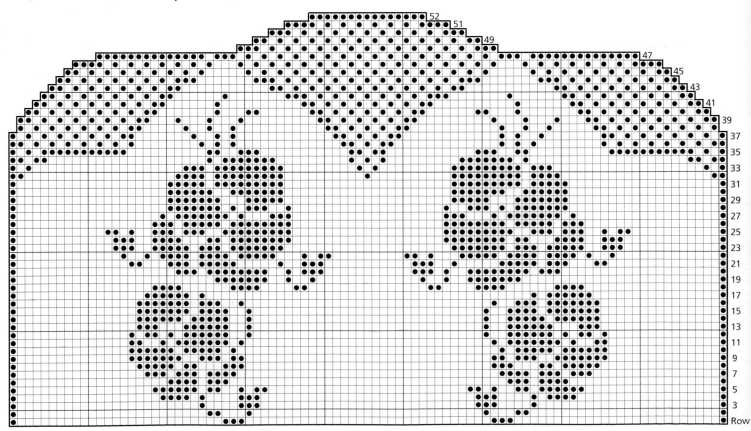

Chart B

Snowbound!

continued from page 13

Rnd 5: Ch 1, sc in same CL; * † (ch 3, sc in next ch-3 sp, ch 3, sc in next CL) twice; ch 5, trc CL in next trc CL; in trc CL just made work (ch 5, sc) 3 times—corner made; ch 5, sk next ch-5 sp †; sc in next CL; rep from * twice more, then rep from † to † once; join in first sc. Finish off.

Rnd 6: Join blue in 2nd ch-5 sp of any corner; ch 3, in same sp work (2 dc, ch 3, 3 dc)—beg corner made; * † 3 dc in each of next 2 ch-5 sps; 2 dc in each of next 4 ch-3 sps; 3 dc in each of next 2 ch-5 sps †; in next ch-5 sp work (3 dc, ch 3, 3 dc)—corner made; rep from * twice more, then rep from † to † once; join in 3rd ch of beg ch-3.

Rnd 7: Sl st in next 2 dc and in next ch-3 sp, in same sp work beg corner; * † (ch 5, sk next 3 dc, sc in next dc) 6 times; ch 5 †; in next corner ch-3 sp work corner; rep from * twice more, then rep from † to † once; join in 3rd ch of beg ch-3.

Finish off and weave in all ends.

Motif B

Work same as Motif A through Rnd 6.

Rnd 7: Sl st in next 2 dc and in next ch-3 sp, beg corner in same sp; (ch 5, sk next 3 dc, sc in next dc) 6 times; ch 5, 3 dc in next corner ch-3 sp; ch 1; hold wrong side of completed motif (see **Diagram A**) facing wrong side of working motif and carefully match sts; on completed motif, sl st in corresponding corner ch-3 sp, ch 1; on working motif, 3 dc in same sp as last 3 dc made; † ch 2; on completed motif, sl st in next ch-5 sp, ch 2; on working motif, sk next 3 dc, sc in next dc †; rep from † to † 5 times more; ch 2; on completed motif, sl st in next ch-5 sp, ch 2; on working motif, sk next 3 dc, 3 dc in next corner ch-3 sp; ch 1; on completed motif, sl st in next corner ch-3 sp, ch 1; on working motif, 3 dc in same sp as last 3 dc made; †† (ch 5, sk next 3 dc, sc in next dc) 6 times; ch 5 ††; corner in next corner ch-3 sp; rep from †† to †† once more; join in 3rd ch of beg ch-3.

Finish off and weave in all ends.

Motif C

Work same as Motif A through Rnd 6.

Rnd 7: Sl st in next 2 dc and in next ch-3 sp, beg corner in same sp; † (ch 5, sk next 3 dc, sc in next dc) 6 times; ch 5 †; corner in next corner ch-3 sp; rep from † to † once; 3 dc in next corner ch-3 sp; ch 1; hold wrong side of completed motif (see **Diagram A**) facing wrong side of working motif and carefully match sts; on completed motif, sl st in corresponding corner ch-3 sp, ch 1; on working motif, 3 dc in same sp as last 3 dc made; ch 2; on completed motif, sl st in next ch-5 sp, ch 2; on working motif, sk next 3 dc, sc in next dc; †† ch 2; on completed motif, sl st in next ch-5 sp, ch 2; on working motif, sk next 3 dc, sc in next dc ††; rep from †† to †† 5 times more; ch 2; on completed motif, sl st in next ch-5 sp, ch 2; on working motif, sk next 3 dc, 3 dc in next corner ch-3 sp; ch 2; on completed motif, sl st in motif joining, ch 2; on working motif, 3 dc in same sp as last 3 dc made; (ch 5, sk next 3 dc, sc in next dc) 6 times; ch 5; join in 3rd ch of beg ch-3.

Finish off and weave in all ends.

C	D	D	D	E
C	D	D	D	E
C	D	D	D	E
C	D	D	D	E
C	D	D	D	E
A	B	B	B	B

Diagram A

Motif D

Work same as Motif A through Rnd 6.

Rnd 7: Sl st in next 2 dc and in next ch-3 sp, beg corner in same sp; (ch 5, sk next 3 dc, sc in next dc) 6 times; ch 5, 3 dc in next corner ch-3 sp; ch 1; hold wrong side of completed motif (see **Diagram A**) facing wrong side of working motif and carefully match sts; on completed motif, sl st in corresponding corner ch-3 sp, ch 1; on working motif, 3 dc in same sp as last 3 dc made; ch 2; on completed motif, sl st in next ch-5 sp, ch 2; on working motif, sk next 3 dc, sc in next dc; * † ch 2; on completed motif, sl st in next ch-5 sp, ch 2; on working motif, sk next 3 dc, sc in next dc †; rep from † to † 5 times more; ch 2; on completed motif, sl st in next ch-5 sp, ch 2; on working motif, sk next 3 dc, 3 dc in next corner ch-3 sp; ch 1; on completed motif, sl st in motif joining, ch 1; on working motif, 3 dc in same sp as last 3 dc made; rep from * once more; (ch 5, sk next 3 dc, sc in next dc) 6 times; ch 5; join in 3rd ch of beg ch-3.

Finish off and weave in all ends.

Motif E

Work same as Motif A through Rnd 6.

Rnd 7: Sl st in next 2 dc and in next ch-3 sp, beg corner in same sp; (ch 5, sk next 3 dc, sc in next dc) 6 times; ch 5, 3 dc in next corner ch-3 sp; ch 1; hold wrong side of completed motif (see **Diagram A**) facing wrong side of working motif and carefully match sts; on completed motif, sl st in corresponding corner ch-3 sp, ch 1; on working motif, 3 dc in same sp as last 3 dc made; † ch 2; on completed motif, sl st in next ch-5 sp, ch 2; on working motif, sk next 3 dc, sc in next dc †; rep from † to † 5 times more; ch 2; on completed motif, sl st in next ch-5 sp, ch 2; on working motif, sk next 3 dc, 3 dc in next corner ch-3 sp; ch 1; on completed motif, sl st in motif joining, ch 1; on working motif, 3 dc in same sp as last 3 dc made; rep from † to † 6 times more; ch 2; on completed motif, sl st in next ch-5 sp, ch 2; on working motif, sk next 3 dc, 3 dc in next corner ch-3 sp; ch 1; on completed motif, sl st in next corner ch-3 sp, ch 1; on working motif, 3 dc in same sp as last 3 dc made; (ch 5, sk next 3 dc, sc in next dc) 6 times; ch 5; join in 3rd ch of beg ch-3.

Finish off and weave in all ends.

Border

Hold afghan with right side facing you and one short end at top; join white in upper right-hand corner ch-3 sp.

Rnd 1 (right side)**:** In same sp work beg trc CL (see Pattern Stitches on page 12); † (ch 4, CL in next ch-5 sp, ch 4, sc in next ch-5 sp) 3 times; ch 4, CL in next ch-5 sp; ch 4, sc in motif joining †; rep from † to † 3 times more; †† (ch 4, CL in next ch-5 sp, ch 4, sc in next ch-5 sp) 3 times; ch 4, CL in next ch-5 sp; ch 4 ††; trc CL in next corner ch-3 sp; rep from † to † 5 times; rep from †† to †† once; trc CL in next corner

continued on page 50

Snowbound!

continued from page 49

ch-3 sp; rep from † to † 4 times; rep from †† to †† once; trc CL in next corner ch-3 sp; rep from † to † 5 times; rep from †† to †† once; join in beg trc CL.

Rnd 2: In same beg trc CL work (beg trc CL, ch 3, trc CL, ch 3, trc CL); † ch 5, in next CL work (CL, ch 3) twice; CL in same CL †; rep from † to † 19 times more; †† ch 5, in next trc CL work (trc CL, ch 3) twice; trc CL in same trc CL ††; rep from † to † 24 times; rep from †† to †† once; rep from † to † 20 times; rep from †† to †† once; rep from † to † 24 times; ch 5; join in beg trc CL.

Rnd 3: Beg CL in same CL; ch 3, in next trc CL work (trc CL, ch 3, trc CL)—corner made; ch 3, CL in next trc CL; ch 5; † sc in next ch-5 sp, ch 3, (sc in next CL, ch 3, sc in next ch-3 sp, ch 3) twice; sc in next CL, ch 3 †; rep from † to † 19 times more; †† sc in next ch-5 sp, ch 5, CL in next trc CL; ch 3, in next trc CL work (trc CL, ch 3, trc CL)—corner made; ch 3, CL in next trc CL; ch 5 ††; rep from † to † 24 times; rep from †† to †† once; rep from † to † 20

times; rep from †† to †† once; rep from † to † 24 times; sc in next ch-5 sp, ch 5; join in beg CL. Finish off.

Rnd 4: Join blue in corner ch-3 sp to left of joining; in same sp work (ch 3, 2 dc, ch 3, 3 dc)—beg corner made; * † 3 dc in next ch-3 sp and in next ch-5 sp; 2 dc in each ch-3 sp to next ch-5 sp; 3 dc in next ch-5 sp and in next ch-3 sp †; in next corner ch-3 sp work (3 dc, ch 3, 3 dc); rep from * twice more, then rep from † to † once; join in 3rd ch of beg ch-3.

Rnd 5: Ch 1, sc in same ch as joining; working in BLs only, sc in next 2 dc, 3 sc in next corner ch-3 sp; * sc in each dc to next corner ch-3 sp; 3 sc in corner ch-3 sp; rep from * twice more; sc in each dc to first sc; join in first sc.

Finish off and weave in all ends.

Snowflake (make 20)

With white, ch 4; join to form a ring.

Rnd 1 (right side): Ch 2, dc in ring; ch 3; * dc CL (see Pattern Stitches on page 12) in ring; ch 3; rep from * 4 times more; ch 3; join in first dc.

Rnd 2: Ch 2, dc in same ch as joining; in dc just made work (ch 3, sc) 3 times; * ch 3, sc in next ch-3 sp, ch 3, dc CL in next dc CL; in dc CL just made work (ch 3, sc) 3 times; rep from * 4 times more; ch 3, sc in next ch-3 sp, ch 3; join in first dc.

Finish off and weave in all ends.

Finishing

Referring to **Photo A** for placement, sew snowflakes to afghan.

Photo A

Holiday Vest

continued from page 9

Row 18: Dc in each rem dc and in 3rd ch of turning ch-3. Finish off, leaving an 18" end for sewing.

Continue with Back.

Size Large:

Row 1 (wrong side): Dc in next ch-1 sp; * dc in next 7 dc and in next ch-1 sp; rep from * 3 times more; dc in next 4 dc—38 dc. Ch 3, turn.

Row 2 (right side): Dc in each rem dc and in 3rd ch of turning ch-3. Ch 3, turn.

Row 3: Dec over next 2 dc [to work dec: (YO, draw up lp in next dc, YO and draw through 2 lps on hook) twice; YO and draw through all 3 lps on hook—dec made]; dec over next 2 dc; dc in each rem dc and in 3rd ch of turning ch-3—36 dc. Ch 3, turn.

Row 4: Dc in each dc to last 3 dc and turning ch-3; dec over next 2 dc; dec over

last dc and 3rd ch of turning ch—34 dc. Ch 3, turn.

Rows 5 and 6: Rep Rows 3 and 4. At end of Row 6—30 dc. Ch 3, turn.

Row 7: (Dec over next 2 dc) twice; dc in each rem dc and in 3rd ch of turning ch-3—28 dc. Ch 3, turn.

Row 8: Dc in each dc to last dc and turning ch-3; dec over last dc and 3rd ch of turning ch—27 dc. Ch 3, turn.

Row 9: Dec over next 2 dc; dc in each rem dc and in 3rd ch of turning ch-3—26 dc. Ch 3, turn.

Rows 10 through 15: Rep Rows 8 and 9 three times more. At end of Row 15—20 dc.

Rows 16 through 18: Rep Row 2. At end of Row 18, do not ch 3. Finish off, leaving an 18" end for sewing.

Back (all sizes)

Hold piece with wrong side facing you; join red in 16th st from left front.

Row 1 (wrong side): Ch 3 (counts as a dc), working in each dc and in each ch-1 sp, dc in next 55 (62, 72) sts—56 (63, 73) dc. Ch 3, turn.

Row 2 (right side): Dc in each dc. Ch 3, turn.

Rows 3 through 15 (17, 17): Rep Row 2.

Right Back Shoulder:

Row 16 (18, 18): Dc in next 15 (16, 19) dc—16 (17, 20) dc. Finish off.

Left Back Shoulder:

Hold back with right side facing you; join red in 25th (30th, 34th) dc from right back shoulder.

Row 16 (18, 18): Ch 3, dc in next 14 (15, 18) dc and in 3rd ch of turning ch-3—16 (17, 20) dc. Finish off.

Right Front

Hold piece with wrong side facing you; join red in 16th st from back.

Size Small Only:

Row 1 (wrong side): Ch 3, dc in next 3 dc and in next ch-1 sp; * dc in next 7 dc and in next ch-1 sp; rep from * once more; dc in next 7 dc and in next 2 chs of turning ch-4—30 dc. Ch 3, turn.

continued on page 51

Holiday Vest

continued from page 50

Row 2 (right side): Dc in each dc and in 3rd ch of turning ch-3. Ch 3, turn.

Row 3: Dc in each dc to last dc and turning ch-3, dec over last dc and 3rd ch of turning ch-3—29 dc. Ch 3, turn.

Row 4: Dec over next 2 dc; dc in each rem dc and in 3rd ch of turning ch-3—28 dc. Ch 3, turn.

Rows 5 through 16: Rep Rows 3 and 4 six times more. At end of Row 16, do not ch 3—16 dc. Finish off, leaving an 18" end for sewing.

Size Medium Only:

Row 1 (wrong side): Ch 3, sk first dc, dc in next ch-1 sp; * dc in next 7 dc and in next ch-1 sp; rep from * twice more; dc in next 7 dc and in first ch of turning ch-4—34 dc. Ch 3, turn, leaving rem 3 chs of turning ch unworked.

Row 2 (right side): Dc in each dc and in 3rd ch of turning ch-3. Ch 3, turn.

Row 3: Dc in next 29 dc, dec over next 2 dc; dec over next dc and 3rd ch of turning ch-3—32 dc. Ch 3, turn.

Row 4: (Dec over next 2 dc) twice; dc in each rem dc and in 3rd ch of turning ch-3—30 dc. Ch 3, turn.

Row 5: Dc in next 27 dc, dec over next dc and 3rd ch of turning ch-3—29 dc. Ch 3, turn.

Row 6: Dec over next 2 dc; dc in each rem dc and in 3rd ch of turning ch-3—28 dc. Ch 3, turn.

Rows 7 through 16: Rep Rows 5 and 6 five times more. At end of Row 16—18 dc.

Row 17: Rep Row 5. At end of row—17 dc.

Row 18: Dc in each rem dc and in 3rd ch of turning ch-3. Finish off, leaving an 18" end for sewing.

Size Large:

Row 1 (wrong side): Ch 3, sk first dc, dc in next 3 dc and in next ch-1 sp; * dc in next 7 dc and in next ch-1 sp; rep from * twice more; dc in next 7 dc and in next 2 chs of turning ch-4—38 dc. Ch 3, turn.

Row 2 (right side): Dc in each rem dc and in 3rd ch of turning ch-3. Ch 3, turn.

Row 3: Dc in next 33 dc, dec over next 2 dc; dec over next dc and 3rd ch of turning ch-3—36 dc. Ch 3, turn.

Row 4: (Dec over next 2 dc) twice; dc in each rem dc and in 3rd ch of turning ch-3—34 dc. Ch 3, turn.

Row 5: Dc in next 29 dc, dec over next 2 dc; dec over next dc and 3rd ch of turning ch-3—32 dc. Ch 3, turn.

Rows 6 and 7: Rep Rows 4 and 5. At end of Row 7—28 dc. Ch 3, turn.

Row 8: Dec over next 2 dc; dc in each rem dc and in 3rd ch of turning ch-3—27 dc. Ch 3, turn.

Row 9: Dc in each dc to last dc and turning ch-3; dec over last dc and 3rd ch of turning ch—26 dc. Ch 3, turn.

Rows 10 through 15: Rep Rows 8 and 9 three times more. At end of Row 15—20 dc.

Rows 16 through 18: Rep Row 2. At end of Row 18, do not ch 3. Finish off, leaving an 18" end for sewing.

With tapestry needle and long ends, sew shoulder seams.

Armhole Edging:

Hold vest with right side facing you and one armhole at top; join red in first unused st at underarm.

Rnd 1: Ch 1, 2 sc in same st as joining; sc in each dc, and in each ch-1 sp; working around armhole in sps formed by each edge dc and turning ch, * 2 sc in next sp; sc in next sp; rep from * around; join in first sc—64 (70, 70) sc.

Rnd 2: Ch 1, sc in same sc; * ch 3, sc in next 6 sc; rep from * 9 (10, 10) times more; ch 3, sc in next 3 sc; join in first sc. Finish off.

Work other armhole edging in same manner.

Lower and Neckline Edging:

Hold vest with right side facing you and lower edge at top; join red in first unused lp of beg ch at base of last V-st in upper right-hand corner.

Rnd 1: Ch 1, 3 sc in same lp—corner made; working across lower edge in unused lps of beg ch and in sps formed by skipped chs, 3 sc in next sp; * sc in next lp, 3 sc in next sp; rep from * across; 3 sc in next lp—corner made; working along right front in

sps formed by edge dc and turning chs, 2 sc in each sp; working along back, sc in each dc; working along center edge in sps formed by edge dc and turning chs, 2 sc in each sp; join in first sc.

Rnd 2: Ch 1, sc in same sc; * ch 3, sc in next 6 sc; rep from * 62 (68, 72) times more; sc in each rem sc; join in first sc.

Finish off and weave in all ends.

Flower (make 9)

With smaller size hook and red, ch 4; join to form a ring.

Rnd 1 (right side): Ch 2 (counts as a dc), 9 dc in ring; join in 2nd ch of beg ch-2—10 dc.

Rnd 2: * Ch 7, sl st in 3rd ch from hook, sc in next ch, hdc in next ch, dc in next 2 chs—petal made; sl st in BL of next 2 dc; rep from * 4 times more; join in unused lp of joining sl st—5 petals.

Rnd 3: Working in front of petals in unused lps of each dc of Rnd 1, * ch 4, sl st in 3rd ch from hook, sc in next ch, sl st in next 2 lps; rep from * 4 times more; join in joining sl st. Finish off, leaving a 12" end for sewing.

Leaf (make 14)

With smaller size hook and dk green, ch 9; sl st in 3rd ch from hook, sc in next ch, hdc in next ch, ch 3, sl st in same hdc—picot made; hdc in next ch, dc in next 2 chs, ch 3, sl st in last dc made—picot made; 3 dc in next ch; working along opposite side in unused lps of beg ch, dc in next lp, ch 3, sl st in same dc—picot made; dc in next lp, hdc in next lp, ch 3, sl st in same hdc—picot made; sc in next lp, sl st in next lp. Finish off, leaving a 12" end for sewing.

Ties (make 2)

With smaller size hook and red, ch 60; sc in 2nd ch from hook and in each rem ch. Finish off, leaving a 6" end for sewing.

Finishing

Step 1: Referring to photo for placement, with tapestry needle and yarn ends, tack flowers and leaves around neckline.

Step 2: Sew one bead to center of each flower.

Step 3: Sew ties to inside front of vest at point where V-neck shaping begins.

Evening of Glamour – Vest *continued from page 22*

Row 8: Sc in next ch-4 sp; * ch 4, sc in 2nd dc of next shell, ch 4, sc in next ch-4 sp; rep from * 5 (7) times more; ch 4, sc in 3rd ch of turning ch-3. Ch 1, turn.

Row 9: Sc in next ch-4 sp, ch 4; * sc in next ch-4 sp, shell in next sc; sc in next ch-4 sp, ch 4; rep from * 5 (7) times more; sc in sp formed by turning ch-4. Ch 1, turn.

Row 10: Sc in next ch-4 sp; * shell in next sc; sc in 2nd dc of next shell, shell in next sc; sc in next ch-4 sp; rep from * 5 (7) times more. Ch 4, turn.

Row 11: Dc in first sc, sc in 2nd dc of next shell, shell in next sc; sc in 2nd dc of next shell; * ch 4, sc in 2nd dc of next shell, shell in next sc; sc in 2nd dc of next shell; rep from * 4 (6) times more; half shell in next sc. Ch 1, turn.

Row 12: Sc in first dc, ch 4, sc in 2nd dc of next shell, ch 4; * sc in next ch-4 sp, ch 4, sc in 2nd dc of next shell, ch 4; rep from * 4 (6) times more; sk next ch of turning ch-4, sc in next ch. Ch 4, turn.

Row 13: Dc in first sc; * † sc in next ch-4 sp, shell in next sc; sc in next ch-4 sp †; ch 4; rep from * 4 (6) times more, then rep from † to † once; half shell in next sc. Ch 1, turn.

Row 14: Sc in first dc; * † shell in next sc; sc in 2nd dc of next shell, shell in next sc †; sc in next ch-4 sp; rep from * 4 (6) times more, then rep from † to † once; sk next ch of turning ch-4, sc in next ch. Ch 4, turn.

Row 15: Dc in first sc; * † sc in 2nd dc of next shell, shell in next sc; sc in 2nd dc of next shell †; ch 4; rep from * 4 (6) times more, then rep from † to † once; half shell in next sc. Ch 1, turn.

Row 16: Sc in first dc; * † ch 4, sc in 2nd dc of next shell, ch 4 †; sc in next ch-4 sp; rep from * 4 (6) times more, then rep from † to † once; sk next ch of turning ch-4, sc in next ch. Ch 4, turn.

Rows 17 through 20: Rep Rows 13 through 16.

Rows 21 through 23: Rep Rows 13 through 15. At end of Row 23, do not ch 1; do not turn. Finish off.

Left Front

Hold piece with wrong side facing you, sk next 3 ch-4 sps from back; make lp on hook and join with an sc in next ch-4 sp.

Row 1 (wrong side): Ch 4, sk next sc; * sc in next ch-4 sp, shell in next sc; sc in next ch-4 sp, ch 4, sk next sc; rep from * 3 (4) times more; sc in next ch-4 sp, half shell in next sc—4 (5) shells. Ch 1, turn.

Row 2 (right side): Sc in next ch-1 sp; * shell in next sc; sc in next ch-4 sp, shell in next sc; sc in 2nd dc of next shell; rep from * 3 (4) times more; shell in next sc; sc in next ch-4 sp—9 (11) shells. Ch 1, turn.

Row 3: Sk first sc, next dc, and next ch-1 sp; sc in next dc, shell in next sc; sc in 2nd dc of next shell; * ch 4, sc in 2nd dc of next shell, shell in next sc; sc in 2nd dc of next shell; rep from * 2 (3) times more; ch 4, sc in 2nd dc of next shell. Ch 4, turn.

Row 4: * † Sc in next ch-4 sp, ch 4, sc in 2nd dc of next shell †; ch 4; rep from * 2 (3) times more, then rep from † to † once. Ch 4, turn.

Row 5: Dc in first sc; * sc in next ch-4 sp, ch 4, sc in next ch-4 sp, shell in next sc; rep from * 2 (3) times more; sc in next ch-4 sp, ch 4, sk next sc, sc in sp formed by turning ch-4. Ch 3, turn.

Row 6: Shell in next sc; * sc in 2nd dc of next shell, shell in next sc; sc in next ch-4 sp, shell in next sc; rep from * 2 (3) times more; sk next ch of turning ch-4, sc in next ch—7 (9) shells. Ch 1, turn.

Row 7: Sk first sc, next dc, and next ch-1 sp; sc in next dc; * ch 4, sc in 2nd dc of next shell, shell in next sc; sc in 2nd dc of next shell; rep from * 2 (3) times more. Ch 3, turn.

Row 8: Sk next dc and next ch-1 sp, sc in next dc; * ch 4, sc in next ch-4 sp, ch 4, sc in 2nd dc of next shell; rep from * once (twice) more; ch 4, sc in next ch-4 sp—6 (8) sc. Ch 4, turn.

Row 9: Dc in first sc; * sc in next ch-4 sp, shell in next sc; sc in next ch-4 sp, ch 4; rep from * once (twice) more; sc in next ch-4 sp, half shell in next sc. Ch 1, turn.

Row 10: Sc in first dc; * shell in next sc; sc in next ch-4 sp, shell in next sc; sc in 2nd dc of next shell; rep from * once (twice) more; shell in next sc; sk next ch of turning ch-4, sc in next ch. Ch 4, turn.

Row 11: Dc in first sc; * sc in 2nd dc of next shell, shell in next sc; sc in 2nd dc of next shell, ch 4; rep from * once (twice)

more; sc in 2nd dc of next shell. Ch 3, turn.

Row 12: * Sc in next ch-4 sp, ch 4, sc in 2nd dc of next shell, ch 4; rep from * once (twice) more; sk next ch of turning ch-4, sc in next ch—4 (6) ch-4 sps. Ch 4, turn.

Row 13: Dc in first sc; * † sc in next ch-4 sp, shell in next sc; sc in next ch-4 sp †; ch 4; rep from * 0 (1) time more, then rep from † to † once; half shell in next sc. Ch 1, turn.

Row 14: Sc in first dc; * † shell in next sc; sc in 2nd dc of next shell, shell in next sc †; sc in next ch-4 sp; rep from * 0 (1) time more, then rep from † to † once; sk next ch of turning ch-4, sc in next ch. Ch 4, turn.

Row 15: Dc in first sc; * † sc in 2nd dc of next shell, shell in next sc; sc in 2nd dc of next shell †; ch 4; rep from * 0 (1) time more, then rep from † to † once; half shell in next sc. Ch 1, turn.

Row 16: Sc in first dc; * † ch 4, sc in 2nd dc of next shell, ch 4 †; sc in next ch-4 sp; rep from * 0 (1) time more, then rep from † to † once; sk next ch of turning ch-4, sc in next ch—4 (6) ch-4 sps. Ch 4, turn.

Rows 17 through 20: Rep Rows 13 through 16.

Rows 21 through 23: Rep Rows 13 through 15. At end of Row 23, do not ch 1; do not turn. Finish off.

Finishing

Sew shoulder and side seams.

Edgings

Armhole Edging:

Join yarn in first ch-4 sp of one underarm, ch 3, working in ch-4 sp and in sps formed by edge dc and turning chs, dc evenly spaced around each armhole so edges remain flat; join in 3rd ch of beg ch-3. Finish off.

Rep in same manner for other armhole edging, have the same number of dc as first edging.

Vest Edging:

Hold vest with right side facing you and beg ch at top; join yarn in first unused lp of beg ch, ch 3 (counts as a dc), 2 dc in same sp—corner made; working in sps formed by 3 skipped chs and in unused lps of each sc; 3 (2) dc in next sp; dc in next lp; * 3 dc in next sp, dc in next lp; rep from * 39 (47) times more; 3 (2) dc in next sp; 3 dc in

continued on page 53

Evening of Glamour – Vest

continued from page 52

next lp—corner made; working along right front in ends of rows in sps formed by edge dc and turning chs, dc evenly along right front, dc evenly spaced across Row 23 of back; working along left front in ends of rows in sps formed by edge dc and turning chs, dc evenly spaced along left front; join in 3rd ch of beg ch-3.

Bottom Border:

Row 1: Sl st in next dc, ch 1, sc in same dc; ch 1, sk next 1 (2) dc; * † sc in next dc, ch 3, sk next 5 dc, in next dc work (trc, ch 2, trc, ch 4, trc, ch 2, trc); ch 3, sk next 5 dc, sc in next dc, ch 1 †; sk next dc; rep from * 10 (12) times more, then rep from † to † once; sk next 1 (2) dc, sc in next dc. Ch 1, turn.

Row 2: Sc in next ch-1 sp; * sk next sc, 3 dc in next ch-3 sp; dc in next trc, 2 dc in next ch-2 sp; dc in next trc, in next ch-4 sp work (3 dc, ch 1, 3 dc); dc in next trc, 2 dc in next ch-2 sp; dc in next trc, 3 dc in next ch-3 sp; sk next sc, sc in next ch-1 sp; rep from * 11 (13) times more.

Finish off and weave in all ends.

Finishing

Sew 4 buttons evenly spaced along left front. Spaces between double crochet along right front opposite buttons form buttonholes.

Evening of Glamour – Shawl

continued from page 23

ch-4 sp) 3 times; ch 4, center sp in next center sp; (ch 4, sc in next ch-4 sp) 4 times; shell in next sc; sc in next ch-4 sp, (ch 4, sc in next ch-4 sp) twice; ch 4, edge sp in turning ch-7. Ch 7, turn.

Row 9: Sc in edge sp, (ch 4, sc in next ch-4 sp) 3 times; shell in next sc; sc in 2nd dc of next shell, shell in next sc; (sc in next ch-4 sp, ch 4) 4 times; center sp in next center sp; (ch 4, sc in next ch-4 sp) 4 times; shell in next sc; sc in 2nd dc of next shell, shell in next sc; (sc in next ch-4 sp, ch 4) 3 times; edge sp in turning ch-7. Ch 7, turn.

Row 10: Sc in edge sp, (ch 4, sc in next ch-4 sp) 3 times; ch 4, sc in 2nd dc of next shell, shell in next sc; sc in 2nd dc of next shell, (ch 4, sc in next ch-4 sp) 4 times; ch 4, center sp in next center sp; (ch 4, sc in next sp) 4 times; ch 4, sc in 2nd dc of next shell, shell in next sc; sc in 2nd dc of next shell, (ch 4, sc in next ch-4 sp) 3 times; ch 4, edge sp in turning ch-7. Ch 7, turn.

Row 11: Sc in edge sp, (ch 4, sc in next ch-4 sp) 4 times; ch 4, sc in 2nd dc of next shell, (ch 4, sc in next ch-4 sp) 5 times; ch 4, center sp in next center sp; (ch 4, sc in next ch-4 sp) 5 times; ch 4, sc in 2nd dc of next shell, (ch 4, sc in next ch-4 sp) 4 times; ch 4, edge sp in turning ch-7. Ch 7, turn.

Row 12: Sc in edge sp, ch 4, sc in next ch-4 sp, shell in next sc; † sc in next ch-4 sp, (ch 4, sc in next ch-4 sp) 3 times; shell in next sc †; rep from † to † once more; (sc in next ch-4 sp, ch 4) twice; center sp in next center sp; (ch 4, sc in next ch-4 sp) twice; shell in next sc; rep from † to † twice; sc in next ch-4 sp, ch 4, edge sp in turning ch-7—6 shells. Ch 7, turn.

Row 13: Sc in edge sp, ch 4; * sc in next ch-4 sp, shell in next sc; sc in 2nd dc of next shell, shell in next sc; (sc in next ch-4 sp, ch 4) twice; rep from * to center sp; center sp in center sp; ** (ch 4, sc in next ch-4 sp) twice; shell in next sc; sc in 2nd dc of next shell, shell in next sc; sc in next ch-4 sp; rep from ** to turning ch-7; ch 4, edge sp in turning ch-7. Ch 7, turn.

Row 14: Sc in edge sp, ch 4, sc in next ch-4 sp, ch 4; * sc in 2nd dc of next shell, shell in next sc; sc in 2nd dc of next shell, (ch 4, sc in next sp) twice; ch 4; rep from * to center sp; center sp in center sp; ch 4; ** (sc in next ch-4 sp, ch 4) twice; sc in 2nd dc of next shell, shell in next sc; sc in 2nd dc of next shell, ch 4; rep from ** to last ch-4 sp and turning ch-7; sc in next ch-4 sp, ch 4, edge sp in turning ch-7. Ch 7, turn.

Row 15: Sc in edge sp, ch 4, (sc in next ch-4 sp, ch 4) twice; * sc in 2nd dc of next shell, ch 4, (sc in next ch-4 sp, ch 4) 3 times; rep from * to center sp; center sp in center sp; ch 4, (sc in next ch-4 sp, ch 4) twice; ** sc in next ch-4 sp, ch 4, sc in 2nd dc of next shell, (ch 4, sc in next ch-4 sp) twice; ch 4; rep from ** to turning ch-7; edge sp in turning ch-7. Ch 7, turn.

Row 16: Sc in edge sp, (ch 4, sc in next ch-4 sp) 3 times; * shell in next sc; sc in next ch-4 sp, (ch 4, sc in next ch-4 sp) 3 times; rep from * to center sp; ch 4, center sp in center sp; (ch 4, sc in next ch-4 sp) 3 times; ** ch 4, sc in next ch-4 sp, shell in next sc; sc in next ch-4 sp, (ch 4, sc in next ch-4 sp) twice; rep from ** to turning ch-7; ch 4, edge sp in turning ch-7. Ch 7, turn.

Row 17: Sc in edge sp, (ch 4, sc in next ch-4 sp) 3 times; * shell in next sc; sc in 2nd dc of next shell, shell in next sc; sc in next ch-4 sp, (ch 4, sc in next ch-4 sp) twice; rep from * to last ch-4 sp before center sp; ch 4, sc in next ch-4 sp, ch 4, center sp in next center sp; (ch 4, sc in next ch-4 sp) 4 times; ** shell in next sc; sc in 2nd dc of next shell, shell in next sc; sc in next ch-4 sp, (ch 4, sc in next ch-4 sp) twice; rep from ** to turning ch-7; ch 4, edge sp in turning ch-7. Ch 7, turn.

Row 18: Sc in edge sp, (ch 4, sc in next ch-4 sp) 3 times; ch 4; * sc in 2nd dc of next shell, shell in next sc; sc in 2nd dc of next shell, (ch 4, sc in next ch-4 sp) twice; ch 4; rep from * to last 2 ch-4 sps before center sp, (sc in next ch-4 sp, ch 4) twice; center sp in center sp; (ch 4, sc in next ch-4 sp) 4 times; ** ch 4, sc in 2nd dc of next shell, shell in next sc; sc in 2nd dc of next shell, (ch 4, sc in next ch-4 sp) twice; rep from ** to last ch-4 sp and turning ch-7; ch 4, sc in next ch-4 sp, ch 4, edge sp in turning ch-7. Ch 7, turn.

Row 19: Sc in edge sp, (ch 4, sc in next ch-4 sp) 4 times; ch 4; * sc in 2nd dc of next shell, (ch 4, sc in next ch-4 sp) 3 times; ch 4; rep from * to last 2 ch-4 sps before center sp; (ch 4, sc in next ch-4 sp) twice; ch 4, center sp in next center sp; (ch 4, sc in next ch-4 sp) 5 times; ** ch 4, sc in 2nd dc of next shell, (ch 4, sc in next ch-4 sp) 3 times; rep from ** to last ch-4 sp and turning ch-7; ch 4, sc in next ch-4 sp, ch 4, edge sp in turning ch-7. Ch 7, turn.

Row 20: Sc in edge sp, ch 4, sc in next ch-4 sp, shell in next sc; sc in next ch-4 sp; * (ch 4, sc in next ch-4 sp) 3 times; shell in next sc; sc in next ch-4 sp; rep from * to last ch-4 sp before center sp; ch 4, sc in next ch-4 sp, ch 4, center sp in next center sp; (ch 4, sc in next ch-4 sp) twice; shell in next sc; sc in next ch-4 sp; ** (ch 4, sc in next ch-4 sp) 3 times; shell in next sc; sc in next ch-4 sp; rep from ** to turning ch-7; ch 4, edge sp in turning ch-7. Ch 7, turn.

continued on page 54

Evening of Glamour – Shawl continued from page 23

Rows 21 through 68: Rep Rows 13 through 20 six times more. At end of Row 68—34 shells.

Rows 69 through 71: Rep Rows 13 through 15. At end of Row 71, do not ch-7; do not turn.

Border

Foundation Row:

Note: Foundation Row is worked around entire shaw.

Sl st in edge sp just made, ch 3 (counts as a dc), dc in same sp; working across top edge of shawl, 2 dc in each edge sp to Row 2; 2 dc in edge sp of Row 2; 5 dc in sp formed by 6 skipped chs of beg ch; dc in next unused lp of beg ch, 5 dc in sp formed by 6 skipped chs of beg ch; 2 dc in each edge sp of Rows 2 through 70; in edge sp of Row 71 work (2 dc, ch 1, 4 dc)—corner made; working across next side, 4 dc in each of next 71 ch-4 sps; in center ch-6 sp work (4 dc, ch 1, 4 dc)—center sp made; working across next side, 4 dc in each of next 71 ch-4 sps; 4 dc in same sp as beg ch-3; ch 1; join in 3rd ch of beg ch-3—corner made. Turn.

Edging:

Note: Edging is worked along two outer edges.

Row 1: Sl st in next ch-1 sp, ch 8 (counts as a trc and a ch-4 sp), in same sp work (trc, ch 2, trc); * ch 3, sk next 6 dc, sc in next dc, ch 2, sk next 2 dc, sc in next dc, ch 3, sk next 6 dc, between last skipped dc and next dc work (trc, ch 2, trc, ch 4, trc, ch 2, trc); rep from * 17 times more; ch 3, sk next 4 dc, in next center ch-1 sp work (sc, ch 2, sc)—center sp made; working along next side, ch 3, sk next 4 dc, between last skipped dc and next dc work (trc, ch 2, trc, ch 4, trc, ch 2, trc); ** † ch 3, sk next 6 dc, sc in next dc, ch 2, sk next 2 dc, sc in next sc, ch 3, sk next 6 dc †; between last skipped dc and next dc work (trc, ch 2, trc, ch 4, trc, ch 2, trc); rep from ** 16 times more, then rep from † to † once; sk next 6 dc, in next corner ch-1 sp work (trc, ch 2, trc, ch 4, trc). Ch 3, turn.

Row 2: 3 dc in next ch-4 sp; dc in next trc, 2 dc in next ch-2 sp; dc in next trc; * 3 dc in next ch-3 sp; sk next sc, sc in next ch-2 sp, sk next sc, 3 dc in next ch-3 sp; dc in next trc, 2 dc in next ch-2 sp; dc in next trc, in next ch-4 sp work (3 dc, ch 1, 3 dc); dc in next trc, 2 dc in next ch-2 sp; dc in next trc; rep from * 17 times more; 3 dc in next ch-3 sp; sk next sc, sc in next center ch-2 sp, 3 dc in next ch-3 sp; ** dc in next trc, 2 dc in next ch-2 sp; dc in next trc, in next ch-4 sp work (3 dc, ch 1, 3 dc); dc in next trc, 2 dc in next ch-2 sp; dc in next trc, 3 dc in next ch-3 sp; sk next sc, sc in next ch-2 sp, sk next sc, 3 dc in next ch-3 sp; rep from ** 17 times more; dc in next trc, 2 dc in next ch-2 sp; dc in next trc, 3 dc over next 4 chs of beg ch-8; dc in next ch. Ch 1, turn.

Row 3: Sc in first dc; † ch 6, sk next 3 dc; keeping last lp of each trc on hook, trc in next dc, sk next 2 dc, trc in next dc, sk next 3 dc, next sc, and next 3 dc; trc in next dc, sk next 2 dc, trc in next dc; YO and draw through all 5 lps on hook; ch 1—cluster made; ch 6, sk next 3 dc, sc in next ch-1 sp †; rep from † to † 17 times more; ch 6, sk next 3 dc; keeping last lp of each trc on hook, trc in next dc, sk next 2 dc, trc in next dc, sk next 3 dc, trc in center sc; YO and draw through all 4 lps on hook; ch 6, dtrc (see Pattern Stitch on page 23) in same center sc, ch 6; keeping last lp of each trc on hook, trc in same center sc, sk next 3 dc, trc in next dc, sk next 2 dc, trc in next dc; YO and draw through all 4 lps on hook; ch 6, sk next 3 dc, sc in next ch-1 sp; rep from † to † 17 times; ch 6, sk next 3 dc; keeping last lp of each trc on hook, trc in next dc, sk next 2 dc, trc in next dc, sk next 3 dc, next sc, and next 3 dc; trc in next dc, sk next 2 dc, trc in next dc, YO and draw through all 5 lps on hook, ch 1—cluster made; ch 6, sk next 3 dc, sc in next sc. Ch 1, turn.

Row 4: In first sc work (sc, ch 1, sc); † ch 3, sk next ch-6 sp, in next ch-1 sp work (trc, ch 2, trc, ch 4, trc, ch 2, trc); ch 3, sk next ch-6 sp, in next sc work (sc, ch 2, sc) †; rep from † to † 17 times more; ch 3, sk next ch-6 sp, in next ch-1 sp work (trc, ch 2, trc, ch 4, trc, ch 2, trc); ch 3, sk next ch-6 sp, in next dtrc work (sc, ch 2, sc)—center sp made; rep from † to † 18 times. Ch 1, turn.

Row 5: Sl st in next ch-2 sp, ch 1, sc in same sp; * 3 dc in next ch-3 sp; dc in next trc, 2 dc in next ch-2 sp; dc in next trc, 7 dc in next ch-4 sp; dc in next trc, 2 dc in next ch-2 sp; dc in next trc, 3 dc in next ch-3 sp; sk next sc; sc in next ch-2 sp; rep from * 37 times more.

Finish off and weave in all ends.

SIMPLY SOFT

SIMPLY THE BEST!

AMERICA'S FAVORITE SOFT YARN! Simply Soft is simply the best, brightest, softest and most versatile yarn for all of your home decor, baby and apparel projects. Now CARON is proud to announce an addition to the family. New Simply Soft Baby Sport has all the softness and brightness you expect, in a 3 ply, 100% acrylic yarn that's perfect for those projects that will be passed down from generation to generation. **AND,** both yarns are now backed by the **GOOD HOUSEKEEPING SEAL** which offers a **2 YEAR, MONEY BACK GUARANTEE** if you are ever dissatisfied with our product. So now, we don't just say its the best, we guarantee it. *If it's color, it's Caron!*

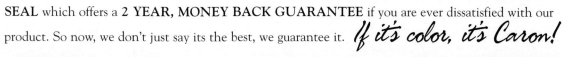

DO YOU LOVE SOFT YARNS... UNTIL YOU WASH THEM?

Red Heart Soft Yarns take to washing like ducks to water.

Now the yarn that is famous for its washability and durability offers you a new family of soft yarns. With Red Heart® Soft™ and Soft Baby™ yarns you'll get cuddle-up softness that lasts wash after wash. With *Bounce-Back®* performance fibers, afghans, sweaters and baby blankets—whatever you create—keep their beautiful shape and soft touch.

You can have it all—softness and wash performance! See for yourself; look for Red Heart Soft and new Soft Baby where you buy your favorite Red Heart yarns.

RED HEART Soft

RED HEART Soft Baby

Contains Genuine PROVEN **Bounce-Back** Fibers Quality Assurance

RED HEART YARNS

Let's Crochet
for Spring

Breathtaking Pansy Bedspread

Spotlight on the Bride – Gown & Accessories

Simply Great Sweaters – Cardigan & Tunic

Pretty Pillow Talk for the Bedroom

Spring Contents

On our cover:
Bridal Gown by Mary Ann Frits, see page 74.

Crocheting On Stage and Off

Crocheting is taking center stage at the Tony Award-Winning Broadway musical, RAGTIME.

During a scene in the Tony Award-Winning Broadway musical "Ragtime," the character of Sarah spends her on-stage time crocheting. Many actresses who have played this role have been given lessons by fellow "Ragtime" New York cast member Valerie Hawkins.

Ms Hawkins learned to crochet just over a year ago, although she has been knitting since the age of 9. "Ragtime" is a three hour musical, and Ms. Hawkins found herself with a good deal of "off-stage" time during each show. She had seen one of the show's dressers (Kathleen) crocheting, and asked her if she would teach her the skill. Valerie had several friends who were about to have babies, and thought that she could spend her "off-stage" time making crocheted baby blankets. "I had always wanted to learn to crochet and after Kathleen showed me a few basic stitches, I just experimented with different possibilities. A door had opened to a whole new world," said Valerie.

Cast members, Tonia Dixon and Dioni Collins, who alternate in the role of Sarah in the musical, asked Valerie to teach them so that when they were "on-stage" they would actually be crocheting, not just pretending.

Soon two of the children in the cast asked to be taught. Pierce Cravens, who plays "The Little Boy" made five scarves for Christmas gifts, each one was different and his own design, Ms. Hawkins proudly proclaims. She is also teaching 10 year-old Dara Page Bloomfield, who is already chaining the yarn fairly consistently. Ms. Hawkins states, "A couple of cast members are expecting

babies this year and I am planning on making blankets for them. I find it very meditative, very zen, it soothes me and stimulates my creativity."

above: Valerie (in make-up) crochets as she waits backstage for her cue

Valerie with baby blanket

Dara crocheting a sweater for her teddy

Pierce works on a scarf for a Christmas gift

Recreate an Antique Treasure

Pansy
Bedspread

We may have come a long way, Baby, but we still haven't created handmade crocheted pieces any more breathtaking than this pansy square design. The antique original, shown on this page, was made in size 30 crochet thread; however we are not inclined to make anything that fine, so we have recreated it using materials which are readily available to us today. The flowers and leaves are crocheted with 6-strand embroidery floss and the beige background is size 10 crochet thread.

Pansy Square

Size:
About 11" x 11"

Materials for each square:
Bedspread-weight crochet cotton,
100 yds ecru
Embroidery floss, 10 skeins each,
floral colors of your choice;
4 skeins shaded greens
*Note: Our photographed square was
made with J. & P. Coats® Knit-Cro-
Sheen®, New Ecru #61; Anchor Floss,
Shaded Pinks #1201; and Shaded
Greens #1215.*
Size 6 steel crochet hook, or size required
for gauge

Gauge:
8 dc = 1"

Pattern Stitches

Double Triple Crochet (dtrc):
YO 3 times; (YO, draw through 2 lps
on hook) 4 times—dtrc made.

Cluster (CL):
* YO twice; insert hook in sp indicated,
draw lp through, (YO, draw through
2 lps on hook) twice; rep from * twice
more; YO, draw through 2 lps on hook;
YO and draw through all 4 lps on
hook—CL made.

Instructions

Square A

First Pansy:
With floral color, ch 7; join to form a ring.

Rnd 1 (right side)**:** Ch 3 (counts as a dc
on this and following rnds), 2 dc in ring;
ch 7; * 3 dc in ring; ch 7; rep from * 3
times more; join in 3rd ch of beg ch-3—
5 ch-7 sps.

Rnd 2: Sl st in next 2 dc and in next ch-7
sp, ch 1, in same sp work (sc, hdc, 11 dc,
hdc, sc)—small petal made; sk next dc, sc
in next dc; * in next ch-7 sp work (sc, hdc,
11 dc, hdc, sc)—small petal made; sk next
dc, sc in next dc; rep from * once more; in
next ch-7 sp work (sc, ch 4, trc); ch 1, in
same sp work [dtrc (see Pattern Stitches),
ch 1] 10 times; in same sp work (dtrc, ch 4,
sc)—large petal made; sk next dc, sc in next
dc, in next ch-7 sp work (sc, ch 4, trc); ch 1,
in same sp work (dtrc, ch 1) 11 times; dtrc
in same sp—large petal made. Finish off.

Our recreation in size 10 thread and embroidery floss.

Second Through Seventh Pansy:
Work same as First Pansy through Rnd 1.

Rnd 2: Sl st in next 2 dc and in next ch-7
sp, ch 1, in same sp work (sc, hdc, 6 dc);
hold wrong side of last completed pansy
facing wrong side of working pansy; on
completed pansy, sl st in BL of 6th dc of
last small petal made; on working pansy, in
same sp work (hdc, sc)—small joined petal
made; sk next dc, sc in next dc; * in next
ch-7 sp work (sc, hdc, 11 dc, hdc, sc)—
small petal made; sk next dc, sc in next dc;
rep from * once more; in next ch-7 sp work
(sc, ch 4, trc); ch 1, in same sp work (dtrc,
ch 1) 10 times; in same sp work (dtrc, ch 4,
sc)—large petal made; sk next dc, sc in next
dc, in next ch-7 sp work (sc, ch 4, trc); ch 1,
in same sp work (dtrc, ch 1) 11 times; dtrc
in same sp—large petal made. Finish off.

Eighth Pansy:
Work same as First Pansy
through Rnd 1.

Rnd 2: Sl st in next 2 dc and
in next ch-7 sp, ch 1, in same
sp work (sc, hdc, 6 dc); hold
wrong side of last completed
pansy facing wrong side of
working pansy; on completed

pansy, sl st in BL of 6th dc of last small
petal made; on working pansy, in same sp
work (5 dc, hdc, sc)—small joined petal
made; sk next dc, sc in next dc; in next ch-7
sp work (sc, hdc, 11 dc, hdc, sc)—small
petal made; sk next dc, sc in next dc, in
next ch-7 sp work (sc, hdc, 6 dc); on completed pansy, sl st in 6th dc of first small
petal; on working pansy, in same sp work
(5 dc, hdc, sc)—joined small petal made; sk
next dc, sc in next dc, in next ch-7 sp work
(sc, ch 4, trc); ch 1, in same sp work (dtrc,
ch 1) 10 times; in same sp work (dtrc, ch 4,
sc)—large petal made; sk next dc, sc in
next dc, in next ch-7 sp work (sc, ch 4, trc);
ch 1, in same sp work (dtrc, ch 1) 11 times;
dtrc in same sp—large petal made.

Finish off and weave in all ends.

Bedspread sizes	Squares needed
Twin size, approx. 66" x 99"	54 squares (6 x 9)
Full size, approx. 77" x 99"	63 squares (7 x 9)
Queen size, approx. 88" x 99"	72 squares (8 x 9)
King size, approx. 99" x 99"	81 squares (9 x 9)

continued on page 106

Our boy and girl bunnies are wonderful spring visitors dressed up in their fine crocheted Easter outfits.

Meet Becca and Brian Bunny

— designed by Candy Clayton

Becca Bunny

Size:
About 16 1/2" tall

Materials:
Worsted weight yarn, 7 oz (490 yds, 210 gms) white; 4 oz (280 yds, 120 gms) dk purple; 2 oz (140 yds, 60 gms) lavender

Note: Our photographed animal was made with Red Heart® Classic™, Light Lavender #579; Amethyst #588; and White #001.

Size F (3.75mm) crochet hook, or size required for gauge

Size 18 tapestry needle

Trimmings:
two sets of 30mm doll joints

two 15mm black animal eyes

18mm animal nose

18" length of black embroidery floss

tacky craft glue or hot glue

polyester fiberfill

black plastic eyelashes

two purple ribbon bows, 1 3/4" long

sewing needle and matching thread

Note: Bunnies have plastic face parts which are not suitable for children under three years of age. If for a young child please embroider faces with floss.

Pattern Stitch

Popcorn (PC):
5 dc in st indicated; drop lp from hook, insert hook in first dc made, draw dropped lp through—PC made.

Gauge:
4 sc = 1"

Instructions

Bunny
With white, work same as Kathy Kitty beginning on page 3, omitting ears and Finishing.

Ear (make 2):
With white, ch 2.

Find more animal pairs in our Summer, Fall, and Winter issues.

Note: *Rnds 1 through 33 are worked in continuous rnds. Do not join; mark beg of rnds.*

Row 1 (right side): 6 sc in 2nd ch from hook.

Rnd 2: 2 sc in each sc—12 sc.

Rnd 3: (Sc in next sc, 2 sc in next sc) 6 times—18 sc.

Rnd 4: (Sc in next 3 sc, 2 sc in next sc) 4 times; sc in next 2 sc—22 sc.

Rnd 5: Sc in each sc.

Rnds 6 through 33: Rep Rnd 5.

Rnd 34: Fold Rnd 33 flat; working through both thicknesses, sc in next 12 sc. Finish off, leaving an 18" end for sewing.

Finishing

Step 1: Stuff body firmly with fiberfill. With tapestry needle and 10" end of body, weave in and out through 12 sts of Rnd 55. Pull to close opening. Weave in end.

Step 2: Fold top of each ear in half; with tapestry needle and 18" end, sew using overcast st (see Crochet Stitch Guide on page 213) across folded top edge of each ear. Sew folded edge of each ear to Rnd 4 of head about 2" apart.

Step 3: Referring to photo for placement, with tapestry needle and embroidery floss, with straight sts (see Embroidery Stitch Guide on page 211) for mouth.

Step 4: For whiskers, refer to Step 5 of Kathy Kitty Finishing on page 44.

Step 5: With sewing needle and matching thread, sew ribbon bows to top of each ear.

Dress

With lavender, ch 32.

Row 1 (wrong side): Sc in 2nd ch from hook and in next 2 chs, (2 sc in next ch, sc in next 3 chs) 7 times—38 sc. Ch 1, turn.

Row 2 (right side): Sc in first 6 sc, 2 sc in each of next 5 sc; sc in next 16 sc, 2 sc in each of next 5 sc; sc in next 6 sc—48 sc. Ch 1, turn.

Row 3: Sc in each sc. Ch 1, turn.

Row 4: Sc in first 6 sc; † 2 sc in next sc; 3 dc in each of next 9 sc; 2 sc in next sc †; sc in next 14 sc; rep from † to † once; sc in next 6 sc—88 sts. Ch 1, turn.

Row 5: Sc in first 7 sts; † 2 sc in next st; dc in next 27 sts, 2 sc in next st †; sc in next 16 sts; rep from † to † once; sc in next 7 sts—92 sts. Ch 1, turn.

Row 6: Sc in first 8 sts; † 2 sc in next st; dc in next 4 sts, 3-sc dec over next 3 sts (to work 3-sc dec: draw up lp in each of next 3 sts, YO and draw through all 4 lps on hook—3-sc dec made); (dc in next 5 sts, dec over next 3 sts) twice; dc in next 4 sts, 2 sc in next st †; sc in next 18 sts; rep from † to † once; sc in next 8 sts—84 sts. Ch 1, turn.

Row 7: Sc in first 9 sts; † 2 sc in next st; dc in next st, trc in next 2 sts, (sl st in next st, dc in next st, trc in next 3 sts, dc in next st, sl st in next st) twice; dc in next st, trc in next 2 sts, dc in next st, 2 sc in next st †; sc in next 20 sts; rep from † to † once; sc in next 9 sts—88 sts. Ch 1, turn.

Row 8: Sc in first 10 sts; † sc dec over next 2 sts; ch 4, sk next 19 sts, sc dec over next 2 sts †; sc in next 22 sts; rep from † to † once; sc in next 10 sts—54 sts. Ch 1, turn.

Row 9: 2 sc in first sc; sc in each st and in each ch to last sc; 2 sc in last sc—56 sc. Ch 1, turn.

Row 10: Sc in each sc. Ch 1, turn.

Row 11: 2 sc in first sc; sc in next 54 sc, 2 sc in next sc—58 sc. Ch 1, turn.

Rows 12 and 13: Rep Row 10.

Row 14: Sc in each sc; join in FL of first sc. Change to dk purple by drawing lp through; cut lavender.

Note: *Remainder of dress is worked in rnds.*

Rnd 1: Ch 3 (counts as a dc on this and following rnds), 2 dc in same lp; working in FLs only, 2 dc in next sc; * 3 dc in next sc; 2 dc in next sc; rep from * 27 times more; join in 3rd ch of beg ch-3—145 dc.

Rnd 2: Ch 3, dc in each dc; join in 3rd ch of beg ch-3.

Rnd 3: Rep Rnd 2.

Rnd 4: Ch 3, dc in next 10 dc; † PC (see Pattern Stitch on page 62) in each of next 2 dc; dc in next 3 dc, PC in each of next 2 dc; dc in next 22 dc †; rep from † to † 3 times more; PC in each of next 2 dc; dc in next 3 dc, PC in each of next 2 dc; dc in next 11 dc; join in 3rd ch of beg ch-3.

Rnd 5: Ch 3, dc in next 8 dc; † (PC in next dc, dc in next 4 sts) twice; PC in next dc; dc in next 18 dc †; rep from † to † 3 times more; (PC in next dc, dc in next 4 sts) twice; PC in next dc; dc in next 9 dc; join in 3rd ch of beg ch-3.

Bear Pair in Summer, page 150

Pig Pair in Fall, page 190

Kitty Pair in Winter, page 2

Rnd 6: Ch 3, dc in next 8 dc; † PC in next PC; dc in next 9 sts, PC in next PC; dc in next 18 dc †; rep from † to † 3 times more; (PC in next PC, dc in next 9 dc) twice; join in 3rd ch of beg ch-3.

continued on page 64

Becca Bunny

continued from page 63

Rnd 7: Ch 3, dc in next 10 sts; † PC in next dc; dc in next 5 dc, PC in next dc; dc in next 22 sts †; rep from † to † 3 times more; PC in next dc; dc in next 5 dc, PC in next dc; dc in next 11 sts; join in 3rd ch of beg ch-3.

Rnd 8: Ch 3, dc in next 12 sts; † PC in next dc; dc in next dc, PC in next dc; dc in next 26 sts †; rep from † to † 3 times more; PC in next dc; dc in next dc, PC in next dc; dc in next 13 sts; join in 3rd ch of beg ch-3.

Rnd 9: Ch 3, dc in next 13 sts; † PC in next dc; dc in next 28 sts †; rep from † to † 3 times more; PC in next dc; dc in next 14 sts; join in 3rd ch of beg ch-3.

Rnd 10: Ch 1, sc in same ch as joining; hdc in next dc, dc in next 3 dc, hdc in next dc; * sc in next dc, hdc in next dc, dc in next 3 sts, hdc in next dc; rep from * 22 times more; sc in next dc; join in first sc—145 sts.

Rnd 11: Ch 1, sc in same ch as joining; * hdc in next hdc, dc in next dc, 3 trc in next dc; dc in next dc, hdc in next hdc, sc in next sc; rep from * 23 times more; join in first sc.

Finish off and weave in all ends.

Collar:
Hold dress with right side of back opening facing you and beg ch at top; join dk purple in first unused lp of beg ch-32 to left of back opening.

Row 1: Ch 1, sc in same lp; 2 sc in next lp; (sc in next lp, 2 sc in next lp) 3 times; sc in next lp, hdc in next 2 lps, 2 dc in each of next 2 lps; hdc in next 2 lps, sl st in next lp, hdc in next 2 lps, 2 dc in each of next 2 lps; hdc in next 2 lps, (sc in next lp, 2 sc in next lp) 4 times; sc in next lp—43 sts. Ch 1, turn.

Row 2: Sc in first 2 sc, (2 sc in next sc, sc in next 2 sts) 4 times; hdc in next hdc, 3 hdc in next dc; 3 dc in each of next 2 dc; 3 hdc in next dc; hdc in next hdc, sc in next hdc, sl st in next sl st, sc in next hdc, hdc in next hdc, 3 hdc in next dc; 3 dc in each of next 2 dc; 3 hdc in next dc; hdc in next hdc, (sc in next 2 sts, 2 sc in next sc) 4 times; sc in next 2 sc. Finish off.

Back Opening Trim and Ties:
Hold dress with right side facing you and neck edge to right; join lavender in first edge sc to right of back opening; ch 1, sc in same sc; working in edge sc of each row; † in next sc work (sl st, ch 24, sl st in 2nd ch from hook and in next 22 chs, sl st) †; sc in next 6 rows; rep from † to † once; sc in next 5 rows; working along next side in edge sc of each row, sc in next 5 rows; rep from † to † once; sc in next 6 rows; rep from † to † once; sc in next sc.

Finish off and weave in all ends.

Feasting on carrots makes Becca feel like dancing.

Brian Bunny

Size:
About 16^{1}/$_{2}$" tall

Materials:
Worsted weight yarn, 7 oz (490 yds,
   210 gms) white; 4 oz (280 yds,
   120 gms) dk purple; 2 oz (140 yds,
   60 gms) lavender
   *Note: Our photographed animal was
   made with Red Heart® Classic™, Light
   Lavender #579; Amethyst # 588; and
   White #001.*
Size F (3.75) crochet hook, or size required
   for gauge
Size 18 tapestry needle

Trimmings:
two sets of 30mm doll joints
two 15mm black animal eyes
18mm animal nose
18" length of black embroidery floss
polyester fiberfill

Gauge:
4 sc = 1"

Instructions

Bunny
With white, work same as Kathy Kitty
beginning on page 3, omitting hair, ears,
and Finishing.

Ear (make 2):
Work same as Becca Bunny Ear, beginning
on page 62.

Finishing
Step 1: Stuff body firmly with fiberfill.
With tapestry needle and 10" end of body,
weave in and out thorugh 12 sts of Rnd 55.
Pull to close opening. Weave in end.

Step 2: Fold top of each ear in half; with
tapestry needle and 18" end, sew using
overcast st (see Crochet Stitch Guide on
page 213) across folded top edge of each
ear. Sew folded edge of each ear to Rnd 4
of head about 2" apart.

Step 3: Referring to photo for placement,
with tapestry needle and embroidery floss,
using straight stitches (see Embroidery
Stitch Guide on page 211) for mouth.

Step 4: For whiskers, refer to Step 5 of
Kathy Kitty Finishing on page 44.

Brian is ready for anything, 'cause he eats his carrots.

Romper
With lavender, ch 32.

Row 1 (wrong side): Sc in 2nd ch from
hook and in next 2 chs, (2 sc in next ch, sc
in next 3 chs) 7 times—38 sc. Ch 1, turn.

Row 2 (right side): Sc in first 6 sc, 2 sc in
each of next 5 sc; sc in next 16 sc, 2 sc in
each of next 5 sc; sc in next 6 sc—48 sc.
Ch 1, turn.

Row 3: Sc in each sc. Ch 1, turn.

Row 4: Sc in first 6 sc; † 2 sc in next sc;
2 dc in each of next 9 sc; 2 sc in next sc †;
sc in next 14 sc; rep from † to † once; sc in
next 6 sc—70 sts. Ch 1, turn.

Row 5: Sc in first 7 sc; † 2 sc in next sc;
dc in next 18 dc, 2 sc in next sc †; sc in
next 16 sc; rep from † to † once; sc in next
7 sc—74 sts. Ch 1, turn.

Row 6: Sc in first 8 sc; † 2 sc in next sc;
dc in next 18 dc, 2 sc in next sc †; sc in
next 18 sc; rep from † to † once; sc in next
8 sc—78 sts. Ch 1, turn.

Row 7: Sc in first 9 sc; † 2 sc in next sc; dc
in next 18 dc, 2 sc in next sc †; sc in next
20 sc; rep from † to † once; sc in next
9 sc—82 sts. Ch 1, turn.

Row 8: Sc in first 10 sc; † sc dec over next
2 sc; ch 4, sk next 16 dc, sc dec over next
2 sts †; sc in next 22 sc; rep from † to
† once; sc in next 10 sc. Ch 1, turn.

Row 9: 2 sc in first sc; sc in each sc and in
each ch to last sc; 2 sc in last sc—56 sc.
Ch 1, turn.

Row 10: Sc in each sc. Ch 1, turn.

Row 11: 2 sc in first sc; sc in each sc to last
sc; 2 sc in last sc—58 sc. Ch 1, turn.

continued on page 98

TERRYSPUN

A soft, textured yarn,
perfect for afghans
and great fashions.

*Available at leading
yarn and craft stores.*

As stylish as an expensive artisan-designed necklace, this stunning lamé bag is practical as well. It can store emergency funds, special pills, your car key or a good luck amulet.

Fiber Fun

Little Amulet Bag

— designed by Kelly Robinson

Size:
About 3" diameter across base

Materials:
Lamé metallic yarn, 1/2 oz (50 yds, 15 gms) silver

Note: Our photographed bag was made with Lion Brand® Lamé Metallic yarn, Silver.

Size 6 (1.80mm) steel crochet hook, or size required for gauge

Gauge:
8 dc = 1"

Instructions

Front
Ch 6, join to form a ring.

Rnd 1 (right side)**:** Ch 3 (counts as a dc), 15 dc in ring; join in 3rd ch of beg ch-3—16 dc.

Rnd 2: Ch 1, sc in same ch as joining; 5 dc in next dc; (sc in next dc, 5 dc in next dc) 7 times; join in first sc—eight 5-dc groups.

Rnd 3: Ch 6 (counts as a dc and a ch-3 sp on following rnds), sk next 2 dc, in next dc work (sc, ch 3, sc); ch 3, sk next 2 dc; * dc in next sc, ch 3, sk next 2 dc, in next dc work (sc, ch 3, sc); ch 3, sk next 2 dc; rep from * 6 times more; join in 3rd ch of beg ch-6—24 ch-3 sps.

Rnd 4: Ch 1, sc in same ch as joining; sk next ch-3 sp, 5 dc in next ch-3 sp; sk next ch-3 sp; * sc in next dc, sk next ch-3 sp, 5 dc in next ch-3 sp; sk next ch-3 sp; rep from * 6 times more; join in first sc.

Rnd 5: Rep Rnd 3.

Rnd 6: Ch 1, sc in same ch as joining; sk next ch-3 sp, 7 trc in next ch-3 sp; sk next ch-3 sp; * sc in next dc, sk next ch-3 sp, 7 trc in next ch-3 sp; sk next ch-3 sp; rep from * 6 times more; join in first sc—64 sts. Do not finish off.

Side:
Row 1: Ch 3, working in BLs only, dc in next 49 sts. Ch 3, turn, leaving rem 15 sts unworked.

Row 2: Dc in each dc and in 3rd ch of beg ch-3. Finish off, leaving an 18" end for sewing.

Back
Rnds 1 through 6: Rep Rnds 1 through 6 of front. Finish off and weave in ends.

Finishing
Step 1: Hold front and back with wrong sides together and back facing you; with tapestry needle and 18" end and using overcast st (see Crochet Stitch Guide on page 213), sew front and back together in back loops only.

Step 2: Join thread in sp formed by turning chs of one side of purse; * ch 5, dc in 5th ch from hook; rep from * 73 times more; sl st in sp formed by edge dc on opposite side. Finish off and weave in ends.

Spring **67**

Pretty Pillow Talk

Remember when young ladies prepared for their romantic future by filling their hope chest with exquisite examples of their needlework? Today's women may not fill a hope chest, but at any stage of their life (married or not) they enjoy creating a little romance in the bedroom. We present here, two pleasing designs to fit standard pillow cases—Battenberg Beauty and Sweethearts.

— designed by Jo Ann Maxwell

Sweethearts Edging

Size:
About 19" long x 4 1/2" wide

Materials:
Bedspread-weight crochet cotton, 100 yds white; 50 yds pink
Note: Our photographed edging was made with J. & P. Coats® Knit-Cro-Sheen®, White #1 and Mid Rose #46A.
Size 6 (1.80mm) steel crochet hook, or size required for gauge
Sewing needle and matching thread

Gauge:
8 dc = 1"

Pattern Stitches

Double Triple Crochet (dtrc):
YO 3 times; draw up lp in st or sp indicated, (YO, draw through 2 lps on hook) 4 times—dtrc made.

Lover's Knot (LK):
Draw up lp on hook 3/8", YO and draw through beg 3/8" lp just made, insert hook in lp on left side (not through beg 3/8" lp) as in **Fig 1**, YO and draw through, YO and draw through 2 lps on hook—LK made.

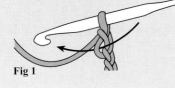

Fig 1

Instructions

Heart (make 5)
With white, ch 5; join to form a ring.

Rnd 1 (right side): Ch 5 (counts as a dtrc), in ring work [trc, 3 dc, trc, 4 dtrc (see Pattern Stitches), trc, 3 dc, trc, 4 dtrc, trc, 3 dc, trc]; join in 5th ch of beg ch-5—24 sts.

Rnd 2: Ch 7 (counts as a trc and a ch-3 sp), trc in same ch as joining; ch 1, (trc in next st, ch 1) 5 times; (trc in next st, ch 2) 5 times; hdc in next dc, ch 1, sc in next dc, ch 1, hdc in next dc, ch 2, (trc in next st, ch 2) 4 times; (trc in next st, ch 1) 6 times; join in 4th ch of beg ch-7.

Rnd 3: Ch 1, sc in same ch as joining and in next ch; 3 sc in next ch; sc in each ch and in each st; join in first sc.

Rnd 4: Sl st in next 2 sc, ch 4 (counts as a dc and a ch-1 sp), LK (see Pattern Stitches); sk next sc, dc in next sc, ch 1, LK; † (sk next 2 sc, dc in next sc, ch 1, LK) 9 times; sk next 2 sc †; hdc in next sc, ch 1, sk next sc, sc in next sc, ch 1, sk next sc, hdc in next sc, ch 1, LK; rep from † to † 9 times; join in 3rd ch of beg ch-4—21 LKs. Change to pink by drawing lp through; cut white.

Rnd 5: Ch 1, in same ch as joining work (sc, ch 3, sl st in same sc—picot made); ch 3; † in next dc work (sc, ch 3, sl st in same sc—picot made); ch 3 †; rep from † to † 9 times more; sc in next hdc and in next ch, sl st in next sc, sc in next ch and in next hdc, ch 3; rep from † to † 9 times; join in first sc at base of first picot. Finish off.

Band
Row 1 (wrong side): With white, ch 5; hold one heart with wrong side facing you, † sc in 2nd picot to right of top center of heart, ch 4, sc in next picot, ch 7, sc in next

picot, ch 4, sc in next picot †; * ch 11; hold next heart with wrong side facing you; rep from † to † once; rep from * 3 times more. Ch 7, turn.

Row 2 (right side): Dc in 4th ch from hook (3 skipped chs count as a dc), in each ch, and in each sc. Ch 4 (counts as first dc and ch-1 sp on following rows), turn.

Row 3: LK; ch 1, sk next 3 dc, dc in next dc; * ch 1, LK; sk next 3 dc, dc in next dc; rep from * 35 times more. Finish off.

Row 4: Hold band with right side facing you and Row 3 at top; join pink in first dc; ch 1, in same dc work (sc, picot); * ch 3, next dc work (sc, picot); rep from * 36 times more.

Finish off and weave in all ends.

Finishing
Step 1: Following Blocking instructions on page 216, block edging.

Step 2: With sewing needle and matching thread, sew to edge of pillowcase along Row 2 of band.

Battenberg Beauty Edging

Size:
About 39" circumference x 5½" at widest point

Materials:
Bedspread-weight crochet cotton, one 225-yd ball white
Note: Our photographed edging was made with J. & P. Coats® Knit-Cro-Sheen®, White #1.
Size 6 (1.80mm) steel crochet hook, or size required for gauge
1½ yd picot-edge pale green satin ribbon, ³/8"-wide
Size 16 tapestry needle
Sewing needle and matching thread

Gauge:
8 dc = 1"

Pattern Stitches

Cluster (CL):
Keeping last lp of each dc on hook, dc in next dc, sk next dc, next ch, next sc, next ch, and next dc, dc in next ch, YO and draw through all 3 lps on hook—CL made.

Small Cluster (small CL):
Keeping last lp of each dc on hook, dc in next ch, sk next CL, dc in next ch, YO and draw through all 3 lps on hook—small CL made.

Instructions

Ch 288; join to form a ring, being careful not to twist ch.

Rnd 1 (right side)**:** Ch 3 (counts as a dc on this and following rnds), dc in each ch; join in 3rd ch of beg ch-3—288 dc.

Rnd 2: Ch 5 (counts as a dc and a ch-2 sp), sk next 2 dc, in next dc work (dc, ch 3, sl st in same dc—picot made); ch 2, sk next 2 dc; * dc in next dc, ch 2, sk next 2 dc, in next dc work (dc, ch 3, sl st in same dc—picot made); ch 2, sk next 2 dc; rep from * 46 times more; join in 3rd ch of beg ch-5—48 picots.

continued on page 97

Rose Petals

Roses are forever when you make and give this lovely afghan to someone close to your heart. Crocheted here in squares of rose and blue, but it would be equally nice with yellow or peach roses.

— designed by Sandy Scoville

Size:
About 48" x 64"

Materials:
Worsted weight yarn, 29 oz (2030 yds, 812 gms) pink; 18 oz (260 yds, 504 gms) each, blue and off white
Note: Our photographed afghan was made with Caron® Wintuk®, Pure Pink #3085; Sky #3254; and Off White #3002.
Size H (5mm) crochet hook, or size required for gauge
Size 16 tapestry needle

Gauge:
4 dc = 1"

Pattern Stitches

Cluster (CL):
Keeping last lp of each trc on hook, 5 trc in sp or st indicated; YO and draw through all 6 lps on hook—CL made.

Beginning Three Double Crochet Cluster (beg 3-dc CL):
Ch 2, keeping last lp of each dc on hook, 2 dc in sp or st indicated; YO and draw through all 3 lps on hook— beg 3-dc CL made.

Three Triple Crochet Cluster (3-trc CL):
Keeping last lp of each trc on hook, 3 trc in sp or st indicated; YO and draw through all 4 lps on hook— 3-trc CL made.

Three Double Crochet Cluster (3-dc CL):
Keeping last lp of each dc on hook, 3 dc in sp or st indicated; YO and draw through all 4 lps on hook— 3-dc CL made.

Double Triple Crochet (dtrc):
YO 3 times; draw up lp in st or sp indicated, (YO and draw through 2 lps on hook) 4 times—dtrc made.

Double Triple Crochet Cluster (dtrc CL):
Keeping last lp of each dtrc on hook, 3 dtrc in st or sp indicated; YO and draw through all 4 lps on hook—dtrc CL made.

Instructions

Square (make 63)
With blue, ch 6; join to form a ring.

Rnd 1 (right side): Ch 1, 16 sc in ring; join in BL of first sc.

Rnd 2: Ch 3 (counts as a dc on this and following rnds), in same lp work (2 dc, ch 3, 3 dc)—beg corner made; working in BLs only, ch 1, sk next 3 sc; * in next sc work (3 dc, ch 3, 3 dc)—beg corner made; ch 1, sk next 3 sc; rep from * twice more; join in 3rd ch of beg ch-3.

Rnd 3: Sl st in next dc, ch 6 (counts as a dc and a ch-3 sp); * † CL (see Pattern Stitches) in next ch-3 sp; ch 3, sk next dc, dc in next dc, ch 1, 3-trc CL (see Pattern Stitches) in next ch-1 sp; ch 1 †; sk next dc, dc in next dc, ch 3; rep from * twice more, then rep from † to † once; join in 3rd ch of beg ch-6. Finish off.

Rnd 4: Join off white in any CL; beg 3-dc CL (see Pattern Stitches) in same CL; ch 3, 3-dc CL (see Pattern Stitches) in same CL—corner made; * 3 dc in next ch-3 sp; 3 dc in each of next 2 ch-1 sps; 3 dc in next ch-3 sp; in next CL work (3-dc CL, ch 3, 3-dc CL)—corner made; rep from * twice more; 3 dc in next ch-3 sp; 3 dc in each of next 2 ch-1 sps; 3 dc in next ch-3 sp; join in beg 3-dc CL.

Rnd 5: Sl st in next ch-3 sp, ch 1, in same sp work (sc, ch 1) 3 times; sc in same sp—corner made; ch 2, sk next 3-dc CL and next dc, sc in next dc; * (ch 2, sk next 2 dc, sc in next dc) 3 times; ch 2, sk next dc and next 3-dc CL, in next ch-3 sp work (sc, ch 1) 3 times; sc in same sp—corner made; ch 2, sk next 3-dc CL and next dc, sc in next dc; rep from * twice more; (ch 2, sk next 2 dc, sc in next dc) 3 times; ch 2, sk next dc and next

3-dc CL and next dc; join in first sc. Finish off.

Rnd 6: Join pink in ch between 2nd and 3rd sc of any corner; ch 1, in same ch work (sc, ch 3, sc)—corner made; ch 1, sc in next ch; * † 3 sc in each of next 5 ch-2 sps; sc in next ch, ch 1 †; in next ch work (sc, ch 3, sc)—corner made; ch 1, sc in next ch; rep from * twice more, then rep from † to † once; join in first sc.

Rnd 7: Sl st in next ch-3 sp, ch 3, in same ch-3 sp work (2 dc, ch 3, 3 dc)—beg corner made; * dc in next ch-1 sp, in next 17 sc, and in next ch-1 sp, in next ch-3 sp work (3 dc, ch 3, 3 dc)—corner made; rep from * twice more; dc in next ch-1 sp, in next 17 dc, and in next ch-1 sp; join in 3rd ch of beg ch-3. Finish off.

Rose Petals:
Join pink in any unused lp of Rnd 1; ch 1, sc in same lp; working in unused lps and in FLs of unused sc, (5 dc in next lp, sk next lp, sc in next lp) twice; 5 dc in next lp; sc in next lp, (5 dc in next lp, sk next lp, sc in next lp) twice; 5 dc in next lp; join in first sc.

Finish off and weave in all ends.

Assembly
Hold two squares with right sides tog, carefully matching stitches. With tapestry needle and pink, and starting and ending in corner ch-3 sps, sew with overcast st (see Crochet Stitch Guide on page 213) along one side through BLs only. Sew other squares tog in same manner, forming 9 rows of 7 squares each.

continued on page 107

Chenille Scrunchie

Need the perfect accessory for that new outfit you're wearing tomorrow? There's still time to make this quick chenille scrunchie.

— designed by Stephanie Hill

Materials:

Worsted weight chenille yarn, 40 yds plum; 20 yds plum sparkle

Note: Our photographed scrunchie was made with Bernat® Chenille, Plum #6310; and Bernat® Chenille Fifth Avenue, Plum Sparkle #8310.

Size I (5.5mm) crochet hook, or size required for gauge

Large elastic band for hair

Gauge:

3 sc = 1"

Instructions

With plum, make lp on hook and join with an sc over elastic band.

Rnd 1: 49 sc over elastic band; join in joining sc—50 sc.

Rnd 2: Working in FLs only, ch 6; * sc in next sc, ch 6; rep from * 49 times more; join in BL of first sc.

Rnd 3: Working in BLs only, ch 6; * sc in next sc, ch 6; rep from * around; join in first sc. Change to plum sparkle by drawing lp through; cut plum.

Rnd 4: Sl st in next ch-6 sp, ch 1, sc in same sp; ch 3; * sc in next ch-6 sp, ch 3; rep from * around; join in first sc. Finish off.

Rnd 5: Make lp on hook and join plum sparkle with an sc in any ch-6 sp on Rnd 2; ch 3; * sc in next ch-6 sp, ch 3; rep from * around; join in first sc.

Finish off and weave in all ends.

There is only one
ORIGINAL
ACCEPT NO SUBSTITUTES

KNITTED DISHCLOTH

MATERIALS: LILY® SUGAR'N CREAM® COTTON (KNIT & CROCHET YARN);
1 skein colour of your choice.
Knitting Needles 1 pair 6.00 mm (U.S. 10, U.K. 4)

Cast on 4 sts. **Row 1:** K, across. **Row 2:** K 2, yo, K to end of row. Repeat Row 2 until there are 43 sts on needle. **Next Dec. Rows:** K 1, K 2 tog. yo, K 2 tog, K to end. Continue working dec. row until 4 st remain. Cast off remaining sts.

ABBREVIATIONS: K = Knit, st(s) = stitch(es), tog = together, YO = yarn over, rep = repeat.

Sugar'n Cream Yarns

IN CANADA: P.O. Box 40, 320 Livingstone Ave. S., Listowel, Ont. N4W 3H3

IN THE U.S.: P.O. Box 435, 378 Niagara St., Lockport, N.Y. 14094-0435

Join us on the Internet http://www.sugarncream.com

Bridal Gown

This picture of loveliness is crocheted with bedspread-weight thread using a beautiful pattern stitch the designer calls "Wedding Shells."

— designed by Mary Ann Frits

Sizing:

Sizes:	Size 2	Size 4	Size 6
Finished Chest Measurement:	30"	32"	34"

Materials:

Bedspread-weight crochet cotton,
24 (28, 32) 250-yd balls white
Note: Our photographed gown was made with Coats Opera size 10, White #500.

For Size 2:
Size 6 (1.80mm) steel crochet hook,
   or size required for gauge
Size 2 (2.25mm) steel crochet hook
Size D (3.25mm) crochet hook

For Size 4:
Size 5 (1.90mm) steel crochet hook,
   or size required for gauge
Size 1 (2.75mm) steel crochet hook
Size E (3.5mm) crochet hook

For Size 6:
Size 4 (2.00mm) steel crochet hook,
   or size required for gauge
Size 0 (3.25mm) steel crochet hook
Size F (3.75mm) crochet hook

Trimmings:

1000 white pearl beads, 4mm
96 white pearl beads, 5mm
20 white pearl buttons, 3/8"-diameter
sewing needle and matching thread

Gauge:

For size 6 hook, 16 dc = 2"
For size 5 hook, 15 dc = 2"
For size 4 hook, 14 dc = 2"

Instructions

Note: Instructions are the same for all sizes. Dress size is determined by crochet hook sizes as specified above.

Right Front Yoke

Starting at top of right shoulder and white smallest size hook, ch 35.

Row 1 (right side)**:** In 7th ch from hook (beg 6 skipped chs count as a ch-3 sp and a dc) work (dc, ch 1) 4 times; dc in same ch—shell made; * † sk next 5 chs, in next ch work (dc, ch 1) 4 times; dc in same ch—shell made; rep from * 3 times more; sk next 3 chs, dc in next ch—5 shells. Ch 1, turn.

Row 2: Sc in first dc and in next ch-1 sp; * † ch 2, sc in next ch-1 sp, ch 3, sc in next ch-1 sp, ch 2 †; sc in next 2 ch-1 sps; rep from * 3 times more, then rep from † to † once; sc in next ch-1 sp, sk next dc, sc in next ch of beg 6 skipped chs. Ch 3, turn.

Row 3: * Shell in next ch-3 sp; dec over next 2 ch-2 sps (to work dec: draw up lp in each of next 2 ch-2 sps, YO and draw through all 3 lps on hook—dec made); rep from * 3 times more; shell in next ch-3 sp; sk next ch-2 sp and next sc, dc in next sc. Ch 1, turn.

Row 4: Sc in first dc and in next ch-1 sp; * † ch 2, sc in next ch-1 sp, ch 3, sc in next ch-1 sp, ch 2 †; sc in next 2 ch-1 sps; rep from * 3 times more, then rep from † to † once; sc in next ch-1 sp, sk next dc, sc in 3rd ch of turning ch-3. Ch 3, turn.

continued on page 76

Bridal Gown

continued from page 74

Rows 5 through 8: Rep Rows 3 and 4 twice more.

Row 9: (Shell in next ch-3 sp, dec) 4 times; shell in next ch-3 sp; sk next ch-2 sp and next sc, in next sc work (dc, ch 1, dc). Ch 1, turn.

Row 10: Sc in first dc and in next 2 ch-1 sps; * † ch 2, sc in next ch-1 sp, ch 3, sc in next ch-1 sp, ch 2 †; sc in next 2 ch-1 sps; rep from * 3 times more, then rep from † to † once; sc in next ch-1 sp, sk next dc, sc in 3rd ch of turning ch-3. Ch 3, turn.

Row 11: (Shell in next ch-3 sp, dec) 4 times; shell in next ch-3 sp; sk next ch-2 sp and next sc, dc in next sc, ch 1, dc in next sc. Ch 1, turn.

Row 12: Rep Row 10.

Row 13: (Shell in next ch-3 sp, dec) 4 times; shell in next ch-3 sp; sk next ch-2 sp and next sc, dc in next sc, ch 1, in next sc work (dc, ch 1, dc). Ch 1, turn.

Row 14: Sc in first dc and in next 3 ch-1 sps; * † ch 2, sc in next ch-1 sp, ch 3, sc in next ch-1 sp †; sc in next 2 ch-1 sps; rep from * 3 times more, then rep from † to † once; sc in next ch-1 sp, sk next dc, sc in 3rd ch of turning ch-3. Ch 3, turn.

Row 15: (Shell in next ch-3 sp, dec) 4 times; shell in next ch-3 sp; sk next ch-2 sp and next sc, (dc in next sc, ch 1) twice; in next sc work (dc, ch 1, dc). Ch 1, turn.

Row 16: Sc in first dc and in next ch-1 sp, ch 3, sc in next ch-1 sp, ch 2, sc in next 2 ch-1 sps; * † ch 2, sc in next ch-1 sp, ch 3, sc in next ch-1 sp †; sc in next 2 ch-1 sps; rep from * 3 times more, then rep from † to † once; sc in next ch-1 sp, sk next dc, sc in 3rd ch of turning ch-3. Ch 3, turn.

Row 17: (Shell in next ch-3 sp, dec) 5 times; shell in next ch-3 sp; sk next sc, dc in next sc—6 shells. Ch 1, turn.

Row 18: Sc in first dc and in next ch-1 sp; * † ch 2, sc in next ch-1 sp, ch 3, sc in next ch-1 sp, ch 2 †; sc in next 2 ch-1 sps; rep from * 4 times more, then rep from † to † once; sc in next ch-1 sp, sk next dc, sc in 3rd ch of turning ch-3. Ch 3, turn.

Row 19: (Shell in next ch-3 sp, dec) 5 times; shell in next ch-3 sp; sk next ch-2 sp and next sc, in next sc work (dc, ch 1, dc). Ch 1, turn.

Row 20: Sc in first dc and in next 2 ch-1 sps; * † ch 2, sc in next ch-1 sp, ch 3, sc in next ch-1 sp, ch 2 †; sc in next 2 ch-1 sps; rep from * 4 times more, then rep from † to † once; sc in next ch-1 sp, sk next dc, sc in 3rd ch of turning ch-3. Ch 3, turn.

Pearls are sewn onto the finished gown for a lustrous look.

Row 21: (Shell in next ch-3 sp, dec) 5 times; shell in next ch-3 sp; sk next ch-2 sp and next sc, dc in next sc, ch 1, in next sc work (dc, ch 1, dc). Ch 1, turn.

Row 22: Sc in first dc and in next 3 ch-1 sps; * † ch 2, sc in next ch-1 sp, ch 3, sc in next ch-1 sp, ch 2 †; sc in next 2 ch-1 sps; rep from * 4 times more, then rep from † to † once; sc in next ch-1 sp, sk next dc, sc in 3rd ch of turning ch-3. Ch 3, turn.

Row 23: (Shell in next ch-3 sp, dec) 5 times; shell in next ch-3 sp; sk next ch-2 sp and next sc, (dc in next sc, ch 1) twice; in next sc work (dc, ch 1, dc). Ch 1, turn.

Row 24: Sc in first dc and in next ch-1 sp, ch 3, sc in next ch-1 sp, ch 2, sc in next 2 ch-1 sps; * † ch 2, sc in next ch-1 sp, ch 3, sc in next ch-1 sp †; sc in next 2 ch-1 sps; rep from * 4 times more, then rep from † to † once; sc in next ch-1 sp, sk next dc, sc in 3rd ch of turning ch-3. Ch 3, turn.

Row 25: Dc in first sc, (shell in next ch-3 sp, dec) 6 times; shell in next ch-3 sp; sk next sc, dc in next sc—7 shells. Finish off and set aside.

Left Front Yoke

Starting at top of left front shoulder and with smallest size hook, ch 35.

Rows 1 through 8: Rep Rows 1 through 8 of Right Front Yoke. At end of Row 8, do not ch 3. Ch 4 (counts as first dc and ch-1 sp on following rows), turn.

Row 9: Dc in first sc; (shell in next ch-3 sp, dec) 4 times; shell in next ch-3 sp; sk next ch-2 sp and next sc, dc in next sc. Ch 1, turn.

Row 10: Sc in first dc and in next ch-1 sp; * † ch 2, sc in next ch-1 sp, ch 3, sc in next ch-1 sp, ch 2 †; sc in next 2 ch-1 sps; rep from * 3 times more, then rep from † to † once; sc in next ch-1 sp, sk next 2 dc, sc in sp formed by turning ch-4 and in 3rd ch of same turning ch. Ch 4, turn.

Row 11: Sk first sc, dc in next sc, (shell in next ch-3 sp, dec) 4 times; shell in next ch-3 sp; sk next ch-2 sp and next sc, dc in next sc. Ch 1, turn.

Row 12: Rep Row 10.

Row 13: Dc in first sc, ch 1, dc in next sc; (shell in next ch-3 sp, dec) 4 times; shell in next ch-3 sp; sk next ch-2 sp and next sc, dc in next sc. Ch 1, turn.

Row 14: Sc in first dc and in next ch-1 sp; * ch 2, sc in next ch-1 sp, ch 3, sc in next ch-1 sp, ch 2, sc in next 2 ch-1 sps; rep from * 4 times more; sc in sp formed by turning ch-4 and in 3rd ch of same turning ch. Ch 4, turn.

Row 15: Dc in first sc, (ch 1, dc in next sc) twice; (shell in next ch-3 sp, dec) 4 times; shell in next ch-3 sp; sk next ch-2 sp and next sc, dc in next sc. Ch 1, turn.

Row 16: Sc in first dc and in next ch-1 sp; * ch 2, sc in next ch-1 sp, ch 3, sc in next ch-1 sp, ch 2, sc in next 2 ch-1 sps; rep from * 4 times more; ch 2, sc in next ch-1 sp, ch 3, sc in sp formed by turning ch-4 and in 3rd ch of same turning ch. Ch 3, turn.

Row 17: (Shell in next ch-3 sp, dec) 5 times; shell in next ch-3 sp; sk next ch-2 sp and next sc, dc in next sc—6 shells. Ch 1, turn.

Row 18: Sc in first dc and in next ch-1 sp; * † ch 2, sc in next ch-1 sp, ch 3, sc in next ch-1 sp, ch 2 †; sc in next 2 ch-1 sps; rep from * 4 times more, then rep from † to † once; sc in next ch-1 sp, sk next dc, sc in 3rd ch of turning ch-3. Ch 4, turn.

Row 19: Dc in first sc, (shell in next ch-3 sp, dec) 5 times; shell in next ch-3 sp; sk next ch-2 sp and next sc, dc in next sc. Ch 1, turn.

Row 20: Sc in first dc and in next ch-1 sp; * † ch 2, sc in next ch-1 sp, ch 3, sc in next ch-1 sp, ch 2 †; sc in next 2 ch-1 sps; rep from * 4 times more, then rep from † to † once; sc in next ch-1 sp, in sp formed by turning ch-4, and in 3rd ch of same turning ch. Ch 4, turn.

Row 21: Dc in first sc, ch 1, dc in next sc, (shell in next ch-3 sp, dec) 5 times; shell in next ch-3 sp; sk next ch-2 sp and next sc, dc in next sc. Ch 1, turn.

Row 22: Sc in first dc and in next ch-1 sp; * ch 2, sc in next ch-1 sp, ch 3, sc in next ch-1 sp, ch 2, sc in next 2 ch-1 sps; rep from * 5 times more; sc in sp formed by turning ch-4 and in 3rd ch of same turning ch. Ch 4, turn.

Row 23: Dc in first sc, (ch 1, dc in next sc) twice; (shell in next ch-3 sp, dec) 5 times; shell in next ch-3 sp; sk next ch-2 sp and next sc, dc in next sc. Ch 1, turn.

Row 24: Sc in first dc, sk next dc, sc in next ch-1 sp; * ch 2, sc in next ch-1 sp, ch 3, sc in next ch-1 sp, ch 2, sc in next 2 ch-1 sps; rep from * 5 times more; ch 2, sc in next ch-1 sp, ch 3, sc in sp formed by turning ch-4 and in 3rd ch of same turning ch. Ch 3, turn.

Row 25: (Shell in next ch-3 sp, dec) 6 times; shell in next ch-3 sp; sk next ch-2 sp and next sc, 2 dc in next sc—7 shells. Ch 1, turn.

Note: On following row, left and right front yoke pieces will be joined.

Row 26: Sc in first 2 dc and in next ch-1 sp; * † ch 2, sc in next ch-1 sp, ch 3, sc in next ch-1 sp, ch 2 †; sc in next 2 ch-1 sps; rep from * 5 times more, then rep from † to † once; sc in next ch-1 sp, sk next dc, sc in 3rd ch of turning ch-3, ch 33; hold wrong side of right front yoke facing you and Row

25 at top; on right front yoke, sc in first dc and in next ch-1 sp; ** ch 2, sc in next ch-1 sp, ch 3, sc in next ch-1 sp, ch 2, sc in next 2 ch-1 sps; rep from ** 5 times more; rep from † to † once; sc in next ch-1 sp, sk next dc, sc in next dc and in 3rd ch of turning ch-3. Ch 3, turn.

Row 27: Sk first sc, dc in next sc, (shell in next ch-3 sp, dec) 6 times; shell in next ch-3 sp; sk next ch-2 sp, next 2 sc, and next ch of next ch-33, (shell in next ch, sk next 5 chs) 5 times; shell in next ch; sk next ch and next 2 sc, (shell in next ch-3 sp, dec) 6 times; shell in next ch-3 sp; sk next ch-2 sp and next sc, dc in next 2 sc—20 shells. Ch 1, turn.

Row 28: Sc in first 2 dc and in next ch-1 sp; * † ch 2, sc in next ch-1 sp, ch 3, sc in next ch-1 sp, ch 2 †; sc in next 2 ch-1 sps; rep from * 18 times more, then rep from † to † once; sc in next ch-1 sp, sk next dc, sc in next dc and in 3rd ch of turning ch-3. Ch 3, turn.

Row 29: Dc in first sc and in next sc, (shell in next ch-3 sp, dec) 19 times; shell in next ch-3 sp; sk next ch-2 sp and next sc, dc in next sc, 2 dc in next sc. Ch 1, turn.

continued on page 78

The sophisticated shell pattern becomes a scalloped edging at hem of sleeve and skirt.

Pearl buttons slip through the shell pattern stitch eliminating the need for button holes.

Row 30: Sc in first 2 dc, sk next 2 dc, sc in next ch-1 sp; * † ch 2, sc in next ch-1 sp, ch 3, sc in next ch-1 sp, ch 2 †; sc in next 2 ch-1 sps; rep from * 18 times more, then rep from † to † once; sc in next ch-1 sp, sk next 2 dc, sc in next dc and in 3rd ch of turning ch-3. Ch 3, turn.

Row 31: Dc in first sc, ch 1, dc in next sc, (shell in next ch-3 sp, dec) 19 times; shell in next ch-3 sp; sk next ch-2 sp and next sc, dc in next sc, ch 1, 2 dc in next sc. Ch 1, turn.

Row 32: Sc in first 2 dc, in next ch-1 sp, in next dc, and in next ch-1 sp; * † ch 2, sc in next ch-1 sp, ch 3, sc in next ch-1 sp, ch 2 †; sc in next 2 ch-1 sps; rep from * 18 times more, then rep from † to † once; sc in next ch-1 sp, sk next dc, sc in next dc, in next ch-1 sp, in next dc, and in 3rd ch of turning ch-3. Ch 4, turn.

Row 33: Dc in first sc, (ch 1, dc in next sc) twice; (shell in next ch-3 sp, dec) 19 times; shell in next ch-3 sp; sk next ch-2 sp and next 2 sc, (dc in next sc, ch 1) twice; in next sc work (dc, ch 1, dc). Ch 1, turn.

Row 34: Sc in first dc; * ch 2, sc in next ch-1 sp, ch 3, sc in next ch-1 sp, ch 2, sc in next 2 ch-1 sps; rep from * 20 times more; ch 2, sc in next ch-1 sp, ch 3, sc in sp formed by turning ch-4, ch 2, sc in 3rd ch of same turning ch. Ch 3, turn.

Row 35: (Shell in next ch-3 sp, dec) 21 times; shell in next ch-3 sp; sk next ch-2 sp, dc in next sc—22 shells. Ch 1, turn.

Row 36: Sc in first dc and in next ch-1 sp; * † ch 2, sc in next ch-1 sp, ch 3, sc in next ch-1 sp, ch 2 †; sc in next 2 ch-1 sps; rep from * 20 times more, then rep from † to † once; sc in next ch-1 sp, sk next dc, sc in 3rd ch of turning ch-3. Ch 3, turn.

Row 37: (Shell in next ch-3 sp, dec) 21 times; shell in next ch-3 sp; sk next ch-2 sp and next sc, dc in next sc—22 shells. Set aside.

Right Back Yoke

Starting at top of left front shoulder and with smallest size hook, ch 35.

Row 1 (right side): In 7th ch from hook work shell; * † sk next 5 chs, in next ch work shell; rep from * 3 times more; sk next 3 chs, dc in next ch—5 shells. Ch 1, turn.

Row 2: Sc in first dc and in next ch-1 sp; * † ch 2, sc in next ch-1 sp, ch 3, sc in next ch-1 sp, ch 2 †; sc in next 2 ch-1 sps; rep from * 3 times more, then rep from † to † once; sc in next ch-1 sp, sk next dc, sc in next ch of beg 6 skipped chs. Ch 9, turn.

Row 3: In 5th ch from hook (4 skipped chs count as a dc and a ch-1 sp) work (dc, ch 1) 3 times; dc in same ch—beg shell made; sk next 3 chs, draw up lp in next ch, sk next 2 sc, draw up lp in next ch-2 sp, YO and draw through all 3 lps on hook; (shell in next ch-3 sp, dec) 4 times; shell in next ch-3 sp; sk next ch-2 sp and next sc, dc in next sc—6 shells. Ch 1, turn.

Row 4: Sc in first dc and in next ch-1 sp, * † ch 2, sc in next ch-1 sp, ch 3, sc in next ch-1 sp, ch 2 †; sc in next 2 ch-1 sps; rep from * 4 times more, then rep from † to † once; sc in sp formed by beg 4 skipped chs of turning ch-9 and in 3rd ch of same skipped chs. Ch 9, turn.

Row 5: In 5th ch from hook work beg shell; sk next 3 chs, draw up lp in next ch, sk next 2 sc, draw up lp in next ch-2 sp, YO and draw through all 3 lps on hook; (shell in next ch-3 sp, dec) 5 times; shell in next ch-3 sp; sk next ch-2 sp and next sc, dc in next sc—7 shells. Ch 1, turn.

Row 6: Sc in first dc and in next ch-1 sp; * † ch 2, sc in next ch-1 sp, ch 3, sc in next ch-1 sp, ch 2 †; sc in next 2 ch-1 sps; rep from * 5 times more, then rep from † to † once; sc in sp formed by beg 4 skipped chs of turning ch-9 and in 3rd ch of same skipped chs. Ch 9, turn.

Row 7: In 5th ch from hook work beg shell; sk next 3 chs, draw up lp in next ch, sk next 2 sc, draw up lp in next ch-2 sp, YO and draw through all 3 lps on hook; (shell in next ch-3 sp, dec) 6 times; shell in next ch-3 sp; sk next ch-2 sp and next sc, dc in next sc—8 shells. Ch 1, turn.

Row 8: Sc in first dc and in next ch-1 sp; * † ch 2, sc in next ch-1 sp, ch 3, sc in next ch-1 sp, ch 2 †; sc in next 2 ch-1 sps; rep from * 6 times more, then rep from † to † once; sc in sp formed by beg 4 skipped chs of turning ch-9 and in 3rd ch of same skipped chs. Ch 9, turn.

Row 9: In 5th ch from hook work beg shell; sk next 3 chs, draw up lp in next ch, sk next 2 sc, draw up lp in next ch-2 sp, YO and draw through all 3 lps on hook; (shell in next ch-3 sp, dec) 7 times; shell in next ch-3 sp; sk next ch-2 sp and next sc, dc in next sc—9 shells. Ch 1, turn.

Row 10: Sc in first dc and in next ch-1 sp; * † ch 2, sc in next ch-1 sp, ch 3, sc in next ch-1 sp, ch 2 †; sc in next 2 ch-1 sps; rep from * 7 times more, then rep from † to † once; sc in sp formed by beg 4 skipped chs of turning ch-9 and in 3rd ch of same skipped chs. Ch 9, turn.

Row 11: In 5th ch from hook work beg shell; sk next 3 chs, draw up lp in next ch, sk next 2 sc, draw up lp in next ch-2 sp, YO and draw through all 3 lps on hook; (shell in next ch-3 sp, dec) 8 times; shell in next ch-3 sp; sk next ch-2 sp and next sc, dc in next sc—10 shells. Ch 1, turn.

Row 12: Sc in first dc and in next ch-1 sp; * † ch 2, sc in next ch-1 sp, ch 3, sc in next ch-1 sp, ch 2 †; sc in next 2 ch-1 sps; rep from * 8 times more, then rep from † to † once; sc in sp formed by beg 4 skipped chs of turning ch-9 and in 3rd ch of same skipped chs. Ch 3 (counts as first dc on following rows), turn.

Row 13: (Shell in next ch-3 sp, dec) 9 times; shell in next ch-3 sp; sk next ch-2 sp and next sc, dc in next sc. Ch 1, turn.

Row 14: Sc in first dc and in next ch-1 sp; * † ch 2, sc in next ch-1 sp, ch 3, sc in next ch-1 sp, ch 2 †; sc in next 2 ch-1 sps; rep from * 8 times more, then rep from † to † once; sc in next ch-1 sp, sk next dc, sc in 3rd ch of turning ch-3. Ch 3, turn.

Rows 15 through 24: Rep Rows 13 and 14 five times more.

Row 25: (Shell in next ch-3 sp, dec) 9 times; shell in next ch-3 sp; sk next ch-2 sp and next sc, 2 dc in next sc. Ch 1, turn.

Row 26: Sc in first 2 dc, sk next dc, sc in next ch-1 sp; * † ch 2, sc in next ch-1 sp, ch 3, sc in next ch-1 sp, ch 2 †; sc in next 2 ch-1 sps; rep from * 8 times more, then rep from † to † once; sc in next ch-1 sp, sk next dc, sc in 3rd ch of turning ch-3. Ch 3, turn.

Row 27: (Shell in next ch-3 sp, dec) 9 times; shell in next ch-3 sp; sk next ch-2 sp and next sc, dc in next 2 sc. Ch 1, turn.

Row 28: Rep Row 26.

Row 29: (Shell in next ch-3 sp, dec) 9 times; shell in next ch-3 sp; sk next ch-2 sp and next sc, dc in next sc, 2 dc in next sc. Ch 1, turn.

Row 30: Sc in first 2 dc, sk next 2 dc, sc in next ch-1 sp; * † ch 2, sc in next ch-1 sp, ch 3, sc in next ch-1 sp, ch 2 †; sc in next 2 ch-1 sps; rep from * 8 times more, then rep from † to † once; sc in next ch-1 sp, sk next dc, sc in 3rd ch of turning ch-3. Ch 3, turn.

Row 31: (Shell in next ch-3 sp, dec) 9 times; shell in next ch-3 sp; sk next ch-2 sp and next sc, dc in next sc, ch 1, 2 dc in next sc. Ch 1, turn.

continued on page 100

Headpiece

Size:
Purchased bridal cap, about 5$^{1/2}$" x 7$^{1/2}$"

Trimmings:
starching supplies (see page 216)
4 small pearl sprays
hot glue or tacky craft glue

Center Piece
With smallest size hook, ch 35.

Rnd 1 (right side): In 7th ch from hook (beg 6 skipped chs count as a ch-3 sp and a dc) work (dc, ch 1) 4 times; dc in same ch—shell made; † sk next 5 chs, in next ch work (dc, ch 1) 4 times; dc in same ch—shell made †; rep from † to † 3 times more; sk next 3 chs, in next ch work (dc, ch 1) 4 times; dc in same ch—shell made; working on opposite side of beg ch in unused lp at base of shells, †† in next unused lp work (dc, ch 1) 4 times; dc in same lp—shell made ††; rep from †† to †† 4 times more; in next ch of beg 6 skipped chs work (dc, ch 1) 3 times; ch 1, sk next 4 skipped chs; join in next ch—ending shell made—12 shells.

Rnd 2: Sl st in next dc and in next ch-1 sp, ch 1, sc in same sp; * † ch 2, sc in next ch-1 sp, ch 3, sc in next ch-1 sp, ch 2 †; sc in next 2 ch-1 sps; rep from * 10 times more, then rep from † to † once; sc in next ch-1 sp, sk next dc; join in first sc.

continued on page 103

Wedding Bells Are Ringing

Lacy, hand-crocheted accessories will add the perfect touch to their special day.

—designed by Jo Ann Maxwell

Bridal Mitts

Size:
About 8" x 11"

Materials:
Bedspread-weight crochet cotton,
   100 yds white
*Note: Our photographed mitt was
made with J. & P. Coats® Knit-
Cro-Sheen®, White #1.*
Size 6 (1.80 mm) steel crochet hook,
   or size required for gauge

Trimmings:
four snaps, size 4/0
sewing needle and matching thread

Gauge:
8 dc = 1"

Pattern Stitches

Double Triple Crochet (dtrc):
YO 3 times; draw up lp in st indicated,
(YO and draw through 2 lps on hook)
4 times—dtrc made.

Triple Triple Crochet (tr trc):
YO 4 times; draw up lp in st indicated,
(YO, draw through 2 lps on hook)
5 times—tr trc made.

Quadruple Triple Crochet (quad trc):
YO 5 times; draw up lp in st indicated,
(YO and draw through 2 lps on hook)
6 times—quad trc made.

Lover's Knot (LK):
Draw up lp on hook 1/2", YO and draw
through beg 1/2" lp just made, insert
hook in lp on left side (not through beg
1/2" lp) as in **Fig 1**, YO and draw
through 2 lps on hook—LK made.

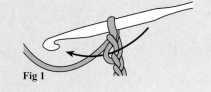

Fig 1

Instructions

Mitt (make 2)
Ch 5, join to form a ring.

Rnd 1 (right side): Ch 7 (counts as a trc and
a ch-3 sp), trc in ring, ch 1, (dc in ring, ch 1)
5 times; in ring work (trc, ch 3, trc); ch 1,
(dc in ring, ch 1) 5 times; join in 4th ch of
beg ch-7.

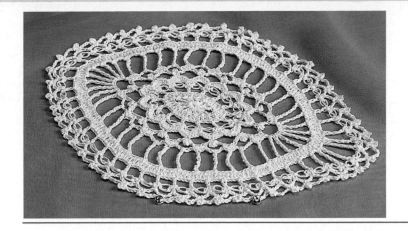

*This simple but lovely accessory will complete the bride's ensemble.
The lacy lover's knots work up quickly and adapt to the bride's hands.*

— designed by Jo Ann Maxwell

Rnd 2: Ch 3 (counts as a dc on this and
following rnds); working in each ch and in
each st, * dc in next st, 3 dc in next st; dc in
next 15 sts, 3 dc in next st; dc in next 13 sts;
join in 3rd ch of beg ch-3—36 dc.

Rnd 3: Ch 4 (counts as a dc and a ch-1 sp),
LK (see Pattern Stitches); (sk next dc, dc in
next dc, ch 1, LK) 3 times; (sk next 2 dc, dc
in next dc, ch 1, LK) 4 times; (sk next dc,
dc in next dc, ch 1, LK) 3 times; (sk next
2 dc, dc in next dc, ch 1, LK) 4 times; join
in 3rd ch of beg ch-4—14 LKs.

Rnd 4: Ch 1, sc in same ch as joining; ch 5,
(sc in next dc, ch 5) 13 times; join in first sc.

Rnd 5: Ch 1, sc in same sc; * † sc in next
ch, 2 hdc in next ch; hdc in next ch of next
ch-5 sp, 2 hdc in next ch; sc in next ch †; sc
in next sc; rep from * 12 times more, then
rep from † to † once; join in first sc.

Rnd 6: Sl st in next sc and in next 3 hdc,
ch 1, in same hdc as last sl st made work
(sc, ch 3, sl st in sc just made—picot made);
ch 7; * sk next 2 hdc, next 3 sc, and next
2 hdc; in next hdc work (sc, ch 3, sl st in
sc just made—picot made); ch 7; rep
from * 12 times more; join in first sc
(beneath picot).

Rnd 7: Sl st in next 3 chs of next ch-7 sp,
ch 1, sc in last sl st made; † 3 hdc in next
ch; sc in next ch, ch 7, sk next 2 chs, next
picot, and next 2 chs; †† sc in next ch, 3 hdc
in next ch; sc in next ch, ch 5 ††; rep from
†† to †† 5 times more; sk next 2 chs, next
picot, and next 2 chs †; sc in next ch; rep
from † to † once; join in first sc.

Rnd 8: Sl st in next 2 hdc, ch 10 (counts as
a quad trc and a ch-3 sp), † quad trc (see

Pattern Stitches) in next ch of next ch-7 sp,
ch 3, (quad trc in next ch, ch 3) 6 times;
†† sk next sc and next hdc, quad trc in next
hdc, ch 4, quad trc in next ch-5 sp, ch 4 ††;
rep from †† to †† 5 times more †; sk next sc
and in next hdc, quad trc in next hdc, ch 3;
rep from † to † once; join in 7th ch of beg
ch-10—40 quad trc.

Rnd 9: Ch 3, dc in each ch and in each
quad trc; join in 3rd ch of beg ch-3.

Rnd 10: Ch 4 (counts as a dc and a ch-1
sp), LK; sk next 3 dc, (trc in next dc, ch 1,
LK, sk next 3 dc) twice; trc in next dc,
ch 1, LK; sk next 3 dc, tr trc (see Pattern
Stitches) in next dc, ch 1, LK; sk next dc,
(quad trc in next dc, ch 1, LK) twice; sk
next dc, (quad trc in next dc, ch 1, LK)
twice; sk next dc, tr trc in next dc, ch 1, LK;
sk next 3 dc, (trc in next dc, ch 1, LK, sk
next 3 dc) 40 times; join in 3rd ch of beg
ch-4—49 LKs.

Rnd 11: Ch 1, sc in same ch as joining;
ch 5, (sc in next trc, ch 5) twice; sc in next
tr trc, ch 5, (sc in next quad trc, ch 5) 4
times; sc in next tr trc, ch 5, (sc in next trc,
ch 5) 40 times; join in first sc.

Rnd 12: Sl st in next 2 chs of next ch-5 sp,
ch 1, sc in same sp, picot; ch 4; * sc in next
ch-5 sp, picot; ch 4; rep from * around; join
in first sc (beneath picot).

Finish off and weave in all ends.

Finishing
With sewing needle and matching thread,
sew snaps to 4th and 8th picots to right of
first picot and to corresponding picots on
opposite side of mitt. Repeat for other mitt.

Cake Topper

Size:
About
Base: 7" diameter
Arch: 7" high
Groom: 5" tall
Bride: 4" tall

Materials:
Bedspread-weight crochet cotton, 150 yds
white; 30 yds ecru (for hair)
*Note: Our photographed cake topper was
made with J. & P. Coats® Knit-Cro-
Sheen®, White #1 and New Ecru #61.*
Size 6 (1.80mm) steel crochet hook, or size
required for gauge

Trimmings:
72, 4mm pearl beads
8" strand fused pearls
6" square white tulle
1½ yds pink satin ribbon, ³/8"-wide
10 pink satin bows with pearls
two 1" diameter Styrofoam® balls
(for bride and groom heads)
small amount of cotton (for top of sleeves
on bride)

*Our delightful bride and groom
under the wedding bells will be a beautiful
crowning touch to the wedding cake and
will become a memento of the happy
couple's special day.*

— designed by Jo Ann Maxwell

sewing needle and matching thread
starching and blocking supplies (see
page 216)
6" Styrofoam® cone
plastic drinking straws
small perscription bottle or lipstick tube
bottle cap

Gauge:
8 dc = 1"

Instructions
*Note: Before beginning, string 32 pearls
onto white crochet thread.*

Base:
Ch 5, join to form a ring.

Rnd 1 (right side): Ch 3 (counts as a dc on
this and following rnds), 19 dc in ring; join
in 3rd ch of beg ch-3—20 dc.

Rnd 2: Ch 3, dc in same ch as joining;
2 dc in each dc; join in 3rd ch of beg
ch-3—40 dc.

continued on page 104

Garter

Size:
Finished Garter—1½" wide x 16"
circumference
Crocheted Center—3¾" x 2½"

Materials:
Bedspread-weight crochet cotton,
40 yds white
*Note: Our photographed garter was
made with J. & P. Coats® Knit-Cro-
Sheen®, White #1.*
Size 6 (1.80mm) steel crochet hook, or size
required for gauge

Trimmings:
starching and blocking supplies (see
page 216)
12" length of fused white pearls
1½ yds white satin ribbon, 1½" wide
8" strand pink ribbon, ³/8"-wide
14" length of white elastic, 1"-wide
small floral spray with pink flowers
6" square pink tulle
hot glue or tacky craft glue
sewing needle and matching thread

Gauge:
8 dc = 1"

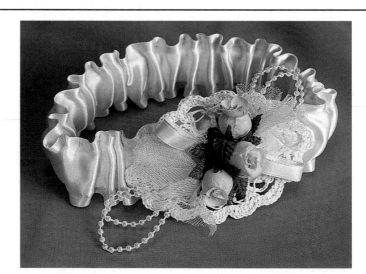

*This lacy accessory
is quick to crochet
and simply attach
to a purchased
plain garter. Who
will be the lucky
guy to catch it?*

*— designed by
Jo Ann Maxwell*

Instructions
Ch 5, join to form a ring.

Rnd 1 (right side): Ch 7 (counts as a trc and
a ch-3 sp), trc in ring, ch 1, (dc in ring, ch 1)
5 times; in ring work (trc, ch 3, trc); ch 1,
(dc in ring, ch 1) 5 times; join in 4th ch of
beg ch-7.

Rnd 2: Ch 3 (counts as a dc), dc in next ch,
3 dc in next ch; (dc in next ch and in next
st) 7 times; dc in next ch, 3 dc in next ch;
(dc in next ch and in next st) 6 times; dc in
next ch; join in 3rd ch of beg ch-3—36 dc.

Rnd 3: Ch 4 (counts as a dc and ch-1 sp),
work LK (see Pattern Stitches on page 81);
(sk next dc, dc in next dc, ch 1, LK) 3 times;
(sk next 2 dc, dc in next dc, ch 1, LK) 4
times; (sk next dc, dc in next dc, ch 1, LK) 3
times; (sk next 2 dc, dc in next dc, ch 1, LK)
3 times; join in 3rd ch of beg ch-4.

Rnd 4: Ch 1, sc in same ch as joining; ch 5,
(sc in next dc, ch 5) 13 times; join in first sc.

Rnd 5: Ch 1, sc in same sc; in next ch-5 sp
work (sc, 2 hdc, dc, 2 hdc, sc); * sc in next

continued on page 105

Single crochet is the workhorse of crochet, probably used more than any other stitch. It's an easy stitch to work, but is also very versatile.

Here are some questions we've been asked about single crochet.

1. When working in single crochet, where do I insert the hook?

There are three places – under both loops, under the front loop, or under the back loop.

Unless a pattern specifies otherwise, always insert the hook under both loops of the stitch (**Fig 1**). This results in a smooth surface fabric.

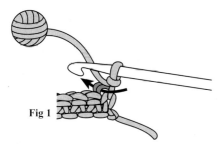

Fig 1

The pattern may specify "sc in front lps only". In that case, insert the hook in just the front loop (**Fig 2**), which is the loop closest to you.

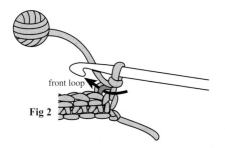

front loop

Fig 2

To "sc in back lps only", insert the hook in just the back loop (**Fig 3**), which is the one farthest from you.

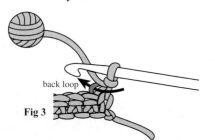

back loop

Fig 3

Working in back loops only on every row creates a ridged fabric.

An sc row worked in back loops only creates a turning ridge (**Fig 4**) to fold a section up, as for a cuff on a hat, or for a hem. For a turning ridge, work one row of sc in back loops only. Then resume working under both loops.

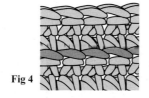

Fig 4

2. Patterns often specify working 3 sc in one st to turn a corner. I don't always like the way this looks. Is there another way?

Yes, several. Experiment on a practice piece with these methods.

A. In corner st work (sc, ch 2, sc); the ch-2 now becomes the corner st.

B. In corner st work (sc, hdc, sc); the hdc now becomes the corner st.

C. Work to st before corner st; 2 sc in this st; hdc in next st, 2 sc in next st. The hdc now becomes the corner st.

3. I find it hard to join pieces of crochet, as for a sweater. How can I do this more neatly?

With right side facing you, work one row of single crochet all around each piece, keeping work flat and working corners as needed. Then sew the seams through the sc row. We don't recommend joining pieces with single crochet or slip stitches, as this makes quite a bulky seam.

4. What does "reverse single crochet" mean?

This stitch, which is worked from left to right, creates a wonderful corded edging. Although it is confusing to work at first, once you've mastered the technique, it's fun, fast and easy. To practice, first work one row of single crochet across a piece.

At end of the row, ch 1, but DO NOT turn. Insert hook in last sc made (**Fig 5**); draw lp through sc—2 lps on hook (**Fig 6**); YO and draw through both lps on hook—one reverse single crochet stitch made. Working left to right, repeat in each sc across.

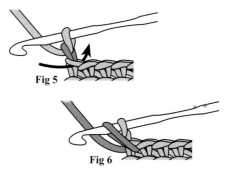

Fig 5

Fig 6

5. What is an extended single crochet?

This is a useful stitch that falls in height between an sc and an hdc.

Work an sc until there are 2 lps on hook (**Fig 7**), hook the yarn and draw it through one lp (**Fig 8**), hook yarn again and draw it through last lp (**Fig 9**).

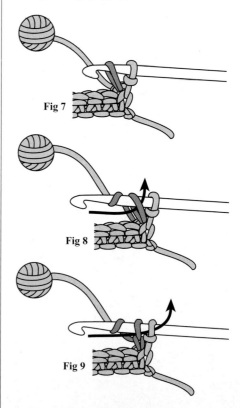

Fig 7

Fig 8

Fig 9

Confetti Tunic

Add pizzazz to your wardrobe with a sweater that crochets quickly in sport weight cotton yarn. Sized to fit comfortably and keep you warm.

— designed by
Melissa Leapman

Sizes:

	Small	Medium	Large
Chest Measurement:	32"- 34"	36"- 38"	40"- 42"
Finished Chest Measurement:	36"	40"	44"

Note: Instructions are written for size small; changes for larger sizes are in parentheses.

Materials:

Sport weight cotton yarn, 34¹/₂ (36, 39) oz [2415 (2520, 2730) yds; 1035 (1080, 1170) gms] variegated; 1³/₄ oz (125 yds, 52¹/₂ gms) each purple, yellow, and rose
Note: Our photographed tunic was made with Lily® "Sugar 'n Cream Sport" Potpourri Print #111; Lilac #09; Yellow #011; and Strawberry Passion #012.
Size F (3.75mm) crochet hook, or size required for gauge
Size E (3.50mm) crochet hook

Gauge:

19 sc = 4"
23 rows = 4"

Pattern Stitch

Long Double Crochet (long dc):
YO, draw up lp in st indicated on 2nd row below, (YO, draw through 2 lps on hook) twice—long dc made.

Instructions

Back

With smaller size hook and variegated, ch 87 (97, 107).

Row 1 (right side): Sc in 2nd ch from hook and in each rem ch—86 (96, 106) sc. Ch 1, turn.

Row 2: Sc in each sc. Change to purple by drawing lp through; cut variegated. Ch 3 (counts as first dc on following rows), turn.

Row 3: Sk first sc, dc in next sc; * ch 2, sk next 2 sc, dc in next 3 sc; rep from * 15 (17, 19) times more; ch 2, sk next 2 sc, dc in next 2 sc. Change to variegated by drawing lp through; cut purple. Ch 1, turn.

Row 4: Sc in first 2 dc; * long dc (see Pattern Stitch) in each of next 2 skipped sc in 2nd row below, sc in next 3 dc; rep from * 15 (17, 19) times more; long dc in each of next 2 skipped sc on 2nd row below, sc in next dc and in 3rd ch of turning ch-3. Ch 1, turn.

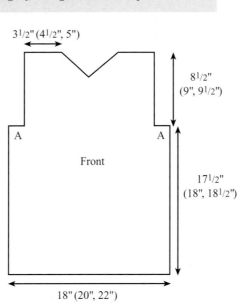

Row 5: Sc in each st. Ch 1, turn.

Row 6: Sc in each sc. Change to yellow by drawing lp through; cut variegated. Ch 3, turn.

Row 7: Sk first sc, dc in next sc; * ch 2, sk next 2 sc, dc in next 3 sc; rep from * 15 (17, 19) times more; ch 2, sk next 2 sc, dc in next 2 sc. Change to variegated by drawing lp through; cut yellow. Ch 1, turn.

Rows 8 and 9: Rep Rows 4 and 5.

Row 10: Sc in each sc. Change to rose by drawing lp through; cut variegated. Ch 3, turn.

Row 11: Sk first sc, dc in next sc; * ch 2, sk next 2 sc, dc in next 3 sc; rep from * 15 (17, 19) times more; ch 2, sk next 2 sc, dc in next 2 sc. Change to variegated by drawing lp through; cut rose. Ch 1, turn.

Rows 12 and 13: Rep Rows 4 and 5. At end of Row 13, change to larger size hook. Ch 1, turn.

Row 14: Sc in each sc. Ch 1, turn.

Rep Row 14 until piece measures 17¹/₂" (18", 18¹/₂") from beg, ending on a wrong side row.

Armhole Shaping:

Row 1 (right side): Sl st in first 8 (10, 12) sc; ch 1, sc in next 70 (76, 82) sc. Ch 1, turn, leaving rem 8 (10, 12) sc unworked.

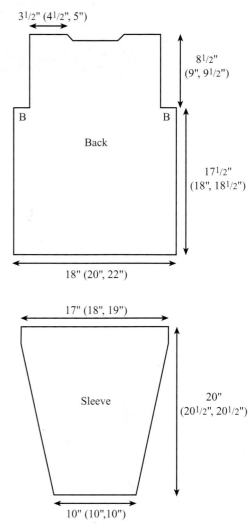

Row 2: Sc in each sc. Ch 1, turn.

Rep Row 2 until armhole measures 7¹/₂" (8", 8¹/₂"), ending by working a wrong side row.

Right Neck Shaping:

Row 1 (right side): Sc in first 18 (21, 24) sc. Ch 1, turn, leaving rem sc unworked.

Row 2: Sc in each sc. Ch 1, turn.

Rows 3 through 5: Rep Row 2. At end of Row 5, do not ch 1; do not turn. Finish off.

Left Neck Shaping:

With right side facing you, sk next 34 sc from right neck shaping; join variegated in next sc.

Row 1 (right side): Sc in each sc. Ch 1, turn.

Rows 2 through 5: Rep Row 1. At end of Row 5, do not ch 1; do not turn. Finish off.

continued on page 107

Shape Up Your Starching

Don't limit yourself to crocheting flat pieces such as doilies or snowflakes just because you are afraid to starch dimensional pieces. This cup and saucer in our Time for Tea pattern look as if they were difficult to starch and shape. They weren't! Try our simple directions for this project, and you'll soon be an expert!

Make sure that you have all the materials needed before you begin starching your project. Some things may need to be purchased when you first start. Once you discover how much fun starching can be, these purchases will only amount to pennies per project.

For this project you will need the following:

• Pinning board, such as a sheet of Styrofoam®
• Plastic wrap to cover the pinning board and to use in shaping crocheted pieces
• Starching solution (a ready-to-use product or a mixture of equal amounts of white craft glue and water)
• Rust-proof pins.
• Styrofoam® ball, 3" diameter
• Small brush (for applying starching solution).
• Margarine tub lid.

As you can see in **Photo A**, all of the crocheted pieces are ready to be starched. You may want to starch a bit of your gauge swatch just to be sure that the starching solution works on the project material without fading or changing the color.

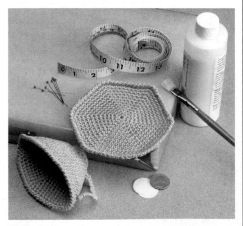

Photo A

Hints: Before starting a starching procedure, ALWAYS have clean hands. Make sure all thread ends are woven in before starching. Once the pieces have been starched, the ends are almost impossible to weave in.

Saucer

First, mist the saucer with water. It is not going to take much shaping since it is almost a flat piece, so pin it off to the side of the board, leaving plenty of room to work with the cup. Once the saucer is pinned to the shape and size desired (see **Photo B**), move on to the cup.

Photo B

Cup

Cut the foam ball in half. Place one half inside the cup. To fill up all the spaces around the ball, remove the ball and add plastic wrap which has been crumpled into the cup (see **Photo C**). Place the ball onto the pinning board flat side down. Place the cup (with the plastic wrap crumpled inside) over the ball. At this point make sure you have enough plastic wrap inside to keep the cup in the desired shape as you apply your starching solution. Pin edges of cup to pinning board.

Photo C

The cup also requires two small circles of plastic to be inserted into the base to stabilize it. The lid of an empty margarine tub works well for this. Using a quarter for a pattern piece, cut out two plastic circles. Place them into the base of the cup (see **Photo D**).

Photo D

Once you have the cup and saucer in the shapes that you want, mist again and proceed with applying your starching solution (see **Photo E**). With a small brush, apply solution thoroughly so as to saturate the pieces. (Saturating the pieces results in the finished project being quite firm.) Once the pieces have been saturated, you can carefully re-shape anything that may have moved as you applied the starching solution.

Photo E

Let these dry overnight and be sure that they are completely dry before removing them from the board. Then brush a light coat of the starching solution to the inside of the cup, to insure its stiffness. Again, let set overnight.

When completely dried, remove cup and saucer from the board and add the crocheted flowers and leaves.

Display the cup and saucer and collect the compliments.

Time for Tea

— designed by Nanette M. Seale

You've always loved the look of Wedgwood china—and now you can recreate your own dainty set in thread crochet. Created in classic blue using size 3 thread and trimmed with pretty garlands of white crocheted blossoms, this set will be treasured as much as expensive china. Patterns begin on page 88.

Cup and Saucer

Size:
About 3" high x 5" diameter

Materials:
Size 3 cotton crochet thread, 3 oz
(210 yds, 90 gms) blue; 1 oz (70 yds,
30 gms) white
*Note: Our photographed set was made
with J. & P. Coats® Speed-Cro-Sheen®,
Blue #4; and White #1.*
Size 0 (2.25mm) steel crochet hook, or size
required for gauge
Size 6 (1.80mm) steel crochet hook (for
roses and leaves)
Size 16 tapestry needle
Starching and blocking supplies (see
page 216)
Hot glue or tacky craft glue

Gauge:
With larger size hook, 5 sc = 1"

Instructions

*Note: Cup and saucer are worked in
continuous rnds. Unless otherwise
stated, do not join; mark beg of rnds.*

Cup

With larger size hook, ch 2.

Rnd 1 (right side): 6 sc in 2nd ch
from hook.

Rnd 2: 2 sc in each sc—12 sc.

Rnd 3: * Sc in next sc, 2 sc in next sc;
rep from * 5 times more—18 sc.

Rnd 4: Working in BLs only, sc in next
2 sc, 2 sc in next sc; rep from * 5 times
more—24 sc.

Rnd 5: * Sc in next 3 sc, 2 sc in next sc; rep
from * 5 times more—30 sc.

continued on page 111

Dessert Plate

Size:
About 10" diameter

Materials:
Size 3 cotton crochet thread, 3 oz
(210 yds, 90 gms) blue; 1 oz (70 yds,
30 gms) white
*Note: Our photographed plate was made
with J. & P. Coats® Speed-Cro-Sheen®,
Blue #4; and White #1*
Size 0 (2.25mm) steel crochet hook, or size
required for gauge
Size 6 (1.80mm) steel crochet hook (for
roses and leaves)
Size 16 tapestry needle
Starching and blocking supplies
(see page 216)
10" dinner plate for shaping
Hot glue or tacky craft glue

Gauge:
With larger size hook, 5 sc = 1"

Instructions

*Note: Plate is worked in continuous rnds.
Do not join; mark beg of rnds.*

With larger size hook, ch 2.

Rnd 1 (right side): 6 sc in 2nd ch
from hook.

Rnd 2: 2 sc in each sc—12 sc.

Rnd 3: * Sc in next sc, 2 sc in next sc; rep
from * 5 times more—18 sc.

Rnd 4: * Sc in next 2 sc, 2 sc in next sc;
rep from * 5 times more—24 sc.

Rnd 5: * Sc in next 3 sc, 2 sc in next sc;
rep from * 5 times more—30 sc.

Rnd 6: * Sc in next 4 sc, 2 sc in next sc;
rep from * 5 times more—36 sc.

Rnd 7: * Sc in next 5 sc, 2 sc in next sc;
rep from * 5 times more—42 sc.

Rnd 8: * Sc in next 6 sc, 2 sc in next sc;
rep from * 5 times more—48 sc.

Rnd 9: * Sc in next 7 sc, 2 sc in next sc;
rep from * 5 times more—54 sc.

Rnd 10: * Sc in next 8 sc, 2 sc in next sc;
rep from * 5 times more—60 sc.

continued on page 112

Purr-fectly Soft For Perfect Results.

The softest yarn ever from the makers of America's favorite yarn—Red Heart.® New TLC® offers beautiful luster, rich drape and exquisite softness. In an exciting range of 43 colors from deep and brilliant tones to gentle-blush pastels,

TLC is the perfect choice for baby blankets, cuddle-up afghans, and ultra-soft apparel.

Make the Purr-Fect choice for your projects—TLC Soft "Purr-Fection" Yarn by the makers of Red Heart.

TLC by the makers of **RED HEART** *Hand Knitting Yarns*

To get the free patterns shown plus a free color chart, send a self-addressed stamped envelope plus $1 for shipping and handling to: TLC Soft Yarn Offer, P.O. Box 865, Stevens Point, WI 54481-0865.

Casual Striped Cardigan

— designed by Melissa Leapman

On days when the sun never comes out or when the nights are cool, you'll look fresh as a spring breeze in this comfortable cardigan.

Sizes:

	Small	Medium	Large
Chest Measurement:	32"- 34"	36"- 38"	40"- 42"
Finished Chest Measurement:	36"	40"	44"

Note: Instructions are written for size small; changes for larger sizes are in parentheses.

All measurements are approximate.

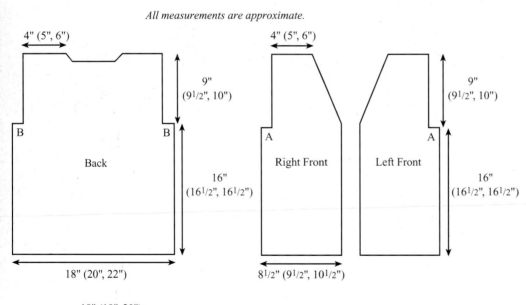

4" (5", 6")

9" (9$^1/2$", 10")

B   B

Back

16" (16$^1/2$", 16$^1/2$")

18" (20", 22")

4" (5", 6")

9" (9$^1/2$", 10")

A   A

Right Front   Left Front

16" (16$^1/2$", 16$^1/2$")

8$^1/2$" (9$^1/2$", 10$^1/2$")

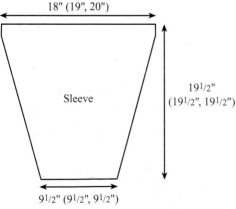

18" (19", 20")

Sleeve

19$^1/2$" (19$^1/2$", 19$^1/2$")

9$^1/2$" (9$^1/2$", 9$^1/2$")

Materials:

Sport weight cotton yarn, 22$^3/4$ (24$^1/2$, 26$^1/4$) oz [1365 (1470, 1575) yds, 682$^1/2$ (712$^1/2$, 742$^1/2$) gms] red; 5$^1/4$ oz (315 yds, 157$^1/2$ gms) each, white and blue
Note: Our photographed cardigan was made with Lily® "Sugar 'n Cream Sport" Red #14; White #001;and Royal Blue #13.
Size F (3.75mm) crochet hook, or size required for gauge
Size E (3.5mm) crochet hook
Six buttons, $^7/8$" diameter
Note: JHB International's "Obsession" style #32282 used on model.
Size 16 tapestry needle
Sewing needle and matching thread

Gauge:

In pattern:
6 sts = 1"
19 rows = 4"

Color Sequence

1 row white
3 rows red
1 row blue
3 rows red

Instructions

Back

With larger size hook and red, ch 108 (120, 132).

Note: On following rows chs count as sts.

Row 1 (right side): Sc in 2nd ch from hook; * ch 1, sk next ch, sc in next ch; rep from * across—107 (119, 131) sts. Ch 1, turn.

Row 2: Sc in first sc and in next ch-1 sp; * ch 1, sc in next ch-1 sp; rep from * 51 (57, 63) times more; sc in next sc. Change to white by drawing lp through; cut red. Ch 1, turn.

Row 3: Sc in first sc; * ch 1, sc in next ch-1 sp; rep from * 51 (57, 63) times more; ch 1, sk next sc, sc in next sc. Change to red by drawing lp through; cut white. Ch 1, turn.

continued on page 109

What's the most difficult crochet stitch?

Just for fun, we asked a group of crochet experts what they consider the most difficult of all crochet stitches—a stitch, not a pattern.

And the winner is —

THE BULLION STITCH!

This is a lovely stitch, which adds rich texture. Sometimes called the Roll Stitch, it is often used in Irish Crochet and in elaborate doilies. It is best worked in crochet thread, which has enough stiffness to hold the shape of the stitch.

The Bullion stitch is basically an extension of the hdc stitch — the yarn is wrapped over the hook, then hook is inserted in next stitch, yarn is hooked and drawn through all lps on hook.

To work the stitch, the thread is first wrapped around the hook (YO) numerous — possibly 10 or 12 or more — times, then the thread is hooked and drawn through all the loops. At first, you'll have trouble with the loops slipping off the hook, and you may want to draw through each loop one at a time; as you become more proficient, you'll draw the yarn through all loops at the same time.

Ready for a challenge? Then try the Practice Piece.

Practice Piece.
Using thread and appropriate size hook, ch 9.

Row 1: Sc in 2nd ch from hook and in each rem ch—8 sc. Ch 2, turn.

Row 2: Hdc in first sc; work bullion stitch in next sc as follows:

Bullion Stitch:
Step 1: YO hook twice (**Fig 1**).

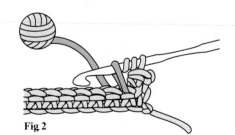

Fig 1

Note: Always wrap yarn around fat part (working area) of hook.

Step 2: Insert hook in next sc, draw up a lp to height of an sc (**Fig 2**).

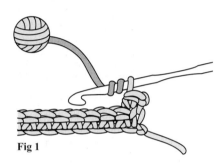

Fig 2

Step 3: Hook yarn and draw through all lps on hook (**Fig 3**).

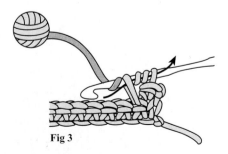

Fig 3

Now let's make it more challenging!

For the next bullion stitch, in Step 1, YO three times; for next stitch, YO four times.

Note: You may need to draw through lps one or two at a time until you have practiced more. Here's a hint that may help. Hold wraps between your left index finger and thumb and turn the hook down while drawing the lp through the wraps.

As you can see, the more YOs, the taller the stitch (**Fig 4**) and the more difficult it becomes to draw the thread through.

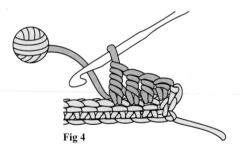

Fig 4

Our Bullion Square uses the 12-YO stitch. For fun, complete the practice row with bullion stitches, adding one more YO in Step 1 each time.

How to Use the Bullion Stitch
The stitch can be used in borders, edgings, or any type of motif.

Page 93 shows one pretty square that can be used for a tablecloth, runner, shawl or doily.

BULLION SQUARE

Materials:
Bedspread-weight crochet cotton
Size 6 (1.80mm) steel crochet hook, or
   size required for gauge

Gauge:
8 sc = 1"

Instructions:
Rnd 1(right side): Ch 2, 8 sc in 2nd ch from hook, join in first sc.

Rnd 2: Ch 4 (does not count as a st), 2 twelve-YO buillion sts in each sc; join with an sc in top of first bullion st—16 bullion sts.

Rnd 3: (Ch 6, sk next bullion st, sc in next bullion st) 7 times; ch 6; join in joining sc—8 ch-6 sps.

Rnd 4: Working behind Rnd 3 in skipped bullion sts, sl st in next skipped bullion st, ch 1, sc in same st; ch 5, (sc in next skipped bullion st, ch 5) 7 times; join in first sc.

Rnd 5: Sl st in next ch-5 sp, ch 4 (counts as a trc), in same sp work (2 trc, ch 3, 3 trc)—beg corner made; 3 trc in next ch-5 sp; * in next ch-5 sp work (3 trc, ch 3, 3 trc)—corner made; 3 trc in next ch-5 sp; rep from * twice more; join in 4th ch of beg ch-4.

Rnd 6: Sl st in next 2 trc and in next ch-3 sp; in same sp work beg corner; † in sp between next two 3-trc groups work (trc, ch 2, trc) †; rep from † to † once more; * in next ch-3 sp work corner; rep from † to † twice; rep from * twice more; join with an sc in 4th ch of beg ch-4.

Rnd 7: Ch 3, sk next trc, sc in next trc; * † in ch-3 sp work (sc, ch 3) 3 times; sc in same sp; sc in next trc, ch 3, sk next trc, sc in next trc, (ch 3, sc in next ch-2 sp) twice; ch 3, sk next trc †; sc in next trc, ch 3, sk next trc, sc in next trc; rep from * twice more, then rep from † to † once; join in joining sc.

Finish off and weave in ends.

Your favorite golfer may not be a professional, but you can show him how important he (or she) is to you with these clever tiger covers for their woods.

Tigers for Your Woods

— designed by Kelly Robinson

Size:
About 12" in length

Materials:
Worsted weight crochet yarn for each cover, 1 oz (70 yds, 30 gms) each, gold, black, and white

Note: Our photographed covers were made with Red Heart® TLC®, Amber #564; Black #5012; and Natural #5017.

Size G (4.25mm) crochet hook, or size required for gauge

Size18 tapestry needle

two 18mm green plastic cat eyes

Gauge:
4 sc = 1"

Pattern Stitches

Long Half Double Crochet (long hdc):
YO, insert hook in next corresponding sc on Rnd 3, draw up lp to height of working rnd, YO and draw through all 3 lps on hook—long hdc made.

Long Double Crochet (long dc):
YO, insert hook in next corresponding sc on Rnd 2, draw up lp to height of working rnd, (YO, draw through 2 lps on hook) twice—long dc made.

Instructions
With white, ch 4; join to form a ring.

Rnd 1 (right side): Ch 1, 8 sc in ring; join in first sc.

Rnd 2: Ch 1, 2 sc in same sc and in each rem sc; join in first sc—16 sc.

Rnd 3: Ch 1, sc in same sc and in each rem sc; join in first sc.

continued on page 114

Tissue Box in Bloom

— designed by Jo Ann Maxwell

Whether it's summer and the pollen count or winter and trying to make it through cold season, you will enjoy the beauty of this gracious floral trimmed tissue box cover.

2 dc in next ch; dc in next 3 chs; join in 3rd ch of beg ch-3—96 dc.

Rnd 2: Ch 6 (counts as a trc and a ch-2 sp); working in BLs only, † [dtrc (see Pattern Stitches) in next dc, ch 2] 8 times; trc in next dc, ch 2, (sk next 2 dc, dc in next dc, ch 3) 11 times; sk next 2 dc, dc in next dc, ch 2 †; trc in next dc, ch 2; rep from † to † once more; join in 4th ch of beg ch-6.

Rnd 3: Ch 3, dc in each ch and in each st; join in 3rd ch of beg ch-3.

Rnd 4: Ch 5 (counts as a dc and a ch-2 sp); working in BLs only, † (sk next dc, trc in next dc, ch 2) twice; (sk next dc, dtrc in next dc, ch 2) twice; sk next dc, tr trc (see Pattern Stitches) in next dc, ch 2, sk next dc, (tr trc in next dc, ch 2) 4 times; sk next dc, tr trc in next dc, (ch 2, sk next dc, dtrc in next dc) twice; ch 2, (sk next dc, trc in next dc, ch 2) twice; sk next dc, dc in next dc, ch 2, sk next 2 dc, sc in next 45 dc, ch 2, sk next 2 dc †; dc in next dc, ch 2; rep from † to † once; join in 3rd ch of beg ch-5.

Rnd 5: Ch 3; † (dc in next 2 chs and in BL of next st) 15 times; ch 3, sc in next sc, (ch 4, sk next 3 sc, sc in next sc) 11 times; ch 3 †; dc in BL of next dc; rep from † to † once; join in 3rd ch of beg ch-3.

Rnd 6: Ch 1, sc in same ch as joining; working in BLs only, † (ch 4, sk next 2 dc, sc in next dc) twice; ch 4, sk next 2 dc, in next dc work (2 trc, ch 5, 2 trc); (ch 4, sk next 2 dc, sc in next dc) 8 times; ch 4, sk next 2 dc, in next dc work (2 trc, ch 5, 2 trc); (ch 4, sk next 2 dc, sc in next dc) 3 times; ch 4, (sc in next ch-4 sp, ch 4) 11 times †; sc in next dc; rep from † to † once; join in first sc.

Rnd 7: Sl st in next 2 chs of next ch-4 sp, ch 1, sc in same sp; (ch 4, sc in next ch-4

Size:
To fit tissue box, 9¹/₂" x 4¹/₂" x 3"

Materials:
Bedspread-weight crochet cotton, one 225-yd ball ecru
Note: Our photographed cover was made with J. & P. Coats® Knit-Cro-Sheen®, New Ecru #61.
Size 6 (1.80mm) steel crochet hook, or size required for gauge
Size 16 tapestry needle

Trimmings:
2 yds dk peach sheer ribbon, 1¹/₂"- wide
6 peach silk roses, 1¹/₄"-diameter
Hot glue or tacky craft glue

Gauge:
8 dc = 1"

Pattern Stitches
Double Triple Crochet (dtrc):
YO 3 times; draw up lp in st indicated, (YO, draw through 2 lps on hook) 4 times—dtrc made.

Triple Triple Crochet (tr trc):
YO 4 times; draw up lp in st indicated, (YO, draw through 2 lps on hook) 5 times—tr trc made.

Instructions
Ch 82; join to form a ring, being careful not to twist ch.

Rnd 1 (right side): Ch 3 (counts as a dc on this and following rnds), dc in same ch as joining; dc in next 5 chs; * 2 dc in next ch; dc in next 5 chs; rep from * 11 times more;

continued on page 113

It Takes a Skein
Pure Elegance

With just one ball of bedspread-weight crochet thread you can create the perfect purse for a bride, the prom or other affairs where your usual leather handbag just won't do!

— designed by Kelly Robinson

Instructions

Flap

Ch 6, join to form a ring.

Row 1 (wrong side)**:** Ch 3 (counts as a dc), 10 dc in ring—11 dc. Ch 1, turn.

Row 2 (right side)**:** Sc in first dc, ch 3, sk next dc; * sc in next dc, ch 3, sk next dc; rep from * 3 times more; sc in 3rd ch of beg ch-3—5 ch-3 sps. Ch 1, turn.

Row 3: Sc in first sc and in next ch-3 sp, ch 3, 5 dc in next ch-3 sp; ch 3, sc in next ch-3 sp, ch 3, 5 dc in next ch-3 sp; ch 3, sc in next ch-3 sp and in next sc. Ch 3 (counts as first dc on following rows), turn.

Row 4: Dc in next sc; † ch 3, 2 dc in each of next 2 dc; dc in next dc, 2 dc in each of next 2 dc; ch 3 †; sc in next sc; rep from † to † once more; dc in next 2 sc. Ch 3, turn.

Row 5: Dc in next dc, ch 3; † (dc in next dc, ch 1) 8 times; dc in next dc, ch 3 †; (sc in next ch-3 sp, ch 3) twice; rep from † to † once more; dc in next dc and in 3rd ch of turning ch-3. Ch 3, turn.

Row 6: Dc in next dc; † ch 3, sk next dc, (sc in next ch-1 sp, ch 3) 8 times; sk next dc and next ch-3 sp †; in next ch-3 sp work (2 dc, ch 3, 2 dc)—shell made; rep from † to † once more; dc in next dc and in 3rd ch of turning ch-3. Ch 3, turn.

Size:
About 4" x 7"

Materials:
Bedspread-weight crochet cotton, 200 yds white

Note: Our photographed purse was made with Caron® Grandma's Best, White #21.

Size 6 (1.80mm) steel crochet hook, or size required for gauge

Gauge:
8 dc = 1"

Pattern Stitches

Beginning Cluster (beg CL)**:**
Keeping last lp of each dc on hook, dc in next sc, sk next ch-1 sp, dc in next sc, YO and draw through all 3 lps on hook—beg CL made.

Cluster (CL)**:**
Keeping last lp of each dc on hook, dc in same sc as last dc made, sk next ch-1 sp, dc in next sc, YO and draw through all 3 lps on hook—CL made.

continued on page 97

Pure Elegance

continued from page 96

Row 7: Dc in next dc; † ch 3, sk next ch-3 sp, (sc in next ch-3 sp, ch 3) 7 times; sk next ch-3 sp †; in ch-3 sp of next shell work shell; rep from † to † once more; dc in next dc and in 3rd ch of turning ch-3. Ch 3, turn.

Row 8: In first dc work (dc, ch 3, 2 dc)—beg shell made; † ch 3, sk next ch-3 sp, (sc in next ch-3 sp, ch 3) 6 times; sk next ch-3 sp †; in next shell work (shell, ch 3, 2 dc); rep from † to † once more; shell in 3rd ch of turning ch-3. Ch 3, turn.

Row 9: Dc in next dc, shell in next ch-3 sp; ch 3; † sk next ch-3 sp, (sc in next ch-3 sp, ch 3) 5 times; sk next ch-3 sp †; (shell in next ch-3 sp, ch 3) twice; rep from † to † once more; shell in next shell; dc in next dc of same shell and in 3rd ch of turning ch-3. Ch 3, turn.

Row 10: Dc in next dc; † ch 3, shell in next shell; ch 3, sk next ch-3 sp, (sc in next ch-3 sp, ch 3) 4 times; sk next ch-3 sp, shell in next shell; ch 3 †; sc in next ch-3 sp; rep from † to † once more; sk next 2 dc of same shell, dc in next dc and in 3rd ch of turning ch-3. Ch 3, turn.

Row 11: Dc in next dc, ch 3, sc in next ch-3 sp, ch 3; † shell in next shell; ch 3, sk next ch-3 sp, (sc in next ch-3 sp, ch 3) 3 times; sk next ch-3 sp, shell in next shell; ch 3 †; (sc in next ch-3 sp, ch 3) twice; rep from † to † once more; sc in next ch-3 sp, ch 3, dc in next dc and in 3rd ch of turning ch-3. Ch 4 (counts as first trc on following rows), turn.

Row 12: Trc in next dc, 5 trc in next ch-3 sp; † ch 3, sk next ch-3 sp, shell in next shell; ch 3, sk next ch-3 sp, (sc in next ch-3 sp, ch 3) twice; sk next ch-3 sp, shell in next shell; ch 3, sk next ch-3 sp †; 9 trc in next ch-3 sp; rep from † to † once more; 5 trc in next ch-3 sp; trc in next dc and in

3rd ch of turning ch-3. Ch 4, turn.

Row 13: Trc in next trc, ch 3, sk next 2 trc; † (trc in next trc, ch 2) twice; trc in next trc, ch 3, sk next ch-3 sp, shell in next shell; ch 3, sk next ch-3 sp, in next ch-3 sp work (sc, ch 7, sc); ch 3, sk next ch-3 sp, shell in next shell; ch 3, (trc in next trc, ch 2) twice; trc in next trc, ch 3 †; sk next trc, trc in next trc, ch 3, sk next trc; rep from † to † once more; sk next 2 trc, trc in next trc and in 4th ch of beg ch-4. Ch 1, turn.

Row 14 (edging): Sc in first 2 trc; † 3 sc in next ch-3 sp; 3 sc in each of next 2 ch-2 sps; 5 sc in next ch-3 sp; sc in next 2 dc, 3 sc in next ch-3 sp; sc in next 2 dc, 5 sc in next ch-3 sp; in next ch-7 sp work (2 sc, 2 hdc, 3 dc, 2 hdc, 2 sc); 5 sc in next ch-3 sp; sk next 2 dc, 3 sc in next ch-3 sp; sc in next 2 dc, 5 sc in next ch-3 sp; 3 sc in each of next 2 ch-2 sps and in next ch-3 sp †; in next trc work (sl st, ch 4, keeping last lp of each trc on hook, 2 trc, YO and draw through all 3 lps on hook; ch 4, sl st); rep from † to † once more; sc in next trc and in 4th ch of turning ch-4; working along edge in sps formed by turning chs, in edge trc, in edge dc, and in edge sc of each row, 2 sc in each of next 10 rows, sc in next 2 rows, 2 sc in next row; sc in center of beg ch-6, 2 sc in next row; sc in next 2 rows, 2 sc in each of next 10 rows; join in first sc. Finish off.

Body

Ch 72.

Row 1 (right side)**:** Keeping last lp of each dc on hook, dc in 5th ch from hook (beg 4 skipped chs count as a dc and ch-1 sp), sk next ch, dc in next ch, YO and draw through all 3 lps on hook; * ch 1, keeping last lp of each dc on hook, dc in same ch as last dc made, sk next ch, dc in next ch, YO and draw through all 3 lps on hook; rep from * 31 times more; ch 1, dc in next ch. Ch 1, turn.

Row 2: Sc in first dc and in next ch-1 sp,

ch 1, sk next CL; * sc in next ch-1 sp, ch 1; rep from * to beg 4 skipped chs; sc in next 2 chs of beg skipped chs. Ch 4 (counts as first dc and ch-1 sp on following rows), turn.

Row 3: Sk first sc, beg CL (see Pattern Stitches on page 96) over next sc, next ch-1 sp and next sc; ch 1; * CL (see Pattern Stitches on page 96) over same sc as last dc made, next ch-1 sp, and next sc; ch 1; rep from * 31 times more; dc in next sc—33 CLs. Ch 1, turn.

Row 4: Sc in first dc and in next ch-1 sp, ch 1, sk next CL; * sc in next ch-1 sp, ch 1; rep from * to turning ch-4; sc in next 2 chs of turning ch. Ch 4, turn.

Rows 5 through 40: Rep Rows 3 and 4 eighteen times more. At end of Row 40, do not ch 4. Finish off.

Edging and Chain:

Hold body with wrong side facing you and beg ch at top; fold in half, placing wrong side of Row 40 facing wrong side of Row 1. Turn so ends of rows are at top and fold is to right. Working through both thicknesses, make lp on hook and join with an sc through Rows 20 and 21; sc in same sp; working in sps formed by edge dc, in turning chs, and in edge sc of each row, (sc in next row, 2 sc in next row) 9 times; sc in next row; * ch 4, keeping last lp of each dc on hook, 2 dc in 3rd ch from hook; YO and draw through all 3 lps on hook; rep from * 59 times more—chain strap made; working through both thicknesses on opposite next side of body in sps formed by edge dc, in turning chs, and in edge sc of each row, (sc in next row, 2 sc in next row) 10 times.

Finish off and weave in all ends.

Finishing

Referring to photo for placement, with wrong side of flap facing right side of body; sew along unused lps of beginning chain of body and in each sc on flap.

Battenberg Beauty Edging

continued from page 69

Rnd 3: Ch 1, sc in same ch as joining; (ch 7, sk next picot, sc in next dc) 24 times; ch 17, sl st in 14th ch from hook, ch 4, (sc in next dc, ch 7, sk next picot, sc in next dc) 23 times; join in first sc.

Rnd 4: Sl st in next ch of next ch-7 sp, ch 3, dc in same ch; † 2 dc in each of next 2 chs; 3 dc in next ch; 2 dc in each of next 3 chs; ch 1, sc in next ch-7 sp, ch 1, 2 dc in next dc †; rep from † to † 10 times more;

2 dc in each of next 2 chs; 3 dc in next ch; 2 dc in each of next 3 chs; ch 1, sk next 3 chs of next ch-7 sp, sc in next ch, picot; sc in next 3 chs, in next sc, and in next 3 chs of next ch-17 lp; ch 1, sl st in next ch (where sl st made); working in chs around next ch-13 lp, in next ch work (sc, hdc); 2 dc in each of next 5 chs; 3 dc in next ch; 2 dc in each of next 5 chs; in next ch work (hdc, sc); sl st in next sl st—battenberg lp

continued on page 98

Battenberg Beauty Edging

continued from page 97

made; sc in next 4 chs, in next sc, and in next 3 chs of next ch-7 sp; sc in next ch, picot; ch 1, 2 dc in next ch of next ch-7 sp; rep from † to † 10 times; 2 dc in each of next 2 chs; 3 dc in next ch; 2 dc in each of next 3 chs; ch 1, sc in next ch-7 sp, ch 1; join in 3rd ch of beg ch-3.

Rnd 5: Sl st in next dc, ch 6 (counts as a dc and a ch-3 sp); † (sk next 2 dc, dc in next dc, ch 3) twice; sk next 2 dc, CL (see Pattern Stitches on page 69) over next 7 sts; ch 3, sk next 2 dc, dc in next dc, ch 3 †; rep from † to † 10 times more; sk next 2 dc, dc in next dc, ch 3, sk next 2 dc, dc in next dc, ch 17, sl st in 14th ch from hook, ch 4, dc in BL of 8th dc of next ch-13 lp, ch 3, sk next 2 dc, dc in BL of next dc, ch 17, sl st in 14th ch from hook, ch 4, sk next dc, dc in BL of next dc, ch 3, sk next 2 dc, dc in BL of next dc, ch 17, sl st in 14th ch from hook, ch 4, dc in 5th dc of next loop, ch 3; rep from † to † 10 times; (sk next 2 dc, dc in next dc, ch 3) twice; sk next 2 dc; to join, YO, draw up lp in next dc, YO, draw through 2 lps on hook, draw up lp in 3rd ch of beg ch-6 and through both lps on hook—3 ch-13 lps.

Rnd 6: Sl st in next ch of next ch-3 sp, ch 3, dc in next 2 chs; † (dc in next dc, picot, dc in next 3 chs) twice; dc in next dc, picot; dc in next 2 chs, small CL (see Pattern Stitches on page 69) over next 3 sts; dc in next 2 chs †; rep from † to † 10 times more; dc in next dc, picot; dc in next 3 chs, dc in next dc, picot; hdc in next 3 chs, sc in next dc and in next 3 chs; * †† sl st in next ch (where sl st made), working around next ch-13 lp, in next ch work (sc, hdc); 2 dc in each of next 5 chs; 3 dc in next ch; 2 dc in each of next 5 chs; in next ch work (hdc, sc); sl st in next sl st—battenberg lp made; sc in next 4 chs ††; (sc in next dc, picot, sc in next 3 chs) twice; rep from * once more, then rep from †† to †† once; sc in next dc, hdc in next 3 chs, dc in next dc, picot; dc in next 3 chs, dc in next dc, picot; dc in next 2 chs, small CL over next 3 sts; dc in next 2 chs; rep from † to † 9 times; (dc in next dc, picot, dc in next 3 chs) twice; dc in next dc, picot; dc in next 2 chs; to join, YO, draw up lp in next ch, YO, draw through 2 lps on hook, sk next CL, draw up lp in 3rd ch of beg ch-3 and draw through both lps on hook. Finish off.

Final Battenberg Loops

Row 1: Hold edging with wrong side facing you and battenberg lps at top; join thread in 4th picot to right of lps; ch 1, sc in same picot; ch 18, sl st in 14th ch from hook, ch 5; working in FLs only, † dc in 8th dc of next battenberg lp, ch 3, sk next 2 dc, dc in next dc †; ch 7, sk next dc, dc in next dc, ch 3, sk next 2 dc, dc in next dc, ch 17, sl st in 14th ch from hook, ch 4; rep from † to † once; ch 17, sl st in 14th ch from hook, ch 4, sk next dc, dc in next dc, ch 3, sk next 2 dc, dc in next dc, ch 17, sl st in 14th ch from hook, ch 4; rep from † to † once; ch 7, sk next dc, dc in next dc, ch 3, sk next 2 dc, dc in next dc, ch 18, sl st in next 14th ch from hook, ch 5, sk next 3 picots, sc in next picot. Ch 1, turn.

Row 2: Sc in first sc, picot; sc in next 5 chs; † sl st in next ch; working around next ch-13 lp, in next ch work (sc, hdc); 2 dc in each of next 5 chs; 3 dc in next ch; 2 dc in each of next 5 chs; in next ch work (hdc, sc); sl st in next sl st (where sl st made)—battenberg lp made †; †† sc in next 4 chs, (sc in next dc, picot, sc in next 3 chs) twice; 3 sc in next ch; (sc in next 3 chs, sc in next dc, picot) twice ††; sc in next 4 chs; rep from † to † once; (sc in next 3 chs, sc in next dc, picot) twice; sc in next 4 chs; rep from † to † once; sc in next 4 chs, (sc in next dc, picot, sc in next 3 chs) twice; rep from † to † once; rep from †† to †† once; sc in next 4 chs; rep from † to † once; sc in next 4 chs, sc in next sc, picot.

Finish off and weave in all ends.

Finishing

Step 1: Hold edging with wrong side of Rnd 2 facing you. With tapestry needle, weave ribbon in and out of Rnd 2. With sewing needle and matching thread, tack ends of ribbon together.

Step 2: With sewing needle and thread, sew edging to pillowcase.

Brian Bunny

continued from page 65

Rows 12 and 13: Rep Row 10.

Row 14: Sc in each sc; join in first sc. Change to dk purple by drawing lp through; cut lavender.

Note: Remainder of romper is worked in rnds.

Rnd 1: Ch 3 (counts as a dc on this and following rnds), dc in next sc, (dc in next 3 sc, 2 dc in next sc) 14 times; join in 3rd ch of beg ch-3—72 dc.

Rnd 2: Ch 3, dc in each dc; join in 3rd ch of beg ch-3.

Rnds 3 and 4: Rep Rnd 2.

Rnd 5: Ch 3, dc in next 7 dc, 2 dc in next dc; (dc in next 8 dc, 2 dc in next dc) 7 times; join in 3rd ch of beg ch-3—80 dc.

Rnds 6 and 7: Rep Rnd 2. At end of Rnd 7, finish off.

Back Flap:

With right side of back opening facing you and Rnd 7 at top; join dk purple in 5th dc to right of joining.

Row 1: Ch 3, dc in next 4 dc, in 3rd ch of beg ch-3, and in next 4 dc—10 dc. Ch 3 (counts as a dc on following rows), turn, leaving rem dc unworked.

Row 2: Dc in each dc and in 3rd ch of beg ch-3.

Row 3: Ch 1, sc in each dc and in 3rd ch of turning ch-3. Finish off, leaving a 10" end for sewing.

Front Flap:

Hold piece with right side of front facing you and Rnd 7 at top; sk next 30 dc to left of back flap; join dk purple in next dc.

Row 1: Ch 3, dc in next 9 dc—10 dc. Ch 3, turn.

Row 2: Dc in each dc and in 3rd ch of beg ch-3. Ch 3, turn.

Row 3: Dc in each dc and in 3rd ch of turning ch-3. Finish off, leaving a 10" end for sewing.

Right Leg:

Hold piece with right side facing you and Rnd 7 at top; join dk purple in next dc to left of back flap.

Rnd 1: Ch 3, dc in next 29 dc; working in sps formed by edge dc and turning chs of each row on flaps, sc dec over next 2 sps;

continued on page 99

Brian Bunny

continued from page 98

(sc dec over same sp just worked and next sp) 3 times; join in 3rd ch of beg ch-3—34 dc.

Rnd 2: Ch 3, dc in each dc; join in 3rd ch of beg ch-3.

Rnds 3 and 4: Rep Rnd 2. At end of Rnd 4, change to lavender by drawing lp through; cut dk purple.

Rnd 5: Ch 1, sc in same ch as joining and in each dc; join in first sc. Finish off.

Left Leg:

Hold piece with right side of front facing you and Rnd 7 at top; join dk purple in next dc to left of front flap.

Rnds 1 through 5: Rep Rnds 1 through 5 of Right Leg.

Collar Trim:

Hold romper with right side of back opening facing you; working in unused lps on opposite side of beg ch-32, join dk purple in first unused lp to left of back opening; ch 1, sc in same lp; (2 sc in next lp, sc in next lp) 15 times—46 sc. Finish off.

Back Opening Trim and Ties:

Hold romper with right side facing you and legs to left; join lavender in first edge sc to right of back opening; ch 1, sc in same sc; working in edge sc of each row, † in next sc work (sl st, ch 24, sl st in 2nd ch from hook and in next 22 chs, sl st) †; sc in next 6 rows; rep from † to † once; sc in next 5 rows; working along next side in edge sc of each row, sc in next 5 rows; rep from † to † once; sc in next 6 rows; rep from † to † once; sc in next sc.

Finish off and weave in all ends.

Heart

With dk purple, ch 4, 4 trc in 4th ch from hook; working in sp formed by edge trc, 3 sc in last edge trc worked; in unused lp of beg ch work (sc, ch 1, sc)—point made; 3 sc in sp formed by beg 3 skipped chs, 2 hdc in next ch; sc in next trc, sl st in next trc, sc in next trc, 2 hdc in next trc; join in first sc. Finish off, leaving a 6" end for sewing. Weave in other end.

Finishing

Step 1: With tapestry needle and 10" end, sew front and back flaps together using overcast st (see Crochet Stitch Guide on page 213). Sew each front flap seam to each leg. Sew each back flap seam to each leg.

Step 2: Referring to photo for placement, with tapestry needle and 6" end, sew heart to center front of romper.

Bridal Gown

continued from page 79

Row 32: Sc in first 2 dc, in next ch-1 sp, in next dc, and in next ch-1 sp; * † ch 2, sc in next ch-1 sp, ch 3, sc in next ch-1 sp, ch 2 †; sc in next 2 ch-1 sps; rep from * 8 times more, then rep from † to † once; sc in next ch-1 sp, sk next dc, sc in 3rd ch of turning ch-3. Ch 3, turn.

Row 33: (Shell in next ch-3 sp, dec) 9 times; shell in next ch-3 sp; sk next ch-2 sp and next 2 sc, (dc in next sc, ch 1) twice; in next sc work (dc, ch 1, dc). Ch 1, turn.

Row 34: Sc in first dc; * † ch 2, sc in next ch-1 sp, ch 3, sc in next ch-1 sp, ch 2 †; sc in next 2 ch-1 sps; rep from * 9 times more, then rep from † to † once; sc in next ch-1 sp, sk next dc, sc in 3rd ch of turning ch-3. Ch 3, turn.

Row 35: (Shell in next ch-3 sp, dec) 10 times; shell in next ch-3 sp; sk next ch-2 sp, dc in next sc—11 shells. Ch 1, turn.

Row 36: Sc in first dc and in next ch-1 sp; * † ch 2, sc in next ch-1 sp, ch 3, sc in next ch-1 sp, ch 2 †; sc in next 2 ch-1 sps; rep from * 9 times more, then rep from † to † once; sc in next ch-1 sp, sk next dc, sc in 3rd ch of turning ch-3. Ch 3, turn.

Row 37: (Shell in next ch-3 sp, dec) 10 times; shell in next ch-3 sp; sk next ch-2 sp and next sc, dc in next sc—11 shells.

Finish off and set aside.

Left Back Yoke

With smallest size hook, ch 35.

Row 1 (right side)**:** In 7th ch from hook work shell; * † sk next 5 chs, in next ch work shell; rep from * 3 times more; sk next 3 chs, dc in next ch—5 shells. Ch 5, turn.

Row 2: Sc in 2nd ch from hook, in next 3 chs, and in next dc; sk next dc, sc in next ch-1 sp; * † ch 2, sc in next ch-1 sp, ch 3, sc in next ch-1 sp, ch 2 †; sc in next 2 ch-1

sps; rep from * 3 times more, then rep from † to † once; sc in next ch-1 sp, sk next dc, sc in next ch of beg 6 skipped chs. Ch 3 (counts as first dc on following rows), turn.

Row 3: * Shell in next ch-3 sp; dec over next 2 ch-2 sps (to work dec: draw up lp in each of next 2 ch-2 sps, YO and draw through all 3 lps on hook—dec made); rep from * 3 times more; shell in next ch-3 sp; draw up lp in next ch-2 sp, sk next sc, draw up lp in next sc, YO and draw through all 3 lps on hook; sk next 3 chs, shell in next sc—6 shells. Ch 5, turn.

Row 4: Sc in 2nd ch from hook, in next 3 chs, and in next dc; sc in next ch-1 sp; * † ch 2, sc in next ch-1 sp, ch 3, sc in next ch-1 sp, ch 2 †; sc in next 2 ch-1 sps; rep from * 4 times more, then rep from † to † once; sc in next ch-1 sp, sk next dc, sc in 3rd ch of turning ch-3. Ch 3, turn.

Row 5: (Shell in next ch-3 sp, dec) 5 times; shell in next ch-3 sp; draw up lp in next ch-2 sp, sk next sc, draw up lp in next sc, YO and draw through all 3 lps on hook; sk next 3 chs, shell in next sc—7 shells. Ch 5, turn.

Row 6: Sc in 2nd ch from hook, in next 3 chs, and in next dc; sc in next ch-1 sp; * † ch 2, sc in next ch-1 sp, ch 3, sc in next ch-1 sp, ch 2 †; sc in next 2 ch-1 sps; rep from * 5 times more, then rep from † to † once; sc in next ch-1 sp, sk next dc, sc in 3rd ch of turning ch-3. Ch 3, turn.

Row 7: (Shell in next ch-3 sp, dec) 6 times; shell in next ch-3 sp; draw up lp in next ch-2 sp, sk next sc, draw up lp in next sc, YO and draw through all 3 lps on hook; sk next 3 chs, shell in next sc—8 shells. Ch 5, turn.

Row 8: Sc in 2nd ch from hook, in next 3 chs, and in next dc; sk next dc, sc in next ch-1 sp; * † ch 2, sc in next ch-1 sp, ch 3, sc in next ch-1 sp, ch 2 †; sc in next 2 ch-1 sps; rep from * 6 times more, then rep from † to † once; sc in next ch-1 sp, sk next dc, sc in 3rd ch of turning ch-3. Ch 3, turn.

Row 9: (Shell in next ch-3 sp, dec) 7 times; shell in next ch-3 sp; draw up lp in next ch-2 sp, sk next sc, draw up lp in next sc, YO and draw through all 3 lps on hook; sk next 3 chs, shell in next sc—9 shells. Ch 5, turn.

Row 10: Sc in 2nd ch from hook, in next 3 chs, and in next dc; sk next dc, sc in next ch-1 sp; * † ch 2, sc in next ch-1 sp, ch 3, sc in next ch-1 sp, ch 2 †; sc in next 2 ch-1 sps; rep from * 7 times more, then rep from † to † once; sc in next ch-1 sp, sk next dc, sc in 3rd ch of turning ch-3. Ch 3, turn.

Row 11: (Shell in next ch-3 sp, dec) 8 times; shell in next ch-3 sp; draw up lp in next ch-2 sp, sk next sc, draw up lp in next sc, YO and draw through all 3 lps on hook; sk next 3 chs, shell in next sc—10 shells. Ch 1, turn.

Row 12: Sc in first dc and in next ch-1 sp; * † ch 2, sc in next ch-1 sp, ch 3, sc in next ch-1 sp, ch 2 †; sc in next 2 ch-1 sps; rep from * 8 times more, then rep from † to † once; sc in next ch-1 sp, sk next dc, sc in 3rd ch of turning ch-3. Ch 3, turn.

Row 13: (Shell in next ch-3 sp, dec) 9 times; shell in next ch-3 sp; sk next ch-2 sp and next sc, dc in next sc. Ch 1, turn.

Row 14: Sc in first dc and in next ch-1 sp; * † ch 2, sc in next ch-1 sp, ch 3, sc in next ch-1 sp, ch 2 †; sc in next 2 ch-1 sps; rep from * 8 times more, then rep from † to † once; sc in next ch-1 sp, sk next dc, sc in 3rd ch of turning ch-3. Ch 3, turn.

Row 15: (Shell in next ch-3 sp, dec) 9 times; shell in next ch-3 sp; sk next ch-2 sp and next sc, dc in next sc. Ch 1, turn.

Rows 16 through 23: Rep Rows 12 and 13 four times more.

Row 24: Rep Row 14.

Row 25: Dc in first sc, (shell in next ch-3 sp, dec) 9 times; shell in next ch-3 sp; sk next ch-2 sp and next sc, dc in next sc. Ch 1, turn.

Row 26: Sc in first dc and in next ch-1 sp, * † ch 2, sc in next ch-1 sp, ch 3, sc in next ch-1 sp, ch 2 †; sc in next 2 ch-1 sps; rep from * 8 times more, then rep from † to † once; sc in next ch-1 sp, sk next dc, sc in next dc and in 3rd ch of turning ch-3. Ch 3, turn.

Row 27: Dc in next sc, (shell in next ch-3 sp, dec) 9 times; shell in next ch-3 sp; sk next ch-2 sp and next sc, dc in next sc. Ch 1, turn.

Row 28: Sc in first dc and in next ch-1 sp; * † ch 2, sc in next ch-1 sp, ch 3, sc in next ch-1 sp, ch 2 †; sc in next 2 ch-1 sps; rep from * 8 times more, then rep from † to † once; sc in next ch-1 sp, sk next dc, sc in next dc and in 3rd ch of turning ch-3. Ch 3, turn.

Row 29: Dc in first sc and in next sc, (shell in next ch-3 sp, dec) 9 times; shell in next ch-3 sp; sk next ch-2 sp and next sc, dc in next sc. Ch 1, turn.

continued on page 101

Bridal Gown

continued from page 100

Row 30: Sc in first dc and in next ch-1 sp; * † ch 2, sc in next ch-1 sp, ch 3, sc in next ch-1 sp, ch 2 †; sc in next 2 ch-1 sps; rep from * 8 times more, then rep from † to † once; sc in next ch-1 sp, sk next 2 dc, sc in next dc and in 3rd ch of turning ch-3. Ch 3, turn.

Row 31: Dc in first sc, ch 1, dc in next sc, (shell in next ch-3 sp, dec) 9 times; shell in next ch-3 sp; sk next ch-2 sp and next sc, dc in next sc. Ch 1, turn.

Row 32: Sc in first dc and in next ch-1 sp; * † ch 2, sc in next ch-1 sp, ch 3, sc in next ch-1 sp, ch 2 †; sc in next 2 ch-1 sps; rep from * 8 times more, then rep from † to † once; sc in next ch-1 sp, sk next dc, sc in next dc, in next ch-1 sp, in next dc, and in 3rd ch of turning ch-3. Ch 4, turn.

Row 33: Dc in first sc, (ch 1, dc in next sc) twice; (shell in next ch-3 sp, dec) 9 times; shell in next ch-3 sp; sk next ch-2 sp and next sc, dc in next sc. Ch 1, turn.

Row 34: Sc in first dc and in next ch-1 sp; * ch 2, sc in next ch-1 sp, ch 3, sc in next ch-1 sp, ch 2, sc in next 2 ch-1 sps; rep from * 9 times more; ch 2, sc in next ch-1 sp, ch 3, sc in sp formed by turning ch-4, ch 2, sc in 3rd ch of same turning ch. Ch 3, turn.

Row 35: (Shell in next ch-3 sp, dec) 10 times; shell in next ch-3 sp; sk next ch-2 sp and next sc, dc in next sc—11 shells. Ch 1, turn.

Row 36: Sc in first dc and in next ch-1 sp; * † ch 2, sc in next ch-1 sp, ch 3, sc in next ch-1 sp, ch 2 †; sc in next 2 ch-1 sps; rep from * 9 times more, then rep from † to † once; sc in next ch-1 sp, sk next dc, sc in 3rd ch of turning ch-3. Ch 3, turn.

Row 37: (Shell in next ch-3 sp, dec) 10 times; shell in next ch-3 sp; sk next ch-2 sp and next sc, dc in next sc. Ch 1, turn.

Note: On following row, back and front pieces will be joined.

Row 38: Sc in first dc and in next ch-1 sp; * † ch 2, sc in next ch-1 sp, ch 3, sc in next ch-1 sp, ch 2 †; sc in next 2 ch-1 sps; rep from * 9 times more, then rep from † to † once; sc in next ch-1 sp, sk next dc, sc in 3rd ch of turning ch-3, ch 15; hold wrong side of front facing you; sc in first dc on front and in next ch-1 sp; ** ch 2, sc in next ch-1 sp, ch 3, sc in next ch-1 sp, ch 2, sc in next 2 ch-1 sps; rep from ** 20 times more;

rep from † to † once; sc in next ch-1 sp, sk next dc, sc in 3rd ch of turning ch-3, ch 15; hold wrong side of right front yoke facing you; sc in first dc on front and in next ch-1 sp; *** ch 2, sc in next ch-1 sp, ch 3, sc in next ch-1 sp, ch 2, sc in next 2 ch-1 sps; rep from *** 9 times more; rep from † to † once; sc in next ch-1 sp, sk next dc, sc in 3rd ch of turning ch-3. Ch 3, turn.

Row 39: (Shell in next ch-3 sp, dec) 10 times; shell in next ch-3 sp; † draw up lp in next ch-2 sp, sk next 2 sc, draw up lp in next ch of next ch-15, YO and draw through all 3 lps on hook; sk next 3 chs, shell in next ch; sk next 5 chs, shell in next ch; sk next 3 chs, draw up lp in next ch, sk next 2 sc, draw up lp in next ch-1 sp, YO and draw through all 3 lps on hook †; (shell in next ch-3 sp, dec) 21 times; shell in next ch-3 sp; rep from † to † once; (shell in next ch-3 sp, dec) 10 times; shell in next ch-3 sp; sk next ch-2 sp and next sc, dc in next sc—48 shells. Ch 1, turn.

Row 40: Sc in first dc, sk next dc, sc in next ch-1 sp; * † ch 2, sc in next ch-1 sp, ch 3, sc in next ch-1 sp, ch 2 †; sc in next 2 ch-1 sps; rep from * 46 times more, then rep from † to † once; sc in next ch-1 sp, sk next dc, sc in 3rd ch of turning ch-3. Ch 3, turn.

Row 41: (Shell in next ch-3 sp, dec) 47 times; shell in next ch-3 sp; sk next ch-2 sp and next sc, dc in next sc. Ch 1, turn.

Rows 42 through 87: Rep Rows 40 and 41 23 times more. At end of Row 87, do not ch 1; join in 3rd ch of turning ch-3 at beg of row.

Note: Remainder of dress is worked in rnds.

Rnd 1: Ch 1, sc in same ch as joining and in next ch-1 sp; * † ch 2, sc in next ch-1 sp, ch 3, sc in next ch-1 sp, ch 2 †; sc in next 2 ch-1 sps; rep from * 46 times more, then rep from † to † once; sc in next ch-1 sp, sk next dc, sc in next dc; join in first sc.

Rnd 2: Ch 3 (counts as a dc on this and following rnds), (shell in next ch-3 sp, dec) 47 times; shell in next ch-3 sp; sk next ch-2 sp and next sc, dc in next sc; join in 3rd ch of beg ch-3.

Rnds 3 and 4: Rep Rnds 1 and 2. At end of Rnd 4, change to next larger size hook.

Rnds 5 through 8: Rep Rnds 1 and 2 twice more. At end of Rnd 8, change to largest size hook.

Rnds 9 through 34: Rep Rnds 1 and 2 thirteen times more.

Rnd 35: Rep Rnd 1.

Rnd 36: Ch 3; * in ch-3 sp of next shell work (dc, ch 1) 6 times; dc in same sp—large shell made; dec; rep from * 46 times more; in ch-3 sp of next shell work (dc, ch 1) 6 times; dc in same sp—large shell made; sk next ch-2 sp and next sc, dc in next sc; join in 3rd ch of beg ch-3.

Rnd 37: Ch 1, sc in same ch as joining and in next ch-1 sp; * † (ch 2, sc in next ch-1 sp,) twice; ch 3, (sc in next ch-1 sp, ch 2) twice †; sc in next 2 ch-1 sps; rep from * 46 times more, then rep from † to † once; sc in next ch-1 sp, sk next dc, sc in next dc; join in first sc.

Rnds 38 and 111: Rep Rnds 36 and 37 thirty-seven times more.

Rnd 112: Rep Rnd 36.

Finish off and weave in all ends.

Sleeve (make 2)
With smallest size hook, ch 47.

Row 1 (right side): In 7th ch from hook work shell; * † sk next 5 chs, shell in next ch; rep from * 5 times more; sk next 3 chs, dc in next ch—7 shells. Ch 1, turn.

Row 2: 2 sc in first dc, sk next dc, sc in next ch-1 sp; * † ch 2, sc in next ch-1 sp, ch 3, sc in next ch-1 sp, ch 2 †; sc in next 2 ch-1 sps; rep from * 5 times more, then rep from † to † once; sc in next ch-1 sp, sk next dc, 2 sc in next ch of beg 6 skipped chs. Ch 4 (counts as first dc and ch-1 sp on following rows), turn.

Row 3: Dc in first sc, ch 1, dc in next sc, (shell in next ch-3 sp, dec) 6 times; shell in next ch-3 sp; sk next ch-2 sp and next sc, dc in next sc, ch 1, in next sc work (dc, ch 1, dc). Ch 1, turn.

Row 4: 2 sc in first dc; (sc in next ch-1 sp and in next dc) twice; sk next dc, sc in next ch-1 sp; * † ch 2, sc in next ch-1 sp, ch 3, sc in next ch-1 sp, ch 2 †; sc in next 2 ch-1 sps; rep from * 5 times more, then rep from † to † once; sc in next ch-1 sp, sk next dc, sc in next dc, in next ch-1 sp, in next dc, and in sp formed by turning ch-4; 2 sc in 3rd ch of same turning ch. Ch 3, turn.

Row 5: Dc in first sc and in next 5 sc, (shell in next ch-3 sp, dec) 6 times; shell in next ch-3 sp; sk next ch-2 sp and next sc, dc in next 5 sc, 2 dc in next sc. Ch 1, turn.

Row 6: Sc in first dc, ch 2, sk next dc, sc in next dc, ch 3, sk next dc, sc in next dc, ch 2,

continued on page 102

sk next sc, sc in next dc, sk next dc, sc in next ch-1 sp; * † ch 2, sc in next ch-1 sp, ch 3, sc in next ch-1 sp, ch 2 †; sc in next 2 ch-1 sps; rep from * 5 times more, then rep from † to † once; sc in next ch-1 sp, sk next dc, sc in next dc, ch 2, sk next dc, sc in next dc, ch 3, sk next dc, sc in next dc, ch 2, sk next dc, sc in 3rd ch of turning ch-3. Ch 4, turn.

Row 7: Dc in first sc, (shell in next ch-3 sp, dec) 8 times; shell in next ch-3 sp; sk next ch-2 sp, in next sc work (dc, ch 1, dc). Ch 1, turn.

Row 8: Sc in first dc, in next ch-1 sp, and in next dc; sk next dc, sc in next ch-1 sp; * † ch 2, sc in next ch-1 sp, ch 3, sc in next ch-1 sp, ch 2 †; sc in next 2 ch-1 sps; rep from * 7 times more, then rep from † to † once; sc in next ch-1 sp, sk next dc, sc in next dc, in sp formed by turning ch-4, and in 3rd ch of same turning ch. Ch 4, turn.

Row 9: Dc in first sc and in next 2 sc; (shell in next ch-3 sp, dec) 8 times; shell in next ch-3 sp; sk next ch-2 sp and next sc, dc in next 2 sc, in next sc work (dc, ch 1, dc). Ch 1, turn.

Row 10: 2 sc in first dc; sc in next ch-1 sp and in next 3 dc, sk next dc, sc in next ch-1 sp; * † ch 2, sc in next ch-1 sp, ch 3, sc in next ch-1 sp, ch 2 †; sc in next 2 ch-1 sps; rep from * 7 times more, then rep from † to † once; sc in next ch-1 sp, sk next dc, sc in next 3 dc and in sp formed by turning ch-4; 2 sc in 3rd ch of same turning ch. Ch 3, turn.

Row 11: Sk first sc, dc in next 5 sc, (shell in next ch-3 sp, dec) 8 times; shell in next ch-3 sp; sk next ch-2 sp and next sc, dc in next 6 sc. Ch 1, turn.

Row 12: Sc in first 6 dc, sk next dc, sc in next ch-1 sp; * † ch 2, sc in next ch-1 sp, ch 3, sc in next ch-1 sp, ch 2 †; sc in next 2 ch-1 sps; rep from * 7 times more, then rep from † to † once; sc in next ch-1 sp, sk next dc, sc in next 5 dc and in 3rd ch of turning ch-3. Ch 4, turn.

Row 13: Dc in first sc and in next 5 sc, (shell in next ch-3 sp, dec) 8 times; shell in next ch-3 sp; sk next ch-2 sp and next sc, dc in next 5 sc, in next sc work (dc, ch 1, dc). Ch 1, turn.

Row 14: Sc in first dc and in next ch-1 sp, ch 2, sk next dc, sc in next dc, ch 3, sk next dc, sc in next dc, ch 2, sk next dc, sc in next

dc, sk next dc, sc in next ch-1 sp; * † ch 2, sc in next ch-1 sp, ch 3, sc in next ch-1 sp, ch 2 †; sc in next 2 ch-1 sps; rep from * 7 times more, then rep from † to † once; sc in next ch-1 sp, sk next dc, sc in next dc, ch 2, sk next dc, sc in next dc, ch 3, sk next dc, sc in next dc, ch 2, sk next dc, sc in sp formed by turning ch-4 and in 3rd ch of same turning ch. Ch 3, turn.

Row 15: Sk first 2 sc, (shell in next ch-3 sp, dec) 10 times; shell in next ch-3 sp; sk next ch-2 sp and next sc, dc in next sc. Ch 1, turn.

Row 16: 2 sc in first dc; sk next dc, sc in next ch-1 sp; * † ch 2, sc in next ch-1 sp, ch 3, sc in next ch-1 sp, ch 2 †; sc in next 2 ch-1 sps; rep from * 9 times more, then rep from † to † once; sc in next ch-1 sp, sk next dc, 2 sc in 3rd ch of turning ch-3. Ch 4, turn.

Row 17: Dc in first sc and in next sc, (shell in next ch-3 sp, dec) 10 times; shell in next ch-3 sp; sk next ch-2 sp and next sc, dc in next sc, in next sc work (dc, ch 1, dc). Ch 1, turn.

Row 18: 2 sc in first dc; sc in next ch-1 sp and in next 2 dc, sk next dc, sc in next ch-1 sp; * † ch 2, sc in next ch-1 sp, ch 3, sc in next ch-1 sp, ch 2 †; sc in next 2 ch-1 sps; rep from * 9 times more, then rep from † to † once; sc in next ch-1 sp, sk next dc, sc in next 2 dc and in sp formed by turning ch-4, 2 sc in 3rd ch of same turning ch. Ch 3, turn.

Row 19: Sk first sc, dc in next 4 sc, (shell in next ch-3 sp, dec) 10 times; shell in next ch-3 sp; sk next ch-2 sp and next sc, dc in next 5 sc. Ch 1, turn.

Row 20: Sc in first 5 dc, sk next dc, sc in next ch-1 sp; * † ch 2, sc in next ch-1 sp, ch 3, sc in next ch-1 sp, ch 2 †; sc in next 2 ch-1 sps; rep from * 9 times more, then rep from † to † once; sc in next ch-1 sp, sk next dc, sc in next 4 dc and in 3rd ch of turning ch-3. Ch 4, turn.

Row 21: Dc in first sc and in next 4 sc, (shell in next ch-3 sp, dec) 10 times; shell in next ch-3 sp; sk next ch-2 sp and next sc, dc in next 4 sc, in next sc work (dc, ch 1, dc). Ch 1, turn.

Row 22: Sc in first dc, ch 2, sk next ch-1 sp, sc in next dc, ch 3, sk next dc, sc in next dc, ch 2, sk next dc, sc in next dc, sk next dc, sc in next ch-1 sp; * † ch 2, sc in next ch-1 sp, ch 3, sc in next ch-1 sp, ch 2 †; sc in next 2 ch-1 sps; rep from * 9 times more,

then rep from † to † once; sc in next ch-1 sp, sk next dc, sc in next dc, ch 2, sk next dc, sc in next dc, ch 3, sk next dc, sc in next dc, ch 2, sk next ch of turning ch-4, sc in next ch. Ch 4, turn.

Row 23: Dc in first sc, (shell in next ch-3 sp, dec) 12 times; shell in next ch-3 sp; sk next ch-2 sp, in next sc work (dc, ch 1, dc). Ch 1, turn.

Row 24: Sc in first dc, in next ch-1 sp, and in next dc; sk next dc, sc in next ch-1 sp; * † ch 2, sc in next ch-1 sp, ch 3, sc in next ch-1 sp, ch 2 †; sc in next 2 ch-1 sps; rep from * 11 times more, then rep from † to † once; sc in next ch-1 sp, sk next dc, sc in next dc, in sp formed by turning ch-4 and in 3rd ch of same turning ch. Ch 3, turn.

Row 25: Dc in first sc and in next 2 sc, (shell in next ch-3 sp, dec) 12 times; shell in next ch-3 sp; sk next ch-1 sp and next sc, dc in next 2 sc, 2 dc in next sc. Ch 1, turn.

Row 26: Sc in first 4 dc, sk next dc, sc in next ch-1 sp; * † ch 2, sc in next ch-1 sp, ch 3, sc in next ch-1 sp, ch 2 †; sc in next 2 ch-1 sps; rep from * 11 times more, then rep from † to † once; sc in next ch-1 sp, sk next dc, sc in next 3 dc and in 3rd ch of turning ch-3. Ch 3, turn.

Row 27: Dc in first sc and in next 3 sc, (shell in next ch-3 sp, dec) 12 times; shell in next ch-3 sp; sk next ch-2 sp and next sc, dc in next 3 sc, 2 dc in next sc. Ch 1, turn.

Row 28: 2 sc in first dc; sc in next 4 dc, sk next dc, sc in next ch-1 sp; * † ch 2, sc in next ch-1 sp, ch 3, sc in next ch-1 sp, ch 2 †; sc in next 2 ch-1 sps; rep from * 11 times more, then rep from † to † once; sc in next ch-1 sp, sk next dc, sc in next 4 dc, 2 sc in 3rd ch of turning ch-3. Ch 3, turn.

Row 29: Dc in first sc and in next 5 sc, (shell in next ch-3 sp, dec) 12 times; shell in next ch-3 sp; sk next ch-2 sp and next sc, dc in next 5 sc, 2 dc in next sc. Ch 1, turn.

Row 30: Sc in first dc, ch 2, sk next dc, sc in next dc, ch 3, sk next dc, sc in next dc, ch 2, sk next dc, sc in next dc, sk next dc, sc in next ch-1 sp; * † ch 2, sc in next ch-1 sp, ch 3, sc in next ch-1 sp, ch 2 †; sc in next 2 ch-1 sps; rep from * 11 times more, then rep from † to † once; sc in next ch-1 sp, sk next dc, sc in next dc, ch 2, sk next dc, sc in next dc, ch 3, sk next dc, sc in next dc, ch 2, sk next dc, sc in 3rd ch of turning ch-3. Ch 3, turn.

continued on page 103

Bridal Gown
continued from page 102

Row 31: Dc in first sc, (shell in next ch-3 sp, dec) 14 times; shell in next ch-3 sp; sk next ch-2 sp and next sc, 2 dc in next sc. Ch 1, turn.

Row 32: 2 sc in first dc; sc in next dc, sk next dc, sc in next ch-1 sp; * † ch 2, sc in next ch-1 sp, ch 3, sc in next ch-1 sp, ch 2 †; sc in next 2 ch-1 sps; rep from * 13 times more, then rep from † to † once; sc in next ch-1 sp, sk next dc, sc in next dc, 2 sc in 3rd ch of turning ch-3. Ch 4, turn.

Row 33: Dc in first sc and in next 2 sc, (shell in next ch-3 sp, dec) 14 times; shell in next ch-3 sp; sk next ch-2 sp and next sc, dc in next 2 sc, in next sc work (dc, ch 1, dc). Ch 1, turn.

Row 34: 2 sc in first dc; sc in next ch-1 sp and in next 3 sc, sk next dc, sc in next ch-1 sp; * † ch 2, sc in next ch-1 sp, ch 3, sc in next ch-1 sp, ch 2 †; sc in next 2 ch-1 sps; rep from * 13 times more, then rep from † to † once; sc in next ch-1 sp, sk next dc, sc in next 3 dc, and in sp formed by turning ch-4; 2 sc in 3rd ch of same turning ch. Ch 3, turn.

Row 35: Dc in first sc and in next 5 sc, (shell in next ch-3 sp, dec) 14 times; shell in next ch-3 sp; sk next ch-2 sp and next sc, dc in next 5 sc, 2 dc in next sc. Ch 1, turn.

Row 36: Sc in first dc, ch 2, sk next dc, sc in next dc, ch 3, sk next dc, sc in next dc, ch 2, sk next dc, sc in next dc, sk next dc, sc in next ch-1 sp; * † ch 2, sc in next ch-1 sp, ch 3, sc in next ch-1 sp, ch 2 †; sc in next 2 ch-1 sps; rep from * 13 times more, then rep from † to † once; sc in next ch-1 sp, sk next dc, sc in next dc, ch 2, sk next dc, sc in next dc, ch 3, sk next dc, sc in next dc, ch 2, sk next dc, sc in 3rd ch of turning ch-3. Ch 3, turn.

Row 37: Dc in first sc, (shell in next ch-3 sp, dec) 16 times; shell in next ch-3 sp; sk next ch-2 sp, 2 dc in next sc. Ch 1, turn.

Row 38: 2 sc in first dc; sc in next dc, sk next dc, sc in next ch-1 sp; * † ch 2, sc in next ch-1 sp, ch 3, sc in next ch-1 sp, ch 2 †; sc in next 2 ch-1 sps; rep from * 15 times more, then rep from † to † once; sc in next ch-1 sp, sk next dc, sc in next dc, 2 sc in 3rd ch of turning ch-3. Ch 2, turn.

Row 39: Sk first sc, dc in next 2 sc, (shell in next ch-3 sp, dec) 16 times; shell in next ch-3 sp; sk next ch-2 sp and next sc, dc in next sc, keeping last lp of each dc on hook, dc in next 2 sc, YO and draw through all 3 lps on hook. Ch 1, turn.

Row 40: Sc in first 2 sts, sk next dc, sc in next ch-1 sp; * † ch 2, sc in next ch-1 sp, ch 3, sc in next ch-1 sp, ch 2 †; sc in next 2 ch-1 sps; rep from * 15 times more, then rep from † to † once; sc in next ch-1 sp, sk next dc, sc in next 2 dc. Ch 3, turn.

Row 41: (Shell in next ch-3 sp, dec) 16 times; shell in next ch-3 sp; sk next ch-2 sp and next 2 sc, dc in next sc. Ch 1, turn.

Row 42: Sc in first dc, sk next dc, sc in next ch-1 sp; * † ch 2, sc in next ch-1 sp, ch 3, sc in next ch-1 sp, ch 2 †; sc in next 2 ch-1 sps; rep from * 15 times more, then rep from † to † once; sc in next ch-1 sp, sk next dc, sc in 3rd ch of turning ch-3. Ch 3, turn.

Row 43: (Shell in next ch-3 sp, dec) 16 times; shell in next ch-3 sp; sk next ch-2 sp and next 2 sc, dc in next sc.

Finish off and weave in all ends.

Assembly
With tapestry needle and thread, sew shoulder seams. Sew sleeves to bodice, matching shoulder seams to centers of sleeves. Sew sleeve seams from underarm to sleeve edge.

Edgings

Neckline Edging
Hold dress with right side of left back opening facing you; join thread in side of Row 10 of left back yoke.

Rnd 1: Ch 1, sc in same sp as joining; working along neckline, down right back opening and up left back opening, sc evenly around, keeping edges flat; join in first sc.

Note: Following rnd is worked from top of left back opening to top of right back opening only.

Rnd 2: Ch 1, sc in same sc as joining; * sk next 2 sc, shell in next sc; sk next 2 sc, sc in next sc; rep from * to top of right back opening, adjusting last rep as necessary. Finish off, leaving rem sts unworked.

Weave in ends.

Finishing
Step 1: Sew buttons evenly spaces along edge of right back opening, having first button at neck edge.

Step 2: With sewing needle and thread, sew 4mm beads to Rows 1 through 10 bodice, having one bead in ch-3 sp at base of each shell. In same manner, sew beads to shells around neckline and shells on sleeves. Sew 5mm beads to Rnds 111 and 112 of skirt.

Headpiece
continued from page 79

Finish off and weave in all ends.

Edging
With smallest size hook, ch 143.

Rnd 1 (right side)**:** In 7th ch from hook (beg 6 skipped chs count as a ch-3 sp and a dc) work (dc, ch 1) 4 times; dc in same ch—shell made; † sk next 5 chs, in next ch work (dc, ch 1) 4 times; dc in same ch—shell made †; rep from † to † 21 times more; sk next 3 chs, in next ch work (dc, ch 1) 4 times; dc in same ch—shell made; working on opposite side of beg ch in unused lp at base of shells, †† in next unused lp work (dc, ch 1) 4 times; dc in same lp—shell made ††; rep from †† to †† 21 times more; in next ch of beg 6 skipped chs work (dc, ch 1) 3 times; ch 1, sk next 4 skipped chs; join in next ch—ending shell made—46 shells.

Rnd 2: Sl st in next dc and in next ch-1 sp, ch 1, sc in same sp; * † ch 2, sc in next ch-1 sp, ch 3, sc in next ch-1 sp, ch 2 †; sc in next 2 ch-1 sps; rep from * 44 times more, then rep from † to † once; sc in next ch-1 sp, sk next dc; join in first sc.

Finish off and weave in all ends.

Finishing
Step 1: Following Starching instructions on page 216, starch piece.

Step 2: Glue center piece to center of hat. Glue one 4mm bead to center of each double shell.

Step 3: Glue edging along edge of hat, beginning at center back and overlapping ends if necessary. Glue one 4mm bead to center of each double shell.

Step 4: Glue two pearl sprays to each side of center back, having ends under crocheted edging.

Cake Topper

continued from page 82

Rnd 3: Ch 3, dc in same ch as joining; dc in next dc, (2 dc in next dc, dc in next dc) 19 times; join in 3rd ch of beg ch-3—60 dc.

Rnd 4: Ch 3, dc in each dc; join in 3rd ch of beg ch-3.

Rnd 5: Ch 3, dc in same ch as joining; dc in next dc, (2 dc in next dc, dc in next dc) 29 times; join in 3rd ch of beg ch-3—90 dc.

Rnd 6: Ch 3, dc in next 12 dc, dec over next 2 dc [to work dec: (YO, draw up lp in next dc, YO and draw through 2 lps on hook) twice; YO and draw through all 3 lps on hook—dec made]; * dc in next 13 dc, dec over next 2 dc; rep from * 4 times more; join in 3rd ch of beg ch-3—84 dc.

Rnd 7: Ch 5 (counts as a dc and a ch-2 sp on this and following rnds), sk next dc; * dc in next dc, ch 2, sk next dc; rep from * 40 times more; join in 3rd ch of beg ch-5.

Rnd 8: Ch 3, dc in each ch and in each dc; join in 3rd ch of turning ch-3—126 dc.

Rnd 9: Ch 6 (counts as a trc and a ch-2 sp), sk next dc; * † dtrc (see Pattern Stitches on page 81) in next dc; ch 2, sk next dc, [tr trc (see Pattern Stitches on page 81) in next dc, ch 2, sk next dc] 4 times; dtrc in next dc, ch 2, sk next dc †; trc in next dc, ch 2, sk next dc; rep from * 7 times more, then rep from † to † once; join in 3rd ch of beg ch-6.

Rnd 10: Ch 1, slide pearl up to hook, ch 2—beg pearl dc made; working in each ch and in each st, * dc in next 5 sts; YO, draw up lp in next st, slide pearl up to hook, (YO and draw through 2 lps on hook) twice—pearl dc made; rep from * 30 times more; dc in next 5 sts; join in 3rd ch of beg pearl dc—32 pearl dc.

Finish off and weave in ends.

Arch

Note: Before beginning, string 8 pearls onto white crochet thread.

Ch 100; join to form a ring, being careful not to twist sts.

Rnd 1 (right side): Ch 1, sc in same ch as joining and in each rem ch; join in first sc—100 sc.

Rnd 2: Ch 5 (counts as a dc and a ch-2 sp),

sk next sc, dc in next sc, (ch 2, sk next sc, dc in next sc) 25 times; ch 3, sk next sc, trc in next sc, ch 3, sk next sc, dtrc in next sc, (ch 3, sk next sc, tr trc in next sc) 4 times; ch 3, sk next sc, dtrc in next sc, ch 3, sk next sc, trc in next sc, ch 3, sk next sc, (dc in next sc, ch 2, sk next sc) 15 times; join in 3rd ch of beg ch-5.

Rnd 3: Ch 1, sc in same ch as joining and in next 2 chs; (sc in next dc and in next 2 chs) 25 times; sc in next dc, hdc in next ch, dc in next 2 chs, pearl dc in next trc; (dc in next 3 chs, pearl dc in next st) 7 times; dc in next 2 chs, hdc in next ch, (sc in next dc and in next 2 chs) 15 times; join in first sc. Finish off and weave in ends.

Bell (make 2)

Note: Before beginning, string 6 pearls onto white crochet thread.

Ch 4, join to form a ring.

Rnd 1: Ch 3 (counts as a dc on this and following rnd), 11 dc in ring; join in 3rd ch of beg ch-3—12 dc.

Rnd 2: Ch 8 (counts as a tr trc and a ch-1 sp), (tr trc in next dc, ch 1) 11 times; join in 7th ch of beg ch-8.

Rnd 3: Ch 3, dc in next ch, pearl dc in next tr trc; (dc in next ch, in next tr trc, and in next ch, pearl dc in next tr trc) 5 times; dc in next ch; join in 3rd ch of beg ch-3.

Finish off and weave in ends.

Bride

Head:

Note: Before beginning, string 16 pearls onto white crochet thread.

Ch 5, join to form a ring.

Rnd 1: Ch 3 (counts as a dc on this and following rnds), 21 dc in ring; join in 3rd ch of beg ch-3—22 dc.

Rnd 2: Ch 2 (counts as an hdc on this and following rnds), hdc in each dc; join in 2nd ch of beg ch-2.

Rnd 3: Ch 2, hdc in each hdc; join in 2nd ch of beg ch-2.

Rnds 4 through 7: Rep Rnd 3.

Insert a Styrofoam® ball.

Rnd 8: Ch 2, sk next hdc, (hdc in next hdc, sk next hdc) 10 times; join in 2nd ch of beg ch-2—11 hdc.

Body:

Rnd 1: Ch 3, dc in same ch as joining; 2 dc in

each hdc; join in 3rd ch of beg ch-3—22 dc.

Rnd 2: Ch 6 (counts as a trc and a ch-2 sp), sk next dc, (trc in next dc, ch 2, sk next dc) 10 times; join in 4th ch of beg ch-6.

Rnd 3: Ch 3, (dc in next 2 chs and in next trc) 10 times; dec over next 2 chs [to work dec: (YO, draw up lp in next ch, YO and draw through 2 lps on hook) twice; YO and draw through all 3 lps on hook—dec made]; join in 3rd ch of beg ch-3—32 dc.

Rnd 4: Ch 1, sc in same ch as joining; ch 1, LK (see Pattern Stitches on page 81); sk next 3 dc, (sc in next dc, ch 1, LK, sk next 3 dc) 7 times; join in first sc—8 LKs.

Rnd 5: Ch 1, sc in same sc; ch 5, (sc in next sc, ch 5) 7 times; join in first sc.

Rnd 6: Sl st in next 2 chs of next ch-5 sp, ch 1, in same sp work (sc, ch 3, sc—picot made); ch 5; * in next ch-5 sp work (sc, ch 3, sc); ch 5; rep from * 6 times more; join in first sc.

Rnd 7: Working behind next picot, sl st in next 2 chs of next ch-5 sp, ch 1, sc in same ch; 3 hdc in next ch; sc in next ch, ch 3; * sk next ch, next picot, and first ch of next ch-5 sp, sc in next ch, 3 hdc in next ch; sc in next ch, ch 3; rep from * 6 times more; join in first sc.

Rnd 8: Sl st in BL of next 2 hdc, ch 9 (counts as a tr trc and a ch-2 sp), tr trc in next ch-3 sp, ch 2; * sk next hdc, tr trc in next hdc, ch 2, tr trc in next ch-3 sp, ch 2; rep from * 6 times more; join in 7th ch of beg ch-9—16 tr trc.

Rnd 9: Ch 1, slip pearl up close to hook, ch 2—beg pearl dc made; dc in next 2 chs; * [YO, draw up lp in next tr trc, slide pearl up to hook, (YO and draw through 2 lps on hook) twice—pearl dc made]; dc in next 2 chs; rep from * 14 times more; join in 3rd ch of beg pearl dc.

Rnd 10: Ch 1, sc in same ch as joining; ch 1, LK; sk next 2 dc; * sc in next dc, ch 1, LK; sk next 2 dc; rep from * 14 times more; join in first sc. Finish off.

Sleeve (make 2):
Ch 4.

Rnd 1: 11 dc in 4th ch from hook (3 skipped chs count as a dc); join in 3rd ch of beg 3 skipped chs—12 dc.

Rnd 2: Ch 3 (counts as a dc on this and following rnds), dc in each dc; join in 3rd ch of beg ch-3.

continued on page 105

Cake Topper

continued from page 104

Stuff with cotton.

Rnd 3: Ch 1, sc in same ch as joining; sk next dc, (sc in next dc, sk next dc) 5 times; join in first sc—6 sc.

Rnd 4: Ch 3, dc in each sc; join in 3rd ch of beg ch-3.

Rnd 5: Ch 3, dc in each dc; join in 3rd ch of beg ch-3.

Rnds 6 and 7: Rep Rnd 5.

Finish off and weave in all ends.

Groom

Head:

Ch 5, join to form a ring.

Rnds 1 through 8: Rep Rnds 1 through 8 of Bride's Head on page 104.

Body:

Rnd 1: Ch 3, dc in same ch as joining; 2 dc in each hdc; join in 3rd ch of beg ch-3—22 dc.

Rnd 2: Ch 3, dc in same ch as joining and in each dc; join in 3rd ch of beg ch-3.

Rnds 3 and 4: Rep Rnd 2.

Rnd 5: Ch 1, sc in same ch as joining and in each dc; join in first sc. Finish off.

Sleeve (make 2):

Ch 4.

Rnd 1: 7 dc in 4th ch from hook (beg 3 skipped chs count as a dc); join in 3rd ch of beg 3 skipped chs—8 dc.

Rnd 2: Ch 3, dc in each dc; join in 3rd ch of beg ch-3.

Rnds 3 through 5: Rep Rnd 2. Finish off.

Leg (make 2):

Ch 4.

Rnd 1: 9 dc in 4th ch from hook (beg 3 skipped chs count as a dc); join in 3rd ch of beg 3 skipped chs—10 dc.

Rnd 2: Ch 3, dc in each dc and in 3rd ch of beg ch-3.

Rnds 3 through 7: Rep Rnd 2.

Rnd 8: Ch 1, sc in same ch as joining and in each dc; join in first sc.

Finish off and weave in all ends.

Hat:

Ch 4, join to form a ring.

Rnd 1: Ch 3 (counts as a dc on this and following rnds), 17 dc in ring; join in 3rd ch of beg ch-3—18 dc.

Rnd 2: Ch 3, working in BLs only, dc in each dc; join in 3rd ch of beg ch-3.

Rnd 3: Ch 3, dc in each dc; join in 3rd ch of beg ch-3.

Rnd 4: Ch 3, dc in same ch as joining; working in BLs only, 2 dc in each dc; join in 3rd ch of beg ch-3.

Finish off and weave in ends.

Finishing

Step 1: Following Starching and Blocking instructions on page 216, starch and block pieces as follows:

> **base and arch**—block flat.
>
> **bells**—shape over finger; reshape as bells dry.
>
> **bride**—block body over 6" cone; block sleeves over plastic straws.
>
> **groom**—block body over perscription bottle or lipstick tube; block sleeves and legs over plastic straws; block hat over bottle cap.

Step 2: For hair, cut one hundred 5" strands of ecru crochet thread. Apply a thin line of glue to top of each head, about 1" in length. Lay 50 strands across top of each head over glue; spread strands out evenly to cover back of head. Trim as desired.

Step 3: For base, cut 14" length of ribbon; with tapestry needle, weave in and out of Rnd 7, beginning and ending on wrong side. Glue 8 ribbon bows with pearls evenly spaced around Rnd 8.

Step 4: For arch, cut 18" length of ribbon; with tapestry needle, weave in and out of Rnd 2, beginning and ending on wrong side opposite pearls; tie ends into bow. Cut 8" length of ribbon; tie into bow; referring to photo for placement, glue bow to top of arch above pearls.

Step 5: For bells, referring to photo for placement, glue one ribbon bow with pearl to each bell; glue bells to arch. Glue arch to base.

Step 6: For bride, referring to photo for placement, glue sleeves to body. Cut tulle into an oval, 3" x 4". Glue oval to bride's head. For headpiece, cut 2" length of fused pearls; glue pearls to veil in a circle. Gather tulle scrap to form bouquet; glue to hold. Cut 4" length of fused pearls; fold; glue to lower edge of tulle bouquet; glue 4 pearls at random on bouquet. Glue bouquet and sleeve ends together.

Step 7: For groom, cut 1" length of ribbon for tie; gather in center and glue to body beneath head. Cut two 1" lengths of ribbon; glue one length around lower edge of each sleeve. Cut 3" length of ribbon; glue around lower edge of body. Cut 3" length of ribbon; fold lengthwise; glue around brim of hat, overlapping ends to form tie. Referring to photo for placement, glue sleeves, legs, and hat to groom.

Garter

continued from page 82

sc, in next ch-5 sp work (sc, 2 hdc, dc, 2 hdc, sc); rep from * 12 times more; join in first sc.

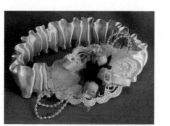

Finish off and weave in ends.

Finishing

Step 1: Following Starching instructions on page 216, starch crocheted piece.

Step 2: Make circle with pink ribbon and glue ends together. Pinch circle in half and glue to center of crocheted piece.

Step 3: Make bow with fused pearls with two 2" loops on each side. Glue bow to top of ribbon.

Step 4: Cut tulle in half. Gather one end of each piece and glue to center of bow over loops. Glue floral spray over tulle ends.

Step 5: To make garter, cut two 26" lengths of white satin ribbon. Place lengths with wrong sides together and sew a scant 1/4" seam on both long sides of ribbon.

Step 6: Pull elastic through ribbon, gathering ribbon. To anchor ends, sew across each end through all thicknesses. Sew ends of garter together with a 1/4" seam. Adjust gathers.

Step 7: Sew or glue crocheted piece to garter over seam.

Pansy Bedspread

continued from page 61

Pansy Edging:

Hold joined pansies with right side facing you; join floral color in first ch-4 sp of first large petal of any pansy; ch 1, sc in same sp; * † ch 3, (sc in next ch-1 sp, ch 3) 11 times; in next ch-4 sp work (sc, ch 3) twice; sk next sc, sc in next sc, ch 3, in next ch-4 sp work (sc, ch 3) twice; (sc in next ch-1 sp, ch 3) 11 times; sc in next dtrc, ch 1 †; sc in ch-4 sp on next large petal of next pansy; rep from * 6 times more, then rep from † to † once; join in first sc.

Finish off and weave in ends.

Center:

With ecru, ch 5; join to form a ring.

Rnd 1 (right side): Ch 1, 8 sc in ring; join in first sc.

Rnd 2: Ch 8 (counts as a trc and a ch 4), sl st in 4th ch from hook—picot made; trc in same sc; * † ch 4, sl st in 4th ch from hook—picot made; in next sc work (trc, ch 4, sl st in 4th ch from hook—picot made; trc); ch 4, sl st in 4th ch from hook—picot made †; in next sc work (trc, ch 4, sl st in 4th ch from hook—picot made; trc); rep from * twice more, then rep from † to † once; join in 4th ch of beg ch-8.

Rnd 3: Ch 7 (counts as a dc and a ch-4 sp); * sk next picot, dc in next trc, ch 4; rep from * 14 times more; join in 3rd ch of beg ch-7. Finish off.

Rnd 4: Join green in any ch-4 sp; ch 1, in same sp work (2 sc, picot, 2 sc); ch 7, sl st in 4th ch from hook—ch-7 picot made; ch 3, sl st in 6th dc of unjoined small petal

of any pansy; * † ch 7, sl st in 4th ch from hook—ch-7 picot made; sl st in base of last picot made, ch 3, in next ch-4 sp work (2 sc, picot, 2 sc); (ch 7, sl st in 4th ch from hook—ch-7 picot made) twice; ch 3, sl st in joining between pansies; ch 7, sl st in 4th ch from hook—ch-7 picot made; sl st in base of 2nd picot made; ch 7, sl st in 4th ch from hook—ch-7 picot made; sl st in base of first picot made; ch 3 †; in next ch-4 sp work (2 sc, picot; 2 sc); ch 7, sl st in 4th ch from hook—ch-7 picot made; ch 3, sl st in 6th dc of unjoined small petal of next pansy; rep from * 6 times more, then rep from † to † once; join in first sc.

Finish off and weave in all ends.

Outside Border:

Hold piece with right side facing you; join ecru in first ch-3 sp to left of joining of any two pansies.

Rnd 1: Ch 7 (counts as a dc and a ch-4 sp), sk next 2 ch-3 sps; * † (dc in next ch-3 sp, ch 4, sk next 2 ch-3 sps) twice; dc in next ch-3 sp, ch 4, sk next 9 ch-3 sps, dc in next ch-3 sp, (ch 4, sk next 2 ch-3 sps, dc in next ch-3 sp) 3 times †; dc in next ch-3 sp on next petal, ch 4, sk next 2 ch-3 sps; rep from * 6 times more, then rep from † to † once; join in 3rd ch of beg ch-7.

Rnd 2: Sl st in next 4 chs, in next dc, and in next ch-4 sp; ch 1, 6 sc in same sp and in each of next 6 ch-4 sps; * † ch 5, turn; with wrong side facing you, sk first 11 sc, sl st in next sc, ch 1, turn; with right side facing you, 7 sc in ch-5 sp just made; sl st in sc at base of same ch-5 †; 6 sc in each of next 7 ch-4 sps; rep from * 5 times more, then rep from † to † once; 6 sc in each of next 6 ch-4 sps; join in first sc.

Rnd 3: Sl st in next 3 sc, ch 1, sc in same sc as last sl st made and in next 24 sc; * † ch 7, sc in 4th sc of next 7-sc group, (ch 7, sc in 4th sc of next 6-sc group) twice; ch 3, in 4th sc of next 6-sc group work (trc, ch 7, trc); ch 3, sc in 4th sc of next 6-sc group, (ch 7, sc in 4th sc of next 6-sc group, ch 7, sc in 4th sc of next 7-sc group, ch 7 †; sk next 2 sc of same 7-sc group and next 3 sc of next 6-sc group, sc in next 25 sc; rep from * twice more, then rep from † to † once; join in first sc.

Rnd 4: Sl st in next 3 sc, ch 1, sc in same sc as last sl st made and in next 18 sc; * † (ch 7, sc in next ch-7 sp) 3 times; ch 3,

sk next ch-3 sp, in next ch-7 sp work [CL (see Pattern Stitches on page 61), ch 1, CL]; ch 5; in same sp work (CL, ch 1, CL); ch 3, sk next ch-3 sp, (sc in next ch-7 sp, ch 7) 3 times †; sk next 3 sc, sc in next 19 sc; rep from * twice more, then rep from † to † once; join in first sc.

Rnd 5: Sl st in next 3 sc, ch 1, sc in same sc as last sl st made and in next 12 sc; * † (ch 7, sc in next ch-7 sp) 3 times; ch 3, CL in next ch-3 sp; ch 1, CL in next ch-1 sp; ch 1, in next ch-5 sp work (CL, ch 1, CL); ch 5, in same sp work (CL, ch 1) twice; CL in next ch-1 sp; ch 1, CL in next ch-3 sp; ch 3, (sc in next ch-7 sp, ch 7) 3 times †; sk next 3 sc, sc in next 13 sc; rep from * twice more, then rep from † to † once; join in first sc.

Rnd 6: Sl st in next 3 sc, ch 1, sc in same sc as last sl st made and in next 6 sc; * † (ch 7, sc in next ch-7 sp) 3 times; ch 3, CL in next ch-3 sp; ch 1, (CL in next ch-1 sp, ch 1) 3 times; in next ch-5 sp work (CL, ch 1, CL); ch 5, in same sp work (CL, ch 1) twice; (CL in next ch-1 sp, ch 1) 3 times; CL in next ch-3 sp; ch 3, (sc in next ch-7 sp, ch 7) 3 times †; sk next 3 sc, sc in next 7 sc; rep from * twice more, then rep from † to † once; join in first sc.

Rnd 7: Sl st in next 3 sc, ch 1, sc in same sc; * † (ch 7, sc in next ch-7 sp) 3 times; ch 3, CL in next ch-3 sp; ch 1, (CL in next ch-1 sp, ch 1) 5 times; in next ch-5 sp work (CL, ch 1, CL); ch 5, in same sp work (CL, ch 1) twice; (CL in next ch-1 sp, ch 1) 5 times; CL in next ch-3 sp; ch 3, (sc in next ch-7 sp, ch 7) 3 times †; sk next 3 sc, sc in next sc; rep from * twice more, then rep from † to † once; join in first sc.

Rnd 8: Sl st in next 3 chs of next ch-7 sp, ch 1, sc in same sp; (ch-7 picot, ch 3, sc in next ch-7 sp) twice; * † ch-7 picot; ch 3, sc in next ch-3 sp; †† ch-7 picot; ch 3, sk next ch-1 sp, sc in next ch-1 sp ††; rep from †† to †† 3 times more; ch-7 picot; ch 3, in next ch-5 sp work (sc, ch 11, sc)—corner made; rep from †† to †† 3 times; ch-7 picot; ch 3, sc in next ch-3 sp †; (ch-7 picot, ch 3, sc in next ch-7 sp) 6 times; rep from * twice more, then rep from † to † once; (ch-7 picot, ch 3, sc in next ch-7 sp) 3 times; ch-7 picot; ch 3; join in first sc.

Finish off and weave in all ends.

continued on page 107

Pansy Bedspread

continued from page 106

Square B

Work same as Square A through Rnd 7.

Rnd 8: Sl st in next 3 chs of next ch-7 sp, ch 1, sc in same sp; (ch-7 picot, ch 3, sc in next ch-7 sp) twice; * † ch-7 picot; ch 3, sc in next ch-3 sp; †† ch-7 picot; ch 3, sk next ch-1 sp, sc in next ch-1 sp ††; rep from †† to †† 3 times more; ch-7 picot; ch 3 †; in next ch-5 sp work (sc, ch 11, sc)—corner made; rep from †† to †† 3 times; ch-7 picot; ch 3, sc in next ch-3 sp †; (ch-7 picot, ch 3, sc in next ch-7 sp) 6 times; rep from * once more, then rep from † to † once; sc in next ch-5 sp, ch 5; hold wrong side of completed square facing wrong side of working square and carefully match sts, sl st in ch-11 sp of any corner; ch 5; on working square, sc in same sp—joined corner made; ††† ch 5, on completed square, sl st in next picot, ch 2, sl st in 4th ch from hook—joined picot made; ch 3, sk next ch-1 sp, sc in next ch-1 sp †††; rep from ††† to ††† twice more; ch 5, on completed square, sl st in next picot, ch 2, sl st in 4th ch from hook—joined picot made; ch 3, sc in next ch-3 sp, (ch 5, on completed square, sl st in next picot, ch 2, sl st in 4th ch from hook—joined picot made; ch 3, sc in next ch-7 sp) 6 times; ch 5, on completed square, sl st in next picot, ch 2, sl st in 4th ch from hook—joined picot made; ch 3, sc in next ch-3 sp; rep from ††† to ††† 4 times; ch 5; on completed square, sl st in next picot, ch 2, sl st in 4th ch from hook—joined picot made; ch 3, sc in next ch-5 sp, ch 5; on completed square, sl st in next corner ch-11 sp, ch 5, on working square, sc in same sp—corner made; rep from †† to †† 3 times; ch-7 picot; ch 3, sc in next ch-3 sp, (ch-7 picot, ch 3, sc in next ch-7 sp) 3 times; ch-7 picot; ch 3; join in first sc.

Finish off and weave in all ends.

Remaining Squares

Work same as Square B, joining sides in similar manner and working corner joinings as necessary.

Rose Petals

continued from page 71

Border:

Hold afghan with right side facing you and one short end at top; join blue in first ch of upper right-hand corner ch-3 sp.

Rnd 1: Ch 4, keeping last lp of each dtrc (see Pattern Stitches on page 71) on hook, 2 dtrc in same lp; YO and draw through all 3 lps on hook—beg dtrc CL made; ch 3—corner made; working in BLs only, sk next ch, dtrc CL in next ch; * † [ch 2, sk next 2 dc, dtrc CL (see Pattern Stitches on page 71) in next dc] 8 times; ch 2, dtrc CL in next ch; ch 2, sk next joining, dtrc CL in next ch on next square †; rep from † to † 5 times more; (ch 2, sk next 2 dc, dtrc CL in next dc) 7 times; ch 2, dtrc CL in next ch; ch 3—corner made; dtrc CL in next ch; working along next side, rep from † to † 8 times; (ch 2, sk next 2 dc, dtrc CL in next dc) 8 times; ch 2, dtrc CL in next ch; ch 3—corner made; sk next ch, dtrc CL in next ch; working along lower edge, rep from † to † 6 times; (ch 2, sk next 2 dc, dtrc CL in next dc) 8 times; ch 2, dtrc in next ch, ch 3—corner made; sk next ch, dtrc CL in next ch; working along next side, rep from † to † 8 times; (ch 2, sk next 2 dc, dtrc in next dc) 8 times; ch 2; join in beg dtrc CL. Finish off.

Rnd 2: Hold afghan with right side facing you and one short end at top; join off white in FL of unused ch of corner ch-3 sp of Rnd 7; in same lp work (beg 3-dc CL, ch 3, 3-dc CL)—beg corner made; working in unused lps of each dc and in unused corner chs, † (ch 1, sk next lp, 3-dc CL in next lp) 13 times; ch 1, 3-dc CL in unused ch of next corner ch-3 sp; ch 1, sk next joining, 3-dc CL in unused ch of next corner ch-3 sp †; rep from † to † 5 times more; (ch 1, sk next dc, 3-dc CL in next dc) 13 times; ch 1, in unused ch of next corner ch-3 sp work (3-dc CL, ch 3, 3-dc CL)—corner made; working along next side, rep from † to † 8 times; (ch 1, sk next dc, 3-dc CL in next dc) 13 times; ch 1, in unused ch of next corner ch-3 sp work (3-dc CL, ch 3, 3-dc CL)—corner made; working along next side, rep from † to † 6 times; (ch 1, sk next dc, 3-dc CL in next dc) 13 times; ch 1, in unused ch of next corner ch-3 sp work (3-dc CL, ch 3, 3-dc CL)—corner made; working along next side, rep from † to † 8 times; (ch 1, sk next dc, 3-dc CL in next dc) 13 times; ch 1; join in beg 3-dc CL.

Finish off and weave in all ends.

Confetti Tunic

continued from page 85

Front

Work same as Back until armhole measures 2 1/2" (2 3/4", 3 1/4"), ending by working a wrong side row.

Left Neck Shaping:

Row 1 (right side): Sc in first 33 (36, 39) sc, dec over last 2 sc (to work dec: draw up lp in each of next 2 sc, YO and draw through all 3 lps on hook—dec made)—34 (37, 40) sc. Ch 1, turn.

Row 2: Dec over first 2 sc; sc in each rem sc—33 (36, 39) sc. Ch 1, turn.

Row 3: Sc in each sc to last 2 sc; dec over next 2 sc—32 (35, 38) sc. Ch 1, turn.

Rows 4 through 9: Rep Rows 2 and 3 three times more. At end of Row 9—26 (29, 32) sc.

Row 10: Sc in each sc. Ch 1, turn.

Row 11: Rep Row 3. At end of row—25 (28, 31) sc.

Rows 12 through 25: Rep Rows 10 and 11 seven times more. At end of Row 25—18 (21, 24) sc.

Rep Row 10 until armhole measures same as back. At end of last row, do not ch 1; do not turn. Finish off.

Right Neck Shaping:

Hold piece with right side facing you, join variegated in same sc as last st made on left neck shaping.

continued on page 108

Confetti Tunic

continued from page 107

Row 1 (right side): Ch 1, dec over next 2 sc; sc in each rem sc—34 (37, 40) sc. Ch 1, turn.

Row 2: Sc in each sc to last 2 sc; dec over last 2 sc—33 (36, 39) sc. Ch 1, turn.

Row 3: Dec over first 2 sc; sc in each rem sc—32 (35, 38) sc. Ch 1, turn.

Rows 4 through 9: Rep Rows 2 and 3 three times more. At end of Row 9—26 (29, 32) sc.

Row 10: Sc in each sc. Ch 1, turn.

Row 11: Rep Row 3. At end of row—25 (28, 31) sc.

Rows 12 through 25: Rep Rows 10 and 11 seven times more. At end of Row 25—18 (21, 24) sc.

Rep Row 10 until armhole measures same as back. At end of last row, do not ch 1. Finish off.

Sleeve (make 2)
With smaller size hook and variegated, ch 47.

Row 1 (right side): Sc in 2nd ch from hook and in each rem ch—46 sc. Ch 1, turn.

Row 2: Sc in each sc. Change to purple by drawing lp through; cut variegated. Ch 3 (counts as first dc on following rows), turn.

Row 3: Sk first sc, dc in next sc; * ch 2, sk next 2 sc, dc in next 3 sc; rep from * 7 times more; ch 2, sk next 2 sc, dc in next 2 sc. Change to variegated by drawing lp through; cut purple. Ch 1, turn.

Row 4: Sc in first 2 dc; * long dc (see Pattern Stitch on page 85) in next 2 skipped sc in 2nd row below, sc in next 3 dc; rep from * 7 times more; long dc in next 2 skipped sc on 2nd row below, sc in next dc and in 3rd ch of turning ch-3. Ch 1, turn.

Row 5: Sc in each st. Ch 1, turn.

Row 6: Sc in each sc. Change to yellow by drawing lp through; cut variegated. Ch 3, turn.

Row 7: Sk first sc, dc in next sc; * ch 2, sk next 2 sc, dc in next 3 sc; rep from * 7 times more; ch 2, sk next 2 sc, dc in next

2 sc. Change to variegated by drawing lp through; cut yellow. Ch 1, turn.

Rows 8 and 9: Rep Rows 4 and 5.

Row 10: Sc in each sc. Change to rose by drawing lp through; cut variegated. Ch 3, turn.

Row 11: Sk first sc, dc in next sc; * ch 2, sk next 2 sc, dc in next 3 sc; rep from * 7 times more; ch 2, sk next 2 sc, dc in next 2 sc. Change to variegated by drawing lp through; cut rose. Ch 1, turn.

Rows 12 and 13: Rep Rows 4 and 5.

Row 14: Sc in each sc. Change to larger size hook. Ch 1, turn.

Size Small Only:

Row 15: 2 sc in first sc; sc in each sc to last sc; 2 sc in last sc—48 sc. Ch 1, turn.

Row 16: Sc in each sc. Ch 1, turn.

Rows 17 and 18: Rep Row 16.

Rows 19 through 54: Rep Rows 15 through 18 nine times more. At end of Row 54—66 sc.

Rows 55 and 56: Rep Rows 15 and 16.

Row 57: Rep Row 15. At end of row—70 sc.

Rows 58 through 62: Rep Row 16.

Row 63: Rep Row 15. At end of row—72 sc.

Rows 64 through 93: Rep Rows 58 through 63 five times more. At end of Row 93—82 sc.

Rep Row 16 until sleeve measures 20" from beg. At end of last row, do not ch 1; do not turn.

Finish off and weave in all ends.

Size Medium Only:

Row 15: 2 sc in first sc; sc in each sc to last sc; 2 sc in last sc—48 sc. Ch 1, turn.

Row 16: Sc in each sc. Ch 1, turn.

Rows 17 and 18: Rep Row 16.

Rows 19 through 86: Rep Rows 15 through 18 seventeen times more. At end of Row 86—82 sc.

Rows 87 and 88: Rep Row 16.

Row 89: Rep Row 15. At end of row—84 sc.

Rows 90 through 94: Rep Row 16.

Row 95: Rep Row 15. At end of row—86 sc.

Rep Row 16 until sleeve measures 20 1/2" from beg.

Finish off and weave in all ends.

Size Large Only:

Row 15: 2 sc in first sc; sc in each sc to last sc; 2 sc in last sc—48 sc. Ch 1, turn.

Row 16: Sc in each sc. Ch 1, turn.

Rows 17 and 18: Rep Row 16.

Rows 19 through 102: Rep Rows 15 through 18 twenty-one times more. At end of Row 102—90 sc.

Rep Row 16 until sleeve measures 20 1/2".

Finish off and weave in all ends.

Assembly
Sew shoulder seams.

Neckband
Hold tunic with right side facing you; with smaller size hook, join variegated in side of last row of back to left of right shoulder seam.

Rnd 1: Ch 1, sc in same sp; working around neckline, sc in side of each row, in each sc across back, and in side of each row along left front to Row 1 of neck shaping; draw up lp in side of Row 1 and in side of Row 1 of right neck shaping, YO and draw through all 3 lps on hook; sc in side of each row to first sc; join in first sc. Change to purple by drawing lp through; cut variegated.

Rnd 2: Reverse sc (see Keeping You in Stitches on page 198) in each sc; join in first reverse sc.

Finish off and weave in ends.

Finishing
Step 1: Sew corners of sleeves to front and back between points **A** and **B** (see diagrams on page 85).

Step 2: Sew sleeve and side seams.

Casual Striped Cardigan

continued from page 90

Row 4: Sc in first sc and in next ch-1 sp; * ch 1, sc in next ch-1 sp; rep from * 51 (57, 63) times more; sc in next sc. Ch 1, turn.

Row 5: Sc in first sc; * ch 1, sc in next ch-1 sp; rep from * 51 (57, 63) times more; ch 1, sk next sc, sc in next sc. Ch 1, turn.

Row 6: Sc in first sc and in next ch-1 sp; * ch 1, sc in next ch-1 sp; rep from * 51 (57, 63) times more; sc in next sc. Change to blue by drawing lp through; cut red. Ch 1, turn.

Row 7: Rep Row 5. At end of row, change to red by drawing lp through; cut blue. Ch 1, turn.

Row 8: Rep Row 4.

Row 9: Rep Row 5.

Rep Row 2 through 9 until back measures 16" (16 1/2", 16 1/2") from beg, ending by working a wrong side row. At end of last row, do not ch 1. Finish off.

Armhole Shaping:

Hold back with right side facing you, continuing in color sequence make lp on larger size hook; sk first 6 sts, join with an sc in next sc; * ch 1, sc in next ch-1 sp; rep from * 45 (51, 57) times more—95 (107, 119) sts. Ch 1, turn, leaving rem 6 sts unworked.

Continue in patt and color sequence until armhole measures 8" (8 1/2", 9") ending by working a wrong side row. Ch 1, turn.

Right Back Shoulder:

Note: Continue working in color sequence as established.

Row 1 (right side)**:** Sc in first sc; * ch 1, sc in next ch-1 sp; rep from * 10 (13, 16) times more; ch 1, sk next sc, sc in next sc—25 (31, 37) sts. Ch 1, turn, leaving rem sts unworked.

Row 2: Sc in first sc and in next ch-1 sp; * ch 1, sc in next ch-1 sp; rep from * 10 (13, 16) times more; sc in next sc. Ch 1, turn.

Rep Rows 1 and 2 until armhole measures

9" (9 1/2", 10"), ending by working a Row 2. At end of last row, do not ch 1. Finish off.

Left Back Shoulder:

Hold back with right side facing you, continuing in color and pattern sequence, make lp on larger size hook; sk next 45 sts from right back shoulder, join with an sc in next sc.

Row 1 (right side)**:** * Ch 1, sc in next ch-1 sp; rep from * 10 (13, 16) times more; ch 1, sk next sc, sc in next sc—25 (31, 37) sts. Ch 1, turn.

Row 2: Sc in first sc and in next ch-1 sp; * ch 1, sc in next ch-1 sp; rep from * 10 (13, 16) times more; sc in next sc. Ch 1, turn.

Row 3: Sc in first sc; * ch 1, sc in next ch-1 sp; rep from * 10 (13, 16) times more; ch 1, sk next sc, sc in next sc—25 (31, 37) sts. Ch 1, turn.

Rep Rows 2 and 3 until armhole measures same as right back shoulder, ending by working a Row 2. At end of last row, do not ch 1. Finish off.

Left Front

With larger size hook and red, ch 52 (58, 64).

Row 1 (right side)**:** Sc in 2nd ch from hook; * ch 1, sk next ch, sc in next ch; rep from * 24 (27, 30) times more—51 (57, 63) sts. Ch 1, turn.

Row 2: Sc in first sc and in next ch-1 sp; * ch 1, sc in next ch-1 sp; rep from * 23 (26, 29) times more; sc in next sc. Change to white by drawing lp through; cut red. Ch 1, turn.

Row 3: Sc in first sc; * ch 1, sc in next ch-1 sp; rep from * 23 (26, 29) times more; ch 1, sk next sc, sc in next sc. Change to red by drawing lp through; cut white. Ch 1, turn.

Row 4: Sc in first sc and in next ch-1 sp; * ch 1, sc in next ch-1 sp; rep from * 23 (26, 29) times more; sc in next sc. Ch 1, turn.

Rep Rows 3 and 4 in same color sequence as back until left front measures same as back to underarm. At end of last row, do not ch 1. Finish off.

Armhole Shaping:

Note: Continue in color sequence as established.

Hold piece with right side facing you, continuing in color sequence, make lp on larger

size hook; sk first 6 sts, join with an sc in next ch-1 sp.

Row 1 (right side)**:** * Ch 1, sc in next ch-1 sp; rep from * 20 (23, 26) times more; ch 1, sk next sc, sc in next sc—45 (51, 57) sts. Ch 1, turn.

Row 2: Sc in first sc and in next ch-1 sp; * ch 1, sc in next ch-1 sp; rep from * 20 (23, 26) times more; sc in next sc. Ch 1, turn.

Row 3: Sc in first sc; * ch 1, sc in next ch-1 sp; rep from * 20 (23, 26) times more; dec over next 2 sc (to work dec: draw up lp in each of next 2 sts, YO and draw through all 3 lps on hook—dec made)—44 (50, 56) sts. Ch 1, turn.

Row 4: Dec over first 2 sc; * sc in next ch-1 sp, ch 1; rep from * 19 (22, 25) times more; sc in next ch-1 sp and in next sc—43 (49, 55) sts. Ch 1, turn.

Row 5: Sc in first sc; * ch 1, sc in next ch-1 sp; rep from * 19 (22, 25) times more; dec—42 (48, 54) sts. Ch 1, turn.

Row 6: Dec; * sc in next ch-1 sp, ch 1; rep from * 18 (21, 24) times more; sc in next ch-1 sp and in next sc—41 (47, 53) sts. Ch 1, turn.

Row 7: Sc in first sc; * ch 1, sc in next ch-1 sp; rep from * 18 (21, 24) times more; dec—40 (46, 52) sts. Ch 1, turn.

Row 8: Sc in first sc; * ch 1, sc in next ch-1 sp; rep from * to last sc; sc in last sc. Ch 1, turn.

Row 9: Sc in first sc; * ch 1, sc in next ch-1 sp; rep from * to last ch-1 sp and last sc; ch 1, dec over last ch-1 sp and last sc— 39 (45, 51) sts. Ch 1, turn.

Row 10: Sc in first sc and next ch-1 sp; * ch 1, sc in next ch-1 sp; rep from * to last sc; sc in last sc. Ch 1, turn.

Row 11: Sc in first sc; * ch 1, sc in next ch-1 sp; rep from * to last 2 sc; dec— 38 (44, 50) sts. Ch 1, turn.

Rows 12 through 35: Rep Rows 8 through 11 six times more. At end of Row 35— 26 (32, 38) sts.

Rows 36 and 37: Rep Rows 8 and 9. At end of Row 37—25 (31, 37) sts.

Row 38: Sc in first sc and in next ch-1 sp; * ch 1, sc in next ch-1 sp; rep from * 10 (13, 16) times more; sc in next sc. Ch 1, turn.

continued on page 110

Casual Striped Cardigan

continued from page 109

Row 39: Sc in first sc; * ch 1, sc in next ch-1 sp; rep from * 10 (13, 16) times more; ch 1, sk next sc, sc in next sc. Ch 1, turn.

Rep Rows 38 and 39 until left front measures same as back, ending by working a wrong side row. At end of last row, do not ch 1. Finish off, leaving an 18" end for sewing.

Right Front

Work same as Left Front to Armhole Shaping. Do not finish off. Ch 1, turn.

Armhole Shaping:

Note: Continue in color sequence as established.

Row 1 (right side)**:** Sc in first sc; * ch 1, sc in next ch-1 sp; rep from * 21 (24, 27) times more—45 (51, 57) sts. Ch 1, turn, leaving rem sts unworked.

Row 2: Sc in first sc and in next ch-1 sp; * ch 1, sc in next ch-1 sp; rep from * 20 (23, 26) times more; sc in next sc. Ch 1, turn.

Row 3: Dec; sc in next ch-1 sp; * ch 1, sc in next ch-1 sp; rep from * 19 (22, 25) times more; ch 1, sk next sc, sc in next sc—44 (50, 56) sts. Ch 1, turn.

Row 4: Sc in first sc and in next ch-1 sp; * ch 1, sc in next ch-1 sp; rep from * 19 (22, 25) times more; dec—43 (49, 55) sts. Ch 1, turn.

Row 5: Dec; sc in next ch-1 sp; * ch 1, sc in next ch-1 sp; rep from * 18 (21, 24) times more; ch 1, sk next sc, sc in next sc—42 (48, 54) sts. Ch 1, turn.

Row 6: Sc in first sc and in next ch-1 sp; * ch 1, sc in next ch-1 sp; rep from * 18 (21, 24) times more; dec—41 (47, 53) sts. Ch 1, turn.

Row 7: Dec; sc in next ch-1 sp; * ch 1, sc in next ch-1 sp; rep from * 17 (20, 23) times more; ch 1, sk next sc, sc in next sc—40 (46, 52) sts. Ch 1, turn.

Row 8: Sc in first sc and in next ch-1 sp; * ch 1, sc in next ch-1 sp; rep from * 17 (20, 23) times more; ch 1, sk next sc, sc in next sc. Ch 1, turn.

Row 9: Dec over first sc and next ch-1 sp; * ch 1, sc in next ch-1 sp; rep from * 17 (20, 23) times more; ch 1, sk next sc, sc in next sc—39 (45, 51) sts. Ch 1, turn.

Row 10: Sc in first 2 sc; * ch 1, sc in next ch-1 sp; rep from * 17 (20, 23) times more; sc in next sc. Ch 1, turn.

Row 11: Dec over first sc and next ch-1 sp; sc in next ch-1 sp; * ch 1, sc in next ch-1 sp; rep from * 16 (19, 22) times more; ch 1, sk next sc, sc in next sc—38 (44, 50) sts. Ch 1, turn.

Row 12: Sc in first sc and next ch-1 sp; * ch 1, sc in next ch-1 sp; rep from * to last 2 sc; ch 1, sk next sc, sc in next sc. Ch 1, turn.

Row 13: Dec over first sc and next ch-1 sp; * ch 1, sc in next ch-1 sp; rep from * to last 2 sc; ch 1, sk next sc, sc in next sc—37 (43, 49) sc. Ch 1, turn.

Row 14: Sc in first sc and next ch-1 sp; * ch 1, sc in next ch-1 sp; rep from * to last sc; sc in last sc. Ch 1, turn.

Row 15: Dec; sc in next ch-1 sp; * ch 1, sc in next ch-1 sp; rep from * to last 2 sc; ch 1, sk next sc, sc in next sc—36 (42, 48) sc. Ch 1, turn.

Row 16: Sc in first sc and next ch-1 sp; * ch 1, sc in next ch-1 sp; rep from * 15 (18, 21) times more; ch 1, sk next sc, sc in next sc. Ch 1, turn.

Row 17: Dec over first sc and next ch-1 sp; * ch 1, sc in next ch-1 sp; rep from * 15 (18, 21) times more; ch 1, sk next sc, sc in next sc—35 (41, 47) sts. Ch 1, turn.

Row 18: Sc in first 2 sc; * ch 1, sc in next ch-1 sp; rep from * 15 (18, 21) times more; sc in next sc. Ch 1, turn.

Row 19: Dec; sc in next ch-1 sp; * ch 1, sc in next ch-1 sp; rep from * 14 (17, 20) times more; ch 1, sk next sc, sc in next sc—34 (40, 46) sts. Ch 1, turn.

Rows 20 through 35: Rep Rows 12 through 15 four times more. At end of Row 35—26 (32, 38) sts.

Rows 36 and 37: Rep Rows 12 and 13. At end of Row 37—25 (31, 37) sts.

Row 38: Sc in first sc and in next ch-1 sp; * ch 1, sc in next ch-1 sp; rep from * 10 (13, 16) times more; sc in next sc. Ch 1, turn.

Row 39: Sc in first sc; * ch 1, sc in next ch-1 sp; rep from * 10 (13, 16) times more; ch 1, sk next sc, sc in next sc. Ch 1, turn.

Rep Rows 38 and 39 until right front measures same as back, ending by working a wrong side row. At end of last row, do not ch 1. Finish off, leaving an 18" end for sewing.

Sleeve (make 2)

With larger size hook and red, ch 58.

Row 1 (right side)**:** Sc in 2nd ch from hook; * ch 1, sk next ch, sc in next ch; rep from * 27 times more—57 sts. Ch 1, turn.

Row 2: 2 sc in first sc; sc in next ch-1 sp; * ch 1, sc in next ch-1 sp; rep from * 26 times more; 2 sc in next sc—59 sts. Change to white by drawing lp through; cut red. Ch 1, turn.

Row 3: Sc in first 2 sc; * ch 1, sc in next ch-1 sp; rep from * 26 times more; ch 1, sk next sc, sc in next 2 sc. Change to red by drawing lp through; cut white. Ch 1, turn.

Row 4: 2 sc in first sc; * ch 1, sc in next ch-1 sp; rep from * 27 times more; ch 1, sk next sc, 2 sc in next sc—61 sts. Ch 1, turn.

Row 5: Sc in first sc; * ch 1, sc in next ch-1 sp; rep from * 28 times more; ch 1, sk next sc, sc in next sc. Ch 1, turn.

Row 6: 2 sc in first sc; sc in next ch-1 sp; * ch 1, sc in next ch-1 sp; rep from * 28 times more; 2 sc in next sc—63 sts. Change to blue by drawing lp through; cut red. Ch 1, turn.

Row 7: Sc in first 2 sc; * ch 1, sc in next ch-1 sp; rep from * 28 times more; ch 1, sk next sc, sc in next 2 sc. Change to red by drawing lp through; cut blue. Ch 1, turn.

Row 8: 2 sc in first sc; ch 1, sk next sc, sc in next ch-1 sp; * ch 1, sc in next ch-1 sp; rep from * 28 times more; ch 1, sk next sc, 2 sc in next sc—65 sts. Ch 1, turn.

Row 9: Sc in first sc; * ch 1, sc in next ch-1 sp; rep from * 30 times more; ch 1, sk next sc, sc in next sc. Ch 1, turn.

Row 10: 2 sc in first sc; sc in next ch-1 sp; * ch 1, sc in next ch-1 sp; rep from * 30 times more; 2 sc in next sc—67 sts. Change to white by drawing lp through; cut red. Ch 1, turn.

Row 11: Sc in first 2 sc; * ch 1, sc in next ch-1 sp; rep from * 30 times more; ch 1, sk next sc, sc in next 2 sc. Change to red by drawing lp through; cut white. Ch 1, turn.

Row 12: 2 sc in first sc; * ch 1, sc in next ch-1 sp; rep from * 31 times more; ch 1, sk next sc, 2 sc in next sc—69 sc. Ch 1, turn.

Row 13: Sc in first sc; * ch 1, sc in next ch-1 sp; rep from * 32 times more; ch 1, sk next sc, sc in next sc. Ch 1, turn.

Row 14: 2 sc in first sc; sc in next ch-1 sp; * ch 1, sc in next ch-1 sp; rep from * 32

continued on page 111

Casual Striped Cardigan

continued from page 110

times more; 2 sc in next sc—71 sts. Change to blue by drawing lp through; cut red. Ch 1, turn.

Row 15: Sc in first 2 sc, ch 1, sk next sc, sc in next ch-1 sp; * ch 1, sc in next ch-1 sp; rep from * 32 times more; ch 1, sk next sc, sc in next 2 sc. Change to red by drawing lp through; cut blue. Ch 1, turn.

Row 16: 2 sc in first sc; * ch 1, sc in next ch-1 sp; rep from * 33 times more; ch 1, sk next sc, 2 sc in next sc—73 sts. Ch 1, turn.

Row 17: Sc in first sc; * ch 1, sc in next ch-1 sp; rep from * 34 times more; ch 1, sk next sc, sc in next sc. Ch 1, turn.

Continue working in patt and color sequence as established, increasing as follows:

Size Small Only:

Inc at each end of every other row 4 times more, then inc at each end every 4th row 14 times, ending on a wrong side row. At end of last row—109 sts.

Continue to work in patt and color sequence without inc until sleeve measures 19½" from beg. At end of last row, do not ch 1.

Finish off and weave in all ends.

Size Mediuim Only:

Inc at each end of every other row 10 times more, then inc at each end every 4th row 11 times. At end of last row—115 sts.

Continue working in patt and color sequence until sleeve measures 19½" from beg. At end of last row, do not ch 1.

Finish off and weave in all ends.

Size Large Only:

Inc at each end of every other row 16 times more, then inc at each end every 4th row 8 times. At end of last row—121 sts.

Continue to work in patt and color sequence without inc until sleeve measures 19½" from beg. At end of last row, do not ch 1.

Finish off and weave in all ends.

Sew shoulder seams.

Front Bands:

Hold cardigan with right side facing you and center right front edge at top; with smaller size hook and red, make lp on hook, join with an sc in side of edge sc on lower right-hand edge.

Row 1: Work along right front edge, sc in side of each row, in each sc across back, and in side of each row along center left front edge. Ch 1, turn.

Row 2: Sc in each sc. Ch 1, turn.

Mark placement of 6 buttonholes evenly spaced along right front edge, having first mark at beg of neckline shaping.

Row 3: * Sc in each sc to first marker; * ch 3, sk next 3 sc—buttonhole made; rep from * 5 times more; sc in each rem sc. Ch 1, turn.

Row 4: Sc in each sc and 3 sc in each ch-3 sp. Ch 1, turn.

Row 5: Sc in each sc.

Finish off and weave in all ends.

Finishing

Step 1: Sew corners of sleeves to front and back between points A and B (see diagrams on page 90).

Step 2: Sew sleeve and side seams.

Step 3: Sew buttons opposite buttonholes.

Time for Tea: Cup and Saucer

continued from page 88

Rnd 6: Sc in each sc.

Rnd 7: * Sc in next 4 sc, 2 sc in next sc; rep from * 5 times more—36 sc.

Rnd 8: Sc in each sc.

Rnd 9: * Sc in next 5 sc, 2 sc in next sc; rep from * 5 times more—42 sc.

Rnd 10: Sc in each sc.

Rnd 11: * Sc in next 6 sc, 2 sc in next sc; rep from * 5 times more—48 sc.

Rnd 12: Sc in each sc.

Rnd 13: * Sc in next 7 sc, 2 sc in next sc; rep from * 5 times more—54 sc.

Rnd 14: Sc in each sc.

Rnd 15: * Sc in next 8 sc, 2 sc in next sc; rep from * 5 times more—60 sc.

Rnd 16: Sc in each sc; join in first sc.

Rnd 17: Ch 1, reverse sc (see Keeping You in Stitches on page 198) in each sc; join in first reverse sc. Finish off.

Base:

Hold cup upside down; join thread in unused lp of any sc on Rnd 3.

Rnd 1: Ch 1, sc in same lp and in each rem unused lp; join in first sc—18 sc.

Rnd 2: Ch 1, sc in same sc and in each rem sc; join in first sc. Finish off.

Handle:

Hold cup right side up; join thread around any sc on Rnd 6; ch 15; join around corresponding sc on Rnd 15; ch 1, reverse sc in each ch; join in joining sl st.

Finish off and weave in all ends.

Saucer

Ch 2.

Rnd 1: 6 sc in 2nd ch from hook.

Rnd 2: 2 sc in each sc—12 sc.

Rnd 3: * Sc in next sc, 2 sc in next sc; rep from * 5 times more—18 sc.

Rnd 4: * Sc in next 2 sc, 2 sc in next sc; rep from * 5 times more—24 sc.

Rnd 5: * Sc in next 3 sc, 2 sc in next sc; rep from * 5 times more—30 sc.

Rnd 6: * Sc in next 4 sc, 2 sc in next sc; rep from * 5 times more—36 sc.

Rnd 7: * Sc in next 5 sc, 2 sc in next sc; rep from * 5 times more—42 sc.

Rnd 8: * Sc in next 6 sc, 2 sc in next sc; rep from * 5 times more—48 sc.

Rnd 9: * Sc in next 7 sc, 2 sc in next sc; rep from * 5 times more—54 sc.

Rnd 10: * Sc in next 8 sc, 2 sc in next sc; rep from * 5 times more—60 sc.

Rnd 11: * Sc in next 9 sc, 2 sc in next sc; rep from * 5 times more—66 sc.

Rnd 12: * Sc in next 10 sc, 2 sc in next sc; rep from * 5 times more—72 sc.

Rnd 13: Ch 1, reverse sc in each sc; join in first reverse sc.

Finish off and weave in ends.

continued on page 112

Time for Tea: Cup and Saucer

continued from page 111

Roses

Note: Roses are made with smaller size hook.

Large Rose (make 3):
Ch 36.

Row 1 (right side): Sc in 6th ch from hook; * ch 3, sk next 2 chs, sc in next ch; rep from * 9 times more. Turn.

Row 2: 5 sc in each of next 2 ch-3 sps; 5 hdc in each of next 3 ch-3 sps; in each of next 5 ch-3 sps work (hdc, 5 dc, hdc); in lp made by beg 5 skipped chs work (hdc, 7 dc, hdc). Finish off.

Medium Rose (make 5):
Ch 24.

Row 1 (right side): Sc in 6th ch from hook; * ch 3, sk next 2 chs, sc in next ch; rep from * 5 times more. Turn.

Row 2: 5 sc in each of next 3 ch-3 sps; 5 hdc in each of next 3 ch-3 sps; in each of next 5 ch-3 sps work (hdc, 5 dc, hdc); 7 hdc in lp made by beg 5 skipped chs. Finish off.

Leaves

Note: Leaves are made with smaller size hook.

Small Leaf (make 12):
Ch 5, keeping last lp of each trc on hook, 4 trc in 5th ch from hook; YO and draw through all 5 lps on hook—trc CL made; ch 3, sl st in top of trc CL just made; ch 4, sl st in same ch as trc CL.

Finish off and weave in ends.

Finishing

Step 1: Referring to Shape up Your Starching article on page 86, starch cup and saucer.

Step 2: For roses, begin at short end of one crocheted rose piece and roll to form a rose and tie ends together to secure. Weave in ends. Repeat with remaining pieces.

Step 3: Glue roses and leaves in place as desired.

Time for Tea: Dessert Plate

continued from page 88

Rnd 11: * Working in FLs only, sc in next 9 sc, 2 sc in next sc; rep from * 5 times more—66 sc.

Rnd 12: * Sc in next 10 sc, 2 sc in next sc; rep from * 5 times more—72 sc.

Rnd 13: * Sc in next 11 sc, 2 sc in next sc; rep from * 5 times more—78 sc.

Rnd 14: * Sc in next 12 sc, 2 sc in next sc; rep from * 5 times more—84 sc.

Rnd 15: * Sc in next 13 sc, 2 sc in next sc; rep from * 5 times more—90 sc.

Rnd 16: * Sc in next 14 sc, 2 sc in next sc; rep from * 5 times more—96 sc.

Rnd 17: * Sc in next 15 sc, 2 sc in next sc; rep from * 5 times more—102 sc.

Rnd 18: * Sc in next 16 sc, 2 sc in next sc; rep from * 5 times more—108 sc.

Rnd 19: * Sc in next 17 sc, 2 sc in next sc; rep from * 5 times more—114 sc.

Rnd 20: * Sc in next 18 sc, 2 sc in next sc; rep from * 5 times more—120 sc.

Rnd 21: * Sc in next 19 sc, 2 sc in next sc; rep from * 5 times more—126 sc.

Rnd 22: * Sc in next 20 sc, 2 sc in next sc; rep from * 5 times more—132 sc.

Rnd 23: * Sc in next 21 sc, 2 sc in next sc; rep from * 5 times more—138 sc.

Rnd 24: * Sc in next 22 sc, 2 sc in next sc; rep from * 5 times more—144 sc.

Rnd 25: * Sc in next 23 sc, 2 sc in next sc; rep from * 5 times more—150 sc.

Rnd 26: * Sc in next 24 sc, 2 sc in next sc; rep from * 5 times more—156 sc.

Rnd 27: * Sc in next 25 sc, 2 sc in next sc; rep from * 5 times more—162 sc.

Rnd 28: Ch 1, reverse sc (see Keeping You in Stitches on page 198) in each sc; join in first reverse sc. Finish off.

Base:

Hold piece upside down; join thread in unused lp of any sc on Rnd 10.

Rnd 1: Ch 1, sc in same lp and in each rem unused lp; join in first sc—60 sc.

Rnd 2: Ch 1, reverse sc in each sc; join in first sc.

Finish off and weave in all ends.

Roses

Note: Roses are made with smaller size hook.

Large Rose (make 10):
Work same as Large Rose above.

Medium Rose (make 10):

Work same as Medium Rose above.

Small Rose (make 36):
Ch 15.

Row 1 (right side): Sc in 6th ch from hook; * ch 3, sk next 2 chs, sc in next ch; rep from * twice more. Turn.

Row 2: 5 sc in each ch-3 sp and in lp made by beg 5 skipped chs.

Finish off and weave in ends.

Leaves

Note: Leaves are made with smaller size hook.

Large Leaf (make 20):
Ch 7, keeping last lp of each dtrc on hook, 4 dtrc (see Pattern Stitch on page 88) in 7th ch from hook, YO and draw through all 5 lps on hook—dtrc CL made; ch 3, sl st in top of dtrc CL just made; ch 6, sl st in same ch as dtrc CL. Finish off and weave in ends.

Small Leaf (make 34):

Work same as Small Leaf above.

Finishing

Step 1: Following Starching instructions on page 216, starch plate and shape over bottom of dinner plate. Allow to dry.

Step 2: For roses, begin at short end of one crocheted rose piece and roll to form a rose and tie ends together to secure. Weave in ends. Repeat with remaining pieces.

Step 3: Glue roses and leaves in place as desired.

Tissue Box in Bloom

continued from page 95

sp) twice;
† ch 4,
2 dc in
2nd ch of
next ch-5
sp; 3 dc in
next ch;
2 dc in
next ch †;
(ch 4, sc in next ch-4 sp) 9 times; rep from
† to † once; (ch 4, sc in next ch-4 sp) 18
times; rep from † to † once; (ch 4, sc in
next ch-4 sp) 9 times; rep from † to † once;
ch 4, (sc in next ch-4 sp, ch 4) 15 times;
join in first sc.

Rnd 8: Sl st in next 2 chs of next ch-4 sp,
ch 1, sc in same sp; (ch 4, sc in next ch-4
sp) twice; † (ch 4, sc in BL of next dc) 7
times; (ch 4, sc in next ch-4 sp) 10 times;
(ch 4, sc in BL of next dc) 7 times †; (ch 4,
sc in next ch-4 sp) 19 times; rep from † to
† once; ch 4, (sc in next ch-4 sp, ch 4) 16
times; join in first sc.

Rnd 9: Sl st in next 2 chs of next ch-4 sp,
ch 1, sc in same sp; * ch 4, sc in next ch-4
sp; rep from * around; join in first sc—88
ch-4 sps.

Rnds 10 through 15: Rep Rnd 9.

Rnd 16: Sl st in next 2 chs of next ch-4 sp,
ch 1, sc in same sp; ch 5; * sc in next ch-4
sp, ch 5; rep from * around; join in first sc.

Rnd 17: Sl st in next ch of next ch-5 sp,
ch 6 (counts as a trc and a ch-2 sp), (trc in
next ch, ch 2) 4 times; * ch 2, dc in next
ch-5 sp, ch 2, trc in next ch of next ch-5 sp,
ch 2, (trc in next ch, ch 2) 4 times; rep from
* around; join in 4th ch of beg ch-6.

Rnd 18: Ch 3, dc in each ch and in each st;
join in 3rd ch of beg ch-3.

Finish off and weave in ends.

Finishing

Step 1: Cover tissue box with several layers
of plastic wrap. Following Starching
instructions on page 216, starch cover and
shape over tissue box. Reshape ruffle as
cover drys.

Step 2: Fold ribbon in thirds lengthwise
with ends tucked under. Weave through
Rnd 2 around top opening and through ch-2
sps on Rnd 4 at each short end of cover.

Step 3: Trim stems from roses. Referring to
photo for placement, glue roses to cover.

Tigers for Your Woods

continued from page 94

Rnd 4: Ch 1, sc in same sc and in next 3 sc; 2 sc in each of next 3 sc, sc in next 6 sc, 2 sc in each of next 3 sc; join in first sc—22 sc.

Note: On following rnds, when changing colors, work last st until 2 lps rem on hook, draw new color through. To carry colors, work over color or colors not in use.

Rnd 5: Ch 1, sc in same sc and in next 3 sc, changing to gold in last sc; carry white; sc in next 2 sc, changing to black in last sc; carry white and gold; sc in next sc, changing to gold; carry white and black; sc in next 2 sc, changing to black in last sc; carry white and gold; sc in next sc, changing to gold; carry white and black; sc in next sc, working over prev rnds, long hdc (see Pattern Stitches on page 94) in next corresponding sc on Rnd 3, 6 long dc (see Pattern Stitches on page 94) in next corresponding sc on Rnd 1; sk next 2 sc on Rnd 4, long hdc in next corresponding sc on Rnd 3, sc in next sc, changing to black; carry white and gold; sc in next sc, changing to gold; carry white and black; sc in next sc, changing to black; carry white and gold; sc in next 2 sc, changing to gold in last sc; carry white and black; sc in next 2 sc, changing to white in last sc; carry gold and black; join in first sc—26 sts.

Note: Continue to carry colors on following rnds.

Rnd 6: Ch 1, sc in same sc and in next 4 sc, change to gold; sc in next sc, change to black; sc in next sc, change to gold; sc in next 2 sc, change to black; sc in next 2 sc, change to gold, sc in next 9 sts, change to black; sc in next sc, change to gold; sc in next sc, change to black; sc in next 2 sc, change to gold; sc in next 2 sc, change to white; join in first sc.

Rnd 7: Ch 1, sc in same sc and in next 4 sc, change to gold; sc in next sc, change to black; sc in next sc, change to gold; sc in next 2 sc, change to black; sc in next 2 sc, change to gold; sc in next 9 sc,

change to black; sc in next sc, change to gold; sc in next sc, change to black; sc in next 2 sc, change to gold; sc in next 2 sc, change to white; join in first sc.

Rnd 8: Ch 1, sc in same sc and in next 4 sc, change to gold; sc in next sc, change to black; sc in next sc, change to gold; sc in next 2 sc, change to black; sc in next 2 sc, change to gold; sc in next 9 sc, change to black; sc in next sc, change to gold; sc in next sc, change to black; sc in next 2 sc, change to gold; sc in next 2 sc, change to white; join in first sc.

Rnd 9: Ch 1, 2 sc in same sc and in each of next 4 sc; change to gold; 2 sc in next sc; change to black; 2 sc in next sc; change to gold; 2 sc in each of next 2 sc; change to black; 2 sc in each of next 2 sc; change to white; 2 sc in each of next 2 sc; change to gold; 2 sc in each of next 6 sc; change to white; 2 sc in each of next 2 sc; change to gold; 2 sc in next sc; change to black; 2 sc in each of next 2 sc; change to gold; 2 sc in each of next 2 sc; change to white; join in first sc—52 sc.

Rnd 10: Ch 1, sc in same sc and in next 9 sc, change to gold; sc in next sc, change to black; sc in next 2 sc, change to gold: sc in next 2 sc, change to black; sc in next sc, change to gold; sc in next sc, change to black; sc in next sc, change to gold; sc in next sc, change to black; sc in next 2 sc, change to white; sc in next 5 sc, change to black; sc in next 12 sc, change to white; sc in next 5 sc, change to gold; sc in next 2 sc, change to black; sc in next 2 sc, change to gold; sc in next sc, change to black; sc in next 2 sc, change to gold; sc in next 2 sc, change to white; join in first sc.

Rnd 11: Ch 1, sc in same sc and in next 9 sc, change to gold; sc in next sc, change to black; sc in next 2 sc, change to gold; sc in next 2 sc, change to black; sc in next sc, change to gold; sc in next sc, change to black; sc in next sc, change to gold; sc in next 2 sc, change to black; sc in next 2 sc, change to white; sc in next 4 sc, change to gold; sc in next 12 sc, change to white; sc in next 5 sc, change to gold; sc in next 3 sc, change to black; sc in next 2 sc, change to gold; sc in next sc, change to black; sc in next 2 sc, change to gold; sc in next sc, change to white; join in first sc.

Rnd 12: Ch 1, sc in same sc and in next sc, dec over next 2 sc [to work dec: draw up lp in each of next 2 sc, YO and draw through all 3 lps on hook—dec made];

(sc in next sc, dec over next 2 sc) twice; change to gold; sc in next sc, change to black; dec over next 2 sc; change to gold; sc in next 2 sc, change to black; sc in next 2 sc, change to gold; sc in next sc, change to black; sc in next sc, change to gold; sc in next 2 sc, change to black; sc in next sc, change to white; sc in next 5 sc, change to black; sc in next 11 sc, change to white; sc in next 4 sc, change to gold; sc in next 3 sc, change to black; sc in next 2 sc, change to gold; dec over next 2 sc; change to black; sc in next sc, change to gold; dec over next 2 sc; change to white; join in first sc—46 sc.

Rnd 13: Ch 1, sc in same sc and in next 7 sc, change to gold; sc in next sc, change to black; sc in next sc, change to gold; sc in next 2 sc, change to black; sc in next 2 sc, change to gold; sc in next sc, change to black; sc in next sc, change to gold; sc in next sc, change to black; sc in next 2 sc, change to gold; sc in next 3 sc, change to black; sc in next sc, change to gold; sc in next 7 sc, change to black; sc in next 2 sc, change to gold; sc in next 4 sc, change to black; sc in next 3 sc, change to gold; sc in next 2 sc, change to black; sc in next sc, change to gold; sc in next 2 sc, change to black; sc in next sc, change to gold; sc in next sc, change to white; join in first sc.

Rnd 14: Ch 1, sc in same sc and in next 8 sc, change to gold; sc in next sc, change to black; sc in next sc, change to gold; sc in next 2 sc, change to black; sc in next sc, change to gold; sc in next 2 sc, change to black; sc in next sc, change to gold; sc in next sc, change to black; sc in next 2 sc, change to gold; sc in next 2 sc, change to black; sc in next sc, change to gold; sc in next 12 sc, change to black; sc in next 3 sc, change to gold; sc in next 2 sc, change to black; sc in next 2 sc, change to gold; sc in next sc, change to black; sc in next sc, change to gold; sc in next sc, change to white; join in first sc.

Rnd 15: Ch 1, sc in same sc and in next 8 sc, change to gold; sc in next sc, change to black; sc in next sc, change to gold; sc in next 2 sc, change to black; sc in next 2 sc, change to gold; sc in next sc, change to black; sc in next sc, change to gold; sc in next sc, change to black; sc in next 2 sc, change to gold; sc in next 2 sc, change to black; sc in next 2 sc, change to gold; sc in next sc, change to black; sc in next 14 sc, change to gold; sc in next 2 sc,

continued on page 115

Tigers for Your Woods

continued from page 114

change to black; sc in next 2 sc, change to gold; sc in next sc, change to black; sc in next sc, change to gold; sc in next sc, change to white; join in first sc.

Rnd 16: Ch 1, sc in same sc and in next 5 sc, (dec, sc in next 2 sc) 4 times; dec; change to black; sc in next 2 sc, dec 4 times; change to white; (dec, sc in next 2 sc) 3 times; join in first sc—34 sc. Mark 9th, 19th, 26th, and 33rd sc for mane.

Note: It is easier to weave in beg ends before you continue.

Rnd 17: Ch 1, sc in same sc and in next 17 sc, change to black; sc in next 2 sc, change to gold; sc in next 3 sc, change to black; sc in next 2 sc, change to white; sc in next 9 sc; join in first sc. Mark 10th, 15th, 26th, and 32nd sc for mane.

Rnd 18: Ch 1, sc in same sc and in next 8 sc, change to gold; sc in next 25 sc, change to white; join in first sc.

Rnds 19 through 31: Rep Rnd 18.

Rnd 32: Ch 1, sc in same sc and in next 7 sc, change to black; sc in next 6 sc, change to gold; sc in next 4 sc, change to black; sc in next 4 sc, change to gold; sc in next 6 sc, change to black; sc in next 6 sc, change to white; join in first sc.

Rnd 33: Ch 1, sc in same sc and in next 9 sc, change to gold; sc in next 4 sc, change to black; sc in next 4 sc, change to gold; sc in next 5 sc, change to black; sc in next 3 sc, change to gold; sc in next 8 sc, change to white; join in first sc.

Rnd 34: Ch 1, sc in same sc and in next 9 sc, change to gold; sc in next 24 sc, change to white; join in first sc.

Rnd 35: Ch 1, sc in same sc and in next 10 sc, change to gold; sc in next 23 sc, change to white; join in first sc.

Rnd 36: Ch 1, sc in same sc and in next 10 sc, change to black; sc in next 23 sc, change to white; join in first sc.

Rnd 37: Ch 1, sc in same sc and in next 10 sc, change to black; sc in next 4 sc, change to gold; sc in next 6 sc, change to black; sc in next 7 sc, change to gold; sc in next 4 sc, change to black; sc in next 2 sc, change to white; join in first sc.

Rnd 38: Ch 1, sc in same sc and in next 9, change to gold; sc in next 24 sc, change to white; join in first sc.

Rnd 39: Ch 1, sc in same sc and in next 8 sc, change to black; sc in next 14 sc, change to gold; sc in next 11 sc, change to white; join in first sc.

Rnd 40: Ch 1, sc in same sc and in next 11 sc, change to black; sc in next 10 sc, change to gold; sc in next 12 sc, change to white; join in first sc.

Rnd 41: Ch 1, sc in same sc and in next 11 sc, change to gold; sc in next 18 sc, change to black; sc in next 3 sc, change to gold; sc in next sc, change to white; join in first sc.

Rnd 42: Ch 1, sc in same sc and in next 11 sc, change to gold; sc in next 8 sc, change to black; sc in next 7 sc, change to gold; sc in next 7 sc; join in first sc.

Rnd 43: Ch 1, sc in same sc and in each rem sc; join in first sc.

Finish off and weave in ends.

Ear (make 2 black and 2 white)
Ch 8, sc in 2nd ch from hook, hdc in next ch, dc in next ch, trc in next ch, dc in next ch, hdc in next ch, sc in next ch.

Finish off and weave in ends.

Club Numbers

Number One:
Starting at bottom, with black, ch 16; 5 dc in 4th ch from hook, ch 3, sl st in same ch; sc in next 9 chs (right side), 3 sc in next ch; sc in next 2 chs. Finish off, leaving a 12" end for sewing.

Number Three:
With black, ch 35; sc in 2nd ch from hook and in next 5 chs (right side), sk next 3 chs, sc in next 4 chs, 3 sc in next ch; sc in next ch, dec over next 2 chs (to work dec: draw up lp in each of next 2 chs, YO and draw through all 3 lps on hook—dec made); (dec over next 2 chs) 7 times; sc in next 3 chs. Finish off, leaving a 12" end for sewing.

Number Five:
With black, ch 35; sc in 2nd ch from hook and in next 5 chs (right side), 3 sc in next ch; sc in next 4 chs, 3 sc in next ch; sc in next 2 chs, dec over next 2 chs (to work dec: draw up lp in each of next 2 chs, YO and draw through all 3 lps on hook—dec made); (dec over next 2 chs) 7 times; sc in next 4 chs. Finish off, leaving a 12" end for sewing.

Finishing

Step 1: Place each eye in center of each white spot on Rnds 10 and 11.

Step 2: For Whiskers: cut three 6" lengths of black; weave 2 strands of black through 5th rnd under long hdc and long dc; weave one strand through 4th rnd of long dc.

Step 3: For Mane: cut sixty-two 4" lengths of white; wrap around each post of next 11 sc from 9th marked sc through 19th marked sc on Rnd 16; tie in knot. Wrap one length around each post of next 8 sc from 26th marked sc through 33rd marked sc on Rnd 16; tie in knot. Wrap one length around each post of next 6 sc from 10th marked sc through 15th marked sc on Rnd 17; tie in knot. Wrap one length around each post of next 7 sc from 26th marked sc through 32nd marked sc on Rnd 17; tie in knot. To make mane fluffy, unravel each yarn end.

Step 4: Hold wrong sides of one white and one black ear together; with tapestry needle and white yarn, sew using overcast st (see Crochet Stitch Guide on page 213) in BLs only of each of next 7 sts. Finish off, leaving an 8" end for sewing. Repeat for other ear.

Step 5: With white side of each ear facing you, sew each ear to head behind mane on Rnds 16 and 17.

Step 6: Referrring to photo for placement, sew numbers to covers.

Step 7: Referring to photo for placement, with tapestry needle and black, make nose using straight stitches (see Embroidery Stitch Guide on page 211).

RELAX & UNWIND

WITH

WINTUK

WINTUK — America's Number one yarn in a 3.5 oz. size. Known for quality, comfort and durability, WINTUK is now backed by the prestigious **GOOD HOUSEKEEPING SEAL.** Trusted by your mother and grandmother, WINTUK is ready for your next project!

If it's color, it's Caron!

1-800-868-9194

CARON®

www.caron.com

Let's Crochet

for Summer

Pretty Summer-weight afghan

Stamp-Out Cold Shoulders – Shrugs!

Sweaters Galore – Tunic and Pullover styles

Scarves, that make 'em look twice!

Summer Contents

On our cover:
Weekend Tunic by Carol Alexander, see page 128.

The Legacy of Elizabeth Hiddleson

You think you have a large collection of crochet patterns?

How would you feel if a giant moving van pulled up in your driveway and deposited seven tons of vintage crochet books?

Jennie Gaskin of Pitkin, Louisiana took it in stride—after all, she already owns a 10 x 44 -foot trailer filled with over 3,000 carefully catalogued crochet books.

Jennie may well be the "Queen of Crochet Books." She runs a small yarn shop next to her isolated home. "I'm located 2 miles from nowhere. Someone really has to want crochet thread or books to drive out here!" she said.

Jennie has been collecting books since 1967, when her grandmother gave her a copy of a 1915 Royal Society pattern book. "Grandmama's notes were in the margins, and it is my real treasure," Jennie said. She sells from her huge inventory at her shop, by direct mail and on her internet site. If you have a special pattern need she'll do a search for you. Her collection includes rare, out of print crochet books.

But what about those seven tons of books?

Elizabeth Hiddleson was a talented and prolific crochet thread designer. Although she held a full time job and had young children, her passion was thread crochet. One day she announced to her family that she was going to take

pictures of four doilies and try to sell the patterns. The family thought she had lost her mind! Years later, Elizabeth was able to buy each of her children a house with the money made from selling her patterns.

Her remarkable designs were all self-published and printed only in black and white.

Sold primarily through small ads in Workbasket, a popular needlework magazine of the time, her books became world-famous, and were even translated into Japanese! Elizabeth's body of work is extensive; in all she published 59 books and over 200 individual patterns. No contemporary designer can match the variety and innovation of her patterns.

After she retired, her daughter, then her granddaughter, continued to sell the books for many years. Now her granddaughter Shirley Siracusa (who doesn't crochet!) has retired, and sold her entire inventory (all seven tons of it) to Jennie!

Elizabeth is leaving a wonderful legacy for all of us; and thanks to Shirley and Jennie, those wonderful books won't be lost to the crochet world.

Jennie Gaskin can be reached at: Country Yarns, 182 Legg Loop, Pitkin, LA 70656-4675

e-mail: jgaskin@camtel.net

website: http://www.countryyarns.com

Double-Take Scarves

Show a spirited approach to fashion with scarves that'll make 'em look twice. Both our Oblong and Triangle shaped designs are crocheted very quickly with wonderful eyelash yarn. Make them to give or make a selection for your own accessory stash!

Triangle Scarf

Size:
About 36" wide x 32" long

Materials:
"Eyelash" type worsted weight yarn, 4³/4 oz (270 yds, 140 gms) multi-colored/silver; 3¹/2 oz (220 yds, 100 gms) black/silver (for fringe)
Size K (6.5mm) crochet hook, or size required for gauge

Gauge:
3 dc = about 1¹/2"

Instructions
Ch 2.

Row 1: Sc in 2nd ch from hook. Ch 1, turn.

Row 2: 3 sc in first sc. Ch 3 (counts as first dc on following rows), turn.

Row 3: Dc in first 2 sc, 2 dc in next sc—5 dc. Ch 3, turn.

Row 4: Dc in first dc and in each dc to turning ch-3; 2 dc in 3rd ch of turning ch-3. Ch 3, turn.

Rep Row 4 until scarf measures about 32". At end of last row, do not ch 3.

Finish off and weave in all ends.

Fringe
Following Fringe instructions on page 211, make Single Knot Fringe. Cut 16" strands of black/silver. Use 4 strands for each knot and tie one knot in each row along each side edge. Trim ends even.

Oblong Scarf

Size:
About 5¹/2" x 62"

Materials:
"Eyelash" type worsted weight yarn, 3¹/2 oz (220 yds, 100 gms) black/gold
Size K (6.5mm) crochet hook, or size required for gauge
Size 16 tapestry needle

Gauge:
5 dc = about 2"

Instructions
Ch 18 loosely.

Row 1 (right side): Dc in 3rd ch from hook (beg 2 skipped chs count as a dc) and in each rem ch—17 dc. Ch 3, turn.

Row 2: Dc in each dc and in 2nd ch of beg 2 skipped chs. Ch 3, turn.

Row 3: Dc in each dc and in 3rd ch of turning ch 3. Ch 3, turn.

Repeat Row 3 until scarf measures about 62". At end of last row, do not ch 3.

Finish off and weave in all ends.

All-American Kid

In-vest in the future of our country! This patriotic red, white and blue vest is perfect for young patriots!

— designed by Jennine Korejko

Sizing:

Size:	4	6	8
Finished Chest Measurement:	25"	26½"	28"

Note: Instructions are written for size 4; changes for larger sizes are in parentheses.

Materials:

Worsted weight yarn, 2½ oz (175 yds, 75 gms) red; 2 oz (140 yds, 60 gms) white; 3 oz (210 yds, 90 gms) blue

Note: Our photographed model was made with Red Heart® Super Saver, Cherry Red #319; Aran #313; and Royal Blue #385.

Size G (4.25mm) crochet hook, or size required for gauge

Size 16 tapestry needle

Gauge:

14 sc = 4"

16 sc rows = 4"

Instructions

With red, ch 67 (71, 77).

Body

Row 1 (right side): Sc in 2nd ch from hook and in each rem ch—66 (70, 76) sc. Ch 1, turn.

Note: When changing colors, work last st until 2 lps rem on hook, draw new color through. Cut old color.

Row 2: 2 sc in first sc; sc in each sc to last sc; 2 sc in last sc, changing to blue in last sc—68 (72, 78) sc. Ch 1, turn.

Row 3: Rep Row 2, changing to white in last sc—70 (74, 80) sc.

Row 4: Rep Row 2. At end of row, do not change color—72 (76, 82) sc.

Row 5: Rep Row 2, changing to red in last sc—74 (78, 84) sc.

Rows 6 through 8: Rep Row 2. At end of Row 8, change to blue in last sc—80 (84, 90) sc.

Row 9: Rep Row 2, changing to white in last sc—82 (86, 92) sc.

Row 10: Rep Row 2. At end of Row 10, do not change color—84 (88, 94) sc. Mark beg and end of Row 10 for edging placement.

Row 11: Rep Row 2, changing to red in last sc—86 (90, 96) sc.

For Sizes 4 and 6 Only:

Row 12: Sc in each sc, changing to blue in last sc. Ch 1, turn.

Row 13: Sc in each sc. Ch 1, turn.

Rows 14 through 18 (20): Rep Row 13.

Row 19 (21): Sc in each sc, changing to red in last sc. Ch 1, turn.

Continue with For All Sizes below.

For Size 8 Only:

Row 12: Sc in each sc. Ch 1, turn.

Row 13: Rep Row 12, changing to blue in last sc. Ch 1, turn.

Rows 14 through 21: Rep Row 12.

Row 22: Rep Row 12, changing to red in last sc. Ch 1, turn.

Row 23: Sc in each sc. Ch 1, turn.

For All Sizes:

Row 20 (22, 24): Sc in each sc, changing to white in last sc. Ch 1, turn.

Row 21 (23, 25): Sc in each sc. Ch 1, turn.

Row 22 (24, 26): Sc in each sc, changing to blue in last sc. Ch 1, turn.

Row 23 (25, 27): Sc in each sc, changing to red in last sc. Ch 1, turn.

Rows 24 (26, 28) and 25 (27, 29): Rep Row 21 (23, 25).

Rows 26 (28, 30) through 29 (31, 33): Rep Rows 20 (22, 24) through 23 (25, 27).

Row 30 (32, 34): Sc in each sc. Ch 1, turn.

Right Front

Row 31 (33, 35): Dec over first 2 sc (to work dec: draw up lp in each of next 2 sts, YO and draw through all 3 lps on hook—dec made); sc in next 18 (19, 21) sc—19 (20, 22) sc. Ch 1, turn, leaving rem sc unworked.

Row 32 (34, 36): Sc in each sc, changing to white in last sc. Ch 1, turn.

Row 33 (35, 37): Dec over first 2 sc; sc in each rem sc—18 (19, 21) sc. Ch 1, turn.

Row 34 (36, 38): Sc in each sc, changing to blue in last sc. Ch 1, turn.

Row 35 (37, 39): Dec; sc in each rem sc, changing to red in last sc—17 (18, 20) sc.

Row 36 (38, 40): Sc in each sc. Ch 1, turn.

Row 37 (39, 41): Dec; sc in each rem sc—16 (17, 19) sc. Ch 1, turn.

Note: On following rows, work in color sequence as established.

Rows 38 (40, 42) through 49 (51, 53): Sc in each sc, dec one st at neck edge every other row, 6 times more. At end of Row 49 (51, 53)—10 (11, 13) sc.

Row 50 (52, 54): Sc in each sc. Ch 1, turn.

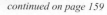

continued on page 159

Part Three – Double Crochet

— by Jean Leinhauser

Here's a stitch with many faces, and many uses. It is the basis of shell stitches, puff stitches, clusters, and many more decorative patterns.

Adjusting Stitch Height

Perhaps the only difficult aspect to double crochet is attaining both row gauge and the stitch gauge given in a pattern—but there's an easy way to solve the problem.

First, use whatever hook size needed to get the stitch gauge. (We know you hate doing gauge swatches, but do it anyway!) Now check the row gauge.

If you have too many rows per inch, you'll need to work your double crochet stitches taller, but don't change hook size! Instead, adjust the double crochet stitches as follows:

Work a double crochet until there are 3 loops on the hook (**Fig 1**); now gently pull up on the loop marked **A** until it is higher than before; keep trying until you achieve the correct height.

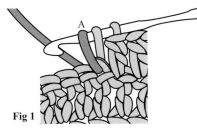

Fig 1

If you have too few rows per inch, your double crochet stitches need to be shorter.

Again, work a double crochet until there are 3 loops on the hook (**Fig 2**); now gently pull down the loop marked **A** until it is shorter than before; keep trying until you achieve the correct height.

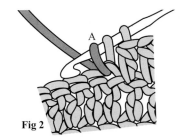

Fig 2

Double Crochet in Filet

The height of a double crochet stitch is especially important in working filet crochet, where you want the stitches and spaces to be perfectly square. The method above should solve the problem.

Turning Chains

When turning rows of double crochet, you can use either two or three chains.

A chain-2 may give a neater edge. Experiment and see which you like better.

Single Crochet Edging

Often you will need to work a round of single crochet as an edging around a double crochet piece. Working the single crochet stitches on the sides of a piece—that is, where the double crochets form the end and beginning of a row—can be confusing. There are two ways to do this.

1. Work a single crochet through the post of each double crochet, then another single crochet in the hole just below the double crochet stitch (**Photo A**).

This method gives a firm neat edge.

Photo A

2. Work two single crochets around the post of each double crochet (**Photo B**).

Photo B

This method will leave a series of holes, which you may want as a decorative accent.

Whichever method you choose, instructions may read …"adjusting stitches to keep work flat". This means that every few stitches, check your work to be sure it is not puckering. If so, go back and skip a stitch here and there.

Double Crochet Post Stitches

Instead of working into the top of a double crochet stitch, you can add nice texture and pattern by working around the post of a stitch.

Front Post Double Crochet (FPdc) is worked as follows:

YO, insert hook from front to back to front around post of stitch (**Fig 3**), YO, draw up lp, (YO and draw through 2 loops on hook) twice.

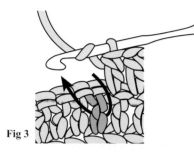

Fig 3

Back Post Double Crochet (BPdc) is worked as follows:

YO, insert hook from back to front to back around post of stitch (**Fig 4**), YO, draw up loop, (YO and draw through 2 loops on hook) twice.

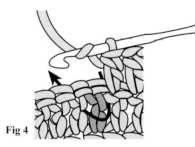

Fig 4

When working post stitches, draw up the yarn to make the double crochets a little taller, as going around the post shortens the stitches.

Post Stitch Variations

Variation 1: Alternating Rows

This variation gives a firm texture, and looks quite different on the front and the back.

Ch 36.

Foundation Row: Dc in 4th ch from hook (beg 3 skipped chs count as a dc) and in each rem ch—34 dc. Ch 3 (counts as first dc on following rows), turn.

Row 1: FPdc around each dc; dc in 3rd ch of beg 3 skipped chs. Ch 3, turn.

Row 2: BPdc around each dc; dc in 3rd ch of turning ch-3. Ch 3, turn.

Rep Rows 1 and 2 for pattern.

Either side can be used as the "right" side (**Photos C** and **D**).

Photo C

Photo D

Variation 2: Checkerboard

Ch 36 and work Foundation Row of Variation 1.

Row 1 (right side)**:** * FPdc around each of next 4 dc; BPdc around each of next 4 dc; rep from * to beg 3 skipped chs, dc in 3rd ch of beg skipped chs. Ch 3, turn.

Rows 2 through 4: Rep Row 1.

Row 5: * BPdc around each of next 4 dc; FPdc around each of next 4 dc; rep from * to turning ch-3, dc in 3rd ch of turning ch. Ch 3, turn.

Rows 6, 7 and 8: Rep Row 5.

Rep Rows 1 through 8 for pattern.

(Example shown in **Photo E**.)

Photo E

Cheery Stripes Dishcloth

It's hard to feel down in the dumps as you wash the dinner dishes with this colorful crocheted cloth.

— designed by Stephanie Hill

Size:
About 8 1/2" x 9 1/2"

Materials:
Worsted weight cotton yarn, 1/2 oz (35 yds, 15 gms) each, white, green, blue, and yellow-green variegated

Note: Our photographed dishcloth made with Lion Brand® Kitchen Cotton, White #100; Lime #174; Morning Glory Blue #108; and Lemon-Lime #239.

Size H (5mm) crochet hook, or size required for gauge

Size 16 tapestry needle

Gauge:
4 dc = 1"

Instructions

Note: When changing colors at the end of a row, work last st until 2 lps rem on hook; draw new color through. Cut old color.

With green, ch 32.

Row 1 (right side)**:** Sc in 2nd ch from hook and in each rem ch—31 sc. Ch 2 (counts as first dc on following rows), turn.

Row 2: Dc in each sc. Ch 5 (counts as first dc and ch-3 sp on following rows), turn.

Row 3: Sk next 2 dc, sl st in next dc; * ch 5, sk next 2 dc, sl st in next dc; rep from * 7 times more; ch 3, sk next 2 dc, dc in 2nd ch of turning ch-2. Ch 5, turn.

Row 4: Sl st in next ch-3 sp, ch 3; * sl st in next ch-5 sp, ch 3; rep from * 8 times more; dc in 2nd ch of turning ch-5. Ch 2, turn.

Row 5: Dc in next ch-3 sp, 3 dc in each of next 9 ch-3 sps; dc in next ch-3 sp and in 2nd ch of turning ch-5, changing to white in last dc—31 dc. Ch 1, turn.

Row 6: Sc in each dc and in 2nd ch of turning ch-2, changing to variegated in last sc. Ch 2, turn.

Row 7: Dc in each sc, changing to blue in last dc. Ch 2 (counts as an hdc on following rows), turn.

continued on page 158

Weekend Tunic

— designed by Carol Alexander

Looks can be deceiving. This comfortable, lacy tunic-style sweater features beautiful stitches that may look complicated but work up quickly and easily in just a couple of days.

Materials:

Size 3 cotton thread, 22 (25, 32) oz [1400 (1600, 2000) yds, 420 (480, 600) gms] blue

Note: Our photographed sweater was made with J. & P. Coats® Speed Cro-Sheen®, Blue #4.

Size F (3.75mm) crochet hook, or size required for gauge

Gauge:

9 sc = 2"
In pattern:
5 Xsts = 3"
Rows 2 through 5 = 1¹/₂"

Pattern Stitch

Cross Stitch (Xst):

YO twice, draw up lp in last st worked, YO, draw through 2 lps on hook; YO, sk next 2 sts, draw up lp in next st, (YO, draw through 2 lps on hook) 4 times; ch 1, dc in center of st (see **Fig 1**)—Xst made.

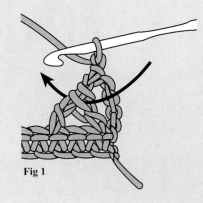

Fig 1

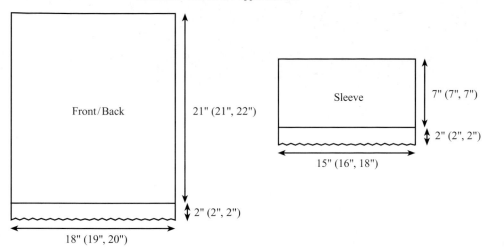

All measurements are approximate.

Front/Back

21" (21", 22")

18" (19", 20")

2" (2", 2")

Sleeve

7" (7", 7")

2" (2", 2")

15" (16", 18")

Sizing:

	X-Small	Small	Medium
Chest Measurement:	(30")	(32")	(34")
Finished Chest Measurement:	(36")	(38")	(40")

Note: Instructions are written for size X-small; changes for larger sizes are in parentheses.

Instructions

Front/Back (make 2)

Ch 92 (98, 104).

Row 1 (wrong side): Sc in 2nd ch from hook and in each rem ch—91 (97, 103) sc. Ch 4 (counts as first trc on following rows), turn.

Row 2 (right side): Xst (see Pattern Stitch) over first 4 sts; * Xst over last st worked and next 3 sts; rep from * 28 (30, 32) times more; trc in same st as last leg of last Xst made—30 (32, 34) Xsts. Ch 1, turn.

Row 3: Sc in first st; * ch 5, sk next 5 sts, sc in next st; rep from * across. Ch 3 (counts as first dc on following rows), turn, leaving turning ch unworked.

Row 4: 6 dc in next ch-5 sp; * keeping last lp of each dc on hook, dc in same ch-5 sp and in next ch-5 sp, YO and draw through all 3 lps on hook—cluster made; 5 dc in same ch-5 sp; rep from * 13 times more; dc in next sc. Ch 1, turn.

Row 5: Sc in each dc and in each cluster. Ch 4, turn, leaving turning ch unworked.

Rows 6 through 53 (53, 57): Rep Rows 2 through 5, 12 (12, 13) times more.

Row 54 (54, 58): Rep Row 2.

Row 55 ((55, 59): Sc in each sc. Finish off.

Sleeve (make 2)

Ch 80 (86, 92).

Row 1 (wrong side): Sc in 2nd ch from hook and in each rem ch—79 (85, 91) sc. Ch 4 (counts as first trc on following rows), turn.

Row 2 (right side): Xst (see Pattern Stitch) over first 4 sts; * Xst over last st worked and next 3 sts; rep from * 24 (26, 28) times more; trc in same st as last leg of last Xst made—26 (28, 30) Xsts. Ch 1, turn.

Row 3: Sc in first st; * ch 5, sk next 5 sts, sc in next st; rep from * across. Ch 3 (counts as first dc on following rows), turn, leaving turning ch unworked.

Row 4: 6 dc in next ch-5 sp; * keeping last lp of each dc on hook, dc in same ch-5 sp and in next ch-5 sp, YO and draw through all 3 lps on hook—cluster made; 5 dc in same ch-5 sp; rep from * 11 (12, 13) times more; dc in next sc. Ch 1, turn.

Row 5: Sc in each dc and in each cluster. Ch 4, turn, leaving turning ch unworked— 79 (85, 91) sc.

Rows 6 through 17: Rep Rows 2 through 5, three times more.

Row 18: Rep Row 2.

Row 19: Sc in each dc and in each cluster. Finish off, leaving turning ch unworked.

Assembly

Hold front and back with wrong sides tog; carefully matching sts, sew shoulder seams from outer edge about 5¹/4" (5 ³/4", 6³/4"). Sew one sleeve to body matching center of Row 19 to shoulder seam. Rep for other sleeve. Sew sleeve and side seams.

Lower Border:

Hold tunic with right side of back facing you and beg ch at top; join yarn in 46th (49th, 52nd) unused lp of beg ch.

Rnd 1: Ch 1, working around lower edge, sc in same lp and in each rem unused lp; join in first sc—182 (194, 206) sc.

Rnd 2: Ch 4 (counts as a dc and a ch-1 sp on this and following rnds), sk next sc; * dc in next sc, ch 1, sk next sc; rep from * around; join in 3rd ch of beg ch-4.

Rnd 3: Ch 1, sc in same ch as joining; ch 5, sk next dc; * sc in next dc, ch 5, sk next dc; rep from * around; join in first sc.

Rnd 4: Sl st in next ch-5 sp, ch 1, 7 sc in same sp and in each rem ch-5 sp; join in first sc.

Rnd 5: Sl st in next 3 sc, ch 1, sc in same sc as last sl st made, ch 3; * sk next 6 sc, sc in next sc, ch 3; rep from * around; join in first sc.

Rnd 6: Sl st in next 2 chs of next ch-3 sp, ch 4, dc in next sc, ch 1; * dc in 2nd ch of next ch-3 sp, ch 1, dc in next sc, ch 1; rep from * around; join in 3rd ch of beg ch-4.

Rnd 7: Sl st in next ch-1 sp, ch 1, in same sp work (sc, ch 3, sc); in each rem ch-1 sp work (sc, ch 3, sc); join in first sc. Finish off.

Sleeve Border:

Hold one sleeve with right side facing you and beg ch at top; join yarn in seam.

Rnd 1: Ch 1, sc in same sp as joining and in each unused lp of beg ch; join in first sc—80 (86, 92) sc.

Rnds 2 through 7: Rep Rnds 2 through 7 of Lower Border.

Work other sleeve border in same manner.

Weave in all ends.

Desert Stripes

Materials:

Sport weight cotton, 10 (10, 12¹/2) oz [640 (640, 800) yds, 280 (280, 350) gms] each, coral and light green; 5 (5, 7¹/2) oz [320 (320, 480) yds, 140 (140, 210) gms] off white

Note: Our photographed sweater was made with Coats & Clark South Maid® "Cotton 8", Coral #815; Moss Green #814; and Cream #803.

Size F (3.75mm) crochet hook, or size required for gauge

Size E (3.5mm) crochet hook

Gauge:

6 sc = 1"

Color Sequence:

5 rows coral
1 row off white
5 rows light green
1 row off white

Instructions

Note: Ch-1 sps count as sts throughout.

Back

With larger size hook and coral, ch 108 (120, 132).

Row 1 (right side): Sc in 2nd ch from hook; * ch 1, sk next ch, sc in next ch; rep from * across—53 (59, 65) ch-1 sps. Ch 1, turn.

Row 2: Sc in first sc and in next ch-1 sp; * ch 1, sc in next ch-1 sp; rep from * 51 (57, 63) times more; sc in next sc. Ch 1, turn.

Row 3: Sc in first sc; * ch 1, sc in next ch-1 sp; rep from * 51 (57, 63) times more; ch 1, sk next sc, sc in next sc. Ch 1, turn.

Rows 4 and 5: Rep Rows 2 and 3. At end of Row 5, change to off white by drawing lp through; cut coral.

Rows 6 through 71: Working in color sequence, rep Rows 2 and 3, 32 times more.

Row 72: In color sequence, rep Row 2. At end of row, do not ch 1, finish off.

Sizing:

Sizes:	Small	Medium	Large
Chest Measurement:	32"- 34"	36"- 38"	40"- 42"
Finished Chest Measurement:	36"	40"	44"

Note: Instructions are written for size small; changes for larger sizes are in parentheses.

All measurements are approximate.

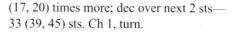

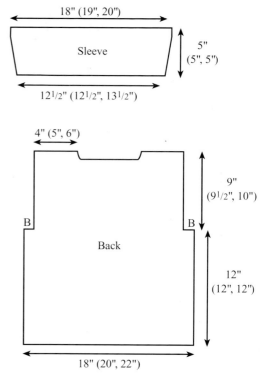

Armhole Shaping:

Hold piece with right side facing you; sk first 6 sts of Row 72, with larger size hook and color in sequence, join in next ch-1 sp.

Row 1 (right side): Ch 1, sc in same sp; * ch 1, sc in next ch-1 sp; rep from * 46 (52, 58) times more—95 (107, 119) sts. Ch 1, turn, leaving rem 6 sts unworked.

Row 2: Sc in first sc and in next ch-1 sp; * ch 1, sc in next ch-1 sp; rep from * 45 (51, 57) times more; sc in next sc. Ch 1, turn.

Row 3: Sc in first sc, ch 1; *sc in next ch-1 sp, ch 1; rep from * 45 (51, 57) times more; sk next sc, sc in next sc. Ch 1, turn.

Continuing in color sequence, rep Rows 2 and 3 until armhole measures 8" (8½", 9"), ending by working a right side row.

Left Back Neck Shaping:

Note: Continue in color sequence as established.

Row 1 (wrong side): Sc in first sc and in next ch-1 sp; * ch 1, sc in next ch-1 sp; rep from * 10 (13, 16) times more; sc in next sc—25 (31, 37) sts. Ch 1, turn, leaving rem sts unworked.

Row 2 (right side): Sc in first sc; * ch 1, sc in next ch-1 sp; rep from * 10 (13, 16) times more; ch 1, sk next sc, sc in next sc. Ch 1, turn.

Row 3: Sc in first sc and in next ch-1 sp; * ch 1, sc in next ch-1 sp; rep from * 10 (13, 16) times more; sc in next sc. Ch 1, turn.

Rep Rows 2 and 3 until armhole measures 9" (9½", 10"). Finish off and weave in all ends.

Right Back Neck Shaping:

Hold back with wrong side facing you; sk next 45 sts from left back neck shaping; with larger size hook and continuing in color sequence, join yarn in next sc.

Row 1 (wrong side): Ch 1, sc in same sc and in next ch-1 sp; * ch 1, sc in next ch-1 sp; rep from * 10 (13, 16) times more; sc in next sc. Ch 1, turn.

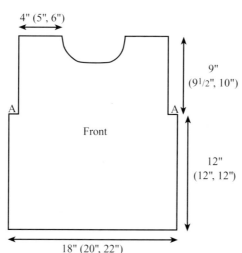

Front

Back

Row 2 (right side): Sc in first sc; * ch 1, sc in next ch-1 sp; rep from * 10 (13, 16) times more; ch 1, sk next sc, sc in next sc. Ch 1, turn.

Row 3: Sc in first sc and in next ch-1 sp; * ch 1, sc in next ch-1 sp; rep from * 10 (13, 16) times more; sc in next sc. Ch 1, turn.

Continuing in color sequence, rep Rows 2 and 3 until armhole measures 9" (9½", 10"). Finish off and weave in all ends.

Front

Work same as for Back until armholes measure 6" (6½", 7"), ending by working a right side row.

Right Front Neck Shaping:

Row 1 (wrong side): Continuing in color sequence, sc in first sc and in next ch-1 sp; * ch 1, sc in next ch-1 sp; rep from * 15 (18, 21) times more; sc in next sc—35 (41, 47) sts. Ch 1, turn.

Row 2 (right side): Dec over first 2 sc (to work dec: draw up lp in each of next 2 sts, YO and draw through all 3 lps on hook—dec made); sc in next ch-1 sp; * ch 1, sc in next ch-1 sp; rep from * 14 (17, 20) times more; ch 1, sk next sc, sc in next sc—34 (40, 46) sts. Ch 1, turn.

Row 3: Sc in first sc and in next ch-1 sp; * ch 1, sc in next ch-1 sp; rep from * 14

(17, 20) times more; dec over next 2 sts—33 (39, 45) sts. Ch 1, turn.

Row 4: Dec; sc in next ch-1 sp; * ch 1, sc in next ch-1 sp; rep from * 13 (16, 19) times more; ch 1, sk next sc, sc in next sc—32 (38, 44) sts. Ch 1, turn.

Row 5: Sc in first sc and in next ch-1 sp; * ch 1, sc in next ch-1 sp; rep from * 13 (16, 19) times more; dec—31 (37, 43) sts. Ch 1, turn.

Row 6: Dec; sc in next ch-1 sp; * ch 1, sc in next ch-1 sp; rep from * 12 (15, 18) times more; ch 1, sk next sc, sc in next sc—30 (36, 42) sts. Ch 1, turn.

Row 7: Sc in first sc and in next ch-1 sp; * ch 1, sc in next ch-1 sp; rep from * 12 (15, 18) times more; dec—29 (35, 41) sts. Ch 1, turn.

Row 8: Dec; sc in next ch-1 sp; * ch 1, sc in next ch-1 sp; rep from * 11 (14, 17) times more; ch 1, sk next sc, sc in next sc—28 (34, 40) sts. Ch 1, turn.

Row 9: Sc in first sc and in next ch-1 sp; * ch 1, sc in next ch-1 sp; rep from * 11 (14, 17) times more; dec—27 (33, 39) sts. Ch 1, turn.

Row 10: Dec; sc in next ch-1 sp; * ch 1, sc in next ch-1 sp; rep from * 10 (13, 16) times more; ch 1, sk next sc, sc in next sc—26 (32, 38) sts. Ch 1, turn.

continued on page 160

Recreate an Antique Treasure
Patriotic Spirit

This crocheter's tribute to Old Glory is as charming today as when it was first created. We've copied this patriotic treasure from the past using bedspread-weight crochet cotton and then framed it.

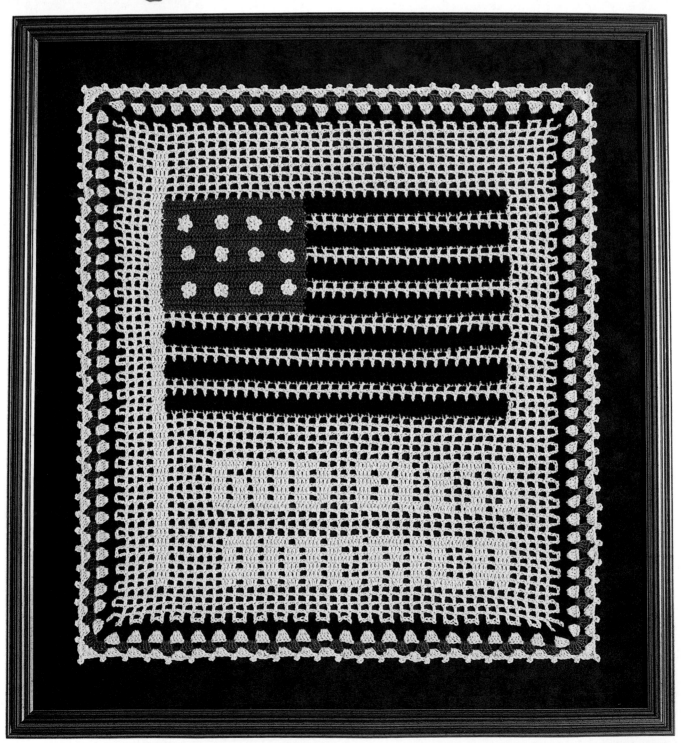

Recreation of original antique

Size:
About 16" x 58"

Materials:
Bedspread-weight crochet cotton, 350 yds off white; 100 yds red; 50 yds blue

Note: Our photographed flag was made with Coats & Clark South Maid®, Cream #430; Victory Red #494; and True Blue #482.

Size 6 (1.80mm) crochet hook, or size required for gauge

Size 16 tapestry needle

Gauge:
6 squares x 6 squares = 2"

Instructions

Note: If you are not familiar with working filet from a chart, please read Filet Review beginning on page 214.

Center
With off white, ch 134.

Row 1 (right side): Dc in 9th ch from hook, (ch 2, sk next 2 chs, dc in next ch) 42 times. Ch 5 (counts as a dc and a ch-2 sp), turn.

Following chart, work Rows 2 through 24.

Note: When changing colors, work last st until 2 lps rem on hook, draw new color through.

Row 25 (right side): Dc in next dc, (ch 2, sk next 2 chs, dc in next dc) 3 times; ch 2, dc in next dc, changing to red, drop off white; (dc in next 2 chs, and in next dc) 32 times; ch 2, dc in next dc, changing to off white, drop red; dc in next 3 dc; (ch 2, sk next 2 chs, dc in next dc) 4 times. Ch 5, turn.

Following chart, work Rows 26 through 36, changing colors as necessary.

Row 37 (right side): Dc in next dc, (ch 2, sk next 2 chs, dc in next

dc) 3 times; ch 2, dc in next dc, changing to red, drop off white; dc in next 60 dc, changing to blue in last dc; drop red; dc in next 38 dc, changing to off white in last dc, drop blue; dc in next 3 dc, (ch 2, sk next 2 chs, dc in next dc) 4 times. Ch 5, turn.

Following chart, work Rows 38 through 59, changing colors as necessary. At end of Row 59, do not ch 5. Finish off.

Edging
Hold piece with right side facing you and Row 59 at top; join red in ch-2 sp in upper right-hand corner.

Rnd 1 (right side):
Ch 3 (counts as a dc on this and following rnds), 3 dc in same sp—beg corner made; † ch 2, 4 dc in next ch-2 sp; (ch 2, sk next ch-2 sp, 4 dc in next ch-2 sp) 20 times; ch 2, 4 dc in next ch-2 sp—

corner made; ch 2, 4 dc in next ch-2 sp; (ch 2, sk next ch-2 sp, 4 dc in next ch-2 sp) 28 times; ch 2 †; 4 dc in next ch-2 sp—corner made; rep from † to † once; join in 3rd ch of beg ch-3. Finish off.

Rnd 2: Join off white in first ch-2 sp to left of upper right-hand corner; ch 3, 3 dc in same sp; † (ch 2, 4 dc in next ch-2 sp) 21 times; ch 4, 4 dc in next ch-2 sp—corner made; (ch 2, 4 dc in next ch-2 sp) 29 times; ch 4 †; 4 dc in next ch-2 sp—corner made; rep from † to † once; join in 3rd ch of beg ch-3. Finish off.

Rnd 3: Join blue in ch-4 sp in upper right-hand corner; ch 3, in same sp work (3 dc, ch 2, 4 dc)—beg corner made; † (ch 2, 4 dc in next ch-2 sp) 21 times; ch 2, in next ch-4 sp work (4 dc, ch 2, 4 dc)—corner made; (ch 2, 4 dc in next ch-2 sp) 29 times; ch 2 †; in next ch-4 sp work (4 dc, ch 2, 4 dc)—corner made; rep from † to † once; join in 3rd ch of beg ch-3. Finish off.

Rnd 4: Join off white in ch-2 sp in upper right-hand corner; ch 3; † in same sp work (3 dc, ch 5, sl st in 5th ch from hook—picot made, 4 dc)—corner made; (ch 5, sl st in 5th ch from hook—picot made, 4 dc in next ch-2 sp) 22 times; ch 5, sl st in 5th ch from hook—picot made; in next ch-2 sp work (4 dc, ch 5, sl st in 5th ch from hook—picot made, 4 dc)—corner made; (ch 5, sl st in

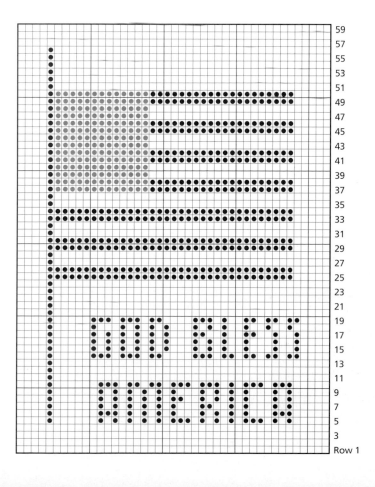

Original work was crocheted with size 20 cotton thread.

continued on page 158

CARON®

Trusted for Generations

When Ovidas Joseph Caron started a small yarn spinning operation in Rochelle, Illinois in 1916, he could never have envisioned that 83 years later crochet enthusiasts the world over would still be using his yarns to create treasured heirlooms for their families and friends. But Ovidas probably wouldn't be surprised to learn that the Good Housekeeping Seal now backs all Caron yarns, a seal that has been assuring quality since 1909.

Today, Caron International now brings 14 different hand-knitting yarns to you, in every texture, weight and color you can imagine. And each yarn offers both value and guaranteed quality, year after year. You probably have an afghan your grandmother made from Caron Wintuk® yarn. Or you may have a sweater that a loving aunt made with Caron Sayelle®. Our yarns have always been developed for lasting beauty from generation to generation.

LIMITED WARRANTY TO CONSUMERS
Good Housekeeping
Promises
REPLACEMENT OR REFUND IF DEFECTIVE

The Acrylic Standard

Looking for a premium 4-ply worsted weight yarn? Our popular Wintuk® and Sayelle® brands have set the standard for quality in rich colors chosen to coordinate with your home decor or to complement your wardrobe. For a great value, look for our no-dye lot Natura®, Perfect Match® and One Pound® brands of 4-ply worsted weight.

Simply the Softest

When you think soft, think Caron! Crocheters across America prefer Caron's Simply Soft® yarn time after time. If you haven't touched (cuddled and snuggled) an afghan made with Simply Soft, you are in for a treat! Even after washing and drying this 4-ply worsted weight acrylic yarn, you can still feel the Simply Soft difference. That's why people say it's "Simply the Softest!"

Yarns for Every Project from CARON®

- Wintuk™
- Sayelle™
- SimplySoft™
- Simply Soft™ Baby Sport
- Perfect Match™
- Natura™
- One Pound™
- Dazzleaire™
- Cuddlesoft™
- Cuddlesoft™ Pomp
- Aunt Lydia's Craft & Rug Yarn
- Victorian Christmas Gold
- Christmas Glitter
- Grandma's Best Cotton Crochet Thread

Have a Very Caron Christmas

When it comes to Christmas yarns, Caron is the leader! Check your local store for seasonal displays of Christmas yarn (traditional red, green, white and ombre). Put some sparkle in your holiday afghans and wearables with Caron Christmas Glitter and Victorian Christmas Gold yarns featuring glittering metallic fibers!

Latch Hook, Too!

Many of our crochet customers are latch hook fans, too. If you haven't tried latch hook, you can give it a whirl with one of Caron's plush latch hook kits in one of your favorite characters. Caron's latch hook kits make this yarn craft easy to learn. Plus our quality yarns and pre-printed canvas ensures success even the first time. Choose from Mickey Unlimited®, Pooh® from Disney as well as the ever-popular Looney Toons® characters from Warner Bros. and NASCAR® designs for racing fans.

Just For Kids

Teach a child to latch hook with our newest line just for children—Krafty Kids® Activity Kits! Recommended for age 7 and up, each Krafty Kids kit includes an 8" x 8" canvas, top quality acrylic yarn, and a latch hook tool. To make latching easier for small fingers, all Krafty Kids canvasses have a slightly larger weave. We've created kid-friendly designs, too, including: Puppy (pictured here), Peace, Kitty, Heart, Panda, Butterfly and WWJD. You can teach yourself and a child at the same time!

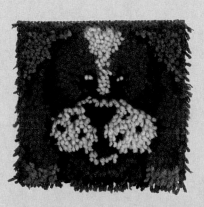

The Good Housekeeping Seal

At Caron, we believe that our customers are vibrant and active and very receptive to new concepts and ideas. Our goal is to meet their creative needs as well as their desire for a top quality yarn product at a fair price. The Caron team takes that goal very seriously, even so far as to seek the coveted Good Housekeeping Seal for all Caron yarn products. Beginning this year, all Caron yarns will bear the Good Housekeeping Seal; Caron yarns are the first and only yarns that bear the Good Housekeeping Seal. Since 1909, all products that bear the Good Housekeeping Seal are backed by a limited two-year warranty. If a product (or something made from the product) bearing the seal proves to be defective at any time within two years from the date it was first purchased, Good Housekeeping will replace the product or refund the purchase price. Well recognized by our consumers, the Good Housekeeping Seal is your guarantee that you are buying the best with Caron!

The Good Housekeeping Guarantee:

"If a product (or something made from the product) bearing the seal proves to be defective at any time within two years from the date it was first purchased, Good Housekeeping will replace the product or refund the purchase price."

CARON®

Set an inviting luncheon table with lovely filet crocheted roses. This timeless design will be enjoyed any season of the year.

Everything's Rosy

— designed by Yalanda Wiese

Size:

About 52" x 52"

Materials:

Size 10 bedspread weight
crochet cotton, 13 (225-yd)
balls white

*Note: Our photographed
tablecloth was made with
J. & P. Coats® Knit-Cro-
Sheen®, White #1.*

Size 6 (1.80mm) steel crochet
hook, or size required
for gauge

Gauge:

8 squares x 8 squares = 2"

Instructions

*Note: If you are not familiar
with working filet from a
chart, please read Filet
Review beginning on
page 214.*

*Please note that on this chart
each open square (or box) is
formed by a ch-1 sp (not a ch-
2 sp) and each closed square
(or box) consists of 3 dc (not
4 dc).*

Ch 424.

Row 1 (right side): Dc in 4th
ch from hook and in each rem
ch. Ch 3 (counts as first dc on
following rows), turn.

Following chart, work
rem rows.

At end of last row, do not
ch 3; do not turn.

Finish off and weave in
all ends.

In the Pink

— *designed by Carol Alexander*

Mothers and young daughters look picture perfect in matching pink sweaters. This is a lightweight style that can be worn for many occasions all through the year. Wear it over a tank top in summer, a turtleneck in the winter or a cotton shirt in the fall.

Junior Miss Pullover

6" (7", 7", 8")

Front

17" (17", 18", 19")

19" (20", 21", 22")

Sizing:

Sizes:	Petite	Small	Medium	Large
Bust Measurement:	32"-34"	35"-37"	38"-40"	41"-43"
Finished Chest Measurement:	38"	40"	42"	44"

Note: Instructions are written for size petite; changes for larger sizes are in parentheses.

Materials:

Size 3 cotton thread, 18 (19½, 22½, 24) oz [1200 (1300, 1400, 1500) yds, 540 (580, 675, 720) gms] pink

Note: Our photographed model was made with J. & P. Coats® Speed-Cro-Sheen®, Mid Rose #46A.

Size G (4.25mm) crochet hook, or size required for gauge

Size 18 tapestry needle

Four ¾" diameter buttons

Sewing needle and matching thread

6" (7", 7", 8")

Back

17" (17", 18", 19")

19" (20", 21", 22")

16" (16", 17", 17")

Sleeve

19" (19", 20", 20")

Gauge:

In pattern:
(sc, ch 3, sc), shell, (sc, ch 3, sc) = 1½"
5 rows = 2"

Instructions

Back

Starting at lower edge, ch 106 (113, 120, 127).

Row 1 (right side): Sc in 2nd ch from hook; * † sk next 2 chs, in next ch work (dc, ch 1) twice; dc in same ch—shell made; sk next 2 chs, sc in next ch †; ch 3, sc in next ch; rep from * 13 (14, 15, 16) times more, then rep from † to † once—15 (16, 17, 18) shells. Ch 7 (counts as a trc and a ch-3 sp on following rows), turn.

Row 2: * † In 2nd dc of next shell work (sc, ch 3, sc); ch 3 †; dc in next ch-3 sp, ch 3; rep from * 13 (14, 15, 16) times more, then rep from † to † once; trc in next sc. Ch 1, turn.

Row 3: Sc in first trc; * † sk next ch-3 sp, shell in next ch-3 sp †; sk next ch-3 sp; in next dc work (sc, ch 3, sc); rep from * 13 (14, 15, 16) times more, then rep from † to † once; sk next 3 chs of turning ch-7, sc in next ch. Ch 7, turn.

Rows 4 through 41 (41, 43, 45): Rep Rows 2 and 3, 19 (19, 20, 21) times more.

Row 42 (42, 44, 46): Rep Row 2.

Row 43 (43, 45, 47): Sc in first trc; * † sk next ch-3 sp, in next ch-3 sp work (hdc, ch 1) twice; hdc in same sp †; sk next ch-3 sp, in next dc work (sc, ch 1, sc); rep from * 13 (14, 15, 16) times more, then rep from † to † once; sk next 3 chs of turning ch-7, sc in next ch. Finish off.

Front

Starting at lower edge, ch 106 (113, 120, 127).

Rows 1 through 3: Work same as Rows 1 through 3 of Back.

Rows 4 through 25 (25, 27, 29): Rep Rows 2 and 3 of Back 11 (11, 12, 13) times more.

Right Front:

For Sizes Petite and Medium Only:

Row 1 (wrong side): * † In 2nd dc of next shell work (sc, ch 3, sc); ch 3, dc in next ch-3 sp, ch 3; rep from * 6 (7) times more; sc in first ch-1 sp of next shell. Ch 3 (counts as

Junior Miss Pullover continued on page 162; Little Sis Pullover on page 140

Little Sis Pullover

All measurements are approximate.

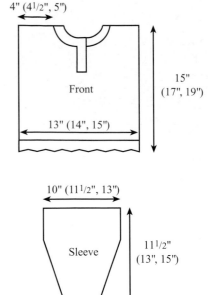

Materials:

Size 3 cotton thread, 12 (13 1/2, 15) oz,
  [800 (900, 1000) yds, 360 (400, 450)
  gms] pink
  *Note: Our photographed sweater was
  made with J. & P. Coats® Speed Cro-
  Sheen®, Mid Rose #46A.*
Size G (4.25mm) crochet hook, or size
  required for gauge
Size 18 tapestry needle
Two 3/8"-diameter white buttons
Sewing needle and matching thread

Gauge:

In pattern:
(sc, ch 3, sc), shell, (sc, ch 3, sc) = 1 1/2"
5 rows = 2"

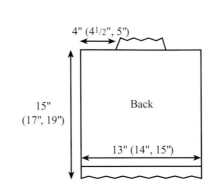

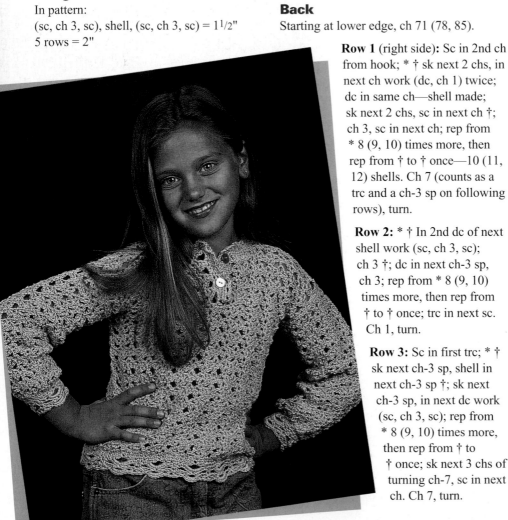

Instructions

Back

Starting at lower edge, ch 71 (78, 85).

Row 1 (right side): Sc in 2nd ch from hook; * † sk next 2 chs, in next ch work (dc, ch 1) twice; dc in same ch—shell made; sk next 2 chs, sc in next ch †; ch 3, sc in next ch; rep from * 8 (9, 10) times more, then rep from † to † once—10 (11, 12) shells. Ch 7 (counts as a trc and a ch-3 sp on following rows), turn.

Row 2: * † In 2nd dc of next shell work (sc, ch 3, sc); ch 3 †; dc in next ch-3 sp, ch 3; rep from * 8 (9, 10) times more, then rep from † to † once; trc in next sc. Ch 1, turn.

Row 3: Sc in first trc; * † sk next ch-3 sp, shell in next ch-3 sp †; sk next ch-3 sp, in next dc work (sc, ch 3, sc); rep from * 8 (9, 10) times more, then rep from † to † once; sk next 3 chs of turning ch-7, sc in next ch. Ch 7, turn.

Rows 4 through 33 (37, 41): Rep Rows 2 and 3, 15 (17, 19) times more.

Row 34 (38, 42): Rep Row 2.

Row 35 (39, 43): Sc in first trc; * † sk next ch-3 sp, in next ch-3 sp work (hdc, ch 1) twice; hdc in same sp †; sk next ch-3 sp; in next dc work (sc, ch 1, sc) †; rep from * 8 (9, 10) times more, then rep from † to † once; sk next 3 chs of turning ch-7, sc in next ch. Finish off.

Front

Starting at lower edge, ch 71 (78, 85).

Rows 1 through 3: Work same as Rows 1 through 3 of Back.

Rows 4 through 23 (27, 31): Rep Rows 2 and 3 of Back 10 (12, 14) times more.

Right Front:

For Sizes 4 and 8 Only:

Row 1 (wrong side): * † In 2nd dc of next shell work (sc, ch 3, sc); ch 3 †; dc in next ch-3 sp, ch 3; rep from * 3 (4) times more, then rep from † to † once; trc in next sc. Ch 1, turn, leaving rem sts unworked.

Row 2 (right side): Sc in first trc; * † sk next ch-3 sp, shell in next ch-3 sp †; sk next ch-3 sp, in next dc work (sc, ch 3, sc); rep from * 3 (4) times more, then rep from † to † once; sk next 3 chs of turning ch-7, sc in next ch. Ch 7, turn.

continued on page 165

Crochet across the generations.

"She thinks that no one cares about craftsmanship these days—that no one takes the time anymore. Wait until I give her this..."

"She thinks crochet is 'old fashioned.' She loves the idea of handmade, but thinks it takes too long. Wait until I give her this..."

Now an exciting new crochet thread from Aunt Lydia's® makes crochet fast, easy and beautiful. Unique heather tones in shades of blue, green, rose and beige give Aunt Lydia's "Denim" Quick Crochet Thread a contemporary look perfect for any number of projects from handbags and vests to doilies, curtains and afghans. The thread works quickly, and the finished project has a soft, heather look. It's the perfect combination for today—handmade quality, in lots less time. Look for Aunt Lydia's "Denim" Quick Crochet Thread today.

To get the free patterns shown above plus a free color chart, send a self-addressed stamped envelope plus $1 for shipping and handling to: Aunt Lydia's Denim Quick Crochet Offer, P.O. Box 865, Stevens Point, WI 54481-0865.

Coats & Clark
4135 South Stream Blvd., Charlotte, NC 28217
In Canada: Coats & Clark, Mississauga, ON L5T 2T5
www.coatsandclark.com

Fashions for Collectibles

— designed by Kelly Robinson

Bathing Beauty

Size:
To fit 9" bean-bag animal

Materials:
Sport weight yarn, 1/2 oz (35 yds, 15 gms) white; small amount of yellow
Note: Our photographed bathing suit was made with Red Heart® Sport, White #1; and Maize #263.
Size G (5mm) crochet hook, or size required for gauge
Hot glue or tacky craft glue

Gauge:
4 sc = 1"

Instructions

Visor
With yellow, ch 36; join to form a ring.

Rnd 1 (right side): Ch 1, sc in same ch as joining and in each rem ch; join in BL of first sc—30 sc.

Rnd 2: Ch 1, sc in same lp as joining; working in BLs only, hdc in next sc, dc in next sc, 2 trc in next sc; 2 dtrc (see Pattern Stitch on page 145) in next sc; 2 trc in next sc; dc in next sc, hdc in next sc, sc in next sc, sl st in next sc. Finish off, leaving rem sts unworked.

Bag
With white, ch 2.

Rnd 1 (right side): 6 sc in 2nd ch from hook; join in first sc.

Rnd 2: Ch 1, 2 sc in same sc and in each rem sc; join in first sc—12 sc.

Note: Rnds 3 through 8 are worked in continuous rnds. Do not join; mark beg of rnds.

Rnd 3: Sc in each sc.

Rnds 4 through 8: Rep Rnd 3. At end of Rnd 8, sl st in next sc. Finish off.

It's even more fun to dress these lovable little animals than it is to collect them. Our Bathing Beauty looks fetching in her yellow polka dot bikini. The Sailor Girl is ready to row away into the sunset with her favorite beau. Dainty Ballerina is a delight in a wonderful pink costume and toe shoes as she warms up for her next performance. While Bedtime Blues gets ready for a dream-filled night in jammies, slippers and nightcap.

Handle:

Hold piece with right side facing you and Rnd 8 at top; join yellow in next sc from ending sl st; ch 24, sk next 5 sc, sl st in next sc.

Finish off and weave in all ends.

Bikini Top (make 2)
With white, ch 2.

Rnd 1 (right side): 6 sc in 2nd ch from hook; join in first sc.

Rnd 2: Ch 1, 2 sc in same sc and in each rem sc; join in first sc—12 sc.

Finish off and weave in ends.

Bikini Bottom
With white, ch 13.

Row 1 (right side): Sc in 2nd ch from hook and in each rem ch—12 sc. Ch 1, turn.

Row 2: Dec over first 2 sc (to work dec: draw up lp in each of first 2 sc, YO and draw through all 3 lps on hook—dec made); sc in next 8 sc, dec over next 2 sc—10 sc. Ch 1, turn.

continued on page 167

Sailor Girl

Size:
To fit 9" bean-bag animal

Materials:
Sport weight yarn, 1 oz (70 yds, 30 gms) blue; 1/2 oz (35 yds, 15 gms) white; small amount of red
Note: Our photographed outfit was made with Red Heart® Sport, Skipper Blue #846; White #1; and Jockey Red #904.
Size G (5mm) crochet hook, or size required for gauge
Hot glue or tacky craft glue

Gauge:
4 sc = 1"

Instructions

Hat
With blue, ch 16; join to form a ring.

Rnd 1 (right side): Ch 1, sc in each ch; join in BL of first sc—16 sc.

Rnd 2: Ch 2, working in BLs only, dc in next sc, dc dec over next 2 sc [to work dc dec: (YO, draw up lp in next sc, YO, draw through 2 lps on hook) twice; YO and draw through all 3 lps on hook—dc dec made]; (dc dec over next 2 sc) 6 times; join in first dc—8 dc.

Rnd 3: Ch 1, draw up lp in same dc as joining and in next dc, YO and draw through all 3 lps on hook—beg sc dec made; sc dec over next 2 dc (to work sc dec: draw up lp in each of next 2 dc, YO and draw through all 3 lps on hook—sc dec made); (sc dec over next 2 sc) twice; join in first sc. Finish off.

continued on page 168

Dainty Ballerina

Size:
To fit 9" bean-bag animal

Materials:
Sport weight yarn, 1¹/₂ oz (105 yds, 45 gms) pink
Note: Our photographed outfit was made with Red Heart® Sport, Pale Rose #755.
Size G (5mm) crochet hook, or size required for gauge
1¹/₄ yds white satin ribbon, ¹/₄"-wide
Hot glue or tacky craft glue

Gauge:
4 sc = 1"

Instructions

Slipper (make 2)
Ch 6.

Rnd 1 (right side): Sc in 2nd ch from hook and in next 3 chs, 3 sc in next ch; working in unused lps on opposite side of beg ch-6, sc in next 4 lps, 3 sc in next lp; join in first sc—14 sc.

Rnd 2: Ch 1, sc in same sc and in next 4 sc, 3 sc in next sc; sc in next 6 sc, 3 sc in next sc; sc in next sc; join in BL of first sc—18 sc.

Rnd 3: Ch 1, sc in same lp; working in BLs only, sc in each sc; join in first sc.

Rnd 4: Ch 1, sc in same sc and in each rem sc; join in first sc.

Rnds 5 and 6: Rep Rnd 4.

Finish off and weave in ends.

Dress

Bodice:
Ch 26, join to form a ring.

Rnd 1 (right side): Ch 3 (counts as a dc on this and following rnds), dc in each ch; join in 3rd ch from hook—26 dc.

Rnd 2: Ch 3, dc in each dc; join in 3rd ch of beg ch-3.

Rnd 3: Rep Rnd 2.

Note: Remainder of bodice is worked in rows from center back to center front.

Left Side:
Row 1 (right side): Ch 3 (counts as a dc), dc in next 3 dc, ch 4, sk next 4 dc—armhole made; dc in next 2 dc, dec over next 2 dc [to work dec: (YO, draw up lp in next dc, YO, draw through 2 lps on hook) twice; YO and draw through all 3 lps on hook—dec made]. Ch 2, turn.

Row 2: Dc in next dc, dec; dc in next 4 chs of next ch-4 sp, in next 3 dc, and in 3rd ch of beg ch-3. Finish off.

Right Side:
Hold piece with right side facing you; join yarn in next unused dc on Rnd 3 from left side.

Row 1 (right side): Ch 2, dc in next 3 dc, ch 4, sk next 4 dc—armhole made; dc in next 6 dc. Ch 3, turn.

Row 2: Dc in next 5 dc and in next 4 chs of next ch-4 sp; dec twice. Finish off.

Edging:
Hold piece with right side and back opening facing you; join yarn in 3rd ch of turning ch-3 of Row 1 of right side; ch 1, reverse sc (see Keeping You in Stitches on page 198) in same ch as joining and in next 10 dc;

working in sps formed by edge dc, 2 sc in each of next 4 sps; sc in next 10 dc. Finish off.

Skirt:
Hold piece with right side facing you and unused lps of beg ch-26 at top; join yarn in first unused lp.

Rnd 1 (right side): Ch 1, sc in same lp, ch 4; working in rem unused lps, * sc in next lp, ch 4; rep from * around; join in first sc—26 ch-4 sps.

Rnd 2: Sl st in next ch-4 sp, ch 1, sc in same sp; ch 5; * sc in next ch-4 sp, ch 5; rep from * around; join in first sc.

Rnd 3: Sl st in next ch-5 sp, ch 1, sc in same lp; ch 10, sc in 5th ch from hook—picot made; ch 6; * sc in next ch-5 sp, ch 10, sc in 5th ch from hook—picot made; ch 6; rep from * around; join in first sc.

Finish off and weave in all ends.

Finishing
Step 1: Cut two 12" lengths of ribbon. Weave one length in and out of Rnd 1 of each slipper. Wrap ends around legs, crisscrossing in back. Tie ends into bows in front. Trim ends even.

Step 2: With remaining ribbon, weave in and out of Rnd 1 of skirt; tie into bow at front. Trim ends even.

Bedtime Blues

Size:
To fit 9" bean-bag animal

Materials:
Sport weight yarn, 1 1/2 oz (105 yds, 45 gms) blue; small amount of white
Note: Our photographed outfit was made with Red Heart® Sport, Blue Jewel #819; and White #1.
Size G (5mm) crochet hook, or size required for gauge
Two 1/2" buttons
Sewing needle and matching thread
Hot glue or tacky craft glue

Gauge:
4 sc = 1"

Pattern Stitch
Double Triple Crochet (dtrc):
YO 3 times; draw up lp in st indicated, (YO, draw through 2 lps on hook) 4 times—dtrc made.

Instructions

Bootie (make 2)
With blue, ch 6.

Rnd 1 (right side): Sc in 2nd ch from hook and in next 3 chs, 3 sc in next ch; working in unused lps on opposite side of beg ch-6, sc in next 4 lps, 3 sc in next lp; join in first sc—14 sc.

Rnd 2: Ch 1, sc in same sc and in next 4 sc, 3 sc in next sc; sc in next 6 sc, 3 sc in next sc; sc in next sc; join in BL of first sc—18 sc.

Rnd 3: Ch 1, sc in same lp; working in BLs only, sc in each sc; join in first sc.

Rnd 4: Ch 1, sc in same sc and in each rem sc; join in first sc.

Rnd 5: Rep Rnd 4.

Rnd 6: Ch 1, sc in same sc and in next 2 sc, sk next sc, dc in next 5 sc, sk next sc, sc in next 6 sc; join in first sc. Finish off.

Night Shirt

Front/Back (make 2):
Starting at top with blue, ch 26.

Row 1 (right side): Sc in 2nd ch from hook and in each rem ch—25 sc. Ch 1, turn.

Row 2: Sc in each sc. Ch 1, turn.

Rows 3 through 11: Rep Row 2.

Row 12: Sl st in first 4 sc; ch 1, sc in same sc as last sl st made and in next 18 sc— 19 sc. Ch 1, turn, leaving rem sc unworked.

Rows 13 through 18: Rep Row 2.

Row 19: Dec over first 2 sc (to work dec: draw up lp in each of next 2 sc, YO and draw through all 3 lps on hook—dec made); sc in next 15 sc, dec over next 2 sc—17 sc. Ch 1, turn.

Row 20: Dec over first 2 sc; sc in next 13 sc, dec over next 2 sc—15 sc. Finish off.

Front Yoke
With white, ch 14, dtrc (see Pattern Stitch) in 7th and 8th chs from hook, trc in next 2 chs, dc in next 2 chs, hdc in next ch, 6 hdc in next ch; working in unused lps on opposite side of beg ch-14, hdc in next lp, dc in next 2 lps, trc in next 2 lps, dtrc in next 2 lps, ch 5, sl st in next ch.

Finish off and weave in ends.

Hat
With white, ch 30; join to form a ring.

Rnd 1 (right side): Ch 1, sc in same ch and in each rem ch; join in first sc—30 sc.

Rnd 2: Ch 1, sc in same sc and in each rem sc; join in first sc.

Rnds 3 through 7: Rep Rnd 2.

Rnd 8: Ch 1, dec over first 2 sc (to work dec: draw up lp in each of next 2 sts, YO and draw through all 3 lps on hook—dec made); sc in next sc; * dec over next 2 sc; sc in next sc; rep from * around; join in first sc—20 sc.

Rnds 9 through 11: Rep Rnd 2.

Rnd 12: Rep Rnd 8. At end of rnd—13 sc.

Rnds 13 through 16: Rep Rnd 2.

Rnd 17: Ch 1, dec over first 2 sc; sc in next sc; * dec over next 2 sc; sc in next sc; rep from * twice more; sc in next sc; join in first sc—9 sc.

Rnds 18 through 21: Rep Rnd 2.

Rnd 22: Ch 1, dec; sc in next sc; (dec, dc in next sc) twice; join in first sc—6 sc.

Rnds 23 through 25: Rep Rnd 2.

Rnd 26: Ch 1, dec 3 times; join in first sc— 3 sc. Finish off.

Edging:
Hold hat with right side facing you and beg ch-30 at top; join blue in first unused lp of beg ch-30; ch 1, sc in same lp; working in unused lps on opposite side of beg ch-30, sc in each lp; join in first sc.

Finish off and weave in all ends.

Pompons
Following Pompon instructions on page 30, make three 2" pompons, one blue and two white.

continued on page 169

Bare shoulders need never be cold! Our simple-to-make shrug is sized for 18" doll, child and adult. Each sleeve is crocheted separately with soft yarn and then joined at the center back. The perfect summer accessory to take along for chilly theaters and restaurants.

Sweet and Simple Shrugs

— designed by Joyce Nordstrom

Sweet & Simple Adult Shrug

Materials:
Worsted weight yarn, 10 oz (700 yds, 300 gms) off white
Note: Our photographed shug was made with Red Heart® TLC®, Natural #5017.
Size K (6.5mm) crochet hook, or size required for gauge
Size 16 tapestry needle

All measurements are approximate.

37"
4¹/₂"
7¹/₂"

Gauge:
In patt:
6 sts = 2"

Instructions

Sleeve (make 2)

Cuff:
Ch 7.

Row 1 (wrong side): Sc in 2nd ch from hook and in next 5 chs—6 sc. Ch 1, turn.

Row 2 (right side): Working in BLs only, sc in each sc. Ch 1, turn.

Rows 3 through 33: Rep Row 2. At end of Row 33, do not turn; do not finish off.

Body:
Row 1 (wrong side): Working along next side in edge sc of each row, in first row work (sc, dc) twice; † sk next row, in next row work (sc, dc) †; rep from † to † 6 times more; sk next row, in next row work (sc, dc) twice; rep from † to † 7 times; sk next row, in next row work (sc, dc) twice—40 sts. Ch 2, turn.

Row 2 (right side): In 2nd ch from hook work (sc, dc); * sk next dc, in next sc work (sc, dc); rep from * 18 times more; sk next dc, in next sc work (sc, dc) twice—44 sts. Ch 3 (counts as first hdc and ch-1 sp on following rows), turn.

Row 3: Sk first 2 sts, hdc in next dc; * ch 1, sk next sc, hdc in next dc; rep from * 19 times more—22 hdc. Ch 3 (counts as first dc on following row), turn, leaving rem sc unworked.

Row 4: 2 dc in each of next 20 ch-1 sps and in sp formed by turning ch-3; dc in 2nd ch of turning ch-3—44 dc. Ch 1, turn.

Row 5: Sc in first dc; * sc in next dc, ch 3, sk next 2 dc, YO, draw up lp in next dc, (YO, draw up lp in same dc) twice; YO and draw through all 7 lps on hook—cluster

made; ch 3, sk next 2 dc; rep from * 6 times more; sc in next sc and in 3rd ch of turning ch-3. Ch 1, turn.

Row 6: Sc in first sc, ch 3, sk next ch-3 sp, 3 sc in next cluster; * ch 3, sk next sc and next ch-3 sp, 3 sc in next cluster; rep from * 5 times more; ch 3, sk next sc, sc in next sc. Ch 3, turn.

Row 7: 2 dc in next ch-3 sp; * dc in next 3 sc, 3 dc in next ch-3 sp; rep from * 5 times more; dc in next 3 sc, 2 dc in next ch-3 sp, dc in next sc—45 dc. Ch 3, turn.

Row 8: Sk first 2 dc; * hdc in next dc, ch 1, sk next dc; rep from * 20 times more; hdc in 3rd ch of turning ch-3—23 hdc. Ch 1, turn.

Row 9: Sc in first hdc, in each of next 21 hdc work (sc, dc); sk next ch of turning ch-3, sc in next ch—44 sts. Ch 1, turn.

Row 10: Sc in first sc; * sk next dc, in next sc work (sc, dc); rep from * 20 times more; sc in next sc. Ch 1, turn.

Rep Row 10 until piece measures 18¹/₂" from beg. At end of last row, do not ch 1; do not turn.

Finish off and weave in all ends.

Assembly
Hold both pieces with right sides together and last rows at top; with tapestry needle, sew last rows together. Starting at cuffs, sew 7" sleeve seams. Turn shrug right side out.

Edging:
Hold shrug with right side facing you; join yarn in one sleeve seam.

Rnd 1 (right side): Ch 1, sc in same sp as joining; working in ends of rows, in edge sc and in sps formed by edge dc, sc in each row; join in first sc.

Rnd 2: Ch 1, in same sc work (sc, ch 3, dc); sk next sc; * in next sc work (sc, ch 3, dc); sk next sc; rep from * around; join in first sc.

Finish off and weave in all ends.

Child & Doll Shrugs continued on page 148

Sweet & Simple
Child Shrug

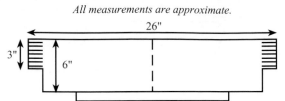

All measurements are approximate.

26"

3"

6"

Materials:

Worsted weight yarn, 5 oz (350 yds, 150 gms) off white

Note: Our photographed shug was made with Red Heart® TLC®, Natural #5017.

Size K (6.5mm) crochet hook, or size required for gauge

Size 16 tapestry needle

Gauge:

In pattern:
6 sts = 2"

Instructions

Sleeve (make 2)

Cuff:

Ch 7.

Row 1 (wrong side): Sc in 2nd ch from hook and in next 5 chs—6 sc. Ch 1, turn.

Row 2 (right side): Working in BLs only, sc in each sc. Ch 1, turn.

Rows 3 through 23: Rep Row 2. At end of Row 23, do not turn; do not finish off.

Body:

Row 1 (wrong side): Working along next side in edge sc of each row, in first row work (sc, dc) twice; sk next row; * in next row work (sc, dc); sk next row; rep from * 9 times more; in next row work (sc, dc) twice—28 sts. Ch 2, turn.

Row 2: In 2nd ch from hook work (sc, dc); * sk next dc, in next sc work (sc, dc); rep from * 12 times more; sk next dc, in next sc work (sc, dc) twice—32 sts. Ch 3 (counts as first hdc and ch-1 sp on following rows), turn.

Row 3: Sk first 2 sts, hdc in next dc; * ch 1, sk next sc, hdc in next dc; rep from * 13 times more—16 hdc. Ch 3 (counts as a dc on following rows), turn, leaving rem sc unworked.

continued on page 169

Sweet & Simple Doll Shrug

Size:

To fit 18" doll

All measurements are approximate.

11"

2"

Materials:

18" doll

Worsted weight yarn, 1/2 oz (35 yds, 15 gms) off white

Note: Our photographed shug was made with Red Heart® TLC®, Natural #5017.

Size K (6.5mm) crochet hook, or size required for gauge

Size 16 tapestry needle

Gauge:

In pattern:
6 sts = 2"

Instructions

Sleeve (make 2)

Cuff:

Ch 3.

Row 1 (right side): Sc in 2nd ch from hook and in next ch—2 sc. Ch 1, turn.

Row 2: Working in BLs only, sc in each sc. Ch 1, turn.

Rows 3 through 11: Rep Row 2. At end of Row 11, do not turn; do not finish off.

continued on page 168

Classy Clotheshangers

— designed by Hannelore Southard

Dress up your closet or make clever hangers for gifts.
Everyone will appreciate how even the finest silks don't slip off these
crochet-covered hangers and into the dark corners of the closet. Top: Seashell, Below: Dainty Chains

Seashell

Size:
Fits a 16¹/₂" long plastic hanger

Materials:
Worsted weight yarn; ¹/₂ oz (35 yds, 15 gms) white
Note: Our photographed cover was made with Patons Canadiana, White #101.

Size I (5.5mm) crochet hook, or size required for gauge
Size 16 tapestry needle
Two decorative buttons, ⁵/₈"-diameter
Sewing needle and matching thread

Gauge:
3 dc = 1"

Instructions

Half (make 2)
Ch 4.

Rnd 1 (right side): 7 dc in 4th ch from hook (beg 3 skipped chs count as a dc); join in 3rd ch of beg 3 skipped chs—8 dc.

continued on page 161

Hello! Brittany and Bobby Bear

These huggable teddies are gracious guests for special tea parties. At 16 1/2" tall they can even become perfect dancing partners for a toddler. This couple looks especially dapper in their colorful outfits.

— *designed by Candy Clayton*

Brittany Bear

Size:
About 16 1/2" tall

Materials:
Worsted weight yarn, 7 oz (490 yds, 210 gms) tan; 4 oz (280 yds, 120 gms) variegated; 2 oz (140 yds, 60 gms) green

Note: Our photographed animal was made with Red Heart® Classic™, Warm Brown #336; Tropical Fruit #951; and Mint Green #681.

Size F (3.75mm) crochet hook, or size required for gauge
Size 18 tapestry needle

Trimmings:
2 sets of 30mm doll joints
two 15mm black animal eyes
18mm animal nose
18" length of black embroidery floss
tacky craft glue or hot glue
polyester fiberfill
black plastic eyelashes
two orange ribbon roses, 1/2"-diameter
sewing needle and matching thread

Gauge:
4 sc = 1"

Instructions

Bear
With tan, work same as Kathy Kitty beginning on page 3, omitting ears and Finishing.

Ear (make 2):

With tan, ch 2.
Note: Rnds 1 through 7 are worked in continuous rnds. Do not join; mark beg of rnds.

Rnd 1 (right side): 6 sc in 2nd ch from hook.

Note: Bears have plastic face parts which are not suitable for children under three years of age. If for a young child please embroider faces with floss.

*Pig Pair
in Fall, page 190*

*Kitty Pair
in Winter, page 2*

*Bunny Pair
in Spring, page 62*

Rnd 2: 2 sc in each sc—12 sc.

Rnd 3: (Sc in next sc, 2 sc in next sc) 6 times—18 sc.

Rnd 4: (Sc in next 2 sc, 2 sc in next sc) 6 times—24 sc.

Rnd 5: Sc in each sc.

Rnds 6 and 7: Rep Rnd 5.

Rnd 8: Fold Rnd 7 flat; working through both thicknesses, sc in next 12 sc. Finish off, leaving an 18" end for sewing.

Finishing

Step 1: Stuff body firmly with fiberfill. With tapestry needle and 10" end of body, weave in and out through 12 sts of Rnd 55. Pull to close opening. Weave in end.

Step 2: Referring to photo for placement, with tapestry needle and floss, make mouth using straight stitches (see Embroidery Stitch Guide on page 211).

Step 3: Sew ears to side of head on Rnds 4 through 12 about 3" apart.

Step 4: On crocheted hair piece, twist each curl down and tack to secure. Sew hair to head between ears.

Step 5: Referring to photo for placement, sew ribbon roses to either side of hair piece.

Dress
Starting at neckline with green, ch 32.

Row 1 (wrong side)**:** Sc in 2nd ch from hook and in next 2 chs, (2 sc in next ch, sc in next 3 chs) 7 times—38 sc. Ch 1, turn.

Row 2 (right side)**:** Sc in first 6 sc, 2 sc in each of next 5 sc; sc in next 16 sc, 2 sc in each of next 5 sc; sc in next 6 sc—48 sc. Ch 1, turn.

Row 3: Sc in each sc. Ch 1, turn.

Row 4: Sc in first 6 sc; † 2 sc in next sc; in next sc work (2 dc, ch 2, 2 dc)—shell made; [sk next sc, in next sc work (2 dc, ch 2, 2 dc)—shell made] 4 times—sleeve made; 2 sc in next sc †; sc in next 14 sc; rep from † to † once; sc in next 6 sc—10 shells. Ch 1, turn.

Row 5: Sc in first 7 sc; † 2 sc in next sc; in ch-2 sp of each of next 5 shells work shell; sk next 2 dc, 2 sc in next sc †; sc in next 16 sc; rep from † to † once; sc in next 7 sc. Ch 1, turn.

Row 6: Sc in first 8 sc; † 2 sc in next sc; shell in each of next 5 shells; sk next 2 dc, 2 sc in next sc †; sc in next 18 sc; rep from † to † once; sc in next 8 sc. Ch 1, turn.

Row 7: Sc in first 9 sc; † 2 sc in next sc; shell in each of next 5 shells; sk next 2 dc, 2 sc in next sc †; sc in next 20 sc; rep from † to † once; sc in next 9 sc. Ch 1, turn.

Row 8: Sc in first 10 sc; † dec over next sc and next ch-2 sp of next shell (to work dec: draw up lp in st and sp indicated, YO and draw through all 3 lps on hook—dec made); ch 4, sk next 3 shells, dec over ch-2 sp of next shell and next sc (skipping 2 dc of shell) †; sc in next 22 sc; rep from † to † once; sc in next 10 sc. Ch 1, turn.

Row 9: 2 sc in first sc; sc in each sc and in each ch to last sc; 2 sc in last sc—56 sc. Ch 1, turn.

Row 10: Sc in each sc. Ch 1, turn.

Row 11: 2 sc in first sc; sc in next 54 sc, 2 sc in next sc—58 sc. Ch 1, turn.

Rows 12 and 13: Rep Row 10.

Row 14: Sc in each sc; join in FL of first sc. Change to variegated by drawing lp through; cut green.

Note: Remainder of dress is worked in rnds.

Rnd 1: Ch 3 (counts as a dc on this and following rnds), in same lp work (dc, ch 2, 2 dc)—beg shell made; sk next sc, working in FLs only, (shell in next sc, sk next sc) 28 times; join in 3rd ch of beg ch-3.

Rnd 2: Sl st in next dc and in next ch-2 sp; beg shell in same sp; shell in each rem shell; join in 3rd ch of beg ch-3.

Rnds 3 through 9: Rep Rnd 2.

Rnd 10: Sl st in next dc and in next ch-2 sp, ch 1, in same sp work (2 sc, ch 1) twice; in each rem shell work (2 sc, ch 1) twice; join in first sc. Finish off.

Collar:
Hold dress with right side of back opening facing you and beg ch at top; join variegated in first unused lp of beg ch to left of back opening.

Row 1: Ch 3, dc in same lp; sk next lp, (shell in next lp, sk next lp) 14 times; 2 dc in next lp. Ch 1, turn.

Row 2: Sc in next 2 dc, sk next 2 dc of next shell, in ch-2 sp of each of next 14 shells work (2 sc, ch 1) twice; sk next 2 dc of shell, sc in next dc and in 3rd ch of beg ch-3. Finish off.

Back Opening Trim and Ties:
Hold dress with right side facing you and skirt to left; join green in first edge sc to

continued on page 152

right of back opening; ch 1, sc in same sc; working in edge sc of each row, † in next sc work (sl st, ch 24, sl st in 2nd ch from hook and in next 22 chs, sl st) †; sc in next 6 rows; rep from † to † once; sc in next 5 rows; working along next side in edge sc of each row, sc in next 5 rows; rep from † to † once; sc in next 6 rows; rep from † to † once; sc in next sc.

Finish off and weave in all ends.

Bobby Bear —————

Size:
About 16¹/₂" tall

Materials:
Worsted weight yarn, 7 oz (490 yds, 210 gms) tan; 4 oz (280 yds, 120 gms) variegated; 2 oz (140 yds, 60 gms) green
Note: Our photographed animal was made with Red Heart® Classic™, Warm Brown #336; Tropicao Fruit #951; and Mint Green #681.
Size F (3.75mm) crochet hook, or size required for gauge
Size 18 tapestry needle

Trimmings:
two sets of 30mm doll joints
two 15mm black animal eyes
18mm animal nose
18" length of black embroidery floss
polyester fiberfill

Gauge:
4 sc = 1"

Instructions

Bear
With tan, work same as Kathy Kitty beginning on page 3, omitting eyelashes, ears, hair, and Finishing.

Ear (make 2):
With tan, work same as Brittany Bear Ear, beginning on page 150.

Finishing
Follow Steps 1 through 3 of Brittany Bear Finishing on page 151.

Romper
Starting at neckline with green, ch 32.

Row 1 (wrong side): Sc in 2nd ch from hook and in next 2 chs, (2 sc in next ch, sc in next 3 chs) 7 times—38 sc. Ch 1, turn.

Row 2 (right side): Sc in first 6 sc, 2 sc in each of next 5 sc; sc in next 16 sc, 2 sc in each of next 5 sc; sc in next 6 sc—48 sc. Ch 1, turn.

Row 3: Sc in each sc. Ch 1, turn.

Row 4: Sc in first 6 sc; † 2 sc in next sc; 2 dc in each of next 9 sc; 2 sc in next sc †; sc in next 14 sc; rep from † to † once; sc in next 6 sc—70 sts. Ch 1, turn.

Row 5: Sc in first 7 sc; † 2 sc in next sc; dc in next 18 dc, 2 sc in next sc †; sc in next 16 sc; rep from † to † once; sc in next 7 sc—74 sts. Ch 1, turn.

Row 6: Sc in first 8 sc; † 2 sc in next sc; dc in next 18 dc, 2 sc in next sc †; sc in next 18 sc; rep from † to † once; sc in next 8 sc—78 sts. Ch 1, turn.

Row 7: Sc in first 9 sc; † 2 sc in next sc; dc in next 18 dc, 2 sc in next sc †; sc in next 20 sc; rep from † to † once; sc in next 9 sc—82 sts. Ch 1, turn.

Row 8: Sc in first 10 sc; † dec over next 2 sc (to work dec: draw up lp in each of next 2 sts, YO and draw through all 3 lps on hook—dec made); ch 4, sk next 16 dc, dec over next 2 sts †; sc in next 22 sc; rep from † to † once; sc in next 10 sc. Ch 1, turn.

Bobby Bear

Row 9: 2 sc in first sc; sc in each sc and in each ch to last sc; 2 sc in last sc—56 sc. Ch 1, turn.

Row 10: Sc in each sc. Ch 1, turn.

Row 11: 2 sc in first sc; sc in each sc to last sc; 2 sc in last sc—58 sc. Ch 1, turn.

Rows 12 and 13: Rep Row 10.

Row 14: Sc in each sc; join in first sc. Change to variegated by drawing lp through; cut green.

Note: Remainder of romper is worked in rnds.

Rnd 1: Ch 3, in first sc work (dc, ch 2, 2 dc)—beg shell made; sk next 2 sc; * in next sc work (2 dc, ch 2, 2 dc)—shell made; sk next 2 sc; rep from * 17 times more; dc in next sc; join in 3rd ch of beg ch-3— 19 shells and one dc.

Rnd 2: Sl st in next dc and in next ch-2 sp, beg shell in same sp; shell in ch-2 sp of each of next 18 shells; sk next 2 dc of same shell, dc in next dc; join in 3rd ch of beg ch-3.

Rnd 3: Sl st in next dc and in next ch-2 sp, beg shell in same sp; shell in each of next 18 shells; sk next 2 dc of same shell, dc in next dc; join in 3rd ch of beg ch-3.

Rnds 4 and 5: Rep Rnd 3.

Rnd 6: Sl st in next dc and in next ch-2 sp, beg shell in same sp; shell in each of next 18 shells; sk next 2 dc of same shell, shell in next dc; join in 3rd ch of beg ch-3— 20 shells. Finish off.

Back Flap:
Hold piece with right side of back facing you and Rnd 6 at top; join variegated in 2nd shell to right of joining.

Row 1: Beg shell in same sp; shell in each of next 2 shells. Turn.

Row 2: Sl st in first 2 dc and in next ch-2 sp; beg shell in same sp; shell in each of next 2 shells. Ch 1, turn.

Row 3: Sc in each dc, in each ch-2 sp, and in 3rd ch of beg ch-3. Finish off, leaving a 10" end for sewing.

Front Flap:
Hold piece with right side of front facing you and Rnd 6 at top; sk next 7 shells from back flap, join variegated in next shell.

Row 1: Beg shell in next shell; shell in each of next 2 shells. Turn.

Rows 2 and 3: Rep Row 2 of Back Flap. At end of Row 3, do not turn. Finish off, leaving a 10" end for sewing.

Right Leg:
Hold piece with right side of back facing you and flaps at top; join variegated in next shell to left of back flap.

Rnd 1: Beg shell in same sp; shell in each of next 6 shells; working in edge dc of front and back flaps, shell in next dc on front flap; sk next row, shell in next dc on back flap; join in 3rd ch of beg ch-3—9 shells.

Rnd 2: Sl st in next dc and in next ch-2 sp, beg shell in same sp; shell in each of next 8 shells; join in 3rd ch of beg ch-3.

Rnds 3 through 5: Rep Rnd 2.

Rnd 6: Sl st in next dc and in next ch-2 sp, ch 1, in same sp work (2 sc, ch 1) twice; in each rem shell work (2 sc, ch 1) twice; join in first sc. Finish off.

Left Leg:
Hold piece with right side of front facing you and leg at top; join variegated in next shell to left of front flap on Rnd 6.

Rnd 1: Beg shell in same sp; shell in each of next 6 shells; working in edge dc of back and front flaps, shell in next dc on back flap; sk next row, shell in next dc on front flap; join in 3rd ch of beg ch-3—9 shells.

Rnds 2 through 6: Rep Rnds 2 through 6 of Right Leg.

Neck Trim:
Hold piece with right side of back facing you and neck at top; join variegated in first unused lp to left of back opening; ch 1, 2 sc in same lp; working in unused lps of beg ch-32, (sc in next lp, 2 sc in next lp) 15 times. Finish off.

Back Opening Trim and Ties:
Hold piece with right side facing you and legs to left; working in edge sc of rows, join green in first edge sc to right of back opening; ch 1, sc in same sc; † in next sc work (sl st, ch 24, sl st in 2nd ch from hook and in next 22 chs, sl st) †; sc in next 6 rows; rep from † to † once; sc in next 5 rows; working along next side in edge sc of rows, sc in next

5 rows; rep from † to † once; sc in next 6 rows; rep from † to † once; sc in next sc.

Finish off and weave in all ends.

Bow Tie
First Half:
With variegated, ch 4.

Row 1 (right side): Sc in 2nd ch from hook and in next 2 chs—3 sc. Ch 1, turn.

Row 2: Sc in each sc. Ch 1, turn.

Row 3: Rep Row 2.

Row 4: 2 sc in first sc; sc in next sc, 2 sc in next sc—5 sc. Ch 1, turn.

Row 5: Sc in each sc. Finish off.

Second Half:
Hold first half with right side facing you and unused lps of beg ch-4 at top; join variegated in first unused lp.

Row 1: Ch 1, sc in same lp and in next 2 lps—3 sc. Ch 1, turn.

Rows 2 through 5: Rep Rows 2 through 5 of First Half. At end of Row 5, do not finish off. Ch 1, turn.

Edging:
2 sc in first sc; † sc in next 3 sc, 2 sc in next sc; working in edge sc of each row on second and first halves, 2 sc in edge sc of same row just worked; sc in next 8 sc, 2 sc in next row †; working across Row 5, 2 sc in same sc just worked; rep from † to † once; join in first sc.

Finish off and weave in ends.

Knot:
With variegated, ch 3.

Row 1: Sc in 2nd ch from hook and in next ch—2 sc. Ch 1, turn.

Row 2: Sc in each sc. Ch 1, turn.

Rows 3 through 5: Rep Row 2. At end of Row 5, do not ch 1. Finish off, leaving an 8" end for sewing.

Finishing
Step 1: With tapestry needle and 8" end, wrap knot over center of bow with Rows 1 and 5 of knot at wrong side of bow. Sew Rows 1 and 5 of knot together. Sew bow tie to center front of romper.

Step 2: With tapestry needle and 10" ends, sew front and back flaps together; sew each front flap to each leg. Sew each back flap to each leg.

Funky Fringe
Trio of Novel Ideas

Fringe doesn't have to be stringy and uninteresting. Here are three new fringe ideas to take your next afghan out of the doldrums.

Fringe is a nice way to finish off a scarf, an afghan or a shawl, but if you'd like to add a bit more style than with the traditional single or double knot fringes, there are many other fun ways to fringe. Here are three of our favorites. Before working fringe, work a foundation row of single crochet in the main color of the piece on each edge to be fringed.

Swinging Hearts
Demonstrate your love with this perky fringe, accented with hearts.

Instructions
Hold piece with right side facing you and edge to be fringed at top; join yarn with an sc in first sc at right-hand edge; ch 3, sk next 2 sc, sc in next sc, ch 10, in 4th ch from hook work (2 dc, 2 hdc, sc, ch 2, sc, 2 hdc, 2 dc, ch 3, sl st)—heart made; sl st in next 6 chs, sl st in same sc as last sc made; ch 3, sk next 2 sc; * in next sc work (sc, hdc, dc, hdc, sc); ch 3, sk next 2 sc, sc in next sc, ch 16, in 4th ch from hook work (2 dc, 2 hdc, sc, ch 2, sc, 2 hdc, 2 dc, ch 3, sl st)—heart made; sl st in next 12 chs, sl st in same sc as last sc made; ch 3, sk next 2 sc, in next sc work (sc, hdc, dc, hdc, sc); ch 3, sk next 2 sc, sc in next sc, ch 10, in

4th ch from hook work (2 dc, 2 hdc, sc, ch 2, sc, 2 hdc, 2 dc, ch 3, sl st)—heart made; sl st in next 6 chs, sl st in same sc as last sc made; ch 3, sk next 2 sc; rep from * across to last 2 sc; sc in last 2 sc.

Finish off and weave in ends.

Work same on opposite end.

Loopy Fringe
This fringe is worked in single crochet and chain stitches with one continuous yarn strand, rather than with short pieces of yarn.

Instructions
Hold piece with right side facing you and edge to be fringed at top; join yarn in first sc at right-hand edge.

Row 1 (right side)**:** * Ch 30, sk next sc, sc in next sc; rep from * across. Ch 30, turn.

Row 2: Working in each unused sc and in front of ch-30 lps, sc in next unused sc; * ch 30, sc in next unused sc; rep from * across.

Finish off and weave in all ends.

Work same on opposite end.

Curlique Fringe
Charming curls form themselves as you crochet this fringe, which is worked with one continuous strand of yarn. To have a different look, you can vary the length of the curls by working more or less chain stitches depending on the length you want.

Instructions
Hold piece with right side facing you and edge to be fringed at top; join yarn with an sc in first sc at right-hand edge; ch 3, sk

continued on page 158

Let's Join Together

Would you like your joinings to go smoothly? Do you really understand join-as-you-go? Read this lesson and you'll be on your way to smooth and neatly finished joinings for all your squares and motifs.

Many wonderful crocheted tablecloths, bedspreads and even afghans are made by joining small motifs together. Joinings can be done either after each motif is finished completely or by joining them as-you-go during the last round. The *Summer Breeze Afghan* on page 156 has examples of both kinds of joinings.

The beauty of the first method is being able to have small pieces that can be carried with you and worked on wherever you go. Waiting for appointments is not annoying because you can use your time crocheting a motif.

We have illustrated the second method—that of joining them together as-you-go in the last round. This provides the opportunity to start joining them together before all motifs are completed and feel a sense of accomplishment sooner as you see the piece begin to take shape. A number of the motifs can still be worked as small individual pieces and joined at a later point in time. Many times a crocheted joining itself can also create its own pattern. In the case of *Summer Breeze Afghan*, the joining is in a different color, so the motif can be completed to the last round and set aside, if desired, for joining as-you-go later.

For a different look, a small group of 4 or more motifs can be joined in the join-as-you-go method to form a square or rectangle, then these larger units are joined. This would still allow for a portable project but allow for a larger portion to be completed at one time. These squares or rectangles could later be sewn together or be assembled using a join-as-you-go method.

Joining Individual Motifs

When joining by the join-as-you-go method, the first motif is worked completely including the last round.

The second motif is then joined to the first in the last round by joining one side to the previous motif. The joining is usually accomplished by using a slip stitch in a corresponding chain space. On the *Summer Breeze Afghan*, the motifs have been joined in the chain-3 spaces of the last round of the motif.

When joining, chain one, slip stitch in the corresponding chain-3 space (see **Photo A**) and then chain one giving you a total of three stitches on the last round of the motif you are stitching—equivalent to the chain three on the last round of the completed motif.

Photo A

When using this method the first row of motifs are joined along one side to the previous motif, then for the second row joinings are along two sides joining one motif to the next motif and also to a motif in the previous row. Corners are joined in the same manner and it is important to make sure that these joinings are secure to avoid holes.

Joining 4-Motif Squares

In the *Summer Breeze Afghan* four motifs are joined in the join-as-you-go method described above to make a 4-motif square (see **Photo B**) and then the 4-motif squares are joined together.

Photo B

To accent the squares, they are crocheted together with a single crochet stitch. Two squares are held with the wrong sides together as a single crochet stitch is worked through the loops of the corresponding stitches at the same time (**Photo C**).

Photo C

This method allows you to continue with your crochet hook and is usually quicker than sewing with needle and yarn.

This fresh blue and white granny is light enough to use on a cool summer evening at the ocean. Practice your newly learned skills in joining motifs as you create this beauty.

— designed by Kathy Wesley

Summer Breeze Afghan

Size:

About 40" x 52"

Materials:

Sport weight yarn, 20 oz (1500 yds, 550 gms) blue; 23 oz (1725 yds, 650 gms) off white

Note: Our photographed afghan was made with J. & P. Coats Luster Sheen®, Bluette #425; and Vanilla #7.

Size F (3.75mm) crochet hook, or size required for gauge

Gauge:

one motif = 4" x 4"

Instructions

Square

(make 35)
Note: Each square consists of 4 joined motifs.

Motif A:

With blue, ch 6; join to form a ring.

Rnd 1 (right side): Ch 3 (counts as a dc), dc in ring; * ch 4, sl st in 4th ch from hook—picot made; 3 dc in ring; rep from * 6 times more; ch 4, sl st in 4th ch from hook—picot made; dc in ring; join in BL of 3rd ch of beg ch-3—8 picots. Change to off white by drawing lp through; cut blue.

Rnd 2: Ch 8 (counts as a dc and a ch-5 sp); working in BLs only, * sk next picot and next dc, dc in next dc, ch 5; rep from * 6 times more; join in 3rd ch of beg ch-8.

Rnd 3: Ch 1, sc in same ch as joining; * † ch 3, in next ch-5 sp work (sc, ch 5, sc)—corner made; ch 3, sc in next dc, ch 3, sc in next ch-5 sp, ch 3 †; sc in next dc; rep from * twice more, then rep from † to † once; join in first sc.

Rnd 4: Sl st in next ch-3 sp, ch 1, sc in same sp, picot; * † ch 2, dc in next ch-5 sp, ch 3, sl st in 3rd ch from hook; dc in same sp, ch 5, sl st in 5th ch from hook; dc in same sp, ch 3, sl st in 3rd ch from hook; dc in same sp—corner made; ch 2, sc in next ch-3 sp, picot; ch 2, sc in next ch-3 sp, ch 3, sc in next ch-3 sp, ch 2 †; sc in next ch-3 sp, picot; rep from * twice more, then rep from † to † once; join in first sc. Finish off.

Rnd 5: With blue, make lp on hook and join with an sc in any corner ch-5 sp, ch 3, sc in same sp—corner made; * † ch 3, dc in next ch-2 sp, ch 3, sk next picot, hdc in next sc, 3 hdc in next ch-3 sp; hdc in next sc, ch 3, sk next picot, dc in next ch-2 sp, ch 3 †; in next ch-5 sp work (sc, ch 3, sc)—corner made; rep from * twice more, then rep from † to † once; join in joining sc.

Finish off and weave in ends.

Motif B:

With blue, ch 6; join to form a ring.

Rnds 1 through 4: Work same as Rnds 1 through 4 of Motif A.

Rnd 5: With blue, make lp on hook and join with an sc in any corner ch-5 sp, ch 3, sc in same sp—corner made; † ch 3, dc in next ch-2 sp, ch 3, sk next picot, hdc in next sc, 3 hdc in next ch-3 sp; hdc in next sc, ch 3, sk next picot, dc in next ch-2 sp, ch 3 †; sc in next corner ch-5 sp, ch 1; holding wrong side of Motif B facing wrong side of Motif A and carefully matching sts; on Motif A, sc in corresponding corner ch-3 sp, ch 1; on Motif B, sc in same corner ch-5 lp, ch 1; on Motif A, sl st in next ch-3 sp, ch 1; on Motif B, dc in next ch-2 sp, ch 1; on Motif A, sl st in next ch-3 sp, ch 1; on Motif B, sk next sc and next picot, hdc in next sc, 3 hdc in next ch-3 sp; hdc in next sc, ch 1; on Motif A, sl st in next ch-3 sp, ch 1; on Motif B, sk next picot, dc in next ch-2 sp, ch 1; on Motif A, sl st in next ch-3 sp, ch 1; on Motif B, sc in next corner ch-5 sp, ch 1; on Motif A, sc in corresponding corner ch-3 sp, ch 1; on Motif B, sc in same corner ch-5 sp; rep from † to † once; in next corner ch-5 sp work (sc, ch 3, sc)—corner made; rep from † to † once; join in joining sc.

Finish off and weave in ends.

Motif C:

With blue, ch 6; join to form a ring.

Rnds 1 through 4: Work same as Rnds 1 through 4 of Motif A.

Rnd 5: With blue, make lp on hook and join with an sc in any corner ch-5 sp, ch 3, sc in same sp—corner made; * † ch 3, dc in next ch-2 sp, ch 3, sk next picot, hdc in next sc, 3 hdc in next ch-3 sp; hdc in next sc, ch 3, sk next picot, dc in next ch-2 sp, ch 3 †; in next corner ch-5 sp work (sc, ch 3, sc)—corner made; rep from † to † once; sc in next corner ch-5 sp, ch 1; holding wrong side of Motif C facing wrong side of Motif A and carefully matching sts, on Motif A, sc in corresponding corner ch-3 sp, ch 1; on Motif C, sc in same corner ch-5 lp, ch 1; on Motif A, sl st in next ch-3 sp, ch 1; on Motif C, dc in next ch-2 sp, ch 1; on Motif A, sl st in next ch-3 sp, ch 1; on Motif C, sk next sc and next picot, hdc in next sc, 3 hdc in next ch-3 sp; hdc in next sc, ch 1; on Motif A, sl st in next ch-3 sp, ch 1; on Motif C, sk next picot, dc in next ch-2 sp, ch 1; on Motif A, sl st in next ch-3 sp, ch 1; on Motif C, sc in next corner ch-5 sp, ch 1; on Motif A, sc in joined corner, ch 1; on Motif C, sc in same corner ch-5 sp; rep from † to † once; join in joining sc.

Finish off and weave in ends.

Motif D:

With blue, ch 6; join to form a ring.

Rnds 1 through 4: Work same as Rnds 1 through 4 of Motif A.

Rnd 5: With blue, make lp on hook and join with an sc in any corner ch-5 sp, ch 3, sc in same sp—corner made; † ch 3, dc in next ch-2 sp, ch 3, sk next picot, hdc in next sc, 3 hdc in next ch-3 sp; hdc in next sc, ch 3, sk next picot, dc in next ch-2 sp, ch 3 †; sc in next corner ch-5 sp; ch 1, holding wrong side of Motif D facing wrong side of Motif C and carefully matching sts, on Motif C, sc in corresponding corner ch-3 sp, ch 1; on Motif D, sc in same corner ch-5 lp; †† ch 1, on prev motif, sl st in next ch-3 sp, ch 1; on Motif D, dc in next ch-2 sp, ch 1; on prev motif, sl st in next ch-3 sp, ch 1; on Motif D, sk next sc and next picot, hdc in next sc, 3 hdc in next ch-3 sp; hdc in next sc, ch 1; on prev motif, sl st in next ch-3 sp, ch 1; on Motif D, sk next ch-2 sp and next picot, dc in next ch-2 sp, ch 1; on prev motif, sl st in next ch-3 sp, ch 1; on Motif D, sc in next corner ch-5 sp ††; ch 1, sc in joined corner, ch 1; on Motif D, sc in same corner ch-5 sp; holding wrong side of Motif D facing wrong side of Motif B, rep from †† to †† once; ch 1; on prev motif, sc in corner ch-3 sp, ch 1; on Motif D, sc in same corner ch-5 sp; rep from † to † once; join in joining sc.

Finish off and weave in ends.

continued on page 158

Summer Breeze Afghan

continued from page 157

Edging:

Hold one square with right side facing you; with blue make lp on hook and join with an sc in any corner ch-3 sp; in same sp work (hdc, ch 1, hdc, sc)—beg corner made; * † sc in next sc, 2 sc in next ch-3 sp; sc in next dc, 2 sc in next ch-3 sp; sc in next 5 hdc, 2 sc in next ch-3 sp; sc in next dc, 2 sc in next ch-3 sp; sc in next sc †; hdc in next corner ch-3 sp (where joined), in motif joining, and in corner ch-3 sp of next motif (where joined); rep from † to † once; in next corner ch-3 sp work (sc, hdc, ch 1, hdc, sc)—corner made; rep from * twice more, then rep from † to † once; hdc in next corner ch-3 sp, in motif joining, and in corner ch-3 sp of next motif; rep from † to † once; join in first sc. Finish off.

Rep with remaining squares.

Assembly

Join squares in 7 rows of 5 squares each. To join squares, hold two squares with wrong sides together. With off white, make lp on hook and join with an sc in corresponding corner ch-1 sps; working in BLs only of both thicknesses, sc in each st. Continue to join squares to form rows, then join rows in same manner.

Afhgan Edging

Hold afghan with right side facing you and one short edge at top; with off white make lp on hook and join with an sc in upper right-hand corner ch-1 sp; ch 3, sc in same sp—corner made; † sc in next hdc; †† ch 3, sk next 2 sts, sc in next st ††; rep from †† to †† 12 times more; * ch 3, sk next hdc and square joining; sc in first hdc on next square; rep from †† to †† 13 times; rep from * 3 times more; sc in next hdc, in next corner ch-1 sp work (sc, ch 3, sc)—corner made; working along next side, sc in next hdc; ** rep from †† to †† 13 times; ch 3, sk next hdc and square joining; sc in first hdc on next square; rep from ** 5 times more; rep from †† to †† 13 times; sc in next hdc †; in next corner ch-1 sp work (sc, ch 3, sc)—corner made; working along next side, rep from † to † once; join in joining sc.

Finish off and weave in all ends.

Cheery Stripes Dishcloth

continued from page 126

Row 8: Hdc in each dc and in 2nd ch of turning ch-2, changing to white in last hdc. Ch 1, turn.

Row 9: Sc in each hdc and in 2nd ch of turning ch-2, changing to green in last sc. Ch 1, turn.

Row 10: Sc in each sc, changing to white in last sc. Ch 1, turn.

Row 11: Sc in each sc, changing to blue in last sc. Ch 2, turn.

Row 12: Hdc in each sc, changing to variegated in last hdc. Ch 2, turn.

Row 13: Dc in each hdc and in 2nd ch of turning ch-2, changing to white in last dc. Ch 1, turn.

Row 14: Sc in each dc and in 2nd ch of turning ch-2, changing to green in last sc. Ch 2, turn.

Rows 15 through 18: Rep Rows 2 through 5. At end of Row 18, do not change color.

Row 19: Sc in each dc and in 2nd ch of turning ch-2.

Finish off and weave in all ends.

Edging

Hold dishcloth with right side facing you and beg ch at top; join white in first unused lp of beg ch; ch 1, 3 sc in same ch as joining; working in unused lps of beg ch, sc in next 29 lps, 3 sc in next lp; † working across next side in each edge st and in sps formed by turning chs, sk next sc row, 2 sc in each of next 4 rows; sc in next row, 2 sc in next row; sc in next 5 rows, 2 sc in next row; sc in next row, 2 sc in each of next 4 rows, sk next sc row †; working across next side, 3 sc in next sc; sc in next 29 sc, 3 sc in next sc; rep from † to † once; join in first sc.

Finish off and weave in ends.

Patriotic Spirit

continued from page 133

5th ch from hook—picot made, 4 dc in next ch-2 sp) 30 times; ch 5, sl st in 5th ch from hook—picot made †; dc in next ch-2 sp; rep from † to † once; join in 3rd ch of beg ch-3.

Finish off and weave in all ends.

Star (make 12):
With off white, ch 4; join to form a ring; (ch 5, sl st in ring) 5 times.

Finish off and weave in ends.

Finishing
Referring to photo for placement, tack stars to blue section of flag.

Funky Fringe
Trio of Novel Ideas

continued from page 154

next 2 sc; * in next sc work [sc, ch 20 (or length desired for curlique), 3 sc in 2nd ch from hook and in next 18 chs, sl st]; ch 3, sk next 2 sc; rep from * across to last sc; sc in last sc.

Finish off and weave in ends.

Work same on opposite end.

All-American Kid

continued from page 123

Rows 51 (53, 55) through 53 (57, 61): Working in color sequence as established, rep Row 50 (52, 54) 3 (5, 7) times more. At end of Row 53 (57, 61), do not ch 1, do not turn.

Finish off, leaving an 18" end for sewing.

Back

Hold piece with right side facing you; sk next 3 sc on Row 30 (32, 34) from right front, join red in next sc.

Row 31 (33, 35): Ch 1, sc in same sc and in next 39 (41, 45) sc—40 (42, 46) sc. Ch 1, turn, leaving rem sc unworked.

Row 32 (34, 36): Sc in each sc, changing to white in last sc. Ch 1, turn.

Row 33 (35, 37): Sc in each sc. Ch 1, turn.

Row 34 (36, 38): Sc in each sc, changing to blue in last sc. Ch 1, turn.

Row 35 (37, 39): Sc in each sc, changing to red in last sc. Ch 1, turn.

Rows 36 (38, 40) through 38 (40, 42): Rep Row 33 (35, 37), changing to white at end of Row 38 (40, 42).

Rows 39 (41, 43) through 50 (52, 54): Rep Rows 33 (35, 37) through 38 (40, 42) twice (twice, three) times more.

For Size 4 Only:

Rows 51 through 53: Rep Rows 33 through 35. At end of Row 53, do not change color; do not ch 1.

Finish off and weave in all ends.

For Size 6 Only:

Rows 53 through 57: Rep Rows 35 through 39. At end of Row 57, do not change color. Do not ch 1.

Finish off and weave in all ends.

For Size 8 Only:

Rows 55 through 60: Rep Rows 37 through 42.

Row 61: Rep Row 37. At end of row, do not ch 1.

Finish off and weave in all ends.

Left Front

Note: When changing colors at end of a row where a dec is made, work dec until 3 lps rem on hook, draw new color through all 3 lps; cut old color.

Hold piece with right side facing you; sk next 3 sc on Row 31 (33, 35) from back, join red in next sc.

Row 31 (33, 35): Ch 1, sc in same sc and in next 17 (18, 20) sc; dec over next 2 sc—19 (20, 22) sc. Ch 1, turn.

Row 32 (34, 36): Sc in each sc, changing to white in last sc. Ch 1, turn.

Row 33 (35, 37): Sc in next 17 (18, 20) sc, dec—18 (19, 21) sc. Ch 1, turn.

Row 34 (36, 38): Sc in each sc, changing to blue in last sc. Ch 1, turn.

Row 35 (37, 39): Sc in next 16 (17, 19) sc, dec, changing to red—17 (18, 20) sc. Ch 1, turn.

Row 36 (38, 40): Sc in each sc. Ch 1, turn.

Row 37 (39, 41): Sc in next 15 (16, 18) sc, dec—16 (17, 19) sc. Ch 1, turn.

Note: On following rows, work in color sequence as established.

Rows 38 (40, 42) through 49 (51, 53): Sc in each sc, dec one st at neck edge every other row, 6 times more. At end of Row 49 (51, 53)—10 (11, 13) sc.

Row 50 (52, 54): Sc in each sc. Ch 1, turn.

Rows 51 (53, 55) through 53 (57, 61): Rep Row 50 (52, 54) 3 (5, 7) times more. At end of Row 53 (57, 61), do not ch 1.

Finish off, leaving an 18" end for sewing.

Sew shoulder seams.

Edgings

Armhole Edgings:

Hold piece with right side facing you; join blue in 2nd skipped sc of Row 30 (32, 34) of body.

Rnd 1 (right side): Ch 1, working in ends of rows in edge sc, work 49 (53, 57) sc evenly around edge; join in first sc.

Rnd 2: Ch 1, sc in same sc and in each rem sc; join in first sc.

Rnd 3: Rep Rnd 2.

Finish off.

Body Edging:

Hold piece with right side facing you and beg ch at top; join blue in first unused lp of beg ch.

Rnd 1 (right side): Ch 1, sc in same lp and in each rem unused lp of beg ch; working along right front in ends of rows in edge sc, 2 sc in first row; sc in next row, 2 sc in each of next 2 rows; sc in next 5 rows, 2 sc in next row (marked row); sc in each row to shoulder seam; sc in right shoulder seam, in each sc across back, and in left shoulder seam; working along left front, sc in each row to marker; 2 sc in marked row; sc in next 5 rows, 2 sc in each of next 2 rows; sc in next row, 2 sc in next row; join in first sc.

Rnd 2: Ch 1, sc in same sc as joining and in each rem sc; join in first sc.

Rnd 3: Rep Rnd 2.

Finish off and weave in all ends.

Finishing

Referring to photo for placement, work stars following diagram.

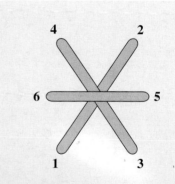

Bring yarn up at 1, down at 2, up at 3, down at 4, up at 5, and down at 6.

Desert Stripes

continued from page 131

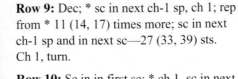

Row 11: Sc in first sc and in next ch-1 sp; * ch 1, sc in next ch-1 sp; rep from * 10 (13, 16) times more; dec—25 (31, 37) sts. Ch 1, turn.

Row 12: Sc in first sc; * ch 1, sc in next ch-1 sp; rep from * 10 (13, 16) times more; ch 1, sk next sc, sc in next sc. Ch 1, turn.

Row 13: Sc in first sc and in next ch-1 sp; * ch 1, sc in next ch-1 sp; rep from * 10 (13, 16) times more; sc in next sc. Ch 1, turn.

Rep Rows 12 and 13 until armhole measures same as for back. At end of last row, do not ch 1. Finish off, leaving an 18" end for sewing.

Left Front Neck Shaping:

Hold front with wrong side facing you; sk next 25 sts from right neck shaping; with larger size hook and continuing in color sequence, join yarn in next sc.

Row 1 (wrong side): Ch 1, sc in same sc and in next ch-1 sp; * ch 1, sc in next ch-1 sp; rep from * 15 (18, 21) times more; sc in next sc—35 (41, 47) sts. Ch 1, turn.

Row 2 (right side): Sc in first sc; * ch 1, sc in next ch-1 sp; rep from * 15 (18, 21) times more; dec—34 (40, 46) sts. Ch 1, turn.

Row 3: Dec; sc in next ch-1 sp; * ch 1, sc in next ch-1 sp; rep from * 14 (17, 20) times more; sc in next sc—33 (39, 45) sts. Ch 1, turn.

Row 4: Sc in first sc; * ch 1, sc in next ch-1 sp; rep from * 14 (17, 20) times more; dec—32 (38, 44) sts. Ch 1, turn.

Row 5: Dec; sc in next ch-1 sp; * ch 1, sc in next ch-1 sp; rep from * 13 (16, 19) times more; sc in next sc—31 (37, 43) sts. Ch 1, turn.

Row 6: Sc in first sc; * ch 1, sc in next ch-1 sp; rep from * 13 (16, 19) times more; dec—30 (36, 42) sts. Ch 1, turn.

Row 7: Dec; sc in next ch-1 sp; * ch 1, sc in next ch-1 sp; rep from * 12 (15, 18) times more; sc in next sc—29 (35, 41) sts. Ch 1, turn.

Row 8: Sc in first sc; * ch 1, sc in next ch-1 sp; rep from * 12 (15, 18) times more; dec—28 (34, 40) sts. Ch 1, turn.

Row 9: Dec; * sc in next ch-1 sp, ch 1; rep from * 11 (14, 17) times more; sc in next ch-1 sp and in next sc—27 (33, 39) sts. Ch 1, turn.

Row 10: Sc in in first sc; * ch 1, sc in next ch-1 sp; rep from * 11 (14, 17) times more; dec—26 (32, 38) sts. Ch 1, turn.

Row 11: Dec; sc in next ch-1 sp; * ch-1, sc in next ch-1 sp; rep from * 10 (13, 16) times more; sc in next sc—25 (31, 37) sts. Ch 1, turn.

Row 12: Sc in first sc; * ch 1, sc in next ch-1 sp; rep from * 10 (13, 16) times more; ch 1, sk next sc, sc in next st. Ch 1, turn.

Row 13: Sc in first sc and in next ch-1 sp; * ch 1, sc in next ch-1 sp; rep from * 10 (13, 16) times more; sc in next sc. Ch 1, turn.

Rep Rows 12 and 13 until armhole measures same as for back. At end of last row, do not ch 1. Finish off, leaving an 18" end for sewing.

Sleeve (make 2)

Note: Ch-1 sps count as sts.

With larger size hook and coral, ch 76 (76, 82).

Row 1 (right side): Sc in 2nd ch from hook; * ch 1, sk next ch, sc in next ch; rep from * 35 (35, 38) times more—75 (75, 81) sts. Ch 1, turn.

Row 2: 2 sc in first sc; sc in next ch-1 sp; * ch 1, sc in next ch-1 sp; rep from * 35 (35, 38) times more; 2 sc in next sc—77 (77, 83) sts. Ch 1, turn.

Row 3: 2 sc in first sc; sc in next sc; * ch 1, sc in next ch-1 sp; rep from * to last 3 sts; ch 1, sk next sc, sc in next sc, 2 sc in next sc—79 (79, 85) sts. Ch 1, turn.

Rows 4 through 11: Working in color sequence, rep Row 3. At end of Row 11—95 (95, 101) sts.

For Size Small Only:

Note: Continue in color sequence.

Row 12: Sc in first 2 sc; * ch 1, sc in next ch-1 sp; rep from * to last 3 sc; ch 1, sk next sc, sc in next 2 sc. Ch 1, turn.

Row 13: 2 sc in first sc; * ch 1, sc in next ch-1 sp; rep from * to last 2 sc; ch 1, sk next sc, 2 sc in next sc—97 sts. Ch 1, turn.

Row 14: Sc in first sc; * ch 1, sc in next ch-1 sp; rep from * to last 2 sc; ch 1, sk next sc, sc in next sc. Ch 1, turn.

Row 15: 2 sc in first sc; sc in next ch-1 sp; * ch 1, sc in next ch-1 sp; rep from * to last sc; 2 sc in last sc—99 sts. Ch 1, turn.

Rows 16 through 23: Rep Rows 12 through 15 twice more.

Rows 24 and 25: Rep Rows 12 and 13. At end of Row 25—109 sts.

Row 26: Sc in first sc; * ch 1, sc in next ch-1 sp; rep from * to last 2 sc; ch 1, sk next sc, sc in next sc. Ch 1, turn.

Row 27: Sc in first sc and in next ch-1 sp; * ch 1, sc in next ch-1 sp; rep from * to last sc; sc in last sc. Ch 1, turn.

Continuing in color sequence, rep Rows 26 and 27 until sleeve measures 5". Finish off.

For Sizes Medium and Large Only:

Note: Continue in color sequence.

Rows 12 through 17: Rep Row 3. At end of Row 17—107 (113) sts.

Row 18: Sc in first 2 sc; * ch 1, sc in next ch-1 sp; rep from * to last 3 sc; ch 1, sk next sc, sc in next 2 sc. Ch 1, turn.

Row 19: 2 sc in first sc; * ch 1, sc in next ch-1 sp; rep from * to last 2 sc; ch 1, sk next sc, 2 sc in next sc—109 (115) sts. Ch 1, turn.

Row 20: Sc in first sc; * ch 1, sc in next ch-1 sp; rep from * to last 2 sc; ch 1, sk next sc, sc in next sc. Ch 1, turn.

Row 21: 2 sc in first sc; sc in next ch-1 sp; * ch 1, sc in next ch-1 sp; rep from * to last sc; 2 sc in last sc—111 (117) sts. Ch 1, turn.

Row 22: Sc in first 2 sc; * ch 1, sc in next ch-1 sp; rep from * to last 3 sc; ch 1, sk next sc, sc in next 2 sc. Ch 1, turn.

Row 23: Rep Row 19. At end of row—113 (119) sts.

Row 24: Rep Row 20.

Row 25: Rep Row 21. At end of row—115 (121) sts.

Row 26: Rep Row 18.

Row 27: Sc in first sc; * ch 1, sc in next ch-1 sp; rep from * to last 2 sc; ch 1, sk next sc, sc in next sc. Ch 1, turn.

Continuing in color sequence, rep Rows 27 and 28 until sleeve measures 5". Finish off.

Assembly

Sew shoulder seams. Sew corners of sleeves between points **A** and **B** (see diagrams on page 131) on front and back. Sew underarm and side seams. *continued on page 161*

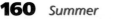

Desert Stripes

continued from page 160

Edgings

Neck Edging:

Hold back with right side facing you; with larger size hook, join off white in 12th ch-1 sp from right back neck shaping.

Rnd 1: Ch 1, sc in same sp; * ch 1, sc in next ch-1 sp; rep from * to left back neck shaping; ch 1, working in edge sc of each row, sc in next row, (ch 1, sk next row, sc in next row) 11 times; working across front, ch 1, sc in next ch-1 sp (already worked), (ch 1, sc in next ch-1 sp) 12 times; ch 1, sc in next ch-1 sp (already worked); working in edge sc of each row, ch 1, sc in next row, (ch 1, sk next row, sc in next row) 11 times; ** ch 1, sc in next ch-1 sp; rep from ** to first sc; join in first sc.

Change to smaller size hook.

Rnd 2: Sl st in next ch-1 sp, ch 1, sc in same sp; ch 1; * sc in next ch-1 sp, ch 1; rep from * around; join in first sc. Finish off.

Sleeve Edging:

Hold one sleeve with beg ch at top; with larger size hook, join off white in sp formed by first skipped ch of beg ch.

Rnd 1: Ch 1, sc in same sp; working in sps formed by rem unused chs, * ch 1, sc in next sp; rep from * around; join in first sc.

Change to smaller size hook.

Rnd 2: Sl st in next ch-1 sp, ch 1, sc in same sp; ch 1; * sc in next ch-1 sp, ch 1; rep from * around; join in first sc. Finish off.

Rep for other sleeve.

Lower Edging:

Hold sweater with right side of back facing you and beg ch at top; with larger size hook, join off white in lp formed by first skipped ch of beg ch.

Rnd 1: Ch 1, sc in same sp; working in sps formed by rem unused chs, ch 1; * sc in next sp, ch 1; rep from * around; join in first sc.

Change to smaller size hook.

Rnd 2: Sl st in next ch-1 sp, ch 1, sc in same sp; ch 1; * sc in next ch-1 sp, ch 1; rep from * around; join in first sc.

Finish off and weave in all ends.

Classy Clotheshangers – Seashell

continued from page 149

Rnd 2: Ch 3 (counts as a dc), dc in same ch as joining; 2 dc in each rem dc; join in 3rd ch of beg ch-3—16 dc.

Rnd 3: Ch 4 (counts as a trc on this and following rnds), 3 trc in same ch as joining; sk next 3 dc; * 4 trc in next dc; sk next 3 dc; rep from * twice more; join in 4th ch of beg ch-4.

Rnd 4: Ch 4, 4 trc in same ch as joining; sk next 3 trc; * 5 trc in next trc; sk next 3 trc; rep from * twice more; join in 4th ch of beg ch-4.

Rnds 5 through 8: Rep Rnd 4.

Rnd 9: Ch 4, 5 trc in same ch as joining; sk next 4 trc; * 6 trc in next trc; sk next 4 trc; rep from * twice more; join in 4th ch of beg ch-4.

Row 10: Rep Rnd 9.

Finish off and weave in ends.

Finishing

Place each piece over hanger. With tapestry needle and carefully matching sts, sew halves together. Sew buttons along seam on one side of hanger.

Dainty Chains

Size:

Fits a 16 1/2" long plastic hanger

Materials:

Worsted weight yarn; 1/2 oz (35 yds, 15 gms) white
> *Note: Our photographed cover was made with Patons Canadiana, White #101.*

Size H (5mm) crochet hook, or size required for gauge
Size 16 tapestry needle
Three decorative buttons, 1/2"-diameter
Sewing needle and matching thread

Gauge:

4 dc = 1"

Instructions

End Section (make 2)

Ch 4.

Rnd 1 (right side)**:** 7 dc in 4th ch from hook (beg 3 skipped chs count as a dc); join in 3rd ch of beg 3 skipped chs—8 dc.

Rnd 2: Ch 3 (counts as a dc on this and following rnds), in same ch as joining work 2 dc, ch 1, 3 dc)—beg shell made; ch 2, sk next 3 dc, in next dc work (3 dc, ch 1, 3 dc)—shell made; ch 2, sk next 3 dc; join in 3rd ch of beg ch-3.

Rnd 3: Sl st in next 2 dc and in next ch-1 sp, in same sp work beg shell; ch 3, in ch-1 sp of next shell work shell; ch 3; join in 3rd ch of beg ch-3.

Rnd 4: Sl st in next 2 dc and in next ch-1 sp, in same sp work beg shell; ch 4, shell in next shell; ch 4; join in 3rd ch of beg ch-3.

Rnd 5: Sl st in next 2 dc and in next ch-1 sp, in same sp work beg shell; ch 5, shell in next shell; ch 5; join in 3rd ch of beg ch-3.

Rnd 6: Sl st in next 2 dc and in next ch-1 sp, in same sp work beg shell; ch 6, shell in next shell; ch 6; join in 3rd ch of beg ch-3.

Rnd 7: Sl st in next 2 dc and in next ch-1 sp, in same sp work beg shell; ch 7, shell in next shell; ch 7; join in 3rd ch of beg ch-3.

Rnd 8: Ch 3, dc in next 2 dc, in next ch-1 sp, and in next 3 dc; ch 7, dc in next 3 dc, in next ch-1 sp, and in next 3 dc; ch 7; join in 3rd ch of beg ch-3.

Rnd 9: Ch 3, dc in next 6 dc, ch 8, dc in next 7 dc, ch 8; join in 3rd ch of beg ch-3.

Rnd 10: Ch 3, dc in next 6 dc, ch 9, dc in next 7 dc, ch 9; join in 3rd ch of beg ch-3.

Rnd 11: Ch 3, dc in next 6 dc, ch 10, dc in next 7 dc, ch 10; join in 3rd ch of beg ch-3.

Rnd 12: Ch 3, dc in next 2 dc, 2 dc in next dc; dc in next 3 dc, ch 11, dc in next 3 dc, 2 dc in next dc; dc in next 3 dc, ch 11; join in 3rd ch of beg ch-3.

Rnd 13: Ch 3, dc in next 7 dc, ch 12, dc in next 8 dc, ch 12; join in 3rd ch of beg ch-3.

Rnd 14: Ch 3, dc in same ch as joining; dc in next 6 dc, 2 dc in next dc; ch 14, 2 dc in next dc, dc in next 6 dc, 2 dc in next dc, ch 14; join in 3rd ch of beg ch-3.

Finish off and weave in all ends.

Finishing

Place each piece over hanger. With tapestry needle and carefully matching stitches, sew end sections together. Sew buttons along seam on one side of hanger.

In the Pink – Junior Miss Pullover

continued from page 139

first dc on following rows), turn, leaving rem sts unworked.

Row 2 (right side): Sk next ch-3 sp, in next dc work (sc, ch 3, sc); * † sk next ch-3 sp, shell in next ch-3 sp †; sk next ch-3 sp, in next dc work (sc, ch 3, sc); rep from * 5 (6) times more, then rep from † to † once; sk next 3 chs of turning ch-7, sc in next ch. Ch 7, turn.

Row 3: * In 2nd dc of next shell work (sc, ch 3, sc); ch 3, dc in next ch-3 sp, ch 3; rep from * 6 (7) times more; sc in 3rd ch of turning ch-3. Ch 3, turn.

Rows 4 through 11: Rep Rows 2 and 3 four times more.

Row 12 (neck shaping): Sc in 2nd ch of next ch-3 sp, 2 sc in next dc; sc in 2nd ch of next ch-3 sp, 2 sc in next ch-3 sp; sc in 2nd ch of next ch-3 sp, in next dc work (sc, ch 3, sc); sk next ch-3 sp; * shell in next ch-3 sp; sk next ch-3 sp, in next dc work (sc, ch 3, sc); sk next ch-3 sp; rep from * 4 (5) times more; shell in next ch-3 sp; sk next 3 chs of turning ch-7, sc in next ch. Ch 7, turn.

Row 13: * † In 2nd dc of next shell work (sc, ch 3, sc); ch 3 †; dc in next ch-3 sp, ch 3; rep from * 4 (5) times more, then rep from † to † once; sc in next ch-3 sp. Ch 1, turn.

Row 14: * † Sk next ch-3 sp, shell in next ch-3 sp †; sk next ch-3 sp, in next dc work (sc, ch 3, sc), rep from * 4 (5) times more, then rep from † to † once; sk next 3 chs of turning ch-7, sc in next ch. Ch 7, turn.

Row 15: * † In 2nd dc of next shell work (sc, ch 3, sc); ch 3, dc in next ch-3 sp †; ch 3; rep from * 3 (4) times more, then rep from † to † once; ch 1, sc in 2nd dc of next shell. Ch 3, turn.

Row 16: Sc in next dc; * † sk next ch-3 sp, shell in next ch-3 sp †; sk next ch-3 sp, in next dc work (sc, ch 3, sc); rep from * 3 (4) times more, then rep from † to † once; sk next 3 chs of turning ch-7, sc in next ch. Ch 7, turn.

Row 17: * In 2nd dc of next shell work (sc, ch 3, sc); ch 3, dc in next ch-3 sp, ch 3; rep

from * 3 (4) times more; sc in 2nd dc of next shell and in 3rd ch of turning ch-3. Ch 2 (counts as first hdc on following row), turn.

Row 18: Sk first sc, hdc in next sc, hdc in 2nd ch of next ch-3 sp; * in next dc work (sc, ch 1, sc); in next ch-3 sp work (hdc, ch 1) twice; hdc in same sp; rep from * 3 (4) times; sk next 3 chs of turning ch-7, hdc in next ch. Finish off.

Continue with Left Front.

For Sizes Small and Large Only:

Row 1 (wrong side): * † In 2nd dc of next shell work (sc, ch 3, sc); ch 3 †; dc in next ch-3 sp, ch 3; rep from * 6 (7) times more, then rep from † to † once; trc in next sc. Ch 1, turn.

Row 2 (right side): Sc in first trc; * † sk next ch-3 sp, shell in next ch-3 sp †; sk next ch-3 sp, in next dc work (sc, ch 3, sc); rep from * 6 (7) times more, then rep from † to † once; sk next 3 chs of turning ch-7, sc in next ch. Ch 7, turn.

Row 3: * † In 2nd dc of next shell work (sc, ch 3, sc); ch 3 †; dc in next ch-3 sp, ch 3; rep from * 6 (7) times more, then rep from † to † once; trc in next sc. Ch 1, turn.

Rows 4 through 11: Rep Rows 2 and 3 four times more. At end of Row 11, do not ch 1. Ch 3, turn.

Row 12 (neck shaping): Dc in 2nd ch of next ch-3 sp, 2 sc in next ch-3 sp; sc in 2nd ch of next ch-3 sp, 2 sc in next dc; sk next ch-3 sp; * shell in next ch-3 sp; sk next ch-3 sp, in next dc work (sc, ch 3, sc); sk next ch-3 sp; rep from * 5 (6) times more; shell in next ch-3 sp; sk next 3 chs of turning ch-7, sc in next ch. Ch 7, turn.

Row 13: * In 2nd dc of next shell work (sc, ch 3, sc); ch 3, dc in next ch-3 sp, ch 3; rep from * 5 (6) times more, sc in 2nd dc of next shell. Ch 2, turn.

Row 14: * Sk next ch-3 sp, in next dc work (sc, ch 3, sc); sk next ch-3 sp, shell in next ch-3 sp; rep from * 5 (6) times more; sk next 3 chs of turning ch-7, sc in next ch. Ch 7, turn.

Row 15: * † In 2nd dc of next shell work (sc, ch 3, sc); ch 3 †; dc in next ch-3 sp, ch 3; rep from * 4 (5) times more, then rep from † to † once; sc in next ch-3 sp. Ch 1, turn.

Row 16: Sk first sc; * † sk next ch-3 sp, shell in next ch-3 sp †; sk next ch-3 sp, in next dc work (sc, ch 3, sc); rep from * 4 (5) times more, then rep from † to † once; sk

next 3 chs of turning ch-7, sc in next ch. Ch 7, turn.

Row 17: * In 2nd dc of next shell work (sc, ch 3, sc); ch 3, dc in next ch-3 sp, ch 3; rep from * 4 (5) times more; sc in 2nd dc of next shell and in next dc of same shell. Ch 2 (counts as first hdc on following row), turn.

Row 18: Sk first sc, hdc in next sc, hdc in 2nd ch of next ch-3 sp, in next dc work (sc, ch 1, sc); sk next ch-3 sp; * † in next ch-3 sp work (hdc, ch 1) twice; hdc in same sp †; sk next ch-3 sp, in next dc work (sc, ch 3, sc); sk next ch-3 sp; rep from * 3 (4) times more, then rep from † to † once; sk next 3 chs of turning ch-7, hdc in next ch. Finish off.

Continue with Left Front.

Left Front:

For Sizes Petite and Medium Only:

Hold piece with wrong side facing you; make lp on hook and join with an sc in next ch-1 sp to left of right front.

Row 1: * Ch 3, dc in next ch-3 sp, ch 3, in 2nd dc of next shell work (sc, ch 3, sc); rep from * 6 (7) times more; ch 3, trc in next sc. Ch 1, turn.

Row 2: Sc in first trc; * sk next ch-3 sp, shell in next ch-3 sp; sk next ch-3 sp, in next dc work (sc, ch 3, sc); rep from * 6 (7) times more; sk next ch-3 sp, dc in next sc. Ch 1, turn.

Row 3: Sc in first dc; * ch 3, dc in next ch-3 sp, ch 3, in 2nd dc of next shell work (sc, ch 3, sc); rep from * 6 (7) times more; ch 3, trc in next sc. Ch 1, turn.

Rows 4 through 11: Rep Rows 2 and 3 four times more.

Row 12 (neck shaping): Sc in first trc; * sk next ch-3 sp, shell in next ch-3 sp; sk next ch-3 sp, in next dc work (sc, ch 3, sc); rep from * 5 (6) times more; sc in 2nd ch of next ch-3 sp, 2 sc in next ch-3 sp; sc in 2nd ch of next ch-3 sp, 2 sc in next dc; sc in 2nd ch of next ch-3 sp, dc in next sc. Finish off.

Hold piece with wrong side facing you, make lp on hook and join with an sc in first ch-3 sp of left front.

Row 13: Ch 3, * † in 2nd dc of next shell work (sc, ch 3, sc); ch 3 †; dc in next ch-3 sp, ch 3; rep from * 4 (5) times more, then rep from † to † once; trc in next sc. Ch 1, turn.

Row 14: Sc in first trc, sk next ch-3 sp; * shell in next ch-3 sp; sk next ch-3 sp, in next dc work (sc, ch 3, sc); sk next ch-3 sp; rep

continued on page 163

In the Pink – Junior Miss Pullover

continued from page 162

from * 4 (5) times more; shell in next ch-3 sp Ch 1, turn.

Row 15: Sl st in first dc, in next ch-1 sp, and in next dc; ch 1, sc in same dc as last sl st made; ch 1, dc in next ch-3 sp, ch 3; * † in 2nd dc of next shell work (sc, ch 3, sc); ch 3 †; dc in next ch-3 sp, ch 3; rep from * of 3 (4) times more, then rep from † to † once; trc in next sc. Ch 1, turn.

Row 16: Sc in first trc; * † sk next ch-3 sp, shell in next ch-3 sp; sk next ch-3 sp †; in next dc work (sc, ch 3, sc); rep from * 3 (4) times more, then rep from † to † once; sc in next dc, dc in next sc. Ch 1, turn.

Row 17: Sc in first dc and in 2nd dc of next shell; * ch 3, dc in next ch-3 sp, ch 3, in 2nd dc of next shell work (sc, ch 3, sc); rep from * 3 (4) times more; ch 3, trc in next sc. Ch 2 (counts as an hdc on following row), turn.

Row 18: Sk next ch-3 sp; * in next ch-3 sp work (hdc, ch 1) twice, hdc in same sp; sk next ch-3 sp, in next dc work (sc, ch 1, sc); sk next ch-3 sp; rep from * 3 (4) times more; hdc in 2nd ch of next ch-3 sp and in next 2 sc.

Finish off and weave in ends.

Continue with Sleeve.

For Sizes Small and Large Only:

Hold piece with wrong side facing you, sk next ch-3 sp to left of right front, join in next sc.

Row 1 (wrong side): Ch 7 (counts as a trc and a ch-3 sp); * † in 2nd dc of next shell work (sc, ch 3, sc); ch 3 †; dc in next ch-3 sp, ch 3; rep from * 6 (7) times more, then rep from † to † once; trc in next sc. Ch 1, turn.

Row 2 (right side): Sc in first trc; * † sk next ch-3 sp, shell in next ch-3 sp †; sk next ch-3 sp, in next dc work (sc, ch 3, sc); rep from * 6 (7) times more, then rep from † to † once; sk next 3 chs of beg ch-7, sc in next ch. Ch 7, turn.

Row 3: * † In 2nd dc of next shell work (sc, ch 3, sc); ch 3 †; dc in next ch-3 sp, ch 3; rep from * 6 (7) times more, then rep from † to † once; trc in next sc. Ch 1, turn.

Row 4: Sc in first trc; * † sk next ch-3 sp, shell in next ch-3 sp †; sk next ch-3 sp, in next dc work (sc, ch 3, sc); rep from * 6 (7)

times more, then rep from † to † once; sk next 3 chs of turning ch-7, sc in next ch. Ch 7, turn.

Rows 5 through 10: Rep Rows 3 and 4 three times more.

Row 11: Rep Row 3.

Row 12 (neck shaping): Sc in first trc; * † sk next ch-3 sp, shell in next ch-3 sp; sk next ch-3 sp †; in next dc work (sc, ch 3, sc); rep from * 5 (6) times more, then rep from † to † once; 2 sc in next dc; sc in 2nd ch of next ch-3 sp, 2 sc in next ch-3 sp; (sk next ch of turning ch-7, sc in next ch) twice. Finish off.

Hold piece with wrong side facing you, make lp on hook and join with an sc in 2nd dc of first shell.

Row 13: * Ch 3, dc in next ch-3 sp, ch 3; in 2nd dc of next shell work (sc, ch 3, sc); rep from * 5 (6) times more; ch 3, trc in next sc. Ch 1, turn.

Row 14: Sc in first trc; * † sk next ch-3 sp, shell in next ch-3 sp †; sk next ch-3 sp, in next dc work (sc, ch 3, sc); rep from * 5 (6) times more; sk next ch-3 sp, ch 1, hdc in next sc. Ch 1, turn.

Row 15: Sc in first ch-3 sp, ch 3; * † in 2nd dc of next shell work (sc, ch 3, sc); ch 3 †; dc in next ch-3 sp, ch 3; rep from * 4 (5) times more, then rep from † to † once; trc in next sc. Ch 1, turn.

Row 16: Sc in first trc; * † sk next ch-3 sp, shell in next ch-3 sp †; sk next ch-3 sp, in next dc work (sc, ch 3, sc); rep from * 4 (5) times more, then rep from † to † once; sk next ch-3 sp, sc in next sc. Ch 1, turn.

Row 17: Sc in first dc of next shell and in next dc of same shell; * ch 3, dc in next ch-3 sp, ch 3, in 2nd dc of next shell work (sc, ch 3, sc); rep from * 4 (5) times more; ch 3, trc in next sc. Ch 2 (counts as first hdc on following row), turn.

Row 18: * Sk next ch-3 sp, in next ch-3 sp work (hdc, ch 1) twice; hdc in same sp; sk next ch-3 sp, in next dc work (sc, ch 1, sc); rep from * 4 (5) times more; dc in 2nd ch of next ch-3 sp and in next 2 sc. Finish off.

Sleeve (make 2)

Ch 51 (51, 56, 56).

Row 1 (right side): Sc in 2nd ch from hook; * † sk next ch, shell in next ch, sk next ch, sc in next ch †; ch 3, sc in next ch; rep from * 8 (8, 9, 9) times more, then rep from † to † once—10 (10, 11, 11) shells.

Row 2: * † In 2nd dc of next shell work (sc, ch 3, sc); ch 3 †; dc in next ch-3 sp, ch 3; rep from * 8 (8, 9, 9) times more, then rep from † to † once; trc in next sc. Ch 1, turn.

Row 3: Sc in first trc; * † sk next ch-3 sp, shell in next ch-3 sp †; sk next ch-3 sp, in next dc work (sc, ch 3, sc); rep from * 8 (8, 9, 9) times more, then rep from † to † once; sk next 3 chs of turning ch-7, sc in next ch. Ch 7, turn.

Rows 4 through 13: Rep Rows 2 and 3 five times more. At end of Row 13, do not ch 7. Ch 4 (counts as a trc on following rows), turn.

Row 14: Trc in first sc, ch 3; * † in 2nd dc of next shell work (sc, ch 3, sc); ch 3 †; dc in next ch-3 sp, ch 3; rep from * 8 (8, 9, 9) times more, then rep from † to † once; 2 trc in next sc. Ch 1, turn.

Row 15: Sc in first 2 trc; * † sk next ch-3 sp, shell in next ch-3 sp; sk next ch-3 sp †; in next dc work (sc, ch 3, sc); rep from * 8 (8, 9, 9) times more, then rep from † to † once; sc in next trc and in 4th ch of turning ch-4. Ch 4, turn.

Row 16: Trc in first trc, 2 trc in next trc; ch 3; * † in 2nd dc of next shell work (sc, ch 3, sc); ch 3 †; dc in next ch-3 sp, ch 3; rep from * 8 (8, 9, 9) times more, then rep from † to † once; 2 trc in each of next 2 sc. Ch 1, turn.

Row 17: Sc in first 4 trc; * † sk next ch-3 sp, shell in next ch-3 sp; sk next ch-3 sp †; in next dc work (sc, ch 3, sc); rep from * 8 (8, 9, 9) times more, then rep from † to † once; sc in next 3 trc and in 4th ch of turning ch-4. Ch 7, turn.

Row 18: Sk first sc, in next sc work (sc, ch 3, sc); ch 3, sk next sc, dc in next sc, ch 3; * † in 2nd dc of next shell work (sc, ch 3, sc); ch 3 †; dc in next ch-3 sp, ch 3; rep from * 8 (8, 9, 9) times more, then rep from † to † once; dc in next sc, ch 3, sk next sc, in next sc work (sc, ch 3, sc); ch 3, trc in next sc. Ch 1, turn.

Row 19: Sc in first trc; * † sk next ch-3 sp, shell in next ch-3 sp †; sk next ch-3 sp, in next dc work (sc, ch 3, sc); rep from * 10 (10, 11, 11) times more, then rep from † to † once; sk next 3 chs of turning ch-7, sc in next ch—12 (12, 13, 13) shells. Ch 7, turn.

Row 20: * † In 2nd dc of next shell work (sc, ch 3, sc); ch 3 †; dc in next ch-3 sp, ch 3; rep from * 10 (10, 11, 11) times more, then rep from † to † once; trc in next sc. Ch 1, turn.

continued on page 164

In the Pink – Junior Miss Pullover

continued from page 163

Row 21: Sc in first trc; * † sk next ch-3 sp, shell in next ch-3 sp †; sk next ch-3 sp, in next dc work (sc, ch 3, sc); rep from * 10 (10, 11, 11) times more, then rep from † to † once; sk next 3 chs of turning ch-7, sc in next ch. Ch 7, turn.

Rows 22 through 27 (27, 29, 29): Rep Rows 20 and 21, 3 (3, 4, 4) times more. At end of Row 27 (27, 29, 29) do not ch-7. Ch 4, turn.

Row 28 (28, 30, 30): Trc in first sc, ch 3; * † in 2nd dc of next shell work (sc, ch 3, sc); ch 3 †; dc in next ch-3 sp, ch 3; rep from * 10 (10, 11, 11) times more, then rep from † to † once; 2 trc in next sc. Ch 1, turn.

Row 29 (29, 31, 31): Sc in first 2 trc; * † sk next ch-3 sp, shell in next ch-3 sp; sk next ch-3 sp †; in next dc work (sc, ch 3, sc); rep from * 10 (10, 11, 11) times more, then rep from † to † once; sc in next trc and in 4th ch of turning ch-4. Ch 4, turn.

Row 30 (30, 32, 32): Trc in first sc, 2 trc in next sc; ch 3; * † in 2nd dc of next shell work (sc, ch 3, sc); ch 3 †; dc in next ch-3 sp, ch 3; rep from * 10 (10, 11, 11) times more, then rep from † to † once; 2 trc in each of next 2 sc. Ch 1, turn.

Row 31 (31, 33, 33): Sc in first 4 trc; * † sk next ch-3 sp, shell in next ch-3 sp; sk next ch-3 sp †; in next dc work (sc, ch 3, sc); rep from * 10 (10, 11, 11) times more, then rep from † to † once; sc in next 3 trc and in 4th ch of turning ch-4. Ch 7, turn.

Row 32 (32, 34, 34): Sk first sc, in next sc work (sc, ch 3, sc); ch 3, sk next sc, dc in next sc, ch 3; * † in 2nd dc of next shell work (sc, ch 3, sc); ch 3 †; dc in next ch-3 sp, ch 3; rep from * 10 (10, 11, 11) times more, then rep from † to † once; dc in next sc, ch 3, sk next sc, in next sc work (sc, ch 3, sc); ch 3, trc in next sc. Ch 1, turn.

Row 33 (33, 35, 35): Sc in first trc; * † sk next ch-3 sp, shell in next ch-3 sp †; sk next ch-3 sp, in next dc work (sc, ch 3, sc); rep from * 12 (12, 13, 13) times more, then rep from † to † once; sk next 3 chs of turning ch-7, sc in next ch—14 (14, 15, 15) shells. Ch 7, turn.

Row 34 (34, 36, 36): * † In 2nd dc of next shell work (sc, ch 3, sc); ch 3 †; dc in next ch-3 sp, ch 3; rep from * 12 (12, 13, 13) times more, then rep from † to † once; trc in next sc. Ch 1, turn.

Row 35 (35, 37, 37): Sc in first trc; * † sk next ch-3 sp, shell in next ch-3 sp †; sk next ch-3 sp, in next dc work (sc, ch 3, sc); rep from * 12 (12, 13, 13) times more, then rep from † to † once; sk next 3 chs of turning ch-7, sc in next ch. Ch 7, turn.

Rows 36 (36, 38, 38) through 41 (41, 43, 43): Rep Rows 34 (34, 36, 36) and 35 (35, 37, 37) 3 times more.

Row 42 (42, 44, 44): Rep Row 34 (34, 36, 36).

Row 43 (43, 45, 45): Sc in first trc; * † sk next ch-3 sp, in next ch-3 sp work (hdc, ch 1) twice; hdc in same sp †; sk next ch-3 sp, in next dc work (sc, ch 1, sc); rep from * 12 (12, 13, 13) times more, then rep from † to † once; sk next 3 chs of turning ch-7, sc in next ch.

Finish off and weave in all ends.

Assembly

Sew shoulder seams. Mark 9" (9 1/2", 10", 10 1/2") from shoulder along outside edges of front and back for armholes. Matching top center of one sleeve to shoulder seam, sew sleeve to armhole, easing as necessary to fit. Repeat with other sleeve. Sew side and sleeve seams, carefully matching row ends.

Borders

Bottom Border:

Hold sweater with right side facing you and beg ch at top; make lp on hook and join with an sc in first unused lp of beg ch of back.

Rnd 1: Working in unused lps of beg ch of back and front, work 151 (159, 175, 183) sc evenly spaced around bottom edge; join in joining sc—152 (160, 176, 184) sc.

Rnd 2: Ch 1, sc in same sc and in next 6 sc; in next sc work (sc, ch 6, sc); * sc in next 7 sc, in next sc work (sc, ch 6, sc); rep from * 17 (18, 20, 21) times more; join in first sc—19 (20, 22, 23) ch-6 sps.

Rnd 3: Sl st in next 3 sc, ch 1, sc in same sc as last sl st made; * † dc in next sc, sc in next sc, sk next 3 sc, 9 sc in next ch-6 sp †; sk next 3 sc, sc in next sc; rep from * 17 (18, 20, 21) times more, then rep from † to † once; sk next sc and beg 2 sl sts; join in first sc.

Rnd 4: Sl st in next dc, ch 1, sc in same dc; * † ch 3, in 5th sc of next 9-sc group work (sc, ch 4, sc); ch 3 †; sc in next dc; rep from * 17 (18, 20, 21) times more, then rep from † to † once; join in first sc.

Rnd 5: Ch 4 (counts as a dc and a ch-1 sp), in same sc work (dc, ch 1, dc); * † sk next ch-3 sp, 6 sc in next ch-4 sp, sk next ch-3 sp †; in next sc work (dc, ch 1) twice; dc in same sc; rep from * 17 (18, 20, 21) times more, then rep from † to † once; join in 3rd ch of beg ch-4. Finish off.

Sleeve Border:

Hold one sleeve with right side facing you and beg ch at top; make lp on hook and join with an sc in underarm seam.

Rnd 1: Work 31 (31, 39, 39) sc evenly spaced around sleeve edge; join in joining sc—32 (32, 40, 40) sc.

Rnd 2: Ch 1, sc in same sc and in next sc; in next sc work (sc, ch 6, sc); * sc in next 7 sc, in next sc work (sc, ch 6, sc); rep from * 2 (2, 3, 3) times more; join in first sc—4 (4, 5, 5) ch-6 sps.

Rnd 3: Sl st in next 3 sc, ch 1, sc in same sc as last sl st made; * † dc in next sc, sc in next sc, sk next 3 sc, 9 sc in next ch-6 sp †; sk next 3 sc, sc in next sc; rep from * 2 (2, 3, 3) times more, then rep from † to † once; sk next sc and beg 2 sl sts; join in first sc.

Rnd 4: Sl st in next dc, ch 1, sc in same dc; * † ch 3, in 5th sc of next 9-sc group work (sc, ch 4, sc); ch 3 †; sc in next dc; rep from * 2 (2, 3, 3) times more, then rep from † to † once; join in first sc.

Rnd 5: Ch 4 (counts as a dc and a ch-1 sp), in same sc work (dc, ch 1, dc); * † sk next ch-3 sp, 6 sc in next ch-4 sp, sk next ch-3 sp †; in next sc work (dc, ch 1) twice; dc in same sc; rep from * 2 (2, 3, 3) times more, then rep from † to † once; join in 3rd ch of beg ch-4. Finish off.

Rep for other sleeve.

Neck Border:

Hold sweater with right side of right front facing you; make lp on hook and join with an sc in end of first row of right front edge opening.

Row 1: Working in ends of rows in edge sts, work 19 sc evenly spaced to neck edge (mark last sc worked for corner); working along right front neck edge, work 19 sc evenly spaced, sc in right shoulder seam (mark for shoulder), work 27 (29, 29, 31) sc across back neck edge, sc in left shoulder seam (mark for shoulder); working along left front neck edge, work 19 sc evenly spaced; working along left front opening, work 20 sc evenly spaced (mark first sc along left front for corner—107 (109, 109, 111) sc. Finish off.

continued on page 165

In the Pink – Junior Miss Pullover

continued from page 164

Place markers for 4 buttonholes evenly spaced on right front opening having first buttonhole 1" from bottom edge and last 1/2" from top edge.

Row 2: Make lp on hook and join with an sc in joining sc of Row 1; sc in each sc to first buttonhole marker, ch 2—buttonhole made; sk next sc; * sc in each sc to next buttonhole marker, ch 2—buttonhole made; sk next sc; rep from * twice more; sc in each sc to corner marker, 3 sc in next sc—corner made; sc in each sc along right front neck to 2 sc before shoulder marker, dec over next 2 sc (to work dec: draw up lp in each of next 2 sc, YO and draw through all 3 lps on hook—dec made); sc in marked sc, dec; sc in each sc across back neck to 2 sc before shoulder marker, dec; sc in marked sc, dec; sc in each sc along left front neck to next corner marker, 3 sc in next sc—corner made; sc in each sc along left edge opening. Finish off.

Row 3: Make lp on hook and join with an sc in joining sc of Row 2; * sc in each sc to next ch-2 sp, 2 sc in next ch-2 sp; rep from * 3 times more; sc in each sc to 2nd sc of next corner, 3 sc in next sc—corner made; sc in each sc to 2 sts before shoulder marker, dec; sc in marked sc, dec; sc in each sc across back to 2 sts before shoulder marker, dec; sc in marked sc, dec; sc in each sc to 2nd sc of next corner, 3 sc in next sc—corner made; sc in each rem sc. Finish off.

Row 4: Make lp on hook and join with an sc in joining sc of Row 3; * ch 3, sk next sc, sc in next sc; rep from * around.

Finish off and weave in all ends.

Sew buttons to Row 3 of left front opening opposite buttonholes.

In the Pink – Little Sis Pullover

continued from page 140

Row 3: * † In 2nd dc of next shell work (sc, ch 3, sc); ch 3 †; dc in next ch-3 sp, ch 3; rep from * 3 (4) times more, then rep from † to † once; trc in next sc. Ch 1, turn.

Rows 4 through 7: Rep Rows 2 and 3 twice more. At end of Row 7, do not ch 1. Ch 3, turn.

Row 8 (neck shaping): Dc in 2nd ch of next ch-3 sp, 2 sc in next ch-3 sp; dc in 2nd ch of next ch-3 sp, in next dc work (sc, ch 3, sc); * † sk next ch-3 sp, shell in next ch-3 sp †; sk next ch-3 sp, in next dc work (sc, ch 3, sc); rep from * 2 (3) times more, then rep from † to † once; sk next 3 chs of turning ch-7, sc in next ch. Ch 7, turn.

Row 9: * In 2nd dc of next shell work (sc, ch 3, sc); ch 3, dc in next ch-3 sp, ch 3; rep from * 2 (3) times more; sc in 2nd dc of next shell. Ch 2, turn, leaving rem sts unworked.

Row 10: Sk first ch-3 sp, in next dc work (sc, ch 3, sc); * † sk next ch-3 sp, shell in next ch-3 sp †; sk next ch-3 sp, in next dc work (sc, ch 3, sc); rep from * once (twice) more, then rep from † to † once; sk next 3 chs of turning ch-7, sc in next ch. Ch 7, turn.

Row 11: * † In 2nd dc of next shell work (sc, ch 3, sc); ch 3 †; dc in next ch-3 sp, ch 3; rep from * once (twice) more, then rep from † to † once; sc in next ch-3 sp. Ch 3, turn.

Row 12: Sk first sc, dc in 2nd ch of next ch-3 sp; * in next ch-3 sp work (hdc, ch 1) twice; hdc in same sp; sk next ch-3 sp, in next dc work (sc, ch 1, sc); rep from * once (twice) more; in next ch-3 sp work (hdc, ch 1) twice; hdc in same sp; sk next 3 chs of turning ch-7, hdc in next ch. Finish off.

Continue with Left Front.

For Size 6 Only:

Row 1 (wrong side): * In 2nd dc of next shell work (sc, ch 3, sc); ch 3, dc in next ch-3 sp, ch 3; rep from * 4 times more; sc in first ch-1 sp of next shell. Ch 3, turn, leaving rem sts unworked.

Row 2 (right side): Sk next ch-3 sp, in next dc work (sc, ch 3, sc); * † sk next ch-3 sp, shell in next ch-3 sp †; sk next ch-3 sp, in next dc work (sc, ch 3, sc); rep from * 3 times more, then rep from † to † once; sk next 3 chs of turning ch-7, sc in next ch. Ch 7, turn.

Row 3: * In 2nd dc of next shell work (sc, ch 3, sc); ch 3, dc in next ch-3 sp, ch 3; rep from * 4 times more; sc in 3rd ch of turning ch-3. Ch 3, turn.

Rows 4 through 7: Rep Rows 2 and 3 twice more.

Row 8 (neck shaping): Sc in 2nd ch of next ch-3 sp, 2 sc in next dc; sc in 2nd ch of next ch-3 sp, shell in next ch-3 sp; sk next ch-3 sp, in next dc work (sc, ch 3, sc); * † sk next ch-3 sp, shell in next ch-3 sp †; sk next ch-3 sp, in next dc work (sc, ch 3, sc); rep from * twice more, then rep from † to † once; sk next 3 chs of turning ch-7, sc in next ch. Ch 7, turn.

Row 9: * In 2nd dc of next shell work (sc, ch 3, sc); ch 3, dc in next ch-3 sp, ch 3; rep from * twice more; in 2nd dc of next shell work (sc, ch 3, sc); ch 2, sc in next ch-3 sp. Ch 1, turn, leaving rem sts unworked.

Row 10: Sk first ch-2 sp, shell in next ch-3 sp; sk next ch-3 sp, in next dc work (sc, ch 3, sc); * † sk next ch-3 sp, shell in next ch-3 sp †; sk next ch-3 sp, in next dc work (sc, ch 3, sc); rep from * once more, then rep from † to † once; sk next 3 chs of turning ch-7, sc in next ch. Ch 7, turn.

Row 11: * In 2nd dc of next shell work (sc, ch 3, sc); ch 3, dc in next ch-3 sp, ch 3; rep from * once more; in 2nd dc of next shell work (sc, ch 3, sc); ch 3, dc in next ch-3 sp, ch 1, sc in 2nd dc of next shell. Ch 3, turn.

Row 12: Sk first sc, dc in next ch-1 sp; * † in next dc work (sc, ch 1, sc); sk next ch-3 sp, in next ch-3 sp work (hdc, ch 1) twice; hdc in same sp †; sk next ch-3 sp; rep from * once more, then rep from † to † once; sk next 3 chs of turning ch-7, hdc in next ch. Finish off.

Continue with Left Front.

Left Front:

For Sizes 4 and 8 only:

Hold piece with wrong side facing you; join in next sc to left of right front.

Row 1 (wrong side): Ch 7 (counts as a trc and a ch-3 sp); * † in 2nd dc of next shell work (sc, ch 3, sc); ch 3 †; dc in next ch-3 sp, ch 3; rep from * 3 (4) times more, then rep from † to † once; trc in next sc. Ch 1, turn.

Row 2 (right side): Sc in first trc; * † sk next ch-3 sp, shell in next ch-3 sp †; sk next ch-3 sp, in next dc work (sc, ch 3, sc); rep from * 3 (4) times more, then rep from † to † once; sk next 3 chs of beg ch-7, sc in next ch. Ch 7, turn.

continued on page 166

In the Pink – Little Sis Pullover

continued from page 165

Row 3: * † In 2nd dc of next shell work (sc, ch 3, sc); ch 3 †; dc in next ch-3 sp, ch 3; rep from * 3 (4) times more, then rep from † to † once; trc in next sc. Ch 1, turn.

Row 4: Sc in first trc; * † sk next ch-3 sp, shell in next ch-3 sp †; sk next ch-3 sp, in next dc work (sc, ch 3, sc); rep from * 3 (4) times more, then rep from † to † once; sk next 3 chs of turning ch-7, sc in next ch. Ch 7, turn.

Rows 5 and 6: Rep Rows 3 and 4.

Row 7: Rep Row 3.

Row 8 (neck shaping): Sc in first trc; * sk next ch-3 sp, shell in next ch-3 sp; sk next ch-3 sp, in next dc work (sc, ch 3, sc); rep from * 3 (4) times more; dc in 2nd ch of next ch-3 sp, 2 sc in next ch-3 sp; (sk next ch of turning ch-7, dc in next ch) twice. Finish off.

Hold piece with wrong side facing you, make lp on hook and join with an sc in 2nd dc of first shell.

Row 9: Ch 3, dc in next ch-3 sp, ch 3; * † in 2nd dc of next shell work (sc, ch 3, sc); ch 3 †; dc in next ch-3 sp, ch 3; rep from * once (twice) more, then rep from † to † once; trc in next sc. Ch 1, turn.

Row 10: Sc in first trc; * sk next ch-3 sp, shell in next ch-3 sp; sk next ch-3 sp, in next dc work (sc, ch 3, sc); rep from * 2 (3) times more, ch 1, sc in next sc. Ch 2, turn.

Row 11: Sc in next ch-3 sp, ch 3, * † in 2nd dc of next shell work (sc, ch 3, sc); ch 3 †; dc in next ch-3 sp, ch 3; rep from * once (twice) more, then rep from † to † once; trc in next sc. Ch 1, turn.

Row 12: Sc in first trc, sk next ch-3 sp; * in next ch-3 sp work (hdc, ch 1) twice, hdc in same sp; in next dc work (sc, ch 1, sc); rep from * once (twice) more; in next ch-3 sp work (hdc, ch 1) twice, hdc in same sp; dc in 2nd ch of next ch-3 and in next sc. Finish off.

Continue with Sleeve.

For Size 6 Only:

Hold piece with wrong side facing you, make lp on hook and join with an sc in ch-1 sp to left of right front joining.

Row 1 (wrong side): Ch 3, dc in next ch-3 sp, ch 3; * † in 2nd dc of next shell work (sc, ch 3, sc); ch 3 †; dc in next ch-3

sp, ch 3; rep from * 3 times more, then rep from † to † once; trc in next sc. Ch 1, turn.

Row 2: Sc in first trc; * sk next ch-3 sp, shell in next ch-3 sp; sk next ch-3 sp, in next dc work (sc, ch 1, sc); rep from * 4 times more; sk next ch-3 sp, dc in next sc. Ch 1, turn.

Row 3: Sc in first dc, ch 3, dc in next ch-3 sp, ch 3; * † in 2nd dc of next shell work (sc, ch 3, sc); ch 3 †; dc in next ch-3 sp, ch 3; rep from * 3 times more, then rep from † to † once; trc in next sc. Ch 1, turn.

Rows 4 through 7: Rep Rows 2 and 3 twice more.

Row 8 (neck shaping): Sc in first trc; * † sk next ch-3 sp, shell in next ch-3 sp †; sk next ch-3 sp, in next dc work (sc, ch 3, sc); rep from * 3 times more, then rep from † to † once; sc in 2nd ch of next ch-3 sp, 2 sc in next dc; sc in 2nd ch of next ch-3 sp, dc in next sc. Finish off.

Hold piece with wrong side facing you, make lp on hook and join with an sc in first ch-3 sp.

Row 9: Ch 2; * † in 2nd dc of next shell work (sc, ch 3, sc); ch 3 †; dc in next ch-3 sp, ch 3; rep from * twice more, then rep from † to † once; trc in next sc. Ch 1, turn.

Row 10: Sc in first trc; * sk next ch-3 sp, shell in next ch-3 sp; sk next ch-3 sp, in next dc work (sc, ch 3, sc); rep from * twice more; sk next ch-3 sp, shell in next ch-3 sp; sc in next sc. Ch 1, turn.

Row 11: Sk first sc, sl st in next dc, in next ch-1 sp and in next dc, ch 1, sc in same dc as last sl st made; ch 1, dc in next ch-3 sp, ch 3; * † in 2nd dc of next shell work (sc, ch 3, sc); ch 3 †; dc in next ch-3 sp, ch 3; rep from * once more, then rep from † to † once; trc in next sc. Ch 2 (counts as first hdc on following row), turn.

Row 12: Sk first ch-3 sp; * in next ch-3 sp work (hdc, ch 1) twice; hdc in same sp; in next dc work (sc, ch 1, sc); rep from * twice more; dc in next ch-1 sp and in next sc. Finish off.

Sleeve (make 2)
Ch 41 (46, 51).

Row 1 (right side): Sc in 2nd ch from hook; * † sk next ch, shell in next ch; sk next ch, sc in next ch †; ch 3, sc in next ch; rep from * 6 (7, 8) times more, then rep from † to † once—8 (9, 10) shells. Ch 7, turn.

Row 2: * † In 2nd dc of next shell work (sc,

ch 3, sc); ch 3 †; dc in next ch-3 sp, ch 3; rep from * 6 (7, 8) times more, then rep from † to † once; trc in next sc. Ch 1, turn.

Row 3: Sc in first trc; * † sk next ch-3 sp, shell in next ch-3 sp †; sk next ch-3 sp, in next dc work (sc, ch 3, sc); rep from * 6 (7, 8) times more, then rep from † to † once; sk next 3 chs of turning ch-7, sc in next ch. Ch 7, turn.

Rows 4 through 25 (29, 33): Rep Rows 2 and 3, 11 (13, 15) times more.

Row 26 (30, 34): Rep Row 2.

Row 27 (31, 35): Sc in first trc; * † sk next ch-3 sp, in next ch-3 sp work (hdc, ch 1) twice; hdc in same sp †; sk next ch-3 sp, in next dc work (sc, ch 1, sc); rep from * 6 (7, 8) times more, then rep from † to † once; sk next 3 chs of turning ch-7, sc in next ch.

Finish off and weave in all ends.

Assembly
Sew shoulder seams. Mark 5" (5 3/4", 6 1/2") from shoulder along outside edges of front and back for armhole. Sew sleeves to body matching center of last row of sleeve to shoulder seam and easing as necessary to fit. Sew side and sleeve seams, matching row ends.

Borders

Lower Edge Border:
Hold sweater with right side facing you and beg ch at top; make lp on hook and join with an sc in first unused lp of beg ch of back.

Rnd 1: Working in unused lps of beg ch of back and front, work 103 (119, 135) sc evenly spaced around bottom edge; join in joining sc—104 (120, 136) sc.

Rnd 2: Ch 1, sc in same sc and in next 6 sc; in next sc work (sc, ch 6, sc); * sc in next 7 sc, in next sc work (sc, ch 6, sc); rep from * 11 (13, 15) times more; join in first sc— 13 (15, 17) ch-6 sps.

Rnd 3: Sl st in next 2 sc, ch 1, sc in same sc as last sl st made; * † dc in next sc, sc in next sc, sk next 3 sc, 9 sc in next ch-6 sp †; sk next 3 sc, sc in next sc; rep from * 11 (13, 15) times more, then rep from † to † once; sk next sc; join in first sc.

Rnd 4: Sl st in next dc, ch 1, sc in same dc; * † ch 3, in 5th sc of next 9-sc group work (sc, ch 4, sc); ch 3 †; sc in next dc; rep from * 11 (13, 15) times more, then rep from † to † once; join in first sc.

continued on page 167

166 *Summer*

In the Pink – Little Sis Pullover

continued from page 166

Rnd 5: Ch 4 (counts as a dc and a ch-1 sp), in same sc work (dc, ch 1, dc); * † sk next ch-3 sp, 6 sc in next ch-4 sp; sk next ch-3 sp †; in next sc work (dc, ch 1) twice; dc in same sc; rep from * 11 (13, 15) times more, then rep from † to † once; join in 3rd ch of beg ch-4. Finish off.

Sleeve Border:

Hold one sleeve with right side facing you and beg ch at top; make lp on hook and join with an sc in sleeve seam.

Rnd 1: Work 23 (23, 31) sc evenly spaced around lower edge; join in joining sc—24 (24, 32) sc.

Rnd 2: Ch 1, sc in same sc and in next 6 sc; in next sc work (sc, ch 6, sc); * sc in next 7 sc, in next sc work (sc, ch 6, sc); rep from * once (once, twice) more; join in first sc—3 (3, 4) ch-6 sps.

Rnd 3: Sl st in next 2 sc, ch 1, sc in same sc as last sl st made; * † dc in next sc, sc in next sc, sk next 3 sc, 9 sc in next ch-6 sp †; sk next 3 sc, sc in next sc; rep from * once (once, twice) more, then rep from † to † once; sk next sc; join in first sc.

Rnd 4: Sl st in next dc, ch 1, sc in same dc; * † ch 3, in 5th sc of next 9-sc group work (sc, ch 4, sc); ch 3 †; sc in next dc; rep from * once (once, twice) more, then rep from † to † once; join in first sc.

Rnd 5: Ch 4 (counts as a dc and a ch-1 sp), in same sc work (dc, ch 1, dc); * † sk next ch-3 sp, 6 sc in next ch-4 sp; sk next ch-3 sp †; in next sc work (dc, ch 1) twice; dc in same sc; rep from * once (once, twice) more, then rep from † to † once; join in 3rd ch of beg ch-4. Finish off.

Rep for other sleeve.

Neck Border:

Hold sweater with right side of right front facing you; make lp on hook and join with an sc in end of first row of right front edge opening.

Row 1: Working in ends of rows in edge sts, work 13 sc evenly spaced to neck edge (mark last sc for corner); working along right front neck edge work 13 sc evenly spaced, sc in right shoulder seam (mark for shoulder), work 23 (23, 25) sc across back neck edge, sc in left shoulder seam (mark for shoulder); working along left front neck edge, work 13 sc evenly spaced, working along left front opening, work 14 sc evenly spaced (mark first sc along opening for corner)—83 (83, 85) sc. Finish off.

Place markers for 2 buttonholes along right front having first buttonhole 1" from bottom edge and second ½" from top edge.

Row 2: Make lp on hook and join with an sc in joining sc of Row 1; sc in each sc to first buttonhole marker, ch 2—buttonhole made; sk next sc, sc in each sc to next buttonhole marker, ch 2—buttonhole made; sk next sc, sc in each sc to corner marker, 3 sc in next sc—corner made; sc in each sc along right front neck to 2 sc before shoulder marker, dec over next 2 sc (to work dec: draw up lp in each of next 2 sc, YO and draw through all 3 lps on hook—dec made); sc in each sc across back neck to shoulder marker, sc in marked sc, dec; sc in each sc across front neck to next corner, 3 sc in next sc—corner made; sc in each sc along left edge opening. Finish off.

Row 3: Make lp on hook and join with an sc in joining sc of Row 2; * sc in each sc to next ch-2 sp, 2 sc in next ch-2 sp; rep from * once more; sc in each sc to 2nd sc of next corner, 3 sc in next sc—corner made; sc in each sc to 2 sc before shoulder marker, dec; sc in each sc across back neck to shoulder marker, sc in marked sc, dec; sc in each sc across left front neck edge to 2nd sc of next corner, 3 sc in next sc—corner made; sc in each rem sc. Finish off.

Row 4: Make lp on hook and join with an sc in joining sc of Row 3; * ch 3, sk next sc, sc in next sc; rep from * along right front, neck edge and left front.

Finish off and weave in all ends.

Sew buttons to Row 3 on left edge of front opening opposite buttonholes.

Fashions for Collectibles – Bathing Beauty

continued from page 143

Row 3: Dec over first 2 sc; sc in next 6 sc, dec over next 2 sc—8 sc. Ch 1, turn.

Row 4: Dec; sc in next 4 sc, dec—6 sc. Ch 1, turn.

Row 5: Dec; sc in next 2 sc, dec—4 sc. Ch 1, turn.

Row 6: Sc in each sc. Ch 1, turn.

Rows 7 and 8: Rep Row 6.

Row 9: 2 sc in first sc; sc in next 2 sc, 2 sc in next sc—6 sc. Ch 1, turn.

Row 10: 2 sc in first sc; sc in next 4 sc, 2 sc in next sc—8 sc. Ch 1, turn.

Row 11: 2 sc in first sc; sc in next 6 sc, 2 sc in next sc—10 sc. Ch 1, turn.

Row 12: 2 sc in first sc; sc in next 8 sc, 2 sc in next sc—12 sc. Ch 1, turn.

Row 13: Sc in each sc.

Finish off and weave in ends.

Polka Dots (make 5)

With yellow, ch 2; 6 sc in 2nd ch from hook; join in first sc.

Finish off and weave in ends.

Finishing

Step 1: Glue three polka dots to front of bikini bottom and glue one polka dot to each piece of bikini top. Tack top pieces together.

Step 2: For bikini ties, cut four 12" lengths and two 8" lengths of white yarn. Glue one 12" length to each top part of wrong side of bikini top and glue one 12" length to each side of wrong side of bikini top. With tapestry needle and one 8" length, weave from front of Row 1 of bikini bottom through back of Row 13 on one side (keeping lengths even on each end). Weave rem 8" length from front of Row 13 through back of Row 1 on rem side (keeping lengths even on each end).

Step 3: Put legs of animal through holes made from 8" yarn lengths and center of bikini bottom. Pull tight and tie two lengths of one end into bow. Repeat on other side.

Step 4: Tie two top 12" lengths of yarn on bikini top into bow around animal's neck and tie two side 12" lengths into bow at back.

Step 5: Place bag and visor on animal.

Fashions for Collectibles –
Sailor Girl

continued from page 143

Brim:

Hold hat with right side facing you and Rnd 3 at top; join blue in any unused lp of Rnd 1.

Rnd 1: Ch 3, working in rem unused lps of Rnd 1, dc in each lp; join in 3rd ch of beg ch-3. Change to white by drawing lp through; cut blue.

Rnd 2: Sl st in each dc; join in joining sl st.

Finish off and weave in all ends.

Dress

With blue, ch 32; join to form a ring.

Rnd 1 (right side): Ch 3 (counts as a dc on this and following rnds), dc in each ch; join in 3rd ch of beg ch-3—32 dc.

Rnd 2: Ch 3, dc in same ch as joining; 2 dc in each rem dc; join in 3rd ch of beg ch-3—64 dc.

Rnd 3: Ch 3, dc in each dc; join in 3rd ch of beg ch-3.

Rnds 4 through 6: Rep Rnd 3. At end of Rnd 6, change to white by drawing lp through; cut blue.

Rnd 7: Ch 1, sc in same ch as joining; working in BLs only, sc in each dc; join in first sc. Finish off.

Trim:

Hold piece with right side facing you and Rnd 7 at top; join red in any unused lp of Rnd 6; working in rem unused lps, sl st in each lp; join in joining sl st. Finish off.

Bodice

Left Front:

Hold piece with right side of rnd joinings facing you and beg ch at top; join blue in 9th unused lp on opposite side of beg ch to left of joining.

Row 1 (right side): Ch 3, dc in next 7 lps. Ch 2, turn.

Row 2: Dc in next 5 dc, dec over next dc and 3rd ch of beg ch-3 [(to work dec: (YO, draw up lp in next st, YO, draw through 2 lps on hook) twice; YO and draw through all 3 lps on hook—dec made)]—6 dc. Ch 2, turn.

Row 3: Dc in next 3 dc, dec over next dc and in 3rd ch of turning ch-3—4 dc. Ch 2, turn.

Row 4: Dc in next dc, dec over next dc and in 3rd ch of turning ch-3—2 dc. Ch 2, turn.

Row 5: Dc in next dc; ch 40—strap made. Finish off.

Left Front Collar:

Hold left front with wrong side facing you; join blue in edge dc of Row 1.

Row 1 (wrong side): Ch 4, 3 trc in same sp; working in sps formed by turning chs and edge dc, 2 dc in next sp; 2 hdc in next sp; 2 sc in each of next 2 sps. Finish off.

Row 2 (right side): Hold left front with wrong side facing you; join red in 4th ch of beg ch-4 on Row 1; sl st in next 11 sts. Finish off.

Right Front:

Hold piece with right side of left front facing you and beg ch at top; join blue in next unused lp to left of left front.

Rows 1 through 5: Rep Rows 1 through 5 of Left Front.

Right Front Collar:

Hold right front with wrong side facing you; join blue in edge dc of Row 5.

Row 1(wrong side): Ch 1, 2 sc in same sp; working in sps formed by turning chs and edge dc, 2 sc in next sp; 2 hdc in next sp; 2 dc in next sp; 4 trc in next sp. Finish off.

Row 2 (wrong side): Hold right front with wrong side facing you; join red in first sc on Row 1; sl st in next 11 sts.

Finish off and weave in all ends.

Finishing

Step 1: Fold wrong side of collars toward right side of front. Referring to photo for placement, with tapestry needle and white, sew one star to each collar.

Step 2: Place dress on animal and tie ends in bow at back of neck. Place hat on top of head.

Sweet and Simple
Doll Shrug

continued from page 148

Body:

Row 1 (wrong side): Working along next side in edge sc of each row, in first row work (sc, dc); * sk next row, in next row work (sc, dc); rep from * 3 times more; sc in next row. Ch 2, turn.

Row 2: In 2nd ch from hook work (sc, dc); * sk next dc, in next sc work (sc, dc); rep from * 3 times more; sk next dc, in next sc work (sc, dc) twice—14 sts. Ch 1, turn.

Row 3: Sk first dc, in next sc work (sc, dc); * sk next dc, in next sc work (sc, dc); rep from * 5 times more. Ch 1, turn.

Rep Row 3 until piece measures 5½" from beg. At end of last row, do not ch 1; do not turn.

Finish off and weave in all ends.

Assembly

Hold both pieces with right sides together and last rows at top; with tapestry needle, sew last rows together. Starting at cuffs, sew 1" sleeve seams. Turn shrug right side out.

Edging:

Hold shrug with right side facing you; join yarn on one sleeve seam.

Rnd 1 (right side): Ch 1, sc in same sp as joining; working in ends of rows, in edge sc and in sps formed by edge dc, sc in each row; join in first sc.

Rnd 2: Ch 1, in same sc work (sc, ch 3, dc); sk next sc; * in next sc work (sc, ch 3, dc); sk next sc; rep from * around; join in first sc.

Finish off and weave in all ends.

Sweet and Simple Child Shrug

continued from page 148

Row 4: 2 dc in each of next 14 ch-1 sps and in sp formed by turning ch-3; dc in 2nd ch of same turning ch-3—32 dc. Ch 1, turn.

Row 5: Sc in first dc; * sc in next dc, ch 3, sk next 2 dc; YO, draw up lp in next dc, (YO, draw up lp in same dc) twice; YO and draw through all 7 lps on hook—cluster made; ch 3, sk next 2 dc; rep from * 4 times more; sc in 3rd ch of turning ch-3. Ch 1, turn.

Row 6: Sc in first sc, ch 3, sk next ch-3 sp, 3 sc in next cluster; * ch 3, sk next sc and next ch-3 sp, 3 sc in next cluster; rep from

* 3 times more; ch 3, sk next sc, sc in next sc. Ch 3, turn.

Row 7: 2 dc in next ch-3 sp; * dc in next 3 sc, 3 dc in next ch-3 sp; rep from * 3 times more; dc in next 3 sc, 2 dc in next ch-3 sp; dc in next sc—33 dc. Ch 3, turn.

Row 8: Sk first 2 dc; * hdc in next dc, ch 1, sk next dc; rep from * 14 times more; hdc in 3rd ch of turning ch-3—17 hdc. Ch 1, turn.

Row 9: Sc in first hdc, in each of next 15 hdc work (sc, dc); sk next ch of turning ch-3, sc in next ch—32 sts. Ch 1, turn.

Row 10: Sc in first sc; * sk next dc, in next sc work (sc, dc); rep from * 14 times more, sc in next sc. Ch 1, turn.

Rep Row 10 until piece measures 13", from beg. At end of last row, do not ch 1; do not turn.

Finish off and weave in all ends.

Assembly

Hold both pieces with right sides together and last rows at top; with tapestry needle, sew last rows together using. Starting at cuffs, sew 6" sleeve seams. Turn shrug right side out.

Edging:

Hold shrug with right side facing you; join yarn in one sleeve seam.

Rnd 1 (right side): Ch 1, sc in same sp as joining; working in ends of rows, in each edge sc and in sps formed by edge dc, sc in each row; join in first sc.

Rnd 2: Ch 1, in same sc work (sc, ch 3, dc); sk next sc; * in next sc work (sc, ch 3, dc); sk next sc; rep from * around; join in first sc.

Finish off and weave in all ends.

Fashions for Collectibles – Bedtime Blues

continued from page 145

Finishing

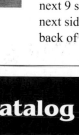

Step 1: Hold front and back with right sides together; with tapestry needle and blue, sew pieces together on each side, starting at Row 17 and sewing up to Row 12 and across slip stitches of Row 12.

Starting at end of each sleeve, sew shoulder seams across six stitches.

Step 2: Referring to photo for placement, sew front piece to center of nightshirt. Sew buttons to center of front piece.

Step 3: Hold nightshirt with right side facing you and lower edge at top; join white in edge sc of Row 16; ch 1, sc in same sp; working in edge sc, sc in next row; † working across lower edge, 2 sc in next sc; sc in next 9 sc, 2 sc in next sc; working along next side, sc in next 2 rows †; working on back of nightshirt, sc in next 2 rows; rep

from † to † once; join in first sc. Finish off.

Step 4: Hold nightshirt with right side of back facing you and one sleeve at top; join white in first sc from sleeve seam; ch 1, sc in same sc; working in edge sc of each row, sc in each row; join in first sc—24 sc. Finish off. Repeat with second sleeve. Weave in all ends.

Step 5: Sew blue pompon to end of hat. Sew one white pompon to top of each bootie.

Let's Crochet
for Fall

**Rugged Individualist –
Sweater for Him**

**Filet Crochet a
Timeless Oval Tablecloth**

**Learn to Crochet
with Beads –
Little Amulet Bag**

**Fall Sweaters –
Sporty and Sunny!**

Fall Contents

On our cover:
Timeless Beauty by Hartmut Hass, see page 182.

Mini Crochet

A size 16 steel crochet hook is so tiny that American manufacturers don't even make it!

Yet it is the favorite crochet tool of Kathi Bacon, who taught herself to crochet from a book at the age of 9. She had an aunt who was involved in textiles, and who taught Kathi to spin at the age of 13.

As a teen she developed a love of lace—bobbin lace, tatting and crochet. Spinning her own fibers meant she could produce very fine threads—and the finer the threads, the more she loved them! Wonderful crochet laces flew off her hook, all of her own original design.

Then one day a friend invited Kathi to join her at a dollhouse miniature show—and Kathi found a whole new world.

Since then, she has been creating tiny, intricate afghans and doilies in the 1" to 1' scale favored by miniaturists. Kathi even spins and dyes her slender threads. Now lucky dollhouses across the country are graced with beautiful lace accessories thanks to Kathi.

Kathi, who lives in Newcastle, WA, with her cats, Tasha and Hazel, is a computer programmer and a technical writer, but her heart is with fiber. In addition to selling her work, she offers classes in spinning, weaving and lace making.

Swirls Tablecloth

Recreate an Antique Treasure

This antique beauty was made with size 30 crochet thread, but you can recapture its loveliness for your own table with size 10 bedspread weight thread following our updated pattern. We've studied this piece and written the new pattern instructions in our usual American School of Needlework® easy-to-follow style.

Swirl Square

Size:
About 4" x 4"

Materials:
Bedspread-weight crochet cotton, 33 yds
Note: Our photographed square was made with J. & P. Coats®, Knit-Cro-Sheen®, White #1.
Size 6 (1.80mm) steel crochet hook, or size required for gauge

Gauge:
5 sc = 1"

Instructions

Square A
Ch 4, join to form a ring.

Note: Rnds 1 through 14 are worked in continuous rnds. Do not join; mark beg of rnd.

Rnd 1 (right side): (Ch 2, sc in ring) 4 times.

Rnd 2: (Ch 2, 3 sc in next ch-2 sp) 4 times.

Rnd 3: (Ch 2, 3 sc in next ch-2 sp, sc in next 2 sc) 4 times.

Rnd 4: (Ch 2, 3 sc in next ch-2 sp, sc in each sc to last sc; sk last sc) 4 times.

Rnds 5 through 7: Rep Rnd 4.

Rnd 8: * Ch 3, sc in next ch-2 sp, ch 3; sk next sc, sc in each sc to last sc, sk last sc; rep from * 3 times more.

Rnd 9: * Ch 3, sc in next sc, ch 3, sc in next ch-3 sp, ch 3, sk next sc, sc in each sc to last sc; sk last sc; rep from * 3 times more.

Rnd 10: * Ch 3, sc in next sc, ch 3, 3 dc in next ch-3 sp, ch 3, sc in next ch-3 sp, ch 3, sk next sc, sc in each sc to last sc, sk last sc;

rep from * 3 times more.

Rnd 11: * Ch 3, sc in next sc, (ch 3, 3 sc in next ch-3 sp) twice; ch 3, sc in next ch-3 sp, ch 3, sk next sc, sc in each sc to last sc; sk last sc; rep from * 3 times more.

Rnd 12: * Ch 3, sc in next sc, ch 3, 3 sc in next ch-3 sp; ch 8, sk next ch-3 sp, 3 sc in next ch-3 sp; ch 3, sc in next ch-3 sp, ch 3, sk next sc, sc in each sc to last sc; sk last sc; rep from * 3 times more.

Rnd 13: * Ch 3, sc in next sc, ch 3, 3 sc in next ch-3 sp; ch 3, 4 dc in next ch-8 sp; ch 3, 3 sc in next ch-3 sp; ch 3, sc in next ch-3 sp, sk next sc, sc in next 2 sc; rep from * 3 times more.

Rnd 14: Sl st in next ch of next ch-3 sp and in same sp; ch 1, sc in same sp; * † ch 3, 3 sc in next ch-3 sp; ch 3, 4 dc in next ch-3 sp; ch 8, 4 dc in next ch-3 sp; ch 3, 3 sc in next ch-3 sp; ch 3 †; sc in next ch-3 sp; rep from * twice more; rep from † to † once; join in first sc.

Rnd 15: Sl st in next ch of next ch-3 sp and in same sp, ch 1, sc in same sp; ch 5, sc in next ch 3 sp; * † ch 5, in next ch-8 sp work (sc, ch 7, sc)—corner made †; (ch 5, sc in next ch-3 sp) 4 times; rep from * twice more, then rep from † to † once; ch 5, (sc in next ch-3 sp, ch 5) twice; join in first sc.

Finish off and weave in ends.

Tablecloth sizes	Squares needed
52" x 52"	169 squares (13 x 13)
45" x 60"	180 squares (12 x 15)
60" x 84"	315 squares (15 x 21)
60" x 104"	390 squares (15 x 26)

Square B
Work same as Square A through Rnd 14.

Rnd 15: Sl st in next ch and in same ch-3 sp, ch 1, sc in same sp; ch 5, sc in next ch-3 sp, * † ch 5, in next ch-8 sp work (sc, ch 7, sc)—corner made †; (ch 5 sc in next ch-3 sp) 4 times; rep from * once more; ch 5, sc in next corner ch-8 sp, ch 3; hold wrong side of Square A facing wrong side of working square and carefully match sts; on completed square, sl st in corresponding corner ch-7 sp; ch 3; on working square, sc in same sp; † ch 2; on completed square, sl st in next ch-5 sp, ch 1; on working motif, sc in next ch-3 sp †; rep from † to † 4 times

continued on page 207

— by Jean Leinhauser

This stitch isn't used as often as sc and dc, but is useful because it creates a more flexible fabric with a better drape than sc, and a fabric that is firmer and keeps its shape better than dc.

At its simplest, a half double crochet stitch (hdc), as its name implies, is half of a double crochet stitch.

The basic hdc is worked as follows:

Step 1:
Bring yarn once over hook from back to front (**Fig 1**).

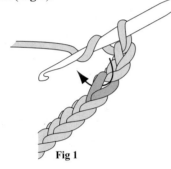

Fig 1

Step 2:
Insert hook in next ch or st, hook yarn and draw it through—3 lps on hook (**Fig 2**).

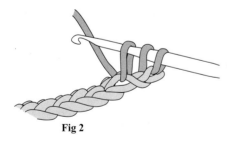

Fig 2

Step 3:
Hook yarn and draw it through all 3 lps on hook (**Fig 3**).

Fig 3

Step 4:
One hdc has been completed (**Fig 4**).

one
half
double
crochet

Fig 4

The turning chain for hdc can be either one or two chs, and your pattern will tell you which to use. Unless a pattern specifies otherwise, the turning chain, as in sc, does not count as a stitch.

The hdc can often be substituted for sc in a pattern. If you're bored working long stretches of plain sc, using hdc instead can speed the process. You can also alternate rows of sc and hdc, and rows of dc and hdc. Always make a swatch when changing a stitch to be sure you like the new look. And be sure to measure the work by inches, not by counting rows.

Decorative patterns using hdc are fun and easy to work. Try this one.

Hdc Berry Stitch

This stitch adds a nice texture to hdc without adding a lot of bulk. It is worked on a multiple of 3 plus 2 stitches.

For Practice:
Ch 24.

Foundation Row:
Sc in 2nd ch from hook and in each rem ch—23 sc. Ch 1, turn (ch 1 does not count as a st).

Row 1: Hdc in first 2 sts; *3 hdc in next st; drop lp from hook and insert hook under both lps of first hdc of 3-hdc group; insert hook in dropped lp , hook yarn and draw through all lps on hook, ch 1—Berry St made; hdc in next 2 sts; rep from * across—6 Berry Sts. Ch 1, turn.

Row 2: Hdc in each hdc and ch-1. Ch 1, turn.

Repeat Rows 1 and 2 for pattern.

Reverse Hdc

A pretty corded edging can be made with hdc. Using hdc yields a dimensional, rope-like finish. Work it as follows:

At end of the row, ch 2, but DO NOT turn. YO, insert hook in last st made (**Fig 5**); draw lp through st—3 lps on hook (**Fig 6**); YO and draw through all 3 lps on hook—one reverse half double crochet stitch made. Working left to right, repeat in each st across.

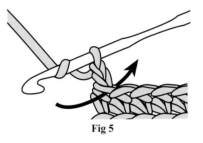

Fig 5

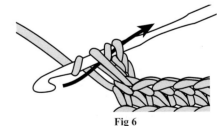

Fig 6

Darling
Baby Booties

Making baby booties while waiting for the new arrival is an old custom that is fun to follow today. These are created in little time and will keep baby's feet nice and cozy.

— designed by Sandy Scoville

Pattern Stitches
Beginning Cluster (beg CL):
Ch 2, keeping last lp of each dc on hook, 3 dc in sp indicated; YO and draw through all 4 lps on hook—beg CL made.

Cluster (CL):
Keeping last lp of each dc on hook, 4 dc in sp indicated; YO and draw through all 5 lps on hook—CL made.

Instructions

Bootie (make 2)

Sole:
Ch 18.

Rnd 1 (right side): Hdc in 3rd ch from hook (2 skipped chs count as an hdc) and in next 14 chs; 3 hdc in next ch; working along opposite side in unused lps of beg ch, hdc in next 15 lps, 2 hdc in next lp; join in 2nd ch of beg 2 skipped chs—36 hdc.

Rnd 2: Ch 2 (counts as an hdc on this and following rnds), hdc in same ch as joining and in next 15 hdc, 2 hdc in next hdc; hdc in next hdc, 2 hdc in next hdc; hdc in next 15 hd 2 hdc in next hdc; hdc in next hdc; join in 2nd ch of beg ch-2—40 hdc.

Rnd 3: Ch 2, hdc in same ch as joining; 2 hdc in each of next 2 hdc; hdc in next 15 hdc, 2 hdc in each of next 5 hdc; hdc in next 15 hdc, 2 hdc in each of next 2 hdc; join in 2nd ch of beg ch-2—50 hdc.

Rnd 4: Ch 2, hdc in same ch as joining; 2 hdc in each of next 3 hdc; hdc in next 21 hdc, 2 hdc in each of next 5 hdc; hdc in next 19 hdc, 2 hdc in next hdc; join in 2nd ch of beg ch-2—60 hdc.

Rnd 5: Ch 2, hdc in next 5 hdc, 2 hdc in next hdc; hdc in next 23 hdc, 2 hdc in next hdc; hdc in next 6 hdc, 2 hdc in next hdc; hdc in next 21 hdc, 2 hdc in next hdc; join in 2nd ch of beg ch-2—64 hdc.

Size:
Newborn to 3 months

Materials:
Bedspread-weight crochet cotton,
    150 yds pink

Note: Our photographed booties were made with Coats Opera 10, Cradle Pink #507.

Size 8 (1.50mm) steel crochet hook, or size required for gauge

Gauge:
8 hdc = 1"

continued on page 206

Back-to-School Plaid Afghan

Send them off to the dorm with an afghan that will remind them that you care.

— *designed by Carol Wilson Mansfield*

Gauge:

With 2 strands of yarn, 9 dc = 4"

Instructions

Center

Note: Center is worked with two strands of yarn. To change colors, work last dc of last row until 2 lps rem on hook; with new color, YO and draw through both lps on hook. Cut old color.

With 2 strands of off white, ch 101.

Row 1 (right side): Dc in 4th ch from hook (beg 3 skipped chs count as a dc) and in next 5 chs; † (ch 1, sk next ch, dc in next ch) 3 times; dc in next 2 chs, ch 1, sk next ch, dc in next 11 chs, ch 1, sk next ch, dc in next 3 chs, (ch 1, sk next ch, dc in next ch) 3 times †; dc in next 26 chs; rep from † to † once; dc in next 6 chs. Ch 3 (counts as first dc on following rows), turn.

Row 2: Dc in next 6 dc; † (ch 1, sk next ch-1 sp, dc in next dc) 3 times; dc in next 2 dc, ch 1, sk next ch-1 sp, dc in next 11 dc, ch 1, sk next ch-1 sp, dc in next 3 dc, (ch 1, sk next ch-1 sp, dc in next dc) 3 times †; dc in next 26 dc; rep from † to † once; dc in next 5 dc and in 3rd ch of beg 3 skipped chs. Ch 3, turn.

Size:

About 44" x 58" (before fringing)

Materials:

Worsted weight yarn, 48 oz (2400 yds, 1440 gms) off white; 18 oz (900 yds, 540 gms) dk blue; 3 oz (150 yds, 90 gms) each gold and red

Note: Our photographed afghan was made with Red Heart® TLC®, Natural #5017; Navy #586; Amber #5644; and Claret #5915.

Size K (6.5mm) crochet hook, or size required for gauge

Size 16 tapestry needle

Row 3: Dc in next 6 dc; † (ch 1, sk next ch-1 sp, dc in next dc) 3 times; dc in next 2 dc, ch 1, sk next ch-1 sp, dc in next 11 dc, ch 1, sk next ch-1 sp, dc in next 3 dc, (ch 1, sk next ch-1 sp, dc in next dc) 3 times †; dc in next 26 dc; rep from † to † once; dc in next 5 dc and in 3rd ch of turning ch-3. Ch 3, turn.

Row 4: Rep Row 3, changing to blue in last dc. Ch 3, turn.

Rep Row 3 in following color sequence:

1 row each of blue, off white, blue, off white, and blue (5 rows total);

3 rows off white;

1 row each of gold, off white, blue, off white, and blue (5 rows total);

3 rows off white;

1 row red;

7 rows off white;

1 row red;

3 rows off white;

1 row each of blue, off white, blue, off white, and gold (5 rows total);

3 rows off white;

1 row each of blue, off white, blue, off white, and blue (5 rows total);

3 rows off white;

1 row each of gold, off white, blue, off white, and blue (5 rows total);

3 rows off white;

1 row red;

7 rows off white;

1 row red;

3 rows off white;

1 row each of blue, off white, blue, off white, and gold (5 rows total);

3 rows off white;

1 row each of blue, off white, blue, off white, and blue (5 rows total);

4 rows off white.

At end of last row, do not ch 3.

Finish off and weave in all ends.

Vertical Stripes

Following color sequence (see diagram), work a vertical stripe in each row of ch-1 sps from bottom edge up to top edge of afghan. To work a vertical stripe, hold afghan with right side facing you and beg ch towards you. With 4 strands of color specified for stripe, make a slip knot on hook, leaving 8" ends to be worked in later as part of fringe. Holding yarn at back of work, insert hook in first ch-1 sp at bottom edge; draw up lp from yarn at back of work and draw through sp and lp on hook— sl st made. Insert hook in ch-1 sp of next row, draw up lp from yarn at back of work and draw through sp and lp on hook—another sl st made. Continue to work sl sts in this manner to top edge. Be sure to work sl sts loosely so as to not pucker or distort the shape of the afghan. Finish off, leaving 8" ends to be worked in later as part of fringe. Continue to work in this manner until all vertical stripes have been completed.

Fringe

Following Fringe instructions on page 211, make Single Knot Fringe. Cut 25" strands of each color. For each knot of off white, use 6 strands. For each knot of gold, red, and blue, use 4 strands each. Working across each short end of afghan, tie knots of fringe in matching colors evenly spaced (about every other st), combining yarn ends with the knots of fringe. Trim ends even.

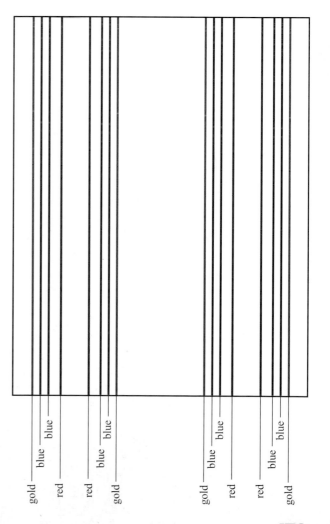

gold · blue · red · blue · red · blue · blue · gold · gold · blue · red · blue · red · blue · blue · gold

Bewitching Boa

A skein of bulky chenille yarn is all the brew you need to create this beguiling boa. Wear it tightly around your neck for warmth or fling it loosely for a spellbinding accessory.

Size:
About 60" long

Materials:
Bulky weight chenille yarn,
   400 yds off white
   Note: *Our photographed boa was made with Lion Brand® Chenille "Thick & Quick", Antique White #098.*
Size K (6.5mm) crochet hook, or size
   required for gauge

Gauge:
2 chs = 1"

Instructions

Loosely ch 130; sl st in 15th ch from hook; * ch 14, sl st in next ch; rep from * to last ch; in last ch work (ch 14, sl st) 3 times; working along opposite side in unused lps of beg ch, ** ch 14, sl st in next lp; rep from ** to last lp; in last lp work (ch 14, sl st) twice.

Finish off and weave in ends.

CREATE DAZZLING CROCHET PROJECTS LIKE A PRO!

Learn to Crochet in Just One Day by Jean Leinhauser — Right-Handed Version — 1146

LEARN TO DO FILET CROCHET IN JUST ONE DAY — 1281 — Welcome — by RITA WEISS

Learn to do Irish Crochet — Easy-to-follow Instructions and 5 Projects — 1291

Complete Guide to Thread Crochet — Everything you ever wanted to know about thread crochet, but didn't know whom to ask — Plus: Instructions for 9 beautiful projects.

Learn To Do Symbol Crochet in Just One Day — by Jean Leinhauser — Book 1: Doilies - 6 projects — 1242

Create spectacular and stunning crochet projects with our easy to follow books. Learn to Crochet In Just One Day or master the art of Filet Crochet. Our designs are current and classic, yet so easy to make! Impress friends and family with your crochet mastery.

BRUSH UP ON YOUR CROCHET SKILLS WITH HOW-TO BOOKS FROM

American School of Needlework ® excellence in instruction

Write to us at:
ASN Publishing
1455 Linda Vista Drive, San Marocs, CA 92069

Visit us on the web at: **www.asnpub.com**

Timeless Beauty

Even in the 21st century we enjoy setting a traditional table for special gatherings. This filet tablecloth is charted for a 60" x 84" size oval which can be used on a rectangular or oval table.

— *designed by Hartmut Hass*

next 5 chs, dc in next 10 chs, (ch 2, sk next 2 chs, dc in next ch) 11 times; dc in next 6 chs, ch 2, sk next 2 chs, dc in next 22 chs, (ch 2, sk next 2 chs, dc in next ch) twice; dc in next 21 chs, ch 2, sk next 2 chs, dc in next 7 chs, (ch 2, sk next 2 chs, dc in next ch) 11 times; dc in next 9 chs, ch 8, sk next 5 chs, dc in next 10 chs, (ch 2, sk next 2 chs, dc in next ch) twice; dc in next 6 chs, (ch 2, sk next 2 chs, dc in next ch) twice; dc in next 6 chs, (ch 2, sk next 2 chs, dc in next ch) twice; dc in next 6 chs, (ch 2, sk next 2 chs, dc in next ch) twice; dc in next 9 chs, ch 8, sk next 5 chs, dc in next 10 chs, (ch 2, sk next 2 chs, dc in next ch) 11 times; dc in next 6 chs, ch 2, sk next 2 chs, dc in next 22 chs, (ch 2, sk next 2 chs, dc in next ch) twice; dc in next 21 chs, ch 2, sk next 2 chs, dc in next 7 chs, (ch 2, sk next 2 chs, dc in next ch) 11 times; dc in next 9 chs, ch 8, sk next 5 chs, dc in next 10 chs; rep from † to † 3 times; (ch 2, sk next 2 chs, dc in next ch) twice; dc in next 9 chs, ch 8, sk next 5 chs, dc in next 10 chs, ch 2, sk next 2 chs, dc in next ch. Ch 5, turn.

Following chart on page 183, work Rows 2 through 128.

Note: For detailed special symbol instructions, see Special Symbol chart on page 183.

Size:
About 60" x 84"

Materials:
Bedspread-weight crochet cotton, twenty-three 225-yd balls white
Note: Our photographed tablecloth was made with J. & P. Coats® Knit-Cro-Sheen®, White #1.
Size 6 (1.80mm) steel crochet hook, or size required for gauge

Gauge:
6 squares x 6 squares = 2"

Instructions
Note: If you are not familiar with working filet from a chart, please read Filet Review beginning on page 214.

First Half
Starting at center, ch 546.

Row 1 (right side)**:** Dc in 9th ch from hook and in next 9 chs, ch 8, sk next 5 chs, dc in next 10 chs; † (ch 2, sk next 2 chs, dc in next ch) twice; dc in next 6 chs †; rep from † to † twice more; (ch 2, sk next 2 chs, dc in next ch) twice; dc in next 9 chs, ch 8, sk

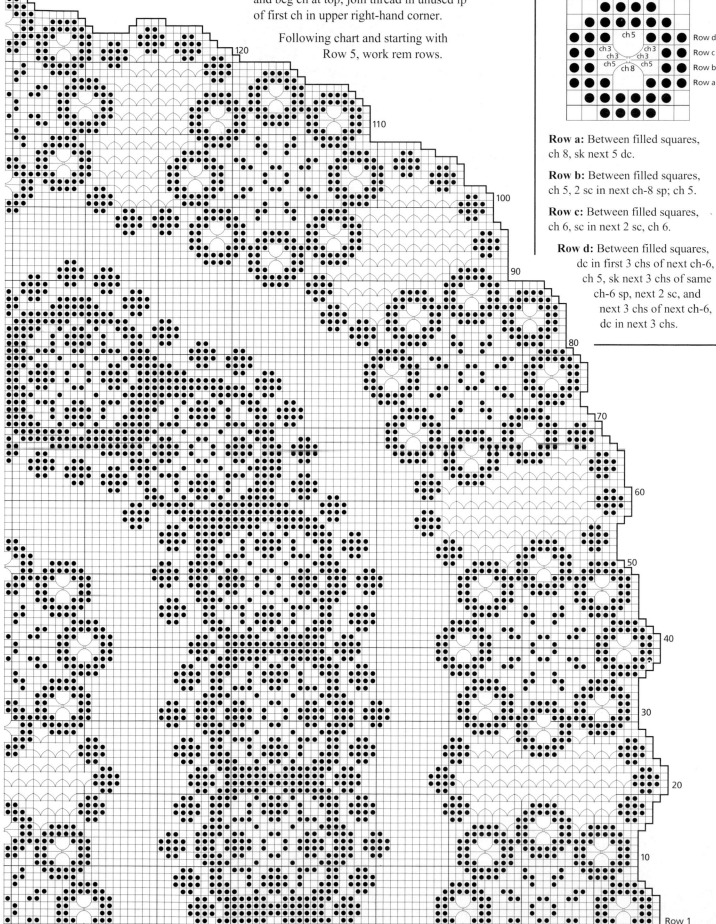

Second Half

Hold piece with wrong side facing you and beg ch at top; join thread in unused lp of first ch in upper right-hand corner.

Following chart and starting with Row 5, work rem rows.

Special Symbol Chart

Row a: Between filled squares, ch 8, sk next 5 dc.

Row b: Between filled squares, ch 5, 2 sc in next ch-8 sp; ch 5.

Row c: Between filled squares, ch 6, sc in next 2 sc, ch 6.

Row d: Between filled squares, dc in first 3 chs of next ch-6, ch 5, sk next 3 chs of same ch-6 sp, next 2 sc, and next 3 chs of next ch-6, dc in next 3 chs.

Chart shows one quarter of tablecloth

You Are My Sunshine

One look at this cheery cardigan sweater and you can't help but smile.

— *designed by Darla Sims*

Materials:

Worsted weight yarn, 24 (24, 30, 30, 38, 38) oz [1680 (1680, 2100, 2100, 2660, 2660) yds, 720 (720, 900, 900, 1140, 1140) gms] yellow
Note: Our photographed sweater was made with Caron® Wintuk®, Jonquil #3256.
Size H (5mm) crochet hook, or size required for gauge
Size F (3.75mm) crochet hook
Size 16 tapestry needle
Sewing needle and matching thread
5 buttons, 7/8"-diameter

Gauge:

In pattern stitch on larger size hook:
7 sts = 2"
8 rows = 3"

Instructions

Back

With larger size hook, ch 67 (73, 81, 87, 95, 101).

Row 1 (right side)**:** Dc in 4th ch from hook (3 skipped chs count as a dc) and in each rem ch—65 (71, 79, 85, 93, 99) dc. Ch 1, turn.

Row 2: Sl st in first dc, hdc in next dc; * sl st in next dc, hdc in next dc; rep from * to beg 3 skipped chs; sl st in 3rd ch of beg 3 skipped chs—65 (71, 79, 85, 93, 99) sts. Ch 2 (counts as first dc on following rows), turn.

Row 3: Dc in each st. Ch 1, turn.

Row 4: Sl st in first dc, hdc in next dc; * sl st in next dc, hdc in next dc; rep from * to turning ch-2; sl st in 2nd ch of turning ch-2. Ch 2, turn.

Rep Rows 3 and 4 until piece measures 21" (21 1/2", 22", 22 1/2", 23", 23 1/2") from beg, ending by working a wrong side row. At end of last row, do not ch 2. Ch 1, turn.

Sizing:

Size	Petite	Small	Medium	Large	X-Large	2X
Chest Measurement:	30"-32"	34"-36"	38"-40"	42"-44"	46"-48"	50"-52"
Finished Chest Measurement:	40"	42"	46"	50"	54"	58"

Note: Instructions are written for size Petite; changes for larger sizes are in parentheses.

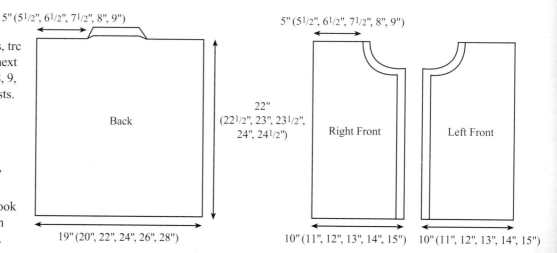

16" (17", 18", 19", 20", 21")

Sleeve

16½" (16½", 16½", 16½", 16½", 16½")

All measurements are approximate.

5" (5½", 6½", 7½", 8", 9")

Back

22" (22½", 23", 23½", 24", 24½")

19" (20", 22", 24", 26", 28")

5" (5½", 6½", 7½", 8", 9")

Right Front

Left Front

10" (11", 12", 13", 14", 15")   10" (11", 12", 13", 14", 15")

Shoulder Shaping:

Next Row: Sc in first 6 (7, 8, 9, 10, 11) sts, hdc in next 6 (7, 8, 9, 10, 11) sts, dc in next 7 (8, 9, 10, 11, 12) sts, trc in next 27 (27, 29, 29, 31, 31) sts, dc in next 7 (8, 9, 10, 11, 12) sts, hdc in next 6 (7, 8, 9, 10, 11) sts, sc in next 6 (7, 8, 9, 10, 11) sts.

Finish off and weave in ends.

Right Front

With larger size hook, ch 33 (37, 41, 43, 47, 51).

Row 1 (right side): Dc in 4th ch from hook (beg 3 skipped chs counts as a dc) and in each rem ch—31 (35, 39, 41, 45, 49) dc. Ch 1, turn.

Row 2: Sl st in first dc, hdc in next dc; * sl st in next dc, hdc in next dc; rep from * to beg 3 skipped chs; sl st in 3rd ch of beg 3 skipped chs—31 (35, 39, 41, 45, 49) sts. Ch 2 (counts as a dc on following rows), turn.

Row 3: Dc in each st. Ch 1, turn.

Row 4: Sl st in first dc, hdc in next dc; * sl st in next dc, hdc in next dc; rep from * to turning ch-2; dc in 2nd ch of turning ch-2. Ch 2, turn.

Rep Rows 3 and 4 until piece measures 18" (18½", 19", 19½", 20", 20½") from beg, ending by working a wrong side row. At end of last row, do not ch 2. Ch 1, turn.

Neck Shaping:

Row 1 (right side): Sl st in next 11 (12, 13, 12, 13, 14) sts; ch 2 (counts as a dc) dc in each rem st—21 (24, 27, 30, 33, 36) dc. Ch 1, turn.

For Sizes Petite, Medium, and X-Large only:

Row 2: Sl st in first dc, hdc in next dc; * sl st in next dc, hdc in next dc; rep from * to beg ch-2; sl st in 2nd ch of beg ch-2. Ch 2, turn.

Row 3: Dec over next 2 sts [to work dec: (YO, draw up lp in next st, YO and draw through 2 lps on hook) twice; YO and draw

through all 3 lps on hook—dec made]; dc in each rem st—20 (26, 32) sts. Ch 1, turn.

Row 4: Sl st in first dc, hdc in next dc; * sl st in next dc, hdc in next dc; rep from * to last dc and turning ch-2; sl st in last dc, hdc in 2nd ch of turning ch-2. Ch 2, turn.

Row 5: Dec over next 2 sts; dc in each rem st—19 (25, 31) sts. Ch 1, turn.

Row 6: Sl st in first dc, hdc in next dc; * sl st in next dc, hdc in next st; rep from * to turning ch-2; sl st in 2nd ch of turning ch-2. Ch 2, turn.

Row 7: Dec; dc in each rem st—18 (24, 30) sts. Ch 1, turn.

Row 8: Rep Row 4.

Row 9 (shoulder shaping): Dc in next 4 (6, 8) sts, hdc in next 6 (8, 10) sts, sc in next 7 (9, 11) sts.

Finish off and weave in ends.

For Sizes Small, Large and 2X only:

Row 2: Sl st in first dc, hdc in next dc; * sl st in next dc, hdc in next dc; rep from * to

last st and beg ch-2; sl st in next st, hdc in 2nd ch of beg ch-2. Ch 2, turn.

continued on page 202

Fiber Fun

Evening
Bun Warmer

We've used a new chenille with metallic yarn to make this quick-to-create elegant bun warmer.

— designed by Kelly Robinson

Size:
About 4¹/2" diameter

Materials:
Worsted weight chenille yarn, 1 oz
   (70 yds, 20 gms)
   Note: Our photographed bun warmer was made with Bernat® Chenille Fifth Avenue, Scarlet Sparkle #8315.
Size E (3.5mm) crochet hook, or size
   required for gauge
Size 18 tapestry needle
Large elastic band for hair

Gauge:
6 dc = 1"

Instructions

Ch 4, join to form a ring.

Rnd 1 (right side)**:** Ch 2, keeping last lp of each dc on hook, 2 dc in ring; YO and draw through all 3 lps on hook—beg cluster made; ch 5; * keeping last lp of each dc on hook, 3 dc in ring; YO and draw through all 4 lps on hook—cluster made; ch 5; rep from * 3 times more; join in beg cluster—5 clusters.

Rnd 2: Ch 1, sc in same cluster; 5 sc in next ch-5 sp; (sc in next cluster, 5 sc in next ch-5 sp) 4 times; join in first sc—30 sc.

Rnd 3: Ch 4 (counts as a dc and a ch-1 sp on this and following rnds), dc in same sc; sk next sc; * in next sc work (dc, ch 1, dc); sk next sc; rep from * 13 times more; join in 3rd ch of beg ch-4.

Rnd 4: Sl st in next ch-1 sp, ch 1, sc in same sp; ch 3, (sc in next ch-1 sp, ch 3) 14 times; join in first sc—15 ch-3 sps.

Rnd 5: Sl st in next ch-3 sp, ch 1, sc in same sp; ch 3, (sc in next ch-3 sp, ch 3) 14 times; join in first sc.

Rnd 6: Ch 4, dc in same sc; in next ch-3 sp work (dc, ch 1, dc); * in next sc work (dc, ch 1, dc); in next ch-3 sp work (dc, ch 1,

dc); rep from * 13 times more; join in 3rd ch of beg ch-4—30 ch-1 sps.

Rnd 7: Sl st in next ch-1 sp, ch 1, sc in same sp; ch 3, sk next 2 dc; * sc in next ch-1 sp, ch 3, sk next 2 dc; rep from * around; join in first sc—30 ch-3 sps.

Rnd 8: Sl st in next ch-3 sp, ch 1, sc in same sp, ch 3; * sc in next ch-3 sp, ch 3; rep from * around; join in first sc.

Rnds 9 and 10: Rep Rnd 8.

Rnd 11: Sl st in next ch-3 sp, ch 1, 2 sc in same sp and in each rem ch-3 sp; join in first sc—60 sc.

Rnd 12: Ch 1, working over elastic band, sc in same sc and in each rem sc; join in first sc.

Finish off and weave in ends.

Rugged Individualist

Classic stripes in masculine shades of brown and beige is a handsome way to show him you care.

Materials:

Worsted weight yarn, 15 oz (985 yds, 425 gms) brown; 9 oz (591 yds, 255 gms) each, heather brown and beige

Note: Our photographed sweater was made with Lion Brand® WoolEase®, Chestnut Heather #179; Natural Heather #98; and Mushroom #403.

Size J (6mm) crochet hook, or size required for gauge

Size I (5.5mm) crochet hook

Size H (5mm) crochet hook

Size G (4.25mm) crochet hook

Gauge:

With largest size hook:

7 dc = 2"

14 dc rows = 7"

Instructions

Back

Ribbing:

With second largest crochet hook and brown, ch 12.

Row 1: Sc in 2nd ch from hook and in each rem ch—11 sc. Ch 1, turn.

Row 2: Working in BLs only, sc in each sc. Ch 1, turn.

Rep Row 2 until ribbing measures about 23". At end of last row, change to largest size hook; ch 3 (counts as first dc on following rows), do not turn.

Body:

Row 1 (right side)**:** Work 84 dc evenly spaced in edge sc of one long side of ribbing—85 dc. Ch 3, turn.

Row 2: Sk first dc, dc in each rem dc and in 3rd ch of beg ch-3. Change to heather brown by drawing lp through; cut brown. Ch 3, turn.

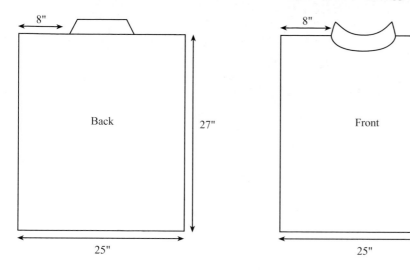

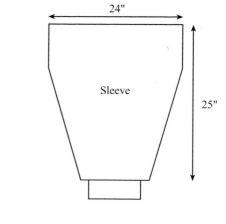

Size:	
	Large
Chest Measurement:	44"- 46"
Finished Chest Measurement:	50"

Rows 3 through 6: Rep Row 2. At end of Row 6, change to brown by drawing lp through; cut heather brown. Ch 3, turn.

Rows 7 and 8: Rep Row 2. At end of Row 8, change to beige by drawing lp through; cut brown. Ch 3, turn.

Rows 9 through 12: Rep Row 2. At end of Row 12, change to brown by drawing lp through; cut beige. Ch 3, turn.

Rows 13 through 47: Rep Row 2 in following color sequence:

    2 rows brown
    4 rows heather brown
    2 rows brown
    4 rows beige
    2 rows brown
    4 rows heather brown
    2 rows brown
    3 rows beige

At end of last row, do not change color; do not ch 3.

Finish off and weave in all ends.

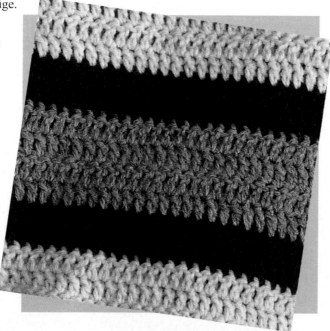

Front

Work same as for back through Row 42.

Left Shoulder Shaping:

Row 1 (right side): With brown, sk first dc, dc in next 36 dc—37 dc. Ch 3, turn, leaving rem dc unworked.

Row 2: Sk first dc, dec over next 2 dc [to work dec: (YO, draw up lp in next dc, YO, draw through 2 lps on hook) twice; YO and draw through all 3 lps on hook— dec made]; dec over next 2 dc; dc in next 31 dc and in 3rd ch of turning ch-3—35 dc. Change to beige by drawing lp through; cut brown. Ch 3, turn.

Row 3: Sk first dc, dc in next 29 dc, (dec over next 2 dc) twice—32 dc. Ch 3, turn, leaving turning ch-3 unworked.

Row 4: Sk first dc, dec twice; dc in next 26 dc and in 3rd ch of turning ch-3—30 dc. Ch 3, turn.

Row 5: Sk first dc, dc in next 24 dc, dec twice—27 dc. Finish off, leaving an 18" end for sewing and leaving turning ch-3 unworked.

Right Shoulder Shaping:

Hold front with right side facing you and Row 42 at top; with largest size hook, join brown in 12th dc from left front shoulder.

Row 1 (wrong side): Ch 3 (counts as first dc), dc in next 35 dc and in 3rd ch of turning ch-3—37 dc. Ch 3, turn.

Row 2 (right side): Sk first dc, dc in next 31 dc, dec twice—34 dc. Change to beige by drawing lp through; cut brown. Ch 3, turn, leaving beg ch-3 unworked.

Row 3: Sk first dc, dec twice; dc in next 28 dc and in 3rd ch of turning ch-3—32 dc. Ch 3, turn.

Row 4: Sk first dc, dc in next 26 dc, dec twice—29 dc. Ch 3, turn, leaving turning ch-3 unworked.

Row 5: Sk first dc, dec twice; dc in next 23 dc and in 3rd ch of turning ch-3—27 dc. Finish off, leaving an 18" end for sewing.

Sew shoulder seams.

Neck Edging:

Hold piece with right side of back facing you; with largest size hook, join brown in first dc to left of right shoulder seam.

Row 1: Ch 1, sc in same dc and in each rem dc across back; working along left front neck edge, 2 sc in side of each of next 5 edge dc and turning ch; sc in each dc across front; working along right front neck edge, 2 sc in side of each of next 5 edge dc; join in first sc. Finish off.

continued on page 201

Animal Pairs

Whether going to market or off to Grandma's house these happily stuffed piggies are wonderful companions.

Patsy and Pierre Pig

— designed by Candy Clayton

Patsy Pig

Size:
About 16 1/2" tall

Materials:
Worsted weight yarn, 7 oz (490 yds, 210 gms) peach; 3 1/2 oz (245 yds, 105 gms) blue; 2 oz (140 yds, 60 gms) white
Note: Our photographed animal was made with Red Heart® Classic™, Sea Coral #246; Light Periwinkle #827; and White #001.
Size F (3.75mm) crochet hook, or size required for gauge
Size 18 tapestry needle

Trimmings:
two sets of 30mm doll joints
two 15mm black animal eyes
36" length black embroidery floss
tacky craft glue or hot glue
polyester fiberfill
black plastic eyelashes
3 blue ribbon roses, 1/2"-diameter
sewing needle and matching thread

Gauge:
4 sc = 1"

Note: Pigs have plastic face parts which are not suitable for children under three years of age. If for a young child please embroider face with floss.

Instructions

Pig
With peach, work same as Kathy Kitty beginning on page 3, omitting ears and Finishing.

Ear (make 2):
With peach, ch 2.

Note: Rnds 1 through 6 are worked in continuous rnds. Do not join; mark beg of rnds.

Rnd 1 (right side): 6 sc in 2nd ch from hook.

Rnd 2: Sc in each sc.

Rnd 3: (Sc in next sc, 2 sc in next sc) 3 times—9 sc.

Rnd 4: (Sc in next sc, 2 sc in next sc) 4 times; sc in next sc—13 sc.

Rnd 5: (Sc in next2 sc, 2 sc in next sc) 4 times; sc in next sc—17 sc.

Rnd 6: Sc in each sc.

Rnd 7: Fold Rnd 6 flat; working through both thicknesses, sc in next 9 sc. Finish off, leaving an 18" end for sewing.

Snout:

With peach, ch 2.

Note: Rnds 1 and 2 are worked in continuous rnds. Do not join; mark beg of rnds.

Rnd 1 (right side): 6 sc in 2nd ch from hook.

Rnd 2: 2 sc in each sc—12 sc.

Rnd 3: Working in BLs only, ch 1, sc in same sc and in each rem sc; join in first sc. Finish off, leaving a 12" end for sewing.

Finishing

Step 1: Stuff body firmly with fiberfill. With tapestry needle and 10" end of body, weave in and out through 12 sts of Rnd 55. Pull to close opening. Weave in end.

Step 2: Stuff snout slightly with fiberfill and sew over Rnds 15 and 16 of face. Referring to photo for placement, with tapestry needle and floss, make two lazy daisy sts (see Embroidery Stitch Guide on page 211) for nostrils. Make mouth using straight stitches (see Embroidery Stitch Guide on page 211).

Step 3: Sew ears to side of head on Rnds 5 through 11 about 2" apart.

Step 4: On crocheted hair piece, twist each curl down and tack to secure. Sew hair to head between ears.

Dress

Starting at neckline with white, ch 32.

Row 1 (wrong side): Sc in 2nd ch from hook and in next 2 chs, (2 sc in next ch, sc in next 3 chs) 7 times—38 sc. Ch 1, turn.

Row 2 (right side): Sc in first 6 sc, 2 sc in each of next 5 sc; sc in next 16 sc, 2 sc in each of next 5 sc; sc in next 6 sc—48 sc. Ch 1, turn.

Row 3: Sc in each sc. Ch 1, turn.

Row 4: Sc in first 6 sc; † 2 sc in next sc; [in next sc work (dc, sc, dc); in next sc work (sc, dc, sc)] 4 times; in next sc work (dc, sc, dc)—sleeve made; 2 sc in next sc †; sc in next 14 sc; rep from † to † once; sc in next 6 sc. Ch 1, turn.

Row 5: Sc in first 7 sc; † 2 sc in next sc; (sc in next dc, dc in next sc) 13 times; sc in next dc, 2 sc in next sc †; sc in next 16 sc; rep from † to † once; sc in next 7 sc. Ch 1, turn.

Row 6: Sc in first 8 sc; † 2 sc in next sc; (dc in next sc, sc in next dc) 13 times; dc in next sc, 2 sc in next sc †; sc in next 18 sc; rep from † to † once; sc in next 8 sc. Ch 1, turn.

Row 7: Sc in first 9 sc; † 2 sc in next sc; (sc in next dc, dc in next sc) twice; 3-sc dec over next dc, next sc, and next dc (to work 3-sc dec: draw up lp in each of 3 sts indicated, YO and draw through all 4 lps on hook—3-sc dec made); †† (dc in next sc, sc in next dc) twice; dc in next sc, 3-sc dec over next dc, next sc, and next dc ††; rep from †† to †† once more; (dc in next sc, sc in next dc) twice; 2 sc in next sc †; sc in next 20 sc; rep from † to † once; sc in next 9 sc. Ch 1, turn.

Row 8: Sc in first 10 sc; † sc dec over next 2 sc (to work sc dec: draw up lp in each of next 2 sts, YO and draw through all 3 lps on hook—sc dec made); ch 4, sk next 19 sts, sc dec over next 2 sc †; sc in next 22 sc; rep from † to † once; sc in next 10 sc. Ch 1, turn.

Row 9: 2 sc in first sc; sc in each sc and each ch to last sc, 2 sc in last sc—56 sc. Ch 1, turn.

Row 10: Sc in each sc. Ch 1, turn.

Row 11: 2 sc in first sc; sc in next 54 sc, 2 sc in next sc—58 sc. Ch 1, turn.

Rows 12 and 13: Rep Row 10.

Row 14: Sc in each sc; join in FL of first sc. Change to blue by drawing lp through; cut white.

Note: Remainder of dress is worked in rnds.

Rnd 1: Ch 1, in same sc work (sc, dc, sc); * in next sc work (dc, sc); in next sc work (dc, sc, dc); in next sc work (sc, dc); in next sc work (sc, dc, sc); rep from * 13 times more; in next sc work (dc, sc, dc); join in first sc—146 sts.

Rnd 2: Ch 3 (counts as a dc on this and following rnds), sc in next dc; * dc in next sc, sc in next dc; rep from * around; join in 3rd ch of beg ch-3.

Rnd 3: Ch 1, sc in same ch as joining; dc in next sc; * sc in next dc, dc in next sc; rep from * around; join in first sc.

Rnds 4 through 15: Rep Rnds 2 and 3 six times more.

Rnd 16: Ch 1, sc in same sc; ch 3, sk next dc; * sc in next sc, ch 3, sk next dc; rep from * around; join in first sc. Finish off.

Find more animal pairs in our Summer, Fall, and Winter issues.

Kitty Pair in Winter, page 2

Bunny Pair in Spring, page 62

Bear Pair in Summer, page 150

Collar:

Hold dress with right side of back opening facing you and beg ch at top; join blue in first unused lp of beg ch-32 to left of back opening.

continued on page 192

Patsy Pig

continued from page 191

Row 1: Ch 1, sc in same lp; 2 sc in next lp; (sc in next lp, 2 sc in next lp) 3 times; sc in next lp, hdc in next 2 lps, 2 dc in each of next 2 lps; hdc in next 2 lps, sl st in next lp, hdc in next 2 lps, 2 dc in each of next 2 lps; hdc in next 2 lps, (sc in next lp, 2 sc in next lp) 4 times; sc in next lp— 43 sts. Ch 1, turn.

Row 2: Sc in first 2 sc, (2 sc in next sc, sc in next 2 sts) 4 times; hdc in next hdc, 3 hdc in next dc; 3 dc in each of next 2 dc; 3 hdc in next dc; hdc in next hdc, sc in next hdc, sl st in next sl st, sc in next hdc, hdc in next hdc, 3 hdc in next dc; 3 dc in each of next 2 dc; 3 hdc in next dc; hdc in next

hdc, (sc in next 2 sts, 2 sc in next sc) 4 times; sc in next 2 sc. Finish off.

Back Opening Trim and Ties:

Hold dress with right side facing you and neck edge to right; working in edge sc of each row on back opening, join white in first edge sc to right of back opening; ch 1, sc in same sc; † in next sc work (sl st, ch 24, sl st in 2nd ch from hook and in next 22 chs, sl st) †; sc in next 6 rows; rep from † to † once; sc in next 5 rows; working along next side in rows of edge sc, sc in next 5 rows; rep from † to † once; sc in next 6 rows; rep from † to † once; sc in next sc.

Finish off and weave in all ends.

Finishing

Sew one ribbon rose to front of bodice and one ribbon rose to each ear.

Pierre Pig

Size:
About 16¹/₂" tall

Materials:
Worsted weight yarn, 7 oz (490 yds, 210 gms) peach; 3¹/₂ oz (245 yds, 105 gms) blue; 2 oz (140 yds, 60 gms) white
Note: Our photographed animal was made with Red Heart® Classic™, Sea Coral #246; Light Periwinkle #82; and White #001.
Size F (3.75mm) crochet hook, or size required for gauge
Size 18 tapestry needle

Trimmings:
2 sets of 30mm doll joints
two 15mm black animal eyes
36" length black embroidery floss
polyester fiberfill

Gauge:
4 sc = 1"

Instructions

Pig
With peach, work same as Kathy Kitty beginning on page 3, omitting eyelashes, ears, hair and Finishing.

Ear (make 2):
With peach, work same as Patsy Pig Ear, beginning on page 190.

Snout:
With peach, work same as Patsy Pig Snout, on page 191.

Finishing
Follow Steps 1 through 3 of Patsy Pig Finishing on page 191.

Romper
Starting at neckband with white, ch 32.

Row 1 (wrong side): Sc in 2nd ch from hook and in next 2 chs, (2 sc in next ch, sc in next 3 chs) 7 times—38 sc. Ch 1, turn.

Row 2 (right side): Sc in first 6 sc, 2 sc in each of next 5 sc; sc in next 16 sc, 2 sc in each of next 5 sc; sc in next 6 sc— 48 sc. Ch 1, turn.

continued on page 205

85 Colors.
One Red Heart.

Red Heart Super Saver,® America's favorite yarn, provides America's most exciting choices. With 85 colors, the possibilities are practically endless. And with Red Heart,® your projects will stay exciting and colorful year after year, wash after wash.

When you choose Red Heart Super Saver, you'll know you're choosing the best in quality and value. That must be why Red Heart has been America's favorite yarn for over 60 years.

Little Treasure Amulet Bag

— *designed by Kelly Robinson*

Perfect for mad money, this precious little bag can be worn instead of a necklace to complete a casual or dressy outfit. The little gold beads are easy to add as you crochet— just take our bead stringing lesson first.

A Lesson in Bead Stringing

Instructions

Cut a 12" length of sewing thread. Join sewing thread to the crochet thread by tying an overhand knot around the crochet thread 1" from end (**Fig A**). Do not cut crochet thread from ball. Select a beading needle that will fit through bead holes. Thread beading needle with untied end of sewing thread. String beads onto beading needle, sliding beads down onto sewing thread, over knot and onto crochet thread (**Fig B**). Continue to string beads until all beads are strung onto crochet thread. Be sure that you have strung the exact number and specified order of beads as indicated in the individual pattern.

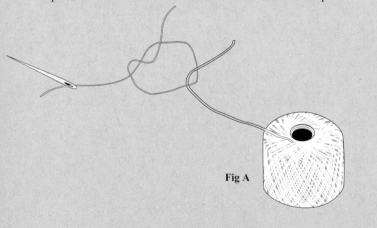

Fig A

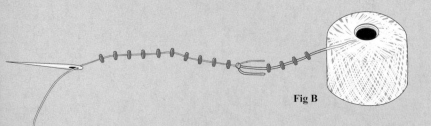

Fig B

Size:
About 5" long

Materials:
Bedspread-weight crochet cotton, 2 oz
  (300 yds, 60 gms) blue
  *Note: Our photographed model made
  with J. & P. Coats® Knit-Cro-Sheen®,
  True Blue #182.*
Size 6 (1.80mm) steel crochet hook, or size
  required for gauge
Size 18 tapestry needle

Trimmings:

636 gold glass seed beads, size 11/0
27 blue glass seed beads, size 11/0
111 gold bugle beads, 7mm
beading needle and matching sewing thread

Gauge:

8 dc = 1"

Instructions

Front/Back (make 2)

Note: String 210 beads onto crochet thread. Slide beads aside until needed.

Ch 21.

Row 1 (right side): Sc in 2nd ch from hook and in each rem ch—20 sc. Ch 1, turn.

Row 2: Slide bead up, sc in first sc; * slide bead up, sc in next sc; rep from * 18 times more—20 beads. Ch 1, turn.

Row 3: Sc in each sc. Ch 1, turn.

Rows 4 through 11: Rep Rows 2 and 3 four times more.

Row 12: Rep Row 2.

Row 13: Dec over first 2 sc (to work dec: draw up lp in each of next 2 sc, YO and draw through all 3 lps on hook—dec made); sc in next 16 sc, dec over next 2 sc—18 sc. Ch 1, turn.

Row 14: Slide bead up, sc in first sc; * slide bead up, sc in next sc; rep from * 16 times more—18 beads. Ch 1, turn.

Row 15: Dec; sc in next 14 sc, dec—16 sc. Ch 1, turn.

Row 16: Slide bead up, sc in first sc; * slide bead up, sc in next sc; rep from * 14 times more—16 beads. Ch 1, turn.

Row 17: Dec; sc in next 12 sc, dec—14 sc. Ch 1, turn.

Row 18: Slide bead up, sc in first sc; * slide bead up, sc in next sc; rep from * 12 times more—14 beads. Ch 1, turn.

Row 19: Dec; sc in next 10 sc, dec—12 sc. Ch 1, turn.

Row 20: Slide bead up, sc in first sc; * slide bead up, sc in next sc; rep from * 10 times more—12 beads. Ch 1, turn.

Row 21: Dec; sc in next 8 sc, dec—10 sc. Ch 1, turn.

Row 22: Slide bead up, sc in first sc; * slide bead up, sc in next sc; rep from * 8 times more—10 beads. Ch 1, turn.

Row 23: Dec; sc in next 6 sc, dec—8 sc. Ch 1, turn.

Row 24: Slide bead up, sc in first sc; * slide bead up, sc in next sc; rep from * 6 times more—8 beads. Ch 1, turn.

Row 25: Dec; sc in next 4 sc, dec—6 sc. Ch 1, turn.

Row 26: Slide bead up, sc in first sc; * slide bead up, sc in next sc; rep from * 4 times more—6 beads. Ch 1, turn.

Row 27: Dec; sc in next 2 sc, dec—4 sc. Ch 1, turn.

Row 28: Slide bead up, sc in first sc; * slide bead up, sc in next sc; rep from * twice more—4 beads. Ch 1, turn.

Row 29: Dec twice—2 sc. Ch 1, turn.

Row 30: Slide bead up, sc in first sc; slide bead up, sc in next sc.

Finish off and weave in ends.

Edging and Chain Strap:

Hold front and back with wrong sides tog and beg chs at top; make lp on hook and join with an sc through both thicknesses and in edge sc of Row 1; working in edge sc of each row, sc in next 28 rows; working across Row 30, 2 sc in each of next 2 sc; working along next side in edge sc of both thicknesses, sc in next 29 rows; ch 200—chain strap made; join in first sc.

Finish off and weave in ends.

Bead Fringe

Using beading needle and single strand of matching sewing thread, secure to inside of bag at 13th sc of edging. Slide two gold seed beads, one bugle bead, (one gold seed bead, one bugle bead) twice; and two gold seed beads onto thread. Bring needle around the bottom seed bead and up through other beads, then take a stitch through sc. Repeat in next 17 sc. Insert needle through next sc, slide four blue seed beads, one bugle bead, (one blue seed bead, one bugle bead) 3 times; and two blue seed beads onto thread. Bring needle around the bottom seed bead and up through other beads, then take a stitch through sc. Repeat twice more in same sc. For next 18 sc, work fringe in same manner as first 18 sc.

Sporty Comfort

Create this cozy sweater in school team colors or any favorite shade of worsted weight yarn and enjoy its comfort and easy styling from fall's first little nip in the air until the daffodils bloom in the spring.

— designed by Darla Sims

Materials:

Worsted weight yarn, 23 (25, 27, 29, 31) oz [1610 (1750, 1890, 2030, 2170) yds, 690 (750, 810, 870, 930) gms] green; 2 (2, 2, 3, 3) oz [140 (140, 140, 210, 210) yds, 60 (60, 60, 180, 180) gms] white *Note: Our photographed sweater was made with Caron® Wintuk®, Fir #3010; and White #3001.*
Size I (5.5mm) crochet hook, or size required for gauge
Size G (4.25mm) crochet hook
Size 16 tapestry needle

Gauge:
In pattern with larger size hook:
3 repeats = 2"

Instructions

Back
With larger size hook and green, ch 56 (62, 68, 74, 80).

Row 1 (right side)**:** In 4th ch from hook (beg 3 skipped chs count as a dc) work (sc, dc); sk next ch; * in next ch work (sc, dc); sk next ch; rep from * to last ch; sc in last ch—54 (60, 66, 72, 78) sts. Ch 3 (counts as first dc on following rows), turn.

Row 2: Sk first sc; * sk next dc, in next sc work (sc, dc); rep from * to beg 3 skipped chs; sc in 3rd ch of beg 3 skipped chs. Ch 3, turn.

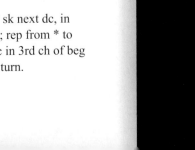

Sizing:

Sizes	Petite	Small	Medium	Large	X-Large
Chest Measurement:	30"-32"	34"-36"	38"-40"	42"-44"	46"-48"
Finished Chest Measurement:	36"	40"	44"	48"	52"

Note: Instructions are written for size Petite; changes for larger sizes are in parentheses.

All measurements are approximate.

5¹/2" (6", 6¹/2", 7", 8")

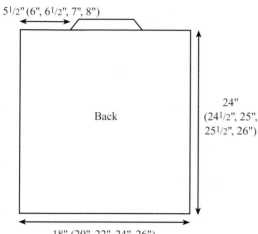

Back

24"
(24¹/2", 25", 25¹/2", 26")

18" (20", 22", 24", 26")

5¹/2" (6", 6¹/2", 7", 8")
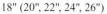

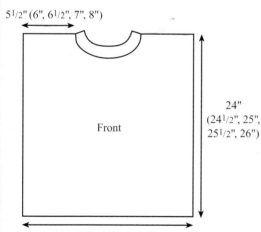

Front

24"
(24¹/2", 25", 25¹/2", 26")

18" (20", 22", 24", 26")

16" (17", 18", 19", 20")

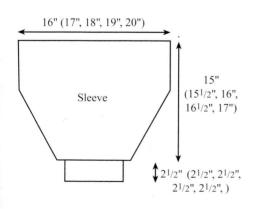

Sleeve

15"
(15¹/2", 16", 16¹/2", 17")

2¹/2" (2¹/2", 2¹/2", 2¹/2", 2¹/2",)

Row 3: Sk first sc; * sk next dc, in next sc work (sc, dc); rep from * to turning ch-3; sc in 3rd ch of turning ch-3. Ch 3, turn.

Rep Row 3 until back measures 16". Mark each end of last row worked for underarm.

Continue in patt as established until piece measures 8" (8¹/2", 9", 9¹/2", 10") from underarm markers. At end of last row, do not ch 3.

Finish off and weave in ends.

Front

Note: When changing color, work until 2 lps of last color rem on hook, draw new color through 2 lps on hook. Carry color not in use along edge of work.

Work same as Back until piece measures same as back to underarm, changing to white in last sc. Mark each end of last row worked for underarm.

Continue in patt as established working 2 rows white and 2 rows green alternately until front measures 3" less than back to shoulder, ending by working a right side row.

Right Neck Shaping:

Row 1 (wrong side): Sk first sc; * sk next dc, in next sc work (sc, dc); rep from * 8 (9, 10, 11, 12) times more—19 (21, 23, 25, 27) sts. Ch 1, turn.

Row 2 (right side): Sk first dc, in next sc work (sc, dc); * sk next dc, in next sc work (sc, dc); rep from * to turning ch-3; sc in 3rd ch of turning ch-3. Ch 3, turn.

Row 3: Sk first sc and next dc; * in next sc work (sc, dc); sk next dc * rep from to last sc; sc in last sc—18 (20, 22, 24, 26) sts. Ch 3, turn.

Row 4: Sk first sc; * sk next dc, in next sc work (sc, dc); rep from * to turning ch-3; sc in 3rd ch of turning ch-3. Ch 3, turn.

Row 5: Sk first sc and next dc; * in next sc work (sc, dc); sk next dc; rep from * to last sc and turning ch-3; sc in last sc and in 3rd ch of turning ch-3—17 (19, 21, 23, 25) sts. Ch 1, turn.

Row 6: Sk first sc, in next sc work (sc, dc); * sk next dc, in next sc work (sc, dc); rep from * to turning ch-3; sc in 3rd ch of turning ch-3. Ch 3, turn.

Row 7: Sk first sc and next dc; * in next sc work (sc, dc); sk next dc; rep from * to last sc; sc in last sc—16 (18, 20, 22, 24) sts. Ch 3, turn.

Row 8: Sk first sc; * sk next dc, in next sc work (sc, dc); rep from * to turning ch-3; sc in 3rd ch of turning ch-3. Ch 3, turn.

Continuing in color sequence and pattern as established, rep Row 8 until front measures same length as back to shoulders. At end of last row, do not ch 3. Finish off.

Left Neck Shaping:

Hold front with wrong side facing you; sk next 17 (19, 21, 23, 25) sts from beg of right neck shaping, working in color sequence as established, make lp on hook and join with an sc in next sc.

Row 1 (wrong side): Dc in same sc; * sk next dc, in next sc work (sc, dc); rep from * 7 (8, 9, 10, 11) times more; sc in 3rd ch of turning ch-3—19 (21, 23, 25, 27) sts. Ch 3, turn.

Row 2 (right side): Sk first sc and next dc; * in next sc work (sc, dc); sk next dc; rep from * to joining sc; in joining sc work (sc, dc). Ch 1, turn.

continued on page 204

Reverse Single Crochet and Reverse Half Double Crochet

Have you ever wished to put a simple edging on your project, but just didn't know how?
We'll show you some effective stitches which create just that kind of edging.

Crochet backwards?

Of course! It's easier than it sounds and with a little practice, reverse sc may well become your favorite edging.

Sometimes called Crab Stitch (because crabs run sideways), this stitch creates an attractive, dimensional cable effect. It is usually worked as the final row or round of a crochet project.

For practice, with desired yarn and appropriate hook, ch 25.

Row 1: Sc in 2nd ch from hook and in each rem ch. Ch 1, turn.

Row 2: Sc in each sc. Ch 1, turn.

Row 3 (right side)**:** Sc in each sc. Do not ch or turn.

Basic Reverse Single Crochet

(Work loosely while you practice; you can adjust tension later).

Ch 1 (**Fig 1**).

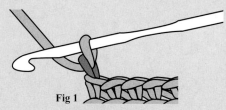
Fig 1

Step 1: With yarn at left of work, insert hook from front to back under both lps of next sc to right (**Fig 2**).

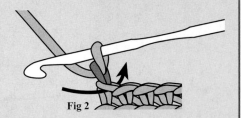
Fig 2

Step 2: YO hook and draw up a lp (**Fig 3**).

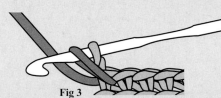
Fig 3

Step 3: YO hook from back to front, turn hook slightly downward (**Fig 4**); draw yarn through both lps on hook—reverse sc made (**Fig 5**).

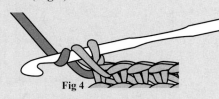
Fig 4

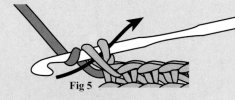
Fig 5

Repeat Steps 1 through 3, 4 times more (**Fig 6**)—5 reverse sc. Do not finish off.

Fig 6

Raised Reverse Single Crochet

This stitch creates a more dimensional edge, achieved by changing the way the yarn goes around the hook in Step 3. Be sure to work loosely as you practice.

Ch 1.

Steps 1 and 2: Rep Steps 1 and 2 of Basic Reverse Single Crochet.

Step 3: YO hook from front to back to front (**Fig 7**); turn hook slightly downward and draw yarn through both lps on hook—raised reverse sc made (**Fig 8**).

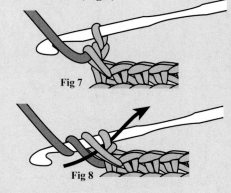
Fig 7

Fig 8

Repeat Steps 1 through 3, 4 times more (**Fig 9**)—5 raised reverse sc. Do not finish off

Fig 9

Look at your work, and compare the two versions. When a pattern calls for reverse sc, you can use either method depending on the look you want. Raised reverse sc uses slightly more yarn.

Reverse Half Double Crochet

For an even more cabled look you can work reverse hdc in the same way. Take care to work loosely.

Ch 2 (**Fig 10**).

Fig 10

Step 1: YO hook as for an hdc; with yarn at left of work, insert hook from front to back under both lps of next sc to right (**Fig 11**).

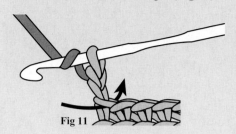
Fig 11

Step 2: YO hook and draw up a lp (**Fig 12**), YO hook and draw through all 3 lps on hook (**Fig 13**)—reverse hdc made.

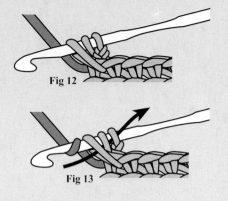
Fig 12

Fig 13

Repeat Steps 1 and 2, five times more. Finish off.

Compare this method with the two preceding. Now it's time to start a project.

Special Note: *Most patterns don't tell you to ch 1 or ch 2 before beginning a row or rnd of reverse sc or reversed hdc. So be sure to add this, as it makes working the first few stitches much easier.*

Coaster with Reverse Single Crochet Edging

Size:
4" diameter

Materials:
Worsted weight yarn, 1/4 oz (8 yds, 7 gms) each of blue and cream
Note: Our photographed coaster was made with Peaches & Cream, Light Blue #26; and Cream #3.
Size H (5mm) crochet hook, or size required for gauge

Gauge:
4 dc = 1"

Instructions
With blue, ch 4; join to form a ring.

Rnd 1 (right side): Ch 1, 8 sc in ring; join in first sc.

Rnd 2: Ch 3 (counts as a dc on this and following rnds), dc in same sc; ch 1 (2 dc in next sc, ch 1) 7 times; join in 3rd ch of beg ch-3—16 dc.

Rnd 3: Ch 3, dc in next dc, 2 dc in next ch-1 sp; (dc in each of next 2 dc, 2 dc in next ch-1 sp) 7 times; join in 3rd ch of beg ch-3— 32 dc. Finish off blue.

Rnd 4: With cream, make lp on hook and join with an sc in 3rd ch of beg ch-3 of prev

rnd; working in BLs only, 2 sc in next dc; * sc in next dc, 2 sc in next dc; rep from * around; join in joining sc—48 sc.

Rnd 5: Ch 1, work reverse sc or raised reverse sc in each sc; join in first st.

Finish off and weave in all ends.

Sunflower Sachet

Take a little time to stitch this optimistic, happy sunflower for someone who needs a cheering up or as a special thank you. This drawstring sachet holds a bar of fragrant soap inside.

—designed by Nanette M. Seale

Size:
About 6¹/2" x 4"

Materials:
Bedspread-weight crochet cotton, one oz (160 yds, 30 gms) white; ¹/2 oz (80 yds, 15 gms) yellow

Embroidery floss, 1 skein brown

Note: Our photographed sachet was made with J. & P. Coats® South Maid®, White #1; and Lemon Peel #499; and Anchor floss, Brown #360.

Size 6 (1.80mm) steel crochet hook, or size required for gauge

Size 18 tapestry needle

Gauge:
2 shells = 1"

Instructions

Body
With white, ch 29.

Row 1 (wrong side): In 6th ch from hook (beg 5 skipped chs count a dc and a ch-2 sp) work (2 dc, ch 2, 2 dc)—shell made; * sk next 3 chs, shell in next ch; rep from * 4 times more; sk next 2 chs, dc in next ch— 6 shells. Ch 3 (counts as a dc on following rows), turn.

Row 2 (right side): Sk next 2 dc; * in ch-2 sp of next shell work shell; rep from * 5 times more; dc in 5th ch of beg 5 skipped chs. Ch 3, turn.

Row 3: Sk next 2 dc, shell in each of next 6 shells; dc in 3rd ch of turning ch-3. Ch 3, turn.

Rows 4 through 30: Rep Row 3. At end of Row 30, do not ch 3; do not turn.

Joining

First Side:
Fold piece in half lengthwise with wrong sides tog (Rows 1 through 15 become back of piece); ch 1; hold piece with edge of front (Rows 16 through 30) facing you and Row 30 to right; working in sps formed by edge dc and turning chs, sc in Row 30, ch 2, sc in Row 1; * ch 2, sc in next row on front, ch 2, sc in next row on back; rep from * 13 times more. Finish off.

Second Side:
Hold piece with opposite side at top; working in sps formed by edge dc and turning chs, join white in Row 16, ch 1, sc in same row; ch 2, sc in Row 15; † ch 2, sc in next row on front, ch 2, sc in next row on back †; rep from † to † 13 times more. Do not finish off.

Ruffle
Rnd 1 (right side): Sc in same sp as last sc worked; 2 sc in next ch-2 sp; sc in next 3 dc; * 2 sc in next ch-2 sp; sc in next 4 dc; rep from * 4 times more; 2 sc in next ch-2 sp; sc in next 3 dc, 2 sc in next ch-2 sp; sc in next sc; working in unused lps and in sps formed by unused chs of beg ch, sc in 3rd ch of beg 5 skipped chs, 2 sc in next

continued on page 201

Sunflower Sachet

continued from page 200

ch-2 sp; † sc in next lp, 3 sc in next ch-3 sp †; rep from † to † 4 times more; sc in next lp, 2 sc in next ch-2 sp; join in first sc—70 sc.

Rnd 2: Ch 4 (counts as a dc and ch-1 sp on this and following rnds), sk next sc; * dc in next sc, ch 1, sk next sc; rep from * 33 times more; join in 3rd ch of beg ch-4—35 dc.

Rnd 3: Ch 1, 2 sc in same sp as joining; * sc in next ch-1 sp and in next dc; rep from * 33 times more; 2 sc in next ch-1 sp; join in first sc—72 sc.

Rnd 4: Ch 3 (counts as a dc on this and following rnds), in same sc work (dc, ch 2, 2 dc)—beg shell made; * sk next 3 sc, in next sc work (2 dc, ch 2, 2 dc)—shell made; rep from * 16 times more; join in 3rd ch of beg ch-3—18 shells.

Rnd 5: Sl st in next dc and in next ch-2 sp, in same sp work beg shell; in ch-2 sp of each rem shell work shell; join in 3rd ch of beg ch-3.

Rnd 6: Sl st in next ch-2 sp, ch 3, 4 dc in same sp; sk next dc, sc in sp between same shell and next shell; * 5 dc in ch-2 sp of next shell, sc in sp between same shell and next shell; rep from * 16 times more; join in 3rd ch of beg ch-3.

Finish off and weave in ends.

Sunflower

Center:

Note: Center is worked in continuous rnds. Do not join; mark beg of rnds.

With 6 strands of floss, ch 3; join to form a ring.

Rnd 1 (right side): 6 sc in ring.

Rnd 2: 2 sc in each sc—12 sc.

Rnd 3: * 2 sc in next sc; sc in next sc; rep from * 5 times more—18 sc.

Rnd 4: * Sc in next 2 sc, 2 sc in next sc; rep from * 5 times more—24 sc. Finish off.

Petals:

Join yellow in BL of first sc on Rnd 4; * ch 8, sl st in 2nd ch from hook, sc in next 6 chs; sl st in BL of next sc on Rnd 4—petal made; rep from * 22 times more; ch 8, sl st in 2nd ch from hook, sc in next 6 chs; join in joining sl st—24 petals. Finish off, leaving a 24" end for sewing.

Cord

With yellow, ch 200; sl st in 2nd ch from hook and in each rem ch. Finish off.

Finishing

Step 1: Referring to photo for placement, with tapestry needle and long end, sew sunflower to front of sachet.

Step 2: Weave cord through ch-1 sps of Rnd 2 of ruffle, beginning and ending in ch-1 sp above left side joining. Tie knots in ends of cord; tie ends together about 1" from ends of cord.

Rugged Individualist

continued from page 189

Neckband:

With brown and 2nd largest size hook, ch 10.

Row 1: Sc in 2nd ch from hook and in next 3 chs; with 3rd largest size hook, sc in next 3 chs; with smallest size hook, sc in next 2 chs—9 sc. Ch 1, turn.

Row 2: Working in BLs only, with smallest size hook, sc in first 2 sc; with 3rd largest size hook, sc in next 3 sc; with 2nd largest size hook, sc in next 4 sc. Ch 1, turn.

Row 3: Working in BLs only, and with 2nd largest size hook, sc in first 4 sc; with 3rd largest size hook, sc in next 3 sc; with smallest size hook, sc in next 2 sc. Ch 1, turn.

Rep Rows 2 and 3 until neckband measures about 24" unstretched at edge using largest size hook.

Fold piece matching dc of last row worked and beg ch; working through both thicknesses, sl st in each st.

Finish off and weave in ends.

Sleeve (make 2)

Ribbing:

Work same as Back ribbing until ribbing measures 9½" slightly stretched.

Body:

Change to largest size hook and work in same color sequence as for Back.

Row 1 (right side): Ch 3 (counts as first dc), work 36 dc evenly spaced in edge sc of one long side of ribbing—37 dc. Ch 3, turn.

Row 2: Dc in first dc; dc in each dc to beg ch-3; 2 dc in 3rd ch of beg ch-3—39 dc. Ch 3, turn.

Row 3: Dc in first dc; dc in each dc to turning ch-3; 2 dc in turning ch-3—41 dc. Ch 3, turn.

Row 4: Sk first dc, dc in each rem dc and in 3rd ch of turning ch-3. Ch 3, turn.

Rows 5 and 6: Rep Row 3.

Rows 7 through 33: Rep Rows 4 through 6 nine times more in same color sequence as for back—81 dc.

Row 34: Rep Row 3—83 dc.

Rep Row 4 in color sequence as established until sleeve measures about 25" from beg. Finish off, leaving a 24" end for sewing.

Finishing

Step 1: Hold widest edge of neck ribbing to right side of neckline; with tapestry needle and brown, sew with an overcast st (see Crochet Stitch Guide on page 213).

Step 2: Mark front and back at side edges 12" down from shoulder seams. With right side of one sleeve and body held together, and matching shoulder seam to center of last row of sleeve, sew seam. Repeat for other sleeve.

Step 3: Sew underarm and side seams.

You Are My Sunshine

continued from page 185

Row 3: Dec over next 2 sts [to work dec: (YO, draw up lp in next st, YO and draw through 2 lps on hook) twice; YO and draw through all 3 lps on hook—dec made]; dc in each rem st—23 (29, 35) sts. Ch 1, turn.

Row 4: Sl st in first dc, hdc in next dc; * sl st in next dc, hdc in next st; rep from * to turning ch-2; sl st in 2nd ch of turning ch-2. Ch 2, turn.

Row 5: Dec over next 2 sts; dc in each rem st—22 (28, 34) sts. Ch 1, turn.

Row 6: Sl st in first dc, hdc in next dc; * sl st in next dc, hdc in next dc; rep from * to last dc and turning ch-2; sl st in last dc, hdc in 2nd ch of turning ch-2. Ch 2, turn.

Row 7: Dec; dc in each rem st—21 (27, 33) sts. Ch 1, turn.

Row 8: Rep Row 4.

Row 9 (shoulder shaping): Dc in next 5 (7, 9) sts, hdc in next 7 (9, 11) sts, sc in next 8 (10, 12) sts.

Finish off and weave in ends.

Left Front

With larger size hook, ch 33 (37, 41, 43, 47, 51).

Row 1 (right side): Dc in 4th ch from hook (beg 3 skipped chs counts as first dc) and in each rem ch—31 (35, 39, 41, 45, 49) dc. Ch 1, turn.

Row 2: Sl st in first dc, hdc in next dc; * sl st in next dc, hdc in next dc; rep from * to beg 3 skipped chs; sl st in 3rd ch of beg 3 skipped chs—31 (35, 39, 41, 45, 49) sts. Ch 2 (counts as first dc on following rows), turn.

Row 3: Dc in each st. Ch 1, turn.

Row 4: Sl st in first dc, hdc in next dc; * sl st in next dc, hdc in next dc; rep from * to turning ch-2; dc in 2nd ch of turning ch-2. Ch 2, turn.

Rep Rows 3 and 4 until piece measures 18" (18¹⁄₂", 19", 19¹⁄₂", 20", 20¹⁄₂") from beg, ending by working a wrong side row.

Neck Shaping:

Row 1 (right side): Dc in next 20 (23, 26, 29, 32, 35) sts—21 (24, 27, 30, 33, 36) dc. Ch 1, turn, leaving rem sts unworked.

For Sizes Petite, Medium, and X-Large only:

Row 2: Sl st in first dc, hdc in next dc; * sl st in next dc, hdc in next dc; rep from * to turning ch-2; sl st in 2nd ch of turning ch-2. Ch 2, turn.

Row 3: Dc in next 17 (23, 29) sts; dec over next 2 sts [to work dec: (YO, draw up lp in next st, YO and draw through 2 lps on hook) twice; YO and draw through all 3 lps on hook—dec made]; dc in next sl st—20 (26, 32) sts. Ch 1, turn.

Row 4: Sl st in first dc, hdc in next st; * sl st in next dc, hdc in next dc; rep from * to last dc and turning ch-2; sl st in last dc, hdc in 2nd ch of turning ch-2. Ch 2, turn.

Row 5: Dc in next 16 (22, 28) sts; dec over next 2 sts; dc in next sl st—19 (25, 31) sts. Ch 1, turn.

Row 6: Sl st in first dc, hdc in next st; * sl st in next dc, hdc in next dc; rep from * to turning ch-2; sl st in 2nd ch of turning ch-2. Ch 2, turn.

Row 7: Dc in next 15 (21, 27) sts; dec; dc in next sl st—18 (24, 30) sts. Ch 1, turn.

Row 8: Sl st in first dc, hdc in next st; * sl st in next dc, hdc in next dc; rep from * to last dc and turning ch-2; sl st in last dc, hdc in 2nd ch of turning ch-2. Ch 1, turn.

Row 9 (shoulder shaping): Sc in first 7 (9, 11) sts, hdc in next 6 (8, 10) sts, dc in next 5 (7, 9) sts.

Finish off and weave in ends.

For Sizes Small, Large and 2X only:

Row 2: Sl st in first dc, hdc in next st; * sl st in next dc, hdc in next dc; rep from * to last dc and turning ch-2; sl st in last dc, hdc in 2nd ch of turning ch-2. Ch 2, turn.

Row 3: Dc in next 20 (26, 32) sts; dec over next 2 sts [to work dec: (YO, draw up lp in next st, YO and draw through 2 lps on hook) twice; YO and draw through all 3 lps on hook—dec made]; dc in next sl st—23 (29, 35) sts. Ch 1, turn.

Row 4: Sl st in first dc, hdc in next dc; * sl st in next dc, hdc in next dc; rep from * to turning ch-2; sl st in 2nd ch of turning ch-2. Ch 2, turn.

Row 5: Dc in next 19 (25, 31) sts; dec over next 2 sts; dc in next sl st—22 (28, 34) sts. Ch 1, turn.

Row 6: Sl st in first dc, hdc in next st; * sl st in next dc, hdc in next dc; rep from * to last dc and turning ch-2; sl st in last dc, hdc in 2nd ch of turning ch-2. Ch 2, turn.

Row 7: Dc in next 18 (24, 30) sts; dec; dc in next sl st—21 (27, 33) sts. Ch 1, turn.

Row 8: Sl st in first dc, hdc in next st; * sl st in next dc, hdc in next dc; rep from * to turning ch-2; sl st in 2nd ch of turning ch-2. Ch 1, turn.

Row 9 (shoulder shaping): Sc in first 8 (10, 12) sts, hdc in next 7 (9, 11) sts, dc in next 6 (8, 10) sts.

Finish off and weave in all ends.

Sleeve (make 2)

With larger size hook, ch 27 (29, 31, 33, 35, 37).

Row 1 (right side): Dc in 4th ch from hook (beg 3 skipped chs count as a dc) and in each rem ch—25 (27, 29, 31, 33, 35) dc. Ch 1, turn.

Row 2: Sl st in first dc, hdc in next dc; * sl st in next dc, hdc in next dc; rep from * to beg 3 skipped chs; sl st in 3rd ch of beg 3 skipped chs. Ch 2 (counts as first dc on following rows), turn.

Row 3: Dc in first sl st; dc in each st to last sl st; 2 dc in last sl st—27 (29, 31, 33, 35, 37) dc. Ch 1, turn.

Row 4: Hdc in first dc; * sl st in next dc, hdc in next dc; rep from * to last dc and turning ch-2; sl st in last dc, hdc in 2nd ch of turning ch-2. Ch 2, turn.

Row 5: Dc in first hdc, and in each st to last hdc; 2 dc in last hdc—29 (31, 33, 35, 37, 39) dc. Ch 1, turn.

Row 6: Sl st in first dc, hdc in next dc; * sl st in next dc, hdc in next dc; rep from * to turning ch-2; sl st in 2nd ch of turning ch-2. Ch 2, turn.

Rows 7 through 34: Rep Rows 3 through 6 seven times. At end of Row 34—57 (59, 61, 63, 65, 67) sts.

For Size Petite only:

Row 35: Dc in each st. Ch 1, turn.

Row 36: Sl st in first dc, hdc in next dc; * sl st in next dc, hdc in next dc; rep from * to turning ch-2; sl st in 2nd ch of turning ch-2. Ch 2, turn.

continued on page 203

You Are My Sunshine

continued from page 202

Rep Rows 35 and 36 until piece measures 16¹/2" from beg, ending by working a wrong side row. At end of last row, do not ch 2. Finish off.

Continue with Collar below.

For Sizes Small and Medium only:

Rows 35 and 36: Rep Rows 3 and 4. At end of Row 36—61 (63) sts.

Row 37: Dc in each st. Ch 1, turn.

Row 38: Hdc in first dc, sl st in next dc; * hdc in next dc, sl st in next dc; rep from * to turning ch-2; hdc in 2nd ch of turning ch-2. Ch 2, turn.

Rep Rows 37 and 38 until piece measures 16¹/2" from beg, ending by working a wrong side row. At end of last row, do not ch 2. Finish off.

Continue with Collar below.

For Sizes Large and X-Large only:

Rows 35 through 38: Rep Rows 3 through 6. At end of Row 38—67 (69) sts.

Row 39: Dc in each st. Ch 1, turn.

Row 40: Sl st in first dc, hdc in next dc; * sl st in next dc, hdc in next dc; rep from * to turning ch-2; sl st in 2nd ch of turning ch-2. Ch 2, turn.

Rep Rows 39 and 40 until piece measures 16¹/2" from beg, ending by working a wrong side row. At end of last row, do not ch 2. Finish off.

Continue with Collar below.

For Size 2X only:

Rows 35 through 38: Rep Rows 3 through 6.

Rows 39 and 40: Rep Rows 3 and 4.

Row 41: Dc in each st. Ch 1, turn.

Row 42: Hdc in first dc, sl st in next st; * hdc in next dc, sl st in next dc; rep from * to turning ch-2; hdc in 2nd ch of turning ch-2. Ch 2, turn.

Rep Rows 41 and 42 until piece measures 16¹/2" from beg, ending by working a wrong side row. At end of last row, do not ch 2. Finish off.

Continue with Collar.

Collar (optional):

With larger size hook, ch 76.

Row 1 (right side)**:** Dc in 4th ch from hook (beg 3 skipped chs count a first dc) and in each rem ch—74 dc. Ch 2 (counts as a dc on following rows), turn.

Row 2: 2 dc in first dc; dc in each dc to beg 3 skipped chs; 3 dc in 3rd ch of beg 3 skipped chs—78 dc. Ch 2, turn.

Row 3: 2 dc in first dc; dc in each dc to turning ch-2; 3 dc in 2nd ch of turning ch-2—82 dc. Ch 2, turn.

Rows 4 through 7: Rep Row 3. At end of Row 7, do not ch 2—98 dc. Ch 1, turn.

Collar Edging:

Rnd 1: 3 sc in first dc; sc in each dc to last dc; 3 sc in last dc—corner made; † working in sps formed by edge sts and turning chs, 2 sc in each of next 7 rows †; working in unused lps of beg ch, sc in each lp; rep from † to † once; join in first sc.

Rnd 2: Ch 1, working from left to right, work reverse sc (see Keeping you in Stitches on page 198) in each sc; join in first sc.

Finish off and weave in all ends.

Assembly:

Sew shoulder seams. Hold one sleeve and jacket with right sides together, matching center of last row of sleeve to shoulder seam; sew seam, easing as necessary to fit. Repeat for other sleeve. Sew underarm and side seams, matching rows.

Edgings

Sweater Edging:

Hold sweater with right side facing you and beg ch at top; with smaller size hook, join yarn in first unused lp of beg ch on left front.

Rnd 1 (right side)**:** Ch 1, 2 sc in same sp as joining—corner made; working in rem unused lps, sc in each lp to last lp of right front; 2 sc in last lp—corner made; working along right front in row edges and turning chs, † 2 sc in each dc row and sc in each hdc row †; working across right front neck edge, 2 sc in first sl st of neck shaping; sc in next 10 (11, 12, 11, 12, 13) sl sts; working in ends of rows and turning chs, rep from † to † to shoulder seam; sc in each st across back to opposite shoulder seam; rep from †

to † to unworked sts of left front neck shaping; sc in each unworked st to last st, 2 sc in last unworked st—corner made; rep from † to † along left front to first sc; join in first sc.

Rnd 2: Ch 1, 2 sc in same sc and in next sc; † sc in each sc to next corner; 2 sc in each corner sc †; rep from † to † twice more; sc in each sc to first sc; join in first sc.

Place markers for 5 buttonholes, evenly spaced along right edge of right front opening.

Rnd 3: Ch 1, sc in same sc; 2 sc in each of next 2 sc; † sc in each sc to 2nd sc of next corner; 2 sc in each corner sc †; working along right front side, * sc in each sc to next marker, ch 3—buttonhole made; sk next 3 sc; rep from * 4 times more; rep from † to † twice; sc in each sc to first sc; join in first sc.

Rnd 4: Ch 1, sc in same sc and in next sc; 2 sc in each of next 2 sc; † sc in each sc to first sc of next corner; 2 sc in each of next 2 sc †; working along right front, * sc in each sc to next ch-3 sp; 3 sc in next ch-3 sp; rep from * 4 times more; then rep from † to † twice; sc in each sc to first sc; join in first sc.

Rnd 5: Ch 1, working from left to right, work reverse sc (see Keeping You in Stitches on page 198) in each sc; join in first sc.

Finish off and weave in all ends.

Sleeve Edging:

Hold one sleeve with right side facing you and beg ch at top; with smaller size hook, join yarn in sleeve seam.

Rnd 1 (right side)**:** Ch 1, sc in same sp and in each unused lp of beg ch; join in first sc.

Rnd 2: Ch 1, working from left to right, reverse sc (see Keeping You in Stitches on page 198) in each sc; join in first sc.

Finish off and weave in ends.

Rep for other sleeve.

Finishing

Sew buttons on Row 3 of edging on left front side to correspond with buttonholes. Referring to photo for placement, sew optional collar to back of sweater if desired.

Sporty Comfort

continued from page 197

Row 3: Sk first dc, sc in next sc; * sk next dc, in next sc work (sc, dc); rep from * to turning ch-3; sc in 3rd ch of turning ch-3—18 (20, 22, 24, 26) sts. Ch 3, turn.

Row 4: Sk first sc, * sk next dc, in next sc work (sc, dc); rep from * to last sc; sc in last sc. Ch 1, turn.

Row 5: Sk first sc; * sk next dc, in next sc work (sc, dc); rep from * to turning ch-3; sc in 3rd ch of turning ch-3—17 (19, 21, 23, 25) sts. Ch 3, turn.

Row 6: Sk first sc; * sk next dc, in next sc work (sc, dc); rep from * across. Ch 1, turn.

Row 7: Sk first dc, sc in next sc; * sk next dc, in next sc work (sc, dc); rep from * to turning ch-3; sc in 3rd ch of turning ch-3—16 (18, 20, 22, 24) sts. Ch 3, turn.

Row 8: Sk first sc; * sk next dc, in next sc work (sc, dc); rep from * to last sc; sc in last sc. Ch 3, turn.

Row 9: Sk first sc; * sk next dc, in next sc work (sc, dc); rep from * to turning ch-3; sc in 3rd ch of turning ch-3. Ch 3, turn.

Rep Row 9 until left front measures same as right front to shoulders.

Finish off and weave in all ends.

Sleeve (make 2)

With larger size hook and green, ch 32 (32, 34, 36, 38).

Row 1 (right side): In 4th ch from hook (beg 3 skipped chs count as a dc) work (sc, dc); sk next ch; * in next ch work (sc, dc); sk next ch; rep from * to last ch; sc in last ch—30 (30, 32, 34, 36) sts. Ch 3 (counts as first dc on following rows), turn.

Note: When changing colors, work until 2 lps of last color rem on hook, with new color draw through 2 lps on hook. Carry color not in use along edge.

Row 2: Sk first sc; * sk next dc, in next sc work (sc, dc); rep from * to beg 3 skipped chs; sc in 3rd ch of beg 3 skipped chs, changing to white. Ch 3, turn.

Row 3: Sk first sc; * sk next dc, in next sc work (sc, dc); rep from * to turning ch-3; sc in 3rd ch of turning ch-3. Ch 1, turn.

Row 4: In first sc work (sc, dc); * sk next dc, in next sc work (sc, dc); rep from * to turning ch-3; in 3rd ch of turning ch-3 work (sc, dc), changing to green in last dc—32 (32, 34, 36, 38) sts. Ch 1, turn.

Row 5: Sk first dc, in next sc work (sc, dc); * sk next dc, in next sc work (sc, dc); rep from * across. Ch 1, turn.

Row 6: Sk first dc, in next sc work (sc, dc); * sk next dc, in next sc work (sc, dc); rep from * across, changing to white in last dc. Ch 1, turn.

Row 7: Rep Row 5.

Row 8: Sc in first dc; * in next sc work (sc, dc); sk next dc; rep from * to last sc; in last sc work (sc, dc, sc), changing to green in last sc—34 (34, 36, 38, 40) sts. Ch 3, turn.

Row 9: Sk first sc; * sk next dc, in next sc work (sc, dc); rep from * to last sc; sc in last sc. Ch 3, turn.

Row 10: Sk first sc; * sk next dc, in next sc work (sc, dc); rep from * to turning ch-3; sc in 3rd ch of turning ch-3, changing to white. Ch 3, turn.

Row 11: Sk first sc; * sk next dc, in next sc work (sc, dc); rep from * to turning ch-3; sc in 3rd ch of turning ch-3. Ch 1, turn.

Row 12: In first sc work (sc, dc); * sk next dc, in next sc work (sc, dc); rep from * to turning ch-3; in 3rd ch of turning ch-3 work (sc, dc), changing to green in last dc—36 (36, 38, 40, 42) sts. Ch 1, turn.

Rows 13 through 20: Rep Rows 5 through 12.

Rows 21 through 24: Rep Rows 5 through 8. At end of Row 24—42 (42, 44, 46, 48) sts. Cut white.

With green, work in patt and color sequence as established, inc at beg and end of every 4th row 3 (4, 5, 6, 7) times more—48 (50, 54, 58, 62) sts.

Continue in patt and color sequence without increasing until sleeve measures 15" (15½", 16", 16½", 17") from beg. At end of last row, do not ch.

Finish off and weave in ends.

Sew sleeve seams.

Sleeve Ribbing:

Foundation Rnd: With smaller size hook and white, make lp on hook and join with an sc in sleeve seam; working in unused lps and skipped chs of beg ch, sc in each of next 30 (30, 32, 34, 36) sts; join in joining sc—31 (31, 33, 35, 37) sc. Ch 11.

Row 1: Sc in 2nd ch from hook and in each rem ch—10 sc; sl st in next 2 sc on foundation rnd. Ch 1, turn.

Row 2: Sk first 2 sl sts, working in BLs only, sc in next 10 sc. Ch 1, turn.

Row 3: Working in BLs only, sc in first sc and in next 9 sc, sl st in next 2 sc on foundation rnd. Ch 1, turn.

Rows 4 through 29 (29, 31, 33, 35): Rep Rows 2 and 3, 13 (13, 14, 15, 16) times more.

Row 30 (30, 32, 34, 36): Rep Row 2. At end of row, do not ch 1.

Finish off, leaving an 18" long end for sewing.

Rep for other sleeve.

Hold one sleeve with right sides of ribbing tog and last row worked facing you, with long end, sew ends of ribbing tog through unused lps of beg ch and FLs of last row. Rep for other sleeve.

Assembly

Sew shoulder seams. Sew side seams beginning with Row 8 and continuing to armhole. Sew sleeves in armhole openings.

Bottom Edging:

Hold sweater with right side facing you and beg ch at top; with smaller size hook and green, make lp on hook and join with an sc in left side seam.

Rnd 1: Working in ends of rows along edge of back, sc in each of next 6 rows, 3 sc in end of next row—corner made; working across back in unused lps of beg ch, sc in each lp; working along next side in ends of rows, 3 sc in first row—corner made; sc in each of next 6 rows and in right side seam; working along next side in ends of rows, sc in each of next 6 rows, 3 sc in next row—corner made; working across front in unused lps of beg ch, sc in each lp; working along next side in ends of rows, 3 sc in first row—corner made; sc in next 6 rows; join in joining sc.

Rnd 2: Ch 1, sc in same sc and in each sc to 2nd sc of next corner; 3 sc in 2nd sc—corner made; * sc in each sc to 2nd sc of next corner; 3 sc in 2nd sc—corner made; rep from * twice more; sc in each sc to first sc; join in first sc.

Finish off and weave in ends.

Neck Ribbing:

Foundation Rnd: Hold sweater with neck

continued on page 205

Sporty Comfort
continued from page 204

edge at top; with smaller size hook and white, make lp on hook and join with an sc in right shoulder seam; sc in each st across back and in left shoulder seam; working along left front in ends of rows, sc in next 6 rows; working across front neck edge, sc in each st; working along right front in ends of rows, sc in next 6 rows; join in joining sc. Ch 6, turn.

Row 1: Sc in 2nd ch from hook and in each rem ch—5 sc; sl st in next 2 sc on foundation rnd. Ch 1, turn.

Row 2: Sk first 2 sl sts, working in BLs only, sc in next 5 sc. Ch 1, turn.

Row 3: Working in BLs only, sc in first sc and in next 4 sc, sl st in next 2 sc on foundation rnd. Ch 1, turn.

Row 4: Sk next 2 sl sts, sc in BLs only of next 5 sc. Ch 1, turn.

Rep Rows 3 and 4 until one sc remains on foundation rnd.

Next Row: Working in BLs only, sc in first sc and in next 4 sc, sl st in next sc on foundation rnd and in next sc (where joining sc was made). Ch 1, turn.

Next Row: Sk next 2 sl sts, sc in BLs only of next 5 sts.

Finish off, leaving an 18" end for sewing.

Finishing
Hold ribbing with right sides together and last row worked facing you, with long end, sew ends of ribbing together through unused lps of beg ch and FLs of last row.

Finish off and weave in ends.

Pierre Pig
continued from page 192

Row 3: Sc in each sc. Ch 1, turn.

Row 4: Sc in first 6 sc; † 2 sc in next sc; 2 dc in each of next 9 sc; 2 sc in next sc—sleeve shaping †; sc in next 14 sc; rep from † to † once; sc in next 6 sc—70 sts. Ch 1, turn.

Row 5: Sc in first 7 sc; † 2 sc in next sc; dc in next 18 dc, 2 sc in next sc †; sc in next 16 sc; rep from † to † once; sc in next 7 sc—74 sts. Ch 1, turn.

Row 6: Sc in first 8 sc; † 2 sc in next sc; dc in next 18 dc, 2 sc in next sc †; sc in next 18 sc; rep from † to † once; sc in next 8 sc—78 sts. Ch 1, turn.

Row 7: Sc in first 9 sc; † 2 sc in next sc; dc in next 18 dc, 2 sc in next sc †; sc in next 20 sc; rep from † to † once; sc in next 9 sc—82 sts. Ch 1, turn.

Row 8: Sc in first 10 sc; † sc dec over next 2 sts (to work sc dec: draw up lp in each of next 2 sts, YO and draw through all 3 lps on hook—sc dec made); ch 4, sk next 16 dc, sc dec over next 2 sts †; sc in next 22 sc; rep from † to † once; sc in next 10 sc. Ch 1, turn.

Row 9: 2 sc in first sc; sc in each sc and in each ch to last sc; 2 sc in last sc—56 sc. Ch 1, turn.

Row 10: Sc in each sc. Ch 1, turn.

Row 11: 2 sc in first sc; sc in each sc to last sc; 2 sc in last sc—58 sc. Ch 1, turn.

Rows 12 and 13: Rep Row 10.

Row 14: Sc in each sc; join in first sc. Change to blue by drawing lp through; cut white.

Note: Remainder of romper is worked in rnds.

Rnd 1: Ch 1, 2 sc in first sc; (sc in next 8 sc, 2 sc in next sc) 6 times; sc in next 2 sc, 2 sc in next sc; join in first sc—66 sc.

Rnd 2: Ch 1, sc in same sc and in next 7 sc; 2 sc in next sc; (sc in next 8 sc, 2 sc in next sc) 5 times; sc in next 12 sc; join in first sc—72 sc.

Rnd 3: Ch 1, sc in same sc and in each rem sc; join in first sc.

Rnd 4: Rep Rnd 3.

Rnd 5: Ch 1, sc in same sc; 2 sc in next sc; (sc in next 8 sc, 2 sc in next sc) 7 times; sc in next 7 sc; join in first sc—80 sc.

Rnds 6 through 12: Rep Rnd 3. At end of Rnd 12, finish off.

Back Flap:
Hold piece with right side facing you and Rnd 12 at top; join blue in 12th sc to right of joining.

Row 1: Ch 1, sc in same sc and in next 23 sc—24 sc. Ch 1, turn.

Row 2: Sc in each sc. Ch 1, turn.

Row 3: (Sc dec over next 2 sc, sc in next 2 sc) 6 times—18 sc. Ch 1, turn.

Row 4: Sc in first 4 sc, sc dec; sc in next sc, sc dec twice; sc in next sc, sc dec; sc in next 4 sc—14 sc. Ch 1, turn.

Row 5: Sc in each sc. Mark first sc and last sc. Ch 1, turn.

Row 6: Sc in first 6 sc, sc dec; sc in next 6 sc—13 sc. Ch 1, turn.

Row 7: Sc in first 3 sc, hdc in next 2 sc, dc dec over next 2 sc [to work dc dec: (YO, draw up lp in next sc, YO, draw through 2 lps on hook) twice; YO and draw through all 3 lps on hook—dc dec made]; hdc dec over next 2 sc [to work hdc dec: (YO, draw up lp in next sc) twice; YO and draw through all 5 lps on hook—hdc dec made]; hdc in next sc, sc in next 3 sc—11 sts. Ch 1, turn.

Row 8: Sc in first 3 sc, hdc in next st, dc in next 2 sts, hdc in next st, sc in next 4 sts. Ch 1, turn.

Row 9: Sc in first 2 sc, hdc in next 2 sts, dc in next 3 sts, hdc in next 2 sts, sc in next 2 sc. Ch 1, turn.

Row 10: Sc in each st. Ch 1, turn.

Row 11: Sc in each sc. Finish off, leaving a 10" end for sewing.

Front Flap:
Hold piece with right side facing you and Rnd 12 at top; sk next 20 sc to left of back flap; join blue in next sc.

Row 1: Ch 1, sc in same sc and in next 15 sc—16 sc. Ch 1, turn.

Row 2: Sc dec; sc in next 3 sc, sc dec 3 times; sc in next 3 sc, sc dec—11 sc. Ch 1, turn.

Row 3: Sc in each sc. Ch 1, turn.

Row 4: Sc in first 2 sc, hdc in next 2 sc, dc in next 3 sc, hdc in next 2 sc, sc in next 2 sc—11 sts. Ch 1, turn.

Row 5: Sc in each st. Mark first sc and last sc. Ch 1, turn.

Rows 6 through 10: Rep Row 3. At end of Row 10, finish off, leaving a 10" end for sewing.

continued on page 206

Pierre Pig
continued from page 205

Right Leg:
Hold piece with right side facing you and Rnd 12 at top; join blue in next sc to left of front flap.

Row 1: Ch 1, sc in same sc and in next 19 sc—20 sc. Ch 1, turn.

Row 2: 2 sc in first sc; sc in next 18 sc, 2 sc in next sc—22 sc. Ch 1, turn.

Row 3: 2 sc in first sc; sc in next 20 sc, 2 sc in next sc—24 sc. Ch 1, turn.

Row 4: 2 sc in first sc; sc in next 22 sc, 2 sc in next sc—26 sc. Turn.

Note: Remainder of leg is worked in rnds.

Rnd 1: Sl st in first 2 sc, ch 1, sc in same sc as last sl st made and in next 23 sc, sc dec over next sc and marked sc on back flap, working in edge sc of each row of back flap, sc in next 6 rows; working in edge sc of each row of front flap, sc in next 6 rows; sc dec over next marked sc and next sl st on Row 4 of leg—38 sc. Ch 1, turn.

Rnd 2: Sl st in next 2 sc, ch 1, sc in same sl st as last sl st made and in next 10 sc; sc dec; sc in next 23 sc, sc dec over next sc and next sl st; join in first sc—36 sc. Ch 1, turn.

Rnd 3: Sc in each sc; join in first sc. Ch 1, turn.

Rnds 4 through 7: Rep Rnd 3. At end of Rnd 7, do not ch 1. Finish off.

Left Leg:
Hold piece with right side facing you and Rnd 12 at top; join blue in next sc to left of back flap.

Rows 1 through 4: Rep Rows 1 through 4 of Right Leg.

Rnd 1: Sl st in first 2 sc, ch 1, sc in same sc as last sl st made and in next 23 sc; sc dec over next sc and marked sc on front flap, working in edge sc of each row of front flap, sc in next 6 rows; working in edge sc of each row of back flap, sc in next 6 rows; sc dec over next marked sc and next sl st on Row 4 of leg—38 sc. Ch 1, turn.

Rnds 2 through 7: Rep Rnds 2 through 7 of Right Leg.

Collar Trim:
Hold romper with right side of back opening facing you; working in unused lps on opposite side of beg ch-32, join blue in first unused lp; ch 1, sc in same lp; (2 sc in next lp, sc in next lp) 15 times—46 sc. Finish off.

Back Opening Trim and Ties:
Hold romper with right side facing you and legs to left; join white in first edge sc to right of back opening; ch 1, sc in same sc; working in edge sc of each row, † in next sc work (sl st, ch 24, sl st in 2nd ch from hook and in next 22 chs, sl st) †; sc in next 6 rows; rep from † to † once; sc in next 5 rows; working along next side in edge sc of each row, sc in next 5 rows; rep from † to † once; sc in next 6 rows; rep from † to † once; sc in next sc.

Finish off and weave in all ends.

Button (make 2)
With blue, ch 2; 7 sc in 2nd ch from hook; join in first sc. Finish off, leaving a 6" end for sewing. Weave in short end.

Finishing
Step 1: With tapestry needle and 10" ends sew front and back flaps together; sew front and back flap seams to each leg.

Step 2: Referring to photo for placement, with tapestry needle and 6" ends, sew buttons to center front of romper.

Darling Baby Booties
continued from page 177

Foot:
Rnd 1: Ch 2, working in BLs only, hdc in each hdc; join in 2nd ch of beg ch-2.

Rnd 2: Ch 1, sc in same ch as joining; ch 3, sk next hdc; * sc in next hdc, ch 3, sk next hdc; rep from * 29 times more; ch 3; join in first sc—32 ch-3 sps.

Rnd 3: Sl st in next ch-3 sp; beg CL (see Pattern Stitches on page 177) in same sp; ch 3, sc in next ch-3 sp, ch 3; * CL (see Pattern Stitches on page 177) in next ch-3 sp; ch 3, sc in next ch-3 sp, ch 3; rep from * 14 times more; join with an sc in beg CL—16 CLs.

Rnd 4: Ch 3, sc in same CL, ch 3; * in each CL work (sc, ch 3) twice; join in joining sc.

Rnd 5: Sl st in next ch-3 sp, ch 1, sc in same sp; * ch 3, CL in next ch-3 sp; ch 3, sc in next ch-3 sp; rep from * 3 times more; ch 11 (for instep), sk next 17 ch-3 sps; ** sc in next ch-3 sp, ch 3, CL in next ch-3 sp; ch 3; rep from ** twice more; join in first sc—7 CLs.

Rnd 6: Sl st in next 3 chs and in next CL, ch 1, in same CL work (sc, ch 3) twice; in each of next 3 CLs work (sc, ch 3) twice; sk next sc and next 3 chs of next ch-11, in next ch work (sc, ch 3) twice; sk next 3 chs, in next ch work (sc, ch 3) twice; sk next 3 chs, next sc, and next 3 chs; in each of next 3 CLs work (sc, ch 3) twice; join in first sc.

Rnd 7: Sl st in next ch-3 sp, ch 1, sc in same sp; ch 3, CL in next ch-3 sp; ch 3; * sc in next ch-3 sp, ch 3, CL in next ch-3 sp; ch 3; rep from * 7 times more; join in first sc—9 CLs.

Rnd 8: Sl st in next 3 chs and in next CL, ch 1, in same CL work (sc, ch 3) twice; in each of next 8 CLs work (sc, ch 3) twice; join with an sc in first ch-3 sp.

Rnd 9: Ch 3, CL in next ch-3 sp; ch 3; * sc in next ch-3 sp, ch 3, CL in next ch-3 sp; ch 3; rep from * 7 times more; join in joining sc.

Rnd 10: Rep Rnd 8.

Rnd 11: Ch 3, sc in same sp; ch 3, CL in next ch-3 sp; ch 3; * in next ch-3 sp work (sc, ch 3) twice; CL in next ch-3 sp; ch 3; rep from * 7 times more; join in first sc.

Finish off.

Instep:
Hold bootie with ch-11 (instep) at top; join thread in first ch.

Row 1: Ch 2 (counts as an hdc), working in unused lps of rem chs, hdc in next 10 chs—11 hdc. Ch 2 (counts as first hdc on following rows), turn.

Row 2: Hdc in each hdc and in 2nd ch of beg ch-2. Ch 2, turn.

Row 3: Hdc in each hdc and in 2nd ch of turning ch-2. Ch 2, turn.

continued on page 207

Darling Baby Booties

continued from page 206

Rows 4 through 7: Rep Row 3. At end of Row 7, do not ch 2; do not turn. Finish off.

Joining:

Hold bootie with right side of instep at top; join thread in side of Row 1; ch 1, sc in same sp; ch 1, sl st in corresponding ch-3 sp on foot (already worked), ch 1; on instep, sc in same sp; ch 3, sk next 2 rows, sc in side of Row 4; † ch 1; on foot, sk next ch-3 sp, sl st in next ch-3 sp, ch 1; on instep, sc in same sp; ch 3 †; sk next 2 rows, sc in side of Row 7; rep from † to † once; sk turning ch-2 and next 2 hdc on Row 7, sc in next hdc; rep from † to † once; sk next 3 hdc, sc in next hdc; rep from † to † once; working along next side, sk next 3 rows, sc in side of Row 4; rep from † to † once; sk next 2 rows, sl st in base of Row 1.

Finish off and weave in all ends.

Tie

Make a chain about 16" long; sc in 2nd ch from hook and in each rem ch.

Finish off and weave in ends.

Beginning and ending at center front, weave tie in and out of Rnd 10. Tie ends into bow.

Swirls Tablecloth

continued from page 175

more; ch 1; on completed square, sl st in next ch-5 sp, ch 1; on working square, sc in next ch-8 sp, ch 1; on completed square, sl st in next ch-5 sp, ch 1; on working square, sc in same sp; ch 5, (sc in next ch-3 sp, ch 5) 3 times; join in first sc.

Finish off and weave in all ends.

Remaining Squares

Work same as Square B, joining sides in similar manner and working corner joinings as necessary.

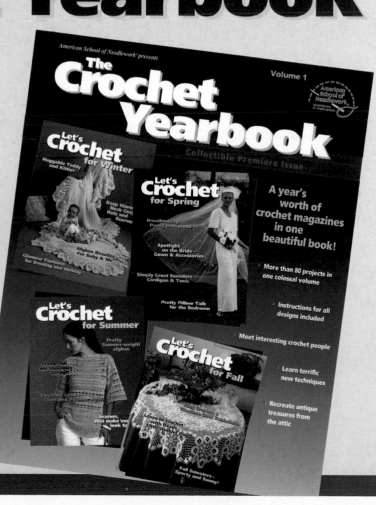

Yearbook
Reference
Guide

Abbreviations and Symbols

beg . . . . begin(ning)

BL(s) . . . . back loop(s)

BPdc . . . . . back post double crochet(s)

ch(s) . . . . chain(s)

CL(s) . . . . cluster(s)

dc . . . . double crochet(s)

dec . . . . decrease(-ing)

dtrc . . . . double triple crochet(s)

FL(s) . . . . front loop(s)

FPdc . . . . . . front post double crochet(s)

FPsc . . . . . . front post single crochet(s)

hdc . . . . half double crochet(s)

LK(s) . . . . Lover's Knot(s)

lp(s) . . . . loop(s)

patt . . . . pattern

PC(s) . . . . popcorn(s)

prev . . . . previous

quad trc . . . . quadruple triple crochet(s)

rem . . . . remain(ing)

rep . . . . repeat(ing)

reverse sc . . . . . . reverse single crochet

rnd(s) . . . . round(s)

sc . . . . single crochet(s)

sk . . . . skip

sl . . . . slip

sl st(s) . . . . slip stitch(es)

sp(s) . . . . space(s)

st(s) . . . . stitch(es)

tog . . . . together

tr trc . . . . triple triple crochet(s)

trc . . . . triple crochet(s)

Xst(s) . . . . cross stitch(es)

YO . . . . yarn over

* An asterisk (or double asterisks **) is used to mark the beginning of a portion of instructions to be worked more than once; thus, "rep from * twice more" means after working the instructions once, repeat the instructions following the asterisk twice more (3 times in all).

† The dagger (or double daggers ††) identifies a portion of instructions that will be repeated again later in the same row or round.

— The number after a long dash at the end of a row or round indicates the number of stitches you should have when the row or round has been completed. The long dash can also be used to indicate a completed stitch such as a decrease, a shell, or a cluster.

( ) Parentheses are used to enclose instructions which should be worked the exact number of times specified immediately following the parentheses, such as "(2 sc in next dc, sc in next dc) twice." They are also used to set off and clarify a group of stitches that are to be worked all into the same space or stitch, such as "(2 dc, ch 1, 2 dc) in corner sp."

[ ] Brackets and ( ) parentheses are used to provide additional information to clarify instructions.

Join - join with a sl st unless otherwise specified.

The patterns in this book are written using United States terminology. Terms which have different English equivalents are noted below.

United States	English
single crochet (sc)	double crochet (dc)
half double crochet (hdc)	half treble (htr)
double crochet (dc)	treble (tr)
triple crochet (trc)	double treble (dtr)
double triple crochet (dtrc)	triple treble (trtr)
quadruple triple crochet (quad trc)	quintuple treble (qt[uin] tr)
skip (sk)	miss
slip stitch (sl st)	slip stitch (ss) or "single crochet"
gauge	tension
yarn over (YO)	yarn over hook (YOH)

A Word about Gauge

A correct stitch gauge is very important. Please take the time to work a stitch gauge swatch about 4" x 4". Measure the swatch. If the number of stitches and rows are fewer than indicated under "Gauge" in the pattern, your hook is too large. Try another swatch with a smaller size hook. If the number of stitches and rows are more than indicated under "Gauge" in the pattern, your hook is too small. Try another swatch with a larger size hook.

Terms

Front loop is the loop toward you at the top of the stitch (**Fig 1**).

Back loop is the loop away from you at the top of the stitch (**Fig 1**).

Post is the vertical part of the stitch.

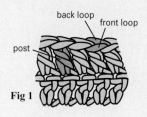

Fig 1

Right Side of the garment means the side that will be seen when it is worn.

Wrong Side of the garment means the side that will be inside when it is worn.

Right Front means the part of the garment that will be worn on the right front.

Left Front means the part of the garment that will be worn on the left front.

Right-hand Side means the side nearest your right hand as you are working.

Left-hand Side means the side nearest your left hand as you are working.

Continue in Pattern as Established is usually used in a pattern stitch, and this means to continue following the pattern stitch as it is already set up (established), working any subsequent inccreases or decreases (usually, worked at the beginning or end of a row) in such a way that the established pattern remains the same.

Work even means to continue to work in the pattern as established, without working any increases or decreases.

A Word about the Yarns and Threads

Each of our patterns specifies the yarn or thread we used for our photographed item, but you may choose to substitute yarn or thread of the same weight that will work to the same gauge.

Fringe

Basic Instructions

Cut a piece of cardboard half as long as specified in instructions for strands plus 1/2" for trimming allowance. Wind yarn loosely and evenly lengthwise around cardboard. When cardboard is filled, cut yarn across one end. Do this several times, then begin fringing; you can wind additional strands as you need them.

Single Knot Fringe

Hold specified number of strands for one knot of fringe together, then fold in half. Hold afghan with right side facing you. Use crochet hook to draw folded end through space or stitch from right to wrong side (**Figs 1** and **2**), pull loose ends through folded section (**Fig 3**) and draw knot up firmly (**Fig 4**). Space knots as indicated in pattern instructions.

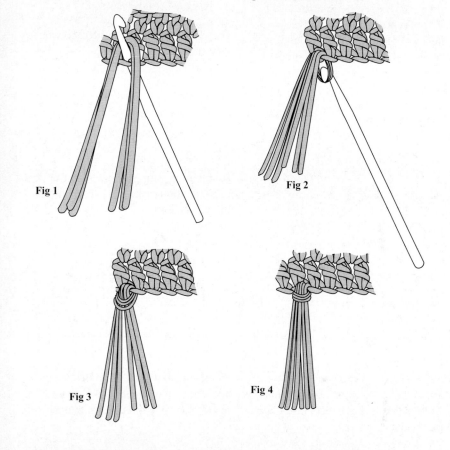

Fig 1

Fig 2

Fig 3

Fig 4

Embroidery Stitch Guide

Lazy Daisy Stitch

Thread tapestry needle with floss. Bring floss up (1), loop floss, insert needle in same hole (2), and bring it up at loop end (3). Pull needle through, adjust loop, and take a small stitch down over loop to secure (4).

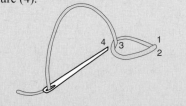

Straight Stitch

Thread tapestry needle with floss. Bring floss up (1) and down (2) to complete one stitch.

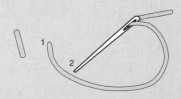

Crochet Stitch Guide

Chain - ch:

Yarn over, draw through loop on hook.

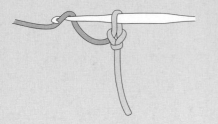

You will never work into the first chain from the hook. Depending on the stitch, you will work into the second, third, fourth, etc. chain from the hook. Excluding the first chain, you will work into every stitch in the chain unless the pattern states differently, but not in the starting slip knot.

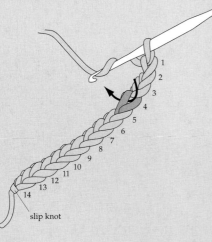

Single Crochet - sc:

Working into chain: Insert hook in stitch through the center of the V and under the back bump, bring yarn over the hook from back to front, and hook the yarn.

Draw yarn through the stitch and well up onto the working area of the hook. You have two loops on the hook.

Again bring yarn over the hook from back to front, hook it and draw through both loops on hook.

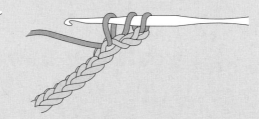

Working into a stitch: To work into a previous row of crochet, insert the hook under both loops of the stitch to be worked into instead of through the center of the V.

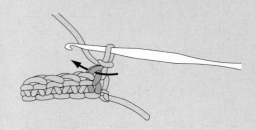

At the end of the row, take care to work in the last stitch which is easy to miss.

Double Crochet - dc:

Working into chain: Bring yarn once over the hook from back to front; skip the first three chains from the hook, then insert hook in the fourth chain.

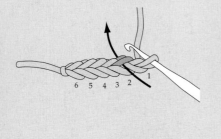

Hook yarn and draw it through the chain stitch and up onto the working area of the hook. You have three loops on the hook.

Hook yarn and draw through the first two loops on hook.

You now have two loops on the hook. Hook yarn and draw through both loops on the hook.

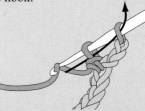

Working into a stitched row: At the beginning of the row, the turning chain counts as a stitch, so skip the first double crochet and work a double crochet in the second stitch (being sure to insert hook under top two loops of stitch).

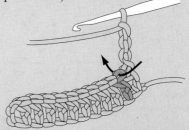

Half Double Crochet - hdc:

Working into chain: Bring yarn over hook from back to front, skip the first two chains, then insert hook in the third chain from the hook.

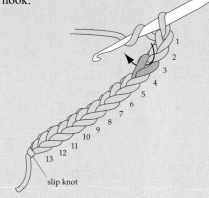

Hook the yarn and draw it through the chain stitch and up onto the working area of the hook. You now have three loops on the hook.

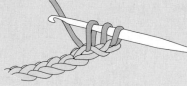

Hook yarn and draw it through all three loops on the hook in one motion.

Working into a stitched row: At the beginning of the row, the turning chain counts as a stitch, so skip the first half double crochet of the previous row and work a half double crochet in the second stitch.

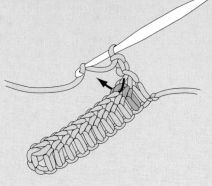

Triple Crochet - trc:

Working into a chain: Bring yarn twice over the hook (from back to front), skip the first four chains, then insert hook into the fifth chain from the hook.

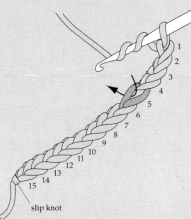

Hook yarn and draw it through the chain stitch and up onto the working area of the hook; you now have four loops on the hook.

Hook yarn and draw it through the first two loops on the hook.

You now have three loops on the hook. Hook yarn again and draw it through the next two loops on the hook.

You now have two loops on the hook. Hook yarn and draw it through both remaining loops on the hook.

Working into a stitched row: At the beginning of the row, the turning chain counts as a stitch, so skip the first triple crochet of the previous row and work a triple crochet in the second stitch.

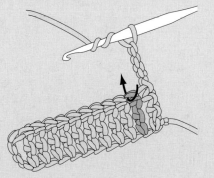

Hint: Remember to work last stitch of each row in turning chain of previous row. Missing this stitch in the turning chain is a common error.

Slip Stitch - sl st:

For Joining a Chain into a Ring: Chain specified number of chains, then insert hook through the first chain you made (next to the slip knot).

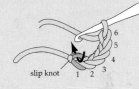

Hook yarn and draw it through the chain and through the loop on hook; you have formed a ring.

For Joining Rounds: Join with a slip stitch into chain indicated in pattern (for example—3rd ch of beg ch-3). Hook yarn and draw it through the chain and through the loop on the hook; you have joined the round.

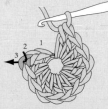

For Moving Yarn Over: Insert hook in stitch, yarn over and draw through both stitch and loop on hook.

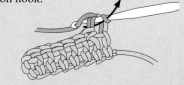

Overcast Stitch is worked loosely to join crochet pieces.

Filet Review

Filet Crochet is a combination of chains, double crochets, single crochets and slip stitches.

These stitches form a series of blocks, some open, some filled (see **Photo A**). The blocks then form beautiful designs.

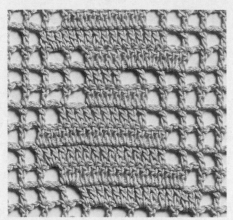

Photo A

Our filet designs are worked from a chart of blocks (squares). On the charts, each vertical line represents one double crochet and each short horizontal line represents a ch-2. A block with a black dot is a filled block.

Open Blocks

An open block is formed by a double crochet, a ch-2 and a double crochet (see **Photo B**).

Photo B

On the chart, a row of open blocks looks like this (**Fig 1**).

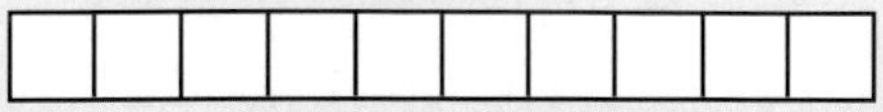

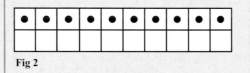

Fig 1

It is worked as follows:

dc in next st, ch 2, sk next 2 sts of prev row, dc in next st

At the beginning of a row, the first dc and the first ch-2 of an open block is formed by a turning ch-5 that is made at the end of the previous row. At the end of a row, the last dc is worked into the 3rd ch of the turning ch-5.

Filled Blocks

A filled block is formed by four double crochets (see **Photo C**).

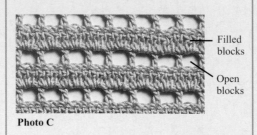

Filled blocks

Open blocks

Photo C

If the filled block is over an open block, it is worked as follows:

dc in next st, 2 dc in next ch-2 sp of prev row, dc in next dc

Note: *Double crochets can be worked into the chains of the ch-2 sp, if desired.*

On this chart, a row of filled blocks is over a row of open blocks (**Fig 2**).

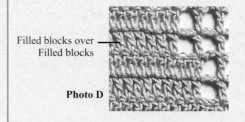

Fig 2

If the filled block is over another filled block, it is worked as follows:

dc in each dc (see **Photo D**).

Filled blocks over Filled blocks

Photo D

On this chart, a row of filled blocks is over another row of filled blocks (**Fig 3**).

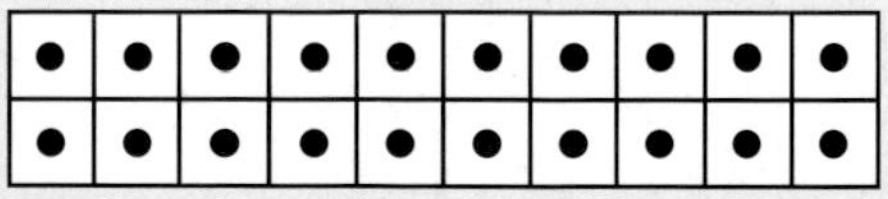

Fig 3

On the charts, the last dc of one block is also the first dc of the following block.

Shaping

Some of the projects are shaped by increasing and decreasing around the edges of the design.

On each chart the number of blocks for each row may increase or decrease (**Fig 4**).

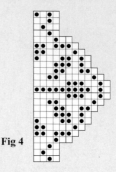

Fig 4

Increases

Open Blocks:

To increase one open block work as follows:

(**a**) At beginning of row:

At the end of the row before the increase, ch 8, turn; dc in first dc of prev row (**Fig 5**).

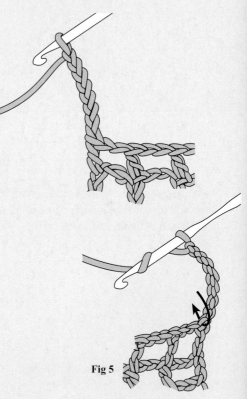

Fig 5

Note: *To work over a turning ch-8, dc in 6th ch of turning ch.*

(b) At end of row:

ch 2, dtrc in same ch as last dc made (**Fig 6**)

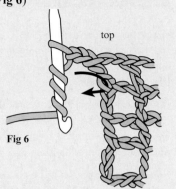

Fig 6

To increase more than one open block:

(a) At beginning of row, work as follows:

At the end of the row before the increase, ch 8 for the first block and then 3 more chains for each additional block; turn; dc in 9th ch from hook and then refer to chart to continue row.

(b) At end of row, work as follows:

For first block, ch 2, dtrc in same ch as last dc made; then work [ch 2, dtrc in center of prev dtrc (**Fig 7**)] for each additional block.

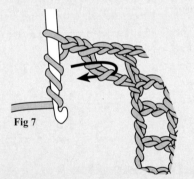

Fig 7

Closed Blocks:

To increase one closed block work as follows:

(a) At beginning of row:

At end of row before the increase, ch 6, turn; dc in 5th and 6th ch from hook and in first dc of prev row (**Fig 8**).

Fig 8

(b) At end of row:

trc in same ch of turning ch as last dc made; trc in base of trc just made (**Fig 9**); (trc in base of last trc made) twice.

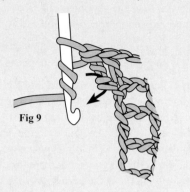

Fig 9

To increase more than one closed block:

(a) At beginning of row, work as follows:

At the end of the row before the increase, ch 8 for the first block and then 3 more chains for each additional block; turn; dc in 4th ch from hook, each rem ch, and in first dc of prev row. Refer to chart to continue row.

(b) At end of row, work as follows:

For first block, trc in same ch of turning ch as last dc made; trc in base of trc just made; (trc in base of last trc made) twice; then work (trc in base of prev trc) 3 times for each additional block.

Decreases

(a) When decrease is at beginning of row, work as follows:

At the end of the row before the decrease, turn without chaining; sk first dc of prev row, sl st in each ch and in each dc to beginning of first block to be worked; ch 5, dc in next dc (**Fig 10**).

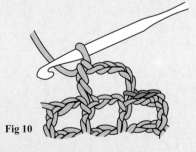

Fig 10

(b) When decrease is at end of row, work as follows:

Work last charted block; ch 5 (for open block) or ch 3 (for closed block), turn, leaving remaining blocks unworked.

Lacet Stitch

An additional stitch used on some of our charts is called a lacet stitch (see **Photo E**).

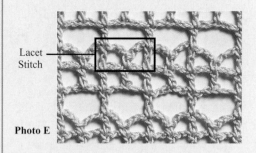

Photo E

It takes the space of two blocks and is worked as follows:

dc in next st, ch 3, sk next 2 sts, sc in next st, ch 3, sk next 2 sts, dc in next st

On the charts it is represented by a V-shaped curved line in a double-wide block (**Fig 11**).

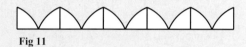

Fig 11

To work over a lacet stitch, work as follows:

dc in next dc, ch 5, dc in next dc

On the charts, it looks like this (**Fig 12**).

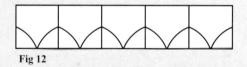

Fig 12

Working From A Chart

When working from a chart remember that for each odd-numbered row (right side of work), you work the chart from right to left; but for each even-numbered row (wrong side of work), you work the chart from left to right.

For Everything's Rosey tablecloth we have charted half of the design. You will work the chart to the center and then work the chart in reverse to complete each row.

For Timeless Beauty tablecloth we have charted a quarter of the design. You will work the quarter chart to the center and then work the chart in reverse to complete the row. To do the second half, work the chart again, starting with the row indicated in the pattern.

To work the short rows at the end of the chart, it will be necessary to finish off and rejoin the thread at various points. When rejoining thread, make sure to stay on the side necessary to continue the pattern.

General Starching Information

Starching Supplies

Before starting this procedure, assemble the following necessary supplies.

1. **Stiffening solution**—use one of the following:

   (a) Commerical stiffening solution used to stiffen crocheted lace (available in your local craft or needlework store).

   (b) White craft glue (such as Elmer's®).

   (c) Thick solution of commerical boil-able starch (liquid or spray starches do not work).

2. **Plastic bag**, the type that locks across the top for soaking crocheted pieces.

3. **Pinning board**, such as a sheet of Styrofoam® (our preference), piece of cardboard or fabric cutting board, for starching flat pieces to shape.

4. **Rust-proof straight pins** to pin out and hold project in shape.

5. **Plastic wrap** to cover pining board so stiffened project will slide off easily when dry.

6. **Blocking form**, as called for in pattern, covered with plastic wrap.

7. **Spray bottle of water**, for dampening pieces (if necessary).

Starching Instructions

Once you have the supplies ready for starching and blocking, proceed as follows:

Step 1. Cover pinning board and blocking form with plastic wrap and pin in place.

Step 2. Pour stiffening solution into a plastic bag and place in a bowl. Immerse piece to be blocked in solution, being sure piece is well coated with starching solution. Remove piece and press out extra solution. Do not squeeze—piece should be very wet, but there should be no solution in the decorative holes (dab with a dry paper towel to absorb excess solution). Any leftover stiffening solution can be stored in the locked plastic bag for a couple days.

Step 3. Place piece on pinning board or over plastic-wrapped form. Shape as necessary being sure to have stitches of design in correct alignment. If necessary pin in place to achieve desired shape. Additional pieces of plastic wrap can be wadded and used for shaping purposes. Let dry thoroughly before removing from form. Refer to individual pattern for further instructions.

Blocking Instructions

Blocking means "setting" the finished project into its final size and shape. To do this, follow these instructions.

If necessary, wash project carefully by hand using a mild soap. Rinse well in warm water. If washing is not needed, lightly dampen project.

Spread project out on a flat padded surface, having the right side facing up. Smooth project out to the correct size, having the design properly aligned with all picots, loops, etc. open. If necessary, use rust-proof pins to hold the edges in place. To retain the blocked dimensions, we suggest lightly spraying with spray starch. Let dry thoroughly before removing.

Hints:

1. Keep hands clean throughout.

2. Keep spray water bottle handy to moisten and reshape as desired.

3. Do not bend stiffened pieces unless slightly damp, as they may crack.

4. Remove pins from piece while slightly damp, as they may stick to piece.

5. Use pastel-colored plastic wrap to cover pinning surface and form to more easily see crocheted piece.

Yarn Suppliers

Caron (Dazzleaire®, Grandma's Best, Wintuk®)

Customer Service
P.O. Box 222
Washington, NC 27889
800-868-9194

Coats & Clark (Red Heart® Classic™, Red Heart® Super Saver, Red Heart® Sport, TLC®, Knit-Cro-Sheen®, Speed-Cro-Sheen®, Luster Sheen®, Big Ball size 20, South Maid® Cotton "8", South Maid® Cotton, Anchor Floss)

Customer Service
P.O. Box 12229
Greer, SC 29650
800-648-1479
www.coatsandclark.com

Coats & Clark Canada (Opera size 10)
6060 Burnside Court
Unit #2
Mississauga, Ontario L5T2T5
800-268-3620

Elmore-Pisgah, Inc. (Peaches & Creme)

204 Oak Street
P.O. Box 187
Spindale, NC 28160
828-286-3665

Lion Brand Yarns (Lion Chenille Sensations, Chenille "Thick and Quick", Wool-Ease®, Lamé Metallic, Kitchen Cotton)

34 West 15th Street
New York, NY 10011
Customer Service:
800-258-9276 (YARN)
www.lionbrand.com

Spinrite Yarns, Ltd. (Bernat® Berella® "4", Bernat Chenille, Bernat Chenille Fifth Avenue, Lily® Sugar 'n Cream Sport, Patons Canadiana)

P.O. Box 40
Listowel, Ontario N4W 3H

Button Supplier

JHB International

1955 S. Quince Street
Denver, CO 80231
800-525-9007

Crochet Hook Supplier

American School of Needlework®

Consumer Division
1455 Linda Vista Drive
San Marcos, CA 92069
800-379-9627

Metric Conversion Charts

INCHES INTO MILLIMETERS & CENTIMETERS (Rounded off slightly)

inches	mm	cm	inches	cm	inches	cm	inches	cm
1/8	3		5	12.5	21	53.5	38	96.5
1/4	6		5 1/2	14	22	56	39	99
3/8	10	1	6	15	23	58.5	40	101.5
1/2	13	1.3	7	18	24	61	41	104
5/8	15	1.5	8	20.5	25	63.5	42	106.5
3/4	20	2	9	23	26	66	43	109
7/8	22	2.2	10	25.5	27	68.5	44	112
1	25	2.5	11	28	28	71	45	114.5
1 1/4	32	3.2	12	30.5	29	73.5	46	117
1 1/2	38	3.8	13	33	30	76	47	119.5
1 3/4	45	4.5	14	35.5	31	79	48	122
2	50	5	15	38	32	81.5	49	124.5
2 1/2	65	6.5	16	40.5	33	84	50	127
3	75	7.5	17	43	34	86.5		
3 1/2	90	9	18	46	35	89		
4	100	10	19	48.5	36	91.5		
4 1/2	115	11.5	20	51	37	94		

mm - millimeter   cm - centimeter

To convert inches to centimeters, multiply the number of inches by 2.5.
(example: 4" x 2.4 = 10cm.

CROCHET HOOKS CONVERSION CHART

U.S.	00	0	1	2	3	4	5	6	7	8	9	10	11	12	13	14
Continental-mm	3.5	3.25	2.75	2.25	2.10	2.00	1.90	1.80	1.65	1.50	1.40	1.30	1.10	1.00	.85	.75

CROCHET HOOKS CONVERSION CHART

U.S.	1/B	2/C	3/D	4/E	5/F	6/G	8/H	9/I	10/J	10 1/2/K	N
Continental-mm	2.25	2.75	3.25	3.5	3.75	4.25	5	5.5	6	6.5	9.0

Index

Designers Index